# RODEO

THE ENVIRONMENT IN MODERN NORTH AMERICA

*Leisl Carr Childers and Michael Childers, Series Editors*

# RODEO
## AN ANIMAL HISTORY

**SUSAN NANCE**

UNIVERSITY OF OKLAHOMA PRESS : NORMAN

Portions of chapter 2 were previously published in Susan Nance, "Who Was Greasy Sal? Outlaw Horses and the Spirit of Calgary in the Automobile Age," in "Tourism in Canada," ed. Jack Little and Ben Bradley, special issue, *Histoire Sociale/Social History* 49, no. 99 (June 2016): 371–89.

Library of Congress Cataloging-in-Publication Data

Names: Nance, Susan, author.
Title: Rodeo : an animal history / Susan Nance.
Description: Norman : University of Oklahoma Press, [2020] | Series: The environment in modern North America ; Volume 3 | Includes bibliographical references and index. | Summary: "Explores how the evolution of rodeo in the United States and Canada has reflected rural western beliefs and assumptions about the natural world against the backdrop of the larger histories of ranching, cattle, horses, and the environment"— Provided by publisher.
Identifiers: LCCN 2019050459| ISBN 978-0-8061-6502-8 (hardcover)
ISBN 978-0-8061-9013-6 (paper)
Subjects: LCSH: Rodeo animals—United States—History. | Rodeo animals—Canada—History. | Human-animal relationships—United States—History. | Human-animal relationships—Canada—History. | Nature—Effect of human beings on—United States. | Nature—Effect of human beings on—Canada. | West (U.S.)—Environmental conditions. | Canada, Western—Environmental conditions.
Classification: LCC GV1834.5 .N36 2020 | DDC 791.8/4—dc23
LC record available at https://lccn.loc.gov/2019050459

*Rodeo: An Animal History* is Volume 3 in the Environment in Modern North America series.

The paper in this book meets the guidelines for permanence and durability of the Committee on Production Guidelines for Book Longevity of the Council on Library Resources, Inc. ∞

Copyright © 2020 by the University of Oklahoma Press, Norman, Publishing Division of the University. Paperback published 2022. Manufactured in the U.S.A.

All rights reserved. No part of this publication may be reproduced, stored in a retrieval system, or transmitted, in any form or by any means, electronic, mechanical, photocopying, recording, or otherwise—except as permitted under Section 107 or 108 of the United States Copyright Act—without the prior written permission of the University of Oklahoma Press. To request permission to reproduce selections from this book, write to Permissions, University of Oklahoma Press, 2800 Venture Drive, Norman OK 73069, or email rights.oupress@ou.edu.

*To Christine and Ric,*
*two of the kindest people you will ever meet*

# Contents

| | |
|---|---|
| List of illustrations | ix |
| Preface | xi |
| | |
| Introduction: The West Wasn't Won on Salad | 1 |
| 1. Busting Steers at the Turn of the Century | 17 |
| 2. Steamboat and Other Early Buckers | 48 |
| 3. Interwar Broncs and Wastage | 76 |
| 4. Mid-century: Bucking Horse of the Year | 100 |
| 5. Bulls and Men of the Late Twentieth Century | 140 |
| 6. Calves and Other Babies of Rodeo into the Twenty-First Century | 177 |
| Epilogue | 213 |
| | |
| Notes | 219 |
| Works Cited | 263 |
| Index | 285 |

# Illustrations

| | | |
|---|---|---|
| 1.1. | Postcard depicting steer busting, Pendleton, Oregon, ca. 1875–1900 | 18 |
| 1.2. | Teasing and goading cattle, 1874 | 29 |
| 1.3. | Roping steer at Cowboy Park rodeo grounds, Ciudad Juárez, Mexico, ca. 1910 | 31 |
| 1.4. | Roping horse observing tied steer and roper, Ontario, Oregon, 1911 | 34 |
| 1.5. | "Testing" a steer, Clark's O.N.T. Spool Cotton thread trade card, ca. 1875–1900 | 35 |
| 1.6. | Probable dead steer at busting competition, Cowboy Park rodeo grounds, Ciudad Juárez, Mexico, ca. 1910 | 38 |
| 1.7. | Still busting at Cheyenne Frontier Days, 1954 | 46 |
| 2.1. | Poetry and imagined monument to Steamboat, *The Billboard*, 1915 | 50 |
| 2.2. | Steamboat | 55 |
| 2.3. | Charles Russell's portrayal of horse breaking, 1899 | 62 |
| 2.4. | Steamboat enduring a spur-and-quirt rider, 1907 | 72 |
| 3.1. | "Let 'Er Buck," Calgary Stampede pennant, 1912 | 83 |
| 3.2. | The bronc "buck," 1930 Calgary Stampede program | 84 |
| 3.3. | Calgary Stampede "Horse List," including Greasy Sal, 1927 | 88 |
| 3.4. | Steele Grey, Calgary Stampede "outlaw" souvenir postcard | 92 |
| 3.5. | Dick Cosgrove and unidentified horse, ca. 1924–27 | 97 |
| 4.1. | War Paint diving, as photographers capture him on film, 1955 | 101 |

| | |
|---|---:|
| 4.2. "High School Horse and His Trainer," comedy act, 1940 | 114 |
| 4.3. Open-top horse trailer, San Angelo, Texas, 1940 | 116 |
| 4.4. Covered horse trailer, Salinas, California, 1958 | 117 |
| 4.5. Kelly Corbin with his car and horse trailer, Pendleton, Oregon, 1964 | 118 |
| 4.6. Christensen tractor-trailer stock haulers, 1947 | 131 |
| 4.7. Christensen Bros.–Rex Allen advertisement, 1957 | 132 |
| 4.8. War Paint, April 18, 1958, photographed for *Life* magazine | 134 |
| 4.9. War Paint and Dallas newspaper reporter, Pendleton, Oregon, 1959 | 135 |
| 4.10. War Paint in wooden bucking chute, Pendleton, Oregon, 1958 | 136 |
| 4.11. Christensen stock unloading at National Finals Rodeo, Dallas, 1959 | 137 |
| 4.12. "Ye Ol' Rodeo Hoss," cartoon by Pete Dixon, 1954 | 138 |
| 5.1. "Lane Frost & Red Rock," offered by Big Country Toys | 142 |
| 5.2. Promotional material for Sloan Williams featuring V61, 1968 | 147 |
| 5.3. Red Rock and Lane Frost, with John Growney in background, 1988 | 152 |
| 5.4. J-31 as "Bodacious! The Master of Disaster," 1996 | 164 |
| 5.5. Professional Bull Riders–branded plush toy of Slingblade | 168 |
| 6.1. Roping calves and horses, San Angelo Fat Stock Show, 1940 | 181 |
| 6.2. Child falling off calf, Sisters, Oregon, 1947 | 183 |
| 6.3. SPCA officer, Callister Park Rodeo, 1943 | 186 |
| 6.4. Clotheslined calf, San Angelo Fat Stock Show, 1940 | 191 |
| 6.5. Scenes from Toots Mansfield's roping school, ca. 1961 | 196 |
| 6.6. Cloverdale Rodeo calf photographed for Vancouver Humane Society, 2006 | 210 |

# Preface

This is a book about rodeo written by an old treeplanter. For a dozen years, beginning at age eighteen, I spent the spring and early summer living outdoors in British Columbia working in silviculture. First I spent four years in the swampy, insanely bug-infested country north of Prince George, earning very little money. There I discovered what it takes to live outdoors 24/7, in all weather, in a tent, to run out of insect repellant, and to be charged by a frightened moose. As a young Vancouverite, I got a profound education on the nature of the Canadian environment. I also saw what it is like in a place where everywhere the land is expected to generate capital. One contract, we worked in a small section of the Bowron Valley, then reputed to be the largest clear-cut on earth ("You can see it from space!" we cynically joked). To allow the timber company to obtain its next logging permit for a patch on the tree line, we planted the middle of that devastated landscape with seedlings supplied from a cooled reefer trailer bearing the timber company's unintentionally cruel slogan "Managed Forests Forever."

In search of better prospects, I thereafter moved south and found work in the Purcell Mountains and the Rocky Mountains just northwest of the Montana border. Promoted to crew manager, I taught myself how to drive a giant crew cab pickup, knowing that loaded timber and gravel trucks tear down the logging roads at top speed and will run smaller vehicles off the road without even noticing. I learned how to dig a truck out of the ditch by myself with just a jack and some flat rocks clawed out of the cut bank. This kind of self-sufficiency was a matter of survival, as often my radio battery was long-dead and there was no other human being within seventy-five miles.

The politics over land use in the West were often on my mind in those years. Near Invermere, the local Ministry of Forests office hired us to replant the site of a forest fire, hoping that in the meantime they could dissuade ranchers with a grazing lease from bringing their stock there. I will never forget returning after a couple of weeks to a parcel we had planted with pine seedlings to find that cows and calves had trampled and defecated on the tiny trees, while deer had finished off the few survivors by browsing off their delicate needles.

These were some of the most difficult times in my life, but I am incredibly grateful for them. When I began work on this book, I realized that these experiences gave me unexpected insight into the worlds of ranching and rodeo—similarly exhausting and political, prone to accidents and reckless behavior, sometimes absurd, always at the mercy of weather, landscape, and animals. And, all quite irresistible.

At the same time, this project has shown me that rodeo is just one of those topics about which the more one learns, the more one realizes there is to learn. So, this book has taken a long time to complete and has often seemed overwhelming. That it has been possible at all is due to the help of the many people I am relieved to finally thank here.

First, many thanks to my editor, Kent Calder, and the production staff at the University of Oklahoma Press, who made a home for this book. Thanks also to the reviewers enlisted by the press for their efforts and wise advice.

This project began over a decade ago with some key funding. I will always be grateful to Richard White, David Kennedy, and the staff at the Bill Lane Center of the West at Stanford University for taking a chance on an unconventional topic and providing an early injection of funding, access to sources, and good ideas on the environmental history angles of this story. Thanks also to the staff of the American Heritage Center of the University of Wyoming for a grant that helped my various visits to Laramie. Thanks finally to the Social Sciences and Humanities Research Council of Canada, which provided the largest chunk of funding to this research in the form of a general research grant. My colleagues at the University of Guelph—Alan Gordon, Donna Andrew, Sandra Sabatini, and Christine Bold—helped me somehow land that funding, and I learned plenty from them about the difficult work of grant writing.

I have spent the bulk of my research time at archives in Laramie, Calgary, and Oklahoma City and I am really glad about it. Many, many thanks to Karen Spilman and other staff at the Donald C. & Elizabeth M. Dickinson Research Center, at the National Cowboy and Western Heritage Museum in Oklahoma City. Equally, the archivists and librarians at the Glenbow Museum in Calgary and the American Heritage Center of the University of Wyoming have received me with politeness and good humor, no matter how many times I insisted on visiting over the last ten years. The University of Guelph interlibrary loan office suffered dearly for this book, but never cut me off or complained about my many requests. I am also grateful for the Library of Congress and the Internet Archive. Thanks to Debra Probert and the staff at the Vancouver Humane Society for rooting around in their files for materials for chapter 6. This work also benefitted from conversations with Richard Slatta, Clay McShane, and assorted others I encountered at animal studies and Western History Association conferences. Finally, way back when, Christi Garneau got this research rolling over one summer by hunting down every possible source and compiling an intimidatingly complete annotated bibliography of every little thing about cattle, horses, ranching, and rodeo.

For help in understanding the principles and findings of animal welfare science, as well as the ways of cattle and horses, I would like to thank Shannon Nicholson, Kimber Sider, Derek Haley, Katrina Merkies, Denna Benn, and the staff at the University of Guelph's Elora Beef and Dairy Units, as well as the Barn 37 and Equine Guelph folks. Thanks also to the hundreds of undergraduate students at the University of Guelph who migrated through my animal history and environmental history classes. Your questions and insights assured me that I might actually be onto something with this project. Over the past decade, the members of the Western Literature Association helped me to pay attention to my writing and to tell a good story. I have struggled to measure up to their incredible energy, optimism, expert writing, and enthusiasm for and support of creative works of all kinds that explore what it is to be western.

Lastly, I must thank the various rodeo and ranching people I have met back of the chutes, at their properties, at conferences, and at my research talks. I was always glad to see cowboy hats in the audience! These are people who listened carefully and did not always agree with me. They made me work harder to know what I was talking about, and how to recognize when I did not. Thanks for being frank with me when you could.

# Introduction

## The West Wasn't Won on Salad

In July 2012, on a Saturday night, I was at Cheyenne Frontier Days to see the last competitive event of the day, the wild horse race. From the back row at the top of the crowded west bleachers, the whole scene of cowboys, horses, arena workers, and audience lay before me. It was extremely hot and the place smelled like grilling hamburgers and spilled beer. Behind me, below in the west parking lot, the Frontier Days carnival was in full operation with its amusement park rides, shopping, food stalls, and see-and-be-seen-in-a-cowboy-hat dating scene. Soon crews would be setting up a stage in the arena for the night show, featuring country music singer Blake Shelton.

In the meantime, pickup riders were pulling in a dozen from the herd of skittish-looking unbroken horses huddled together on the east side of the arena, brought in from "wild ranges down in Texas," as the rodeo announcer said. Staff at Frontier Days are proud to tell you that for roping events they use "fresh stock," namely wild horses, steers, and calves who have not been to a rodeo before and therefore do not know what is coming when they enter the noisy rodeo arena. Each wild horse, already wearing a halter bearing a five-foot lead, was dragged into the fenced-off west section and handed off to a three-man team waiting in line there. To the triumphant sounds of Strauss's *Also Sprach Zarathustra* blaring over the PA system, the horses fought, stepping blindly backward, snaking their necks around in their halters, or futilely resisting, straight-legged with hooves dug into the dirt. The rodeo announcer chatted along, explaining the meaning of the "action" the crowd was witnessing. "If you want to glance back to the way it used to be . . . this is shades of the Old West, all over again. And for one hundred and sixteen years that's what they've been doing at old Cheyenne," he proclaimed just as a chestnut mare jerked herself head-over-hooves backward into the dirt.

A gunshot started the race. Now to the accompaniment of the Surfaris' 1963 hit, "Wipe Out," men on each team hauled on the lead ropes and, when they could get close enough, hung off the horses' crests and withers as a predator would, while teammates scrambled to cinch on a saddle. As the energy level escalated, the horses became more desperate. Many appeared sincerely terrified, snorting, screeching, and breathing hard with the whites of their eyes showing. Roped horses ran into other horses and men. Some bucked and kicked at their captors, but then tripped, landing head-first, jamming dirt into their eyes, nostrils, and mouths.

It was late afternoon, so the audience was made up of ropers and riders who had competed earlier in the day, their family members, and people from Cheyenne, Laramie, Denver, or beyond (like me). They represented ranching people, town dwellers, urbanite tourists, and rodeo regulars. Everyone seemed delighted by the mayhem down below, laughing and pointing at the horses, or yelling advice to the men with whom the horses struggled. Below me in the bleachers a young woman in a cowboy hat sported a T-shirt that stated on the back, "P.E.T.A. People Eating Tasty Animals," in reference to the animal rights organization People for the Ethical Treatment of Animals and their attacks on rodeo sports. She was laughing especially hard at the dusty mess of men and horses fighting one another in the arena. Many of these spectators were—it occurred to me, somewhat paradoxically—horse people. They were avowed horse lovers who, if asked, would speak confidently and at length about their love of western horses, and those horses' nature, behavior, and needs.

Suddenly, there was blood on the ground. A man on one team had been kicked squarely in the face by the mare his team was working to saddle. From the top of the bleachers, even I could see that his nose had been completely crushed. On his knees, now with blood pouring down his face, bleary-eyed and obviously rattled, he reached up over his head to hold out to one of his teammates the lead rope he was still clutching. The teammates managed to get a saddle on that horse, and one rode her around the arena to finish the race as the injured cowboy crawled out of the way. And the audience laughed at him, too. "Who are these westerners?" I wondered while noting the sheer violence of the scene. How do they claim that this is a sensibly western thing to do? That hot Saturday evening, the wild horse race seemed to expose how the rural cultures of the West, only periodically on display in town at the yearly rodeo, belong to people who imagine they are still fighting to survive. Perhaps they raced terrified wild horses in a ritual of dark humor that explores their struggle to control the land, weather, and animals of the West?

In truth, I should already have had this figured out. It was not my first rodeo, so to speak. I had seen horses and men die at rodeos, and countless animals and people limping out or taken away on a stretcher. And always an ambulance to the side of the arena was parked pointing out toward the pavement in the direction of the nearest emergency room. Somehow, that particular 2012 horse race revealed to me the taxing but committed relationship many in the West have with their animals and environment. It is something rancher Judy Blunt once analyzed as the "choice we made to live where we lived, the quarrel we took up with the land and passed along."[1] The fellow with the broken nose, the laughing spectators, and those struggling wild horses were suddenly evocative of a stubborn western desire to do difficult things simply because others—outsiders, tenderfoots, tourists, city people—cannot. Or choose not to.

The rodeo community is diverse, of course. Still, the institution is essentially a celebration of rural and ranch life in the West. It romanticizes and lampoons the precarious, exhausting work since the late nineteenth century of cajoling the environment on a remote piece of property into producing market cattle and horses who can be broken. In a way, rodeo is the long-term product of the commodification of the western environment, over which rural westerners have claimed custodial authority for generations.[2] Many have taken this difficult road, insisting on isolated, rural living that discounts or outright ignores the limits of animals, the land, and themselves. Rodeo has helped many normalize this approach to the environment as the ostensible responsibility of self-sufficient people who seek independence and freedom. What is especially amazing is that westerners, including rodeo people, have managed this feat while performing before a modern backdrop of environmental uncertainty and shrinking rural autonomy. For instance, in recent decades many ranges have been better managed in order to repair the grievous damage caused by what geographer Paul Starrs called the "rapacious use of lands" between the 1880s and World War I. However, in many places the West still copes with serious environmental degradation caused by extensive ranching.[3] So has the creeping and oft-resented control of territory by the U.S. Bureau of Land Management, the U.S. Forest Service, and the Canadian Crown and their grazing fees both subsidized rural living and caused troubling political divisions. Extensive ranching has for decades been barely profitable, often unsustainable financially without a job on the side.[4] All the while, rodeo's organizers, competitors, stock contractors, fans, and families kept alive the nineteenth-century hope for the West—many years ago Henry Nash Smith named it the "myth of the garden"—as a freely available, abundant environment that enriches brave, independent men and women willing to do the work.[5] Rodeo is their defense of that choice to quarrel with the land and its ambivalent consequences.

Certainly, other interpretations of rodeo and its history abound. Several decades ago Elizabeth Atwood Lawrence persuasively explained rodeo's contests between humans and livestock as ritual dramas of settler expansion across the West, played out over and over again as symbolic struggles between human versus animal, tame versus wild, and culture versus nature.[6] Other explanations are equally as true as Lawrence's, depending upon one's perspective:[7] rodeo as a community ritual that affirms shared values[8]; as venue for cowboy folklore and performance[9]; as working-class sport affirming the democratic potential of society and the economy[10]; and as a way to express racial, gender, or class identities through an athletic celebration of horsemanship and horsewomanship.[11]

This century, I think we need to ask if there is even more to rodeo. To paraphrase Donald Worster, there are those historians who can ignore the role of animals in the past, but I am not one of them.[12] To be human is not normative, but just one of thousands of ways to experience the world. To me, all of rodeo's animals have their own story to tell about the violence inherent in the sport and about how the common cultures of rodeo have mediated social and environmental change as rural and small-town westerners experienced it, and city people appropriated it. Consider that California's Rodeo Salinas and the Omak Stampede in Washington relish their mountain race in which riders race horses down a treacherously steep trail, the Calgary Stampede features its chuckwagon races, and Cheyenne has its chaotic wild horse race and old-time steer busting. From the remote, local dirt-road affair drawing less than one hundred spectators to marquee Ticketmaster events, most rodeos include at least one such reckless, routinely deadly-to-people-and-livestock event as a showstopper. Even in carefully regulated roping and riding events, people and animals are injured and even killed with regularity. Of course, no rodeo producer, publicist, or arena veterinarian will tell you how many horses and cattle are euthanized back of the chutes, in the stockyards, or back at the ranch due to injuries suffered at the show. No ambulance stands by at the arena for the livestock. Rodeo is a dangerous sport in many respects and reveals many westerners to be people who are proudly tolerant of danger and violence, and are ready to impose these values on their animals.

American settler communities founded the first rodeos, the roping and riding contests initially known as "cowboy tournaments," by drawing from Hispanic *charreada* traditions (equestrian and bull festivals) to give birth to modern rodeo at a moment historian Richard White has called "a great divide in the history of the American west." Specifically, the later nineteenth century was a time in which Indigenous societies for whom "animals were persons" lost cultural and political dominance. As homesteaders, laborers, speculators, American Civil War veterans, and others flooded into the West from around the globe, the region became integrated into national markets for food and raw materials requiring that "animal persons yielded to animals of enterprise."[13] Rodeo helped people cope with the shift from subsistence hunting and farming to extraction of animals from the land to feed commercial markets. Beginning in Hispanic and later settler cowboy tournaments that developed into twentieth-century rodeo, the sport was a way to come to terms with the quarrel with the land that the shift required, as well as the uneven results it produced for individual people, families, and communities. All the while, Indigenous Peoples with their own generations-old horse traditions equally adapted ranching and rodeo to their own interests, although always within a critique of American and Canadian conquests of the West. While at times they disagreed with the settler community about, in the early days, whether cattle should be hunted like game or killed in a slaughterhouse or, later, what constituted a "wild" horse, legally speaking, they shared a belief that people had the right to use and kill these animals.[14]

Broad historical paradigms such as historian Richard White's idea about a transition for western animals from "animal persons" to "animals of enterprise" can gloss over the irregularities and exceptions in the past, for people and animals. Still this paradigm matches my own research on animal modernity outside the West since the mid-nineteenth century, especially in the cities.[15] Although the paradigm manifested somewhat differently in the cities, there we find the same polarity as more animals became commodities. Modern people both monetized animal life and felt bad about it, mirroring what White calls the pairing of "money and pity" in people's understanding of animals in the West in this period.[16] Because animals are sentient and responsive in ways that the land, water, or weather are not, western animals like the wild horses I saw that afternoon in Cheyenne became characters in rodeo's normalization of the "great divide" in the West. Yet, some said, those beings deserved a degree of human sympathy as a way to honor their vulnerability to human power, or at least to believe one was wielding power judiciously without the inconvenience of substantially changing one's work or consumption practices.

Richard White's work is part of the New Western History movement, which is not so new anymore these days. Still, many appreciate its "myth-breaking spirit" and habit of "draining the majesty from the history of westering," as Stephen Aron wrote some years ago.[17] Especially since the 1980s, historians have created an inclusive and frank history of western Canada and the United States that adds great complexity to the old nineteenth-century ideal of settler expansion across the continent as innocently and uniformly progressive, egalitarian, inevitable, and triumphant. This expansion was certainly characterized by what historians now explain as "relentless violence" as settler communities, private interests, military, and government authorities took control of animals, land, and other resources in the West, and the dominant actors employed "coercive violence" to consolidate their power.[18]

Historians have retold this story with respect to colonization and race, class and gender conflict, human-driven environmental change, animal extinctions and eradication programs, and inequalities and disappointments of all kinds.[19] There is no doubting that the late-nineteenth century West could be a violent place. It was so, not only for the few shoot-outs and lynchings, the more common race riots and mine disasters, the unfathomable horrors of the Indian Wars, the anguish of women and children trapped in abusive situations in remote locations, or the homesteaders and ranchers who ran out of water, money, or hope in the face of a landscape and weather that refused to cooperate. More than that, for animals, the human West was an exceptionally violent place. Settlers hunted, trapped, poisoned, and tortured predators and valuable fur-bearing species; worked horses, mules, and burros past their limits; and neglected livestock on frigid, drought-stricken, or overstocked ranges.

Rodeo's place in that story has escaped scrutiny until now. To understand how rodeo's animals became surrogates for the trials of rural life in the West and the violence in its history, what if we proceed from some unconventional questions that help us to really see the animals of rodeo as beings who had lives beyond the arena? Given that to produce a rodeo or perform in one has always been difficult, dirty, hands-on, and often dangerous work, what would rodeo history look like if we took it as a record not of human triumph and resilience but of human imperfection and stubbornness? Since we know that rodeo has always changed over time, and is still a living tradition, what would rodeo history look like if we asked not what makes rodeo historically authentic or inauthentic but what has made it modern and adaptable? If we think about rodeo as the live-performance component of the Western in entertainment, what would rodeo history look like if we asked about not just the champions and the arena triumphs but what goes on backstage before, during, and after "the show"?[20] Given that the rodeo community is a large, disparate group that cannot be accurately described by lumping people together, likewise what would rodeo history look like if, when possible, we examined its animals as diverse collections of individuals? Ask these questions and perhaps the seeming contradictions in human-animal relationships that have played out in rodeo competitions appear less a problem to ignore or explain away. Instead they are a defining characteristic that has kept rodeo relevant for one hundred and forty years.

This book tells a story about rodeo livestock in the context of the common culture of rodeo, one dominated by settlers and their descendants but which minority communities also shared and appropriated across Canada, the United States, and border regions of Mexico to which non-Spanish-speaking people traveled for rodeos. Of course, Hispanic *charreada*, from which rodeo was derived, continued on in parallel. Native American, First Nations, African American competitors, the LGBTQ community, prisons, high schools and colleges—they all adapted rodeo to their own cultures over the course of the twentieth century. Still, in the beginning it was settler communities that had the capital and media access to mainstream the common culture of rodeo and convince so many that rodeo sports were native to the whole trans-Mississippi West and western Canada. "The West" was equally an idea that reached out to not-so-western places like New York's Madison Square Garden when westerners shipped a load of animals there and held a rodeo before Manhattan audiences without expecting any locals to compete. It was a place existing both in the past and the present, an imagined space of hardy people who succeeded in life because they valued individualism and self-reliance in a presumed-meritocratic society.

Rodeo has always been a way to tell stories for local and distant audiences about western history and myth.[21] In fact, all sorts of people have claimed a stake in the broader commercial "Wild West" and other stereotypes that portrayed the West as a place of adventure, quick riches, dramatic action, or nostalgic violence. People found these ideas in western-styled entertainment, advertising, books, magazines, newspapers, art, and souvenirs,[22] as well as community rituals like roundups or local cowboy tournaments.[23] Collectively, despite the diversity of their attitudes and behavior, rodeo people became the caretakers of these myths of the West. Many westerners used them to express a loosely united identity that defied national boundaries and offered a promotional brand—the mythical West—to tourists and other outsiders, although often that message was shaped to serve the interests of local elites.[24] This mythical West was represented by rodeo's winners, like early feminist rodeo icons Lucille Mulhall and Mabel Strickland, pathbreaking competitors of color like Tom Threepersons and Fred Whitfield, celebrity cowboys like Casey Tibbs and Ty Murray, and utterly dominant athletes like barrel racer Charmayne James.

Equally, some years ago Elizabeth Lawrence explained rodeo as a "ritual of the beef empire."[25] Indeed, rodeo is the beef (and sheep and dude ranch) industry's contribution to the world of entertainment through which rodeo people carved out a place for themselves and their ideas in crowded national entertainment and sports markets. Rural people have used rodeo as a platform to advocate for meat production and a whole range of attitudes and politics associated with extensive ranching in the West. By 2010, Vern Kimball, then-CEO of the Calgary Stampede, would explain his rodeo to a journalist just so: "It's an opportunity to teach youth about a way of life, and to teach people about where food comes from."[26] As long as people fueled consumer demand for cheap beef and wool, disposable horses, or cowboy-themed dude ranch vacations, rodeo offered a way explain the modern West and animals' place in it to westerners and visitors as inevitable and crucial to consumers everywhere.

All the while, rodeos helped perpetuate a nineteenth-century attitude toward the natural world that brought about the environmental crisis in which we find ourselves today. Of course, we cannot be too presentist and hold historical rodeo participants responsible for that crisis now. Even if over time they argued about range health, stocking densities, water rights, the damage done to the land and waterways by camping tourists or cattle hooves, no one understood until very recently the environmental toll that beef and other meat consumption would take on the planet.[27] In rodeo's foundational years, an age of massive government-facilitated immigration, industrial development, and calorie production, the concept of climate change was nonexistent. Still, rodeo naturalized and promoted as "traditional" and "heritage" modes of land and animal use that have become unsustainable as the global population pushes past seven billion. It has permitted gradual land-use reform to tick along while keeping alive old stories of the limitless abundance of the

West, with the romantic figure of the cowboy or cowgirl in the leading role. As consumers, whether beef-eaters or not, we are all implicated in that story of rodeo and the uses of animals and land that it required.

The common culture of rodeo was founded upon another ubiquitous but seldom scrutinized western belief: the myth of animal consent to their use in the settling of the West.[28] The myth had two forms. The most obvious was in rodeo marketing and Western art and literature that boasted of roping steers, bucking horses, and raging bulls so mean that there were just hankering for a fight. Their very existence was an irresistible invitation to the brave cowboys and cowgirls of the West looking to test themselves in roping, riding, or wrestling those creatures. Rodeo people took all that with a grain of salt most of the time, and would say privately that they knew full well that calves did not wish to be roped or that bucking was no fun for horses. Yet, publicly, rodeo people relied on this concept every time they described a bucking bull as intelligent and ornery, or insisted that this bronc or that "just loves to buck!"

In its second form in work-a-day life at farms, ranches, or the rodeo grounds, the myth of animal consent to their use was grounded in a belief that livestock had entered into what Stephen Budiansky has called an "ancient contract." Cattle, horses, sheep, and others exchanged their freedom and self-determination for the occasional bale of hay and an unfrozen bucket of water in winter. In return, as the logic goes, people had a right to make life and death decisions for them, abscond with their offspring, and exploit their labor.[29] The ancient contract element of the myth of consent often was grounded in a very old human habit of justifying human supremacy by imagining a captive animal as a "sagacious animal," a being who understands and endorses human motivations and activities, although he or she is not actually free to walk away.[30] In rodeo, stockmen and women purpose-bred cattle and horses for the sport: roping, hazing (assisting a rider in bulldogging by directing running calves or steers in a straight line), barrel racing, and cutting horses, equine and bovine buckers among them. When these animals produced the behaviors rodeo required, whether cooperative or resistant, and were able to tolerate the necessary hours of travel and practice training behind the scenes, many rodeo and other rural people believed they were in a sense consenting to working in rodeo since they thus avoided ranch work or the slaughterhouse.

The myth of domesticated animals' consent to their use in the settling of the West served as an anchor in times of immense economic, cultural, and environmental change. Rodeo performed the myth as live entertainment because it offered a dominionist ideology that held human needs and activities to be supreme, but which also resolved contradictions between animal behavior that people witnessed and the meanings they applied to that behavior.[31] Animals who struggled, disobeyed, or ran away and chose to be feral were somehow only more western by their will to be free of human control and thus the challenge they presented to western people who sought to exploit them. Rodeo gracefully captured both that adversarial attitude toward nature, in events in which a human and nonhuman squared off, and the "partnership" ideal. The latter was represented initially by roping horses and other equines ridden in the arena, although in time many rodeo people would imagine bucking horses and bulls as enthusiastic, knowing partners in competition with cowgirls and cowboys.[32]

The western myth of animal consent further asserted that animals somehow endorsed or did not mind any violence that took place in the settling of the West or in contemporary western life, even violence directed at them. The New Western historians have documented how settlers were "traumatized" by the resistance of Indigenous people and, I would add, the harsh, unforgiving environment and unsympathetic behavior of wild animals in many places. As Walter Hixson tells us, people thus "internalized a propensity for traumatic, righteous violence, and a quest for total security," in a struggle for control. Many early settlers believed that to be truly western, they should impose their will on nonwhites, the land, and animals by any means necessary.[33] From that perspective, settlers were not aggressors or perpetrators of injustice when they engaged in violence to become supreme. They interpreted any resistance to their activities and aspirations on the part of native people, animals, or the environment as attacks of a sort that transformed settlers themselves into "beleaguered" victims of villainous and "savage" regressive forces that sought to impede the spread of "civilization" and economic prosperity.[34] Popular representations of conflict in the West have often romanticized any violence by settlers toward people, animals, or the land as moral, necessary, and decisive.[35]

Many settlers viewed animals who simply acted in their own self-interest, doing what made sense to them—hunting, reproducing, grazing and browsing, running, fighting, or existing at all—as an attack on their goals and culture. According to this worldview, any action settlers took to destroy, control, or exploit those animals was moral and a matter of self-preservation. Animal and environmental historians have documented that mode of thinking with respect to wolves, bison, prairie dogs, and others, wherein westerners believed those animals were "enemies" challenging settler control of resources and thus metaphorically asking to be killed, or captured and put to work.³⁶ To help people digest and justify their part in this process, rodeo performed this concept with livestock as prey and humans in the role of rightful apex predator. In rodeo's action-oriented, fast-paced events, animals were roughly thrown down or set upon so they would fight, kick, and struggle with all their might. No less than the "Attack on the Deadwood Coach" in Buffalo Bill Cody's Wild West or today's "Gunfight shows at Noon, 2 and 3:30 PMDaily" at the OK Corral Historic Complex in Tombstone, Arizona, here was a way to make entertainment out of the violence in western history.³⁷ The Western itself, as a style of entertainment and literature, reimagined collective and sustained patterns of violence in western history as stories of individual conflict and honorable triumph.³⁸ This is how rodeo reimagined human-animal relations in the West, too. It symbolically boiled down millions of interactions across a vast territory over hundreds of years into simple contests between human and animal in an arena where there would be only one winner at a time.

The myth of animal consent in rodeo referred to many westerners' quarrel with the land, although in ways outsiders might not particularly notice. It equally functioned to "conceal traumas" in the past, as anthropologists would explain it.³⁹ Well-meaning ranchers who lost a Bureau of Land Management or Forest Service contract and went bust, cattle who froze to death over an epic winter, land that became infested with inedible plants due to the labor of carrying market cattle or sheep (or wild horses, some insisted)—these historical injustices or mistakes were papered over by rodeo's competitions, in which anyone could be a winner and there was always another critter waiting in the chute. On the ground in Wyoming, British Columbia, or Texas, even when water, weather, land or plants would not cooperate, animals could be made to do so.⁴⁰ To many, the dramatic energy of roping or riding competitions authenticated them because animals could not "act" or dissimulate in performance, so rodeo offered live animals expressing their individual experience on the spot. With every buck bucked and rope tied around hoofed legs, rodeos both capitalized upon animal resistance to humans and discounted its moral significance. Rodeo people were only reflecting an ideology of human dominion shared by most North Americans, after all.

For those seeking self-reliance in the West, life on the land was defined by hard work and suffering, which differentiated the real cowboys and cowgirls from city people and tourists. By these agricultural values, it was certainly not the responsibility of humankind to protect animals from work or suffering, either. Many rural westerners would further have pointed out that it was a modern folly of the tenderfoot or urbanite to lump all nonhumans into the blanket moral category of "animals" in any event. To pet and praise one's pickup horse and sell to the cannery "a real mean one" who bit and kicked was no contradiction since not all animals deserved identical material treatment or moral consideration. The entire diagnosis of any *contradiction* in western human-animal relationships, many would point out, showed how many people were uninformed about the work that must be done to produce food for people who will not do it for themselves.[41] Plenty of westerners disagreed, of course. Still, the myths of western individualism, moral certainty, and self-reliance that were everywhere in the twentieth-century West depended upon the myth of animal consent to their use in rural western life, especially by way of extensive ranching.

As diverse as the West has always been, here was something about which everyone—white, Indigenous, Hispanic, man, woman, urban or rural, Canadian or American—could agree. Perhaps because horses and cattle coexisted closely with humans and helped dislodge native animals from western lands, some people persuaded themselves that horses and cattle somehow consented to participation in human ventures. Certainly, domesticated animals who provided labor, companionship, and raw materials (their bodies) were unknowing tools of conquest.[42] Again, Indigenous Peoples also appropriated horses and cattle to increase their own autonomy and power. Even if in some places and times they developed varying modes of animal husbandry that settlers might criticize, they too agreed that people had a right to make use of animals and that modern westerners did so to stay in close contact with the land.[43]

Sports journalism and the popular literature about rodeo and its history usually have the myth of animal consent firmly embedded in them. Some authors may note questions over animal use in rodeo in passing but generally minimize them as a controversy stirred up by ill-informed outsiders to rodeo, and generally a distraction to be avoided.[44] Typically, if we glimpse rodeo animals at all, we only do so by way of accounts of their few seconds in the arena, their buck-off statistics, or the glamorized lore about a famous bronc, bull, or roping horse as the meanest or most faithful one ever.[45] Rodeo's animals feature in the sport's history only so much as they facilitate tales of human "illustrious champions" and individual triumph that come richly decorated with silver buckles, prize saddles, iconic arena performances, and roaring crowds.[46] Not incidentally, when writers emphasize all the firsts and bests in rodeo history, they also exclude much of what rodeos have been to the competitors who did not win, and the families, businesses, communities, and visitors who depended upon rodeos socially and financially.

This book, then, is a history of some of rodeo's animals. Three chapters are dedicated to cattle and three to horses in competitive rodeo events: steer and calf roping, bronc and bull riding. It tells some of their stories with the aim of exposing larger patterns in rodeo sports and the histories of animals in the West. Some of the stories are famous ones told in new ways; other stories are previously unknown or have not been told for many decades. They span a period beginning with the ad hoc cowboy tournaments of the 1880s and 1890s and then travel through the complex forty-year period around the turn of the century during which organized community rodeos and travelling Wild West shows coexisted and popularized Western horse and cattle sports outside the ranching community. With the demise of Wild West shows in the interwar years, the book follows the "professionalization" and segmentation of rodeo after World War II. This process culminated in the birth of the Professional Bull Riders bull-riding-only tour in 1992, as well as a changing role for community rodeos in the urbanizing West by the early twenty-first century. The stories take place against the backdrop of beef production and family ranching, from the Beef Bonanza bubble and Big Die-Up of the 1880s, through the advent of industrial feedlot-based cattle production, to the advent of specialty rodeo roughstock ranching by the second half of the twentieth century. The stories are also crucial to explaining rodeo's meaning to and total integration into the lives of so many individuals, families, and communities as a way to "celebrate survival" in the rural West.[47]

An equally important backdrop to the story of rodeo's animals is the evolution of humane and animal advocacy organizations in the United States and Canada. One persistent obstacle to the goals of this book is that critics of rodeo within the rodeo community can be extremely difficult to find in the historical record. Locals who disliked rodeo and stayed away, or rodeo people who resented particular events but kept quiet, are largely ignored by rodeo's historians and the material record that rodeos produce from year to year. Although rodeo people have disagreed about every conceivable element of the sport, self-censorship persists among them and the residents of towns and cities politically or financially reliant upon the sport. Consequently, the voices of humane and animal advocacy organizations frequently offer the only counterpoints to the publicity and nostalgic histories rodeo people put forward to celebrate themselves. Thus, these stories of rodeo's animals are also explained with respect to the rise of progressive animal-welfare groups in the West between the 1880s and World War II, often humane associations or local chapters of the Society for the Prevention of Cruelty to Animals. Thereafter, other advocacy organizations, some of them nationally based and better funded, challenged rodeo with animal rights–based arguments that sought abolition of particular events or of rodeo as a whole: the Humane Society of the United States (HSUS), People for the Ethical Treatment of Animals (PETA), Showing Animals Respect and Kindness (SHARK), the Animal Liberation Front, and even some regional humane societies that adopted an animal rights philosophy. Rodeo has always been controversial—since the very beginning—so the voices of animal advocates are at times crucial to the story if we are to understand how rodeo has adapted and persisted all these years in spite of it all.

If one really appreciates its breadth and adaptability, rodeo is an amazing but intimidating topic. To attempt to write an inclusive, synthetic history of rodeo, in all its diversity across one hundred and forty years in the United States, Canada, and the border regions of Mexico, is challenging and perhaps foolhardy. The range of western animals—historically contingent individuals varying by breed, origin, and life experience—involved in rodeo over time is equally broad. Still, I volunteer to give it a try since my goal is for readers to *really see* those animals, not simply as the ornaments or background noise of rodeo, but as beings who had lives, who passed through rodeo but were not solely defined by it.

The stories we can tell about rodeo's animals are further shaped by the dilemmas of rodeo's historical sources. Those who controlled the animals moving into and out of rodeos left few records of their day-to-day work. Two large caches of business records in Laramie and Calgary do tell of the day-to-day labors of running the Cheyenne Frontier Days rodeo and the Calgary Stampede. The countless smaller community rodeos and private-ranch competitions left far fewer records—perhaps just an advertisement, a few photographs, or competition results posted in an old newspaper. I have combed through plenty of these as well, and found ways to tell the stories of some of rodeo's animals through them. Memoirs and old-timer stories, photographs, and editorials in rodeo papers and western-lifestyle magazines also help us understand the contexts and the people that animals contended with, and, for some famous animals, the conditions of their lives.

Readers should thus take this book as a starting point for the history of rodeo's animals, and an invitation for more questions and more research that does justice to the breadth and diversity of rodeo, its contradictions, and its staying power. My efforts to document some of this history necessarily meant making some choices, leaving many valuable topics and questions to other authors. Certainly, the universe of Mexican and Mexican American rodeos deserves renewed attention and a full history, as do junior rodeo and, probably the most universally prominent rodeo event today, barrel racing.[48]

The folksy bumper-sticker maxim "The West Wasn't Won on Salad" is true and not true. For instance, to those who oversaw the blooming of California in the early twentieth century as the irrigated produce capital for the United States and Canada, it is not the main story of the West. But for those who sat in the stands or loitered back of the chutes at a rodeo, small or large, it might be just about the whole story. From its very beginning, rodeo sports were really a public reflection of the triad of beef, rural politics, and agricultural attitudes toward animals and the land that supported continental food production and western tourism. Rodeo celebrated the imposition of the concept of private property onto the West grounded in early settlers' decision to overturn the societies and ecologies they found and to reshape the region toward national and global commodity markets, by violence if necessary.[49] Rodeo has been both a stubborn celebration of that rural quarrel with the land and a coping mechanism for dealing with the limits of people, animals, and the land when they failed to live up to human aspirations.

A brief note on terminology: Especially later in this study, the term "animal welfare" appears, but it has multiple meanings. In its most general terms, animal welfare science (AWS) researchers operate from an ethological point of view assuming, among other things, that cattle and horses have versatile mental abilities even if those abilities are not always immediately apparent to human perception. AWS research and the related discipline of domestic animal ethology have greatly improved scientists' understanding of bovine and equine cognition, learning, and experience as well as the evolutionary advantages that come with having complex mental lives. Largely extinct now is the twentieth-century belief among scientists that nonhuman animals are "stimulus-response machines" who exhibit behaviors but are unfeeling and unthinking. Of course, many westerners have always known that horses and cattle learn from experience, act on their environments in their own interests, and have emotional and physical experiences ranging from fear and pain to contentment and happiness. Still, people might debate how much that was so for this or that calf or pony.

AWS research is driven by a respect for the scientific method and being "led by data not feelings," as such researchers say. It also contains an ethical and practical argument that all sentient animals should have "five freedoms" (from hunger and thirst; from discomfort; from pain, injury, or disease; from fear and distress; and the freedom to express behaviors typical to their species). These findings proceed from the idea that, if the five freedoms are accommodated by people, both human and nonhuman life will improve. It posits that complex mental lives—including emotions like anxiety, grief, and joy—should be assumed in other species since they promote social cohesion and survival. Lastly, in the AWS field, "animal welfare problems" are by definition caused by people (either out of ignorance, inattention, lack of resources, or other factors), so AWS has been a way to evaluate the welfare primarily of domesticated and captive animals.[50]

To stock and rodeo people, "animal welfare" has been more loosely defined. In common usage, it generally indicates a utilitarian attitude justifying human use of animals as necessary and moral. Still, it urges those who own, manage, or ride horses and cattle to refrain from excessive infliction of pain or fear that promotes balkiness, weight loss, or serious physical injuries like broken limbs. Loosely defined and debated among stock and rodeo people themselves, the ranching and farming definition of "animal welfare" is elastic enough to accommodate "accidents" that occur in ranch work and the rodeo game. To many stock and rodeo people, animals who are at times thirsty, frightened, in pain, too cold, too hot, or frustrated and cramped up by too many hours riding in a stock trailer without a break can still have overall "good welfare" if they are decently fed, they see a veterinarian once in a while, and their caregivers believe they are doing the best they can. Both senses of the term "animal welfare" here must be distinguished from "animal rights," which, broadly defined, indicates a political position that precludes human use of animals in many settings, including for entertainment or sport.

CHAPTER 1

# Busting Steers at the Turn of the Century

Steer busting was one of rodeo's original timed events and probably the best-kept secret in the sport's history. Perhaps seeking not to criticize the sport's early founders, most rodeo historians discuss steer busting only in vague terms. They refrain from lengthy descriptions of what went on, noting simply that steer busting was controversial because it was "too hard on the stock" and so was ostensibly banned in many places.[1] In fact, there was no such simple reform or resolution. Instead, if we actually look closely at steer busting and its controversies, we can understand how rodeo people would learn to adapt their contests just enough to survive their critics and carry on, while still claiming legitimate stewardship over western livestock.

Although in the late nineteenth and early twentieth century the sport was routinely called "steer roping" or "steer tying," as a competition between individual ropers, generally it was practiced as steer busting.[2] The goal was to chase down and rope a steer on horseback, then dismount and tie him in the shortest possible time. In 1896, the newspapers described the particulars of "busting" or tripping the steer like this:

> The contestant, mounted on a thoroughly trained horse, is stationed at a point twenty-five yards from the flagman. When all are ready the vaqueros single out a steer and with a yell such as only cowboys can give, they start him across the line by the flagman at break-neck speed. Just as [the steer] passes the "dead line," the flagman swings his flag down as a signal for the cowboy to start. His spurs no sooner touch the horse's flanks than he is off with a jump and rapidly catching up with the steer. A whirl or two of the lariat over his head and then the noose darts out and neatly drops over the head of the steer. This done, the rider draws the rope along the right side of the animal and reining his horse to

A famous postcard depicting steer busting, photographed a decade after numerous supposed bans on the practice. "Harry Walters wins championship trick riding contest," 1919, Cheyenne, Wyoming, Doubleday-Foster Photo Co. Inc., Bruce McCarroll Collection of the Bonnie & Frank McCarroll Rodeo Archives, National Cowboy & Western Heritage Museum, RC2006.076.0620, Gift of Bruce McCarroll.

the left, at right angles to the course of the animal, brings the rope across the hind legs of the animal. The rope is then wrapped about the pommel of the saddle and all slack is taken up. Throwing his weight with the horse from the steer, the animal's head is drawn around to the right, his hind legs crowded to the right, and almost as quick as a flash he is lying in a heap.[3]

The goal of throwing the steer in the air, or tripping him, was to land him on his head, thus stunning him so he would be easier to tie. Tripping steers also enhanced the action and drama for spectators of the competition.

Many people disliked steer busting from the beginning, and humane organizations spoke out almost immediately. For others, the controversy around the event and the ostensible toughness of its participants was actually part of its cachet. Ever since then, rodeo has been marked by this contradiction as rodeo people defied their critics, the disputes were never fully resolved, and livestock were caught in the middle. Steer busting was and remains (it is still practiced) a sensational reinterpretation of the range work of capturing a steer, calf, or cow at large on the land. It became a foundational rodeo event because it conveyed the idea that rugged, unsentimental conflict with resistant animals helped westerners to be western, which was a self-exoticizing cliché upon which competitive rodeos and Wild West shows would come to trade.

Violent entertainments seemed western in those days because plenty of people endorsed, participated in, or at least tolerated the collective and individual violence by which settlers forcibly repurposed space, animals, and resources toward settler control and the production of commodities like beef. No one expected this process to be easy, and many relished the struggle in order to express their identities as rural westerners.[4] Steer roping competitions communicated this idea while supporting a broader habit on the part of some travel writers, journalists, western boosters, and rodeo promoters of portraying the West as a place of extremes and the incredible, which in turn encouraged many to internalize American exceptionalism more broadly.[5]

Not yet known as "rodeo," "cowboy tournaments" or simply "roping competitions" organized by promoters coexisted with informal cowboy contests at private ranches that had always taken place anywhere there were friends, food, whiskey, and a bucking horse to mount or some cattle to rope.[6] Cowboy tournaments were rare in Canada until after the turn of the century, so that region awaits chapter 3. The present chapter charts the origins of steer busting competitions from ad hoc cowboy tournaments and exhibitions of the 1880s to a moment of public crisis in the first decade of the twentieth century when legislation ostensibly banning the practice appeared around the West. The West that people conjured through steer roping competitions in those years was the recent past of the Beef Bonanza. In the 1870s and early 1880s, private investors fueled a speculative bubble in which it seemed anyone might become a millionaire cattle baron. Acting largely unsupervised and unregulated by government, men put as many cattle as they could on grasslands recently confiscated from Indigenous nations by the federal government.[7] By 1885, rangelands had become devastated from overgrazing while barbed wire and sod-busting homesteaders limited access to remaining free grazing land that cattlemen required if they were ever to turn a profit. Yet, the downturn only seemed to make steer busting more compelling as nostalgic entertainment. Every rider who chased down and roped a head of livestock was metaphorically resurrecting the abundance of the free grass days and the Beef Bonanza a few years earlier. To many, steer busting celebrated a moment of seemingly infinite potential in the recent past, which communities could in turn use in the present to propose that there was another bounty in the near future.

Steer busting purported to present not only the storied free-grass, open-range cowboy in action but also the "wild and untamed steers of the Texas prairies."[8] Many people imagined semi-feral or wild cattle, sharp-horned and powerful, to be quintessentially western animals. Fierce and freedom-loving, they would be subdued only by the most fierce and fearless cowboys. By their very independence and efforts to flee or defend themselves, these cattle were just begging for a fight, and thus they metaphorically consented to the steer busting contest. Actual living steers bore the burden of living up to those myths when they were demonized by rodeo promoters, captured by stockmen, and employed in busting. This chapter tells what it can of their story.

The first steer busting competition organized by and for settlers appears to have taken place in 1882 when ten ropers in Austin, Texas, competed for a $300 saddle donated by John Neff, a Confederate veteran and local saloon proprietor.[9] The contest was a novel feature attached to the five-day Capital State Fair in Austin, and one newspaper claimed the steer busting competition had been "the most exciting sport of the fair, [which] attracted the greatest attention."[10] It was certainly a showy affair. Trotting in from the nearby country, cowboys appeared in Austin that week and conspicuously strode about "rigged out in the panoply of their profession."[11] It was the height of the Beef Bonanza bubble. Several years of maximum cattle production and record beef prices were peaking that fall due to an unusually warm winter the previous year and an influx of foreign investment that fueled the hiring of range cowboys.[12]

Now, perhaps flush with a little more cash than usual, many young cowboys of the period flaunted their unique relationship to the land and livestock by competing in pricey silver-and-leather cowboy accoutrements like elaborate or expensive hats, chaps, vests, bandannas, spurred boots, and sometimes guns.[13] Tournament organizers encouraged such showmanship with prizes of richly decorated saddles, sombreros, and other western garb. Cowboy winners also earned some notoriety and praise from their feats in these competitions because the papers always named steer roping finalists, their relative times, and winnings at these self-consciously western events. People were delighted and "astonished" by the sight of these cowboy competitors in Austin that November. "When the cowboys entered for the contest, they rode into the field and tied their horses to a tree near the pen, there was quite a buzz of excitement, and many visitors critically examined the roping saddles, lariats, etc.," said one local paper.[14] It was only November 1882, and Bill Cody—that famed storyteller of western history for audiences far and wide—would not found his traveling Wild West show company in North Platte, Nebraska, for another six months.[15]

Austin was primed for such a show just then. The small city sat on the Colorado River at the southern end of new rail lines and near the storied Chisholm Trail, the dirt highway leading north along which drovers and cattlemen herded Texan cattle, mostly longhorns, to railheads in Kansas after the Civil War.[16] Austin also had an ostentatious new statehouse under construction and an impressive new university in operation. People in Austin were just then experimenting with ways of adapting the storied Wild West found in for-profit entertainments, like dime novels, into a city brand that could promote regional investment. Cowboy tournaments were an opportunity to adapt some of those emerging western stereotypes to the then-current trend of boostering civic festivals. Counterintuitively to many, cowboy tournaments applied a Wild West civic branding theme to a town or region to claim that it was proceeding past "the pioneer stage" of boom and bust, and was thus ripe for sensible investment.[17]

Nationally, such civic celebrations included classics like New Orleans' Mardi Gras and newly established events like St. Louis's Veiled Prophet Festival, Los Angeles' Fiesta de los Flores, and San Diego's Cabrillo Celebration, as well as countless agricultural fairs and themed "jubilee" or fiesta days in smaller cities and towns. As with the big-city civic festivals and fairs, festival days in the West often appeared democratic in participation and spectatorship—especially if staged on July 4th to impose patriotic feeling upon the community—but largely represented the work of a local elite to assert their cultural authority. The crowds of folks who showed up to watch a parade or participate in a cowboy or agricultural competition were deemed by some to be endorsing the powerful locals who organized the celebration.[18]

Not everyone at Austin's Capital State Fair would have predicted that steer busting would become so central to that celebration since there was plenty else to see. Founded in 1875, the fair featured agricultural, technological, and industrial exhibits, as well as various sporting entertainments that encouraged wagering, like horse racing, shooting tournaments, cockfights, baseball games, and, one year, "deer chasing," in which a single deer was trapped in an enclosure with a group of hunting dogs and frantically tried to escape by running herself against the fencing.[19] On the question of how cowboy tournaments even related to western character (whatever that might even be in an era of such heavy in-migration), one Texas critic insisted in 1882 that the horse races and baseball game had been more crowded with spectators than the first-ever steer roping feature. "This could have been of no special interest," he said of the cowboy roping, "save to people from other states."[20]

Although local people appreciated steer roping and other cowboy sports thereafter, the Texan had a point. To promote land sales and business investment from points north and east, promoters at Austin's fair were the first of many community boosters, land speculators, newspapermen, and others who began sponsoring steer busting and cowboy tournaments of their own. Beginning in Texas and the Southwest, the tournaments followed the expanding cattle trade north and west, often just as a novelty added to local agricultural fairs, civic festivals, or Fourth of July celebrations. By the mid-1880s, community-sponsored cowboy contests at fairs and festivals were becoming a way to associate one's city or town with the "myth of the garden" West, unfettered and environmentally abundant, teeming with cattle and other resources to harvest.[21] The press was especially integral to the spread of steer busting, explaining the logistics and regulation of the competition for far-flung audiences and promoters looking for a novelty for their own festival.[22]

Soon, people in, Wyoming, Oregon, or Colorado were wondering if steer busting, bronc riding, and other cowboy events were novelties from the Southwest that they could borrow and claim as authentically and broadly western. As it happened, in many places people began thinking in these terms just when the western myth of the garden was in serious crisis, during the years of the Big Die-Up. In 1886 and 1887, just as the cattle trade had spread to Montana and Wyoming, millions of these animals died in unusually harsh winters after having been neglected on drought-stricken or depleted rangelands.[23] It was a moment of environmental, animal, and human crisis in which people's lives were changing quickly and cowboy sports helped people digest what was happening by imagining a more abundant West. These sports jostled around in American culture with other entertainments, such as stereo cards, illustrations of "western scenes," dime novels, and traveling shows about the West, in which fiction and reality would be mixed.[24] Audiences of steer busting surely understood they were witnessing reckless, sensational stunts by (probably drunken) cowboys with little sympathy for animals, save a favored horse. Still, cowboys who competed in steer busting generally worked in remote locations with limited supervision.²⁵ What actually went on out there was difficult for many people to know with complete certainty, including their cattleman employers.

Many took steer busting to be one of various "most grotesque exhibitions of . . . cowpuncher merriment" that one could find in the West and that tapped into the apparent audience appetite for violence, feeding off old ideas about cowboys as wild men who teased or terrorized cattle when drunk or bored.²⁶ A "cowpuncher" was a stock pusher, that is, a cowboy or stockman who hurried animals along into a chute at the stockyards with a long board or pole. To explain the sensational brutality of early cowboy sports, some blamed the influence of old vaquero games and were suspicious of Hispanic cowboys who appeared at some tournaments and who worked across the Southwest for ranch operations of all kinds. Mexican and Mexican American *charreada* or *charrería* traditions included bull baiting with bears, bull fighting, horse tripping, trick and fancy horse riding, and other skill competitions for cowboys, with plenty of wagering on the results. Bull tailing, in particular, seemed a precursor to steer busting. In San Francisco before annexation, for example, vaqueros practiced what one observer called "a local version of bull-fighting—*colea el toro*—in which the object was to torment a bull and then attempt to overturn the creature by seizing its tail." In another telling, vaqueros specifically sought to frighten steers: "In mid-flight chasing the steer, the vaquero would grasp the tail and with a sudden jerk and twist somersault the panic-stricken animal and easily tie him down."²⁷ Some critics appear to have found tailing and busting dishonorable specifically because the cowboy or vaquero made his own work easier by the tripping, and thus did not engage in a fair fight.

These kinds of Spanish-era slaughter-day fiesta sports informed but actually had a tenuous presence at settler-sponsored events.²⁸ For instance, "bullfights in the true Spanish style" only appeared very occasionally in settler venues and routinely produced a public outcry since the sight of blood and dead animals was guaranteed.²⁹ In several places, tournament promoters nonetheless tried out old vaquero games of skill like "jerking the heads off chickens buried up to their necks in the sand while riding by at full speed."³⁰ In at least one case, an anti-cruelty advocate obstructing such a contest was placated when organizers wrung the necks of the chickens before burying them in the sand of the arena.³¹

From an official point of view, as city boosters in Austin and elsewhere might have hoped the press would explain it, steer busting was a novel way to draw attention to a community. With its vaquero origins and wild-man portrayal of cowboys, it was familiarly exotic. It turned violence against market steers, a disliked or unknown creature to most Americans in any event, into broadly accessible sporting entertainment that normalized the idea that such engagement with animals was uniquely western. At the same time, any cowboy might win, so cowboy contests in general encouraged popular ideas about the democratic promise of the West.[32] Young male competitors vying with their peers to dominate an animal and be declared "winner" also bore strong resemblance to the archetypal male heroes within American culture who proved themselves through a violent trial in the wilderness or on the battlefield.[33]

From a cowboy's point of view, steer busting was deeply subversive. Consider that it sometimes also appeared as a group challenge called a "steer roping exhibition." This was an old Californio-Mexican practice that predated and rejected regulated, individual-competitor challenges, which would soon take over rodeo to treat competitors as individuals, not a more powerful collective. In roping exhibitions, spectators witnessed a cowboy-centric satire, like this one at the horse track in Aspen, Colorado, in 1898:

> Five steers were turned loose at once and all the cowboys took after them, yelling like mad. The steers gave them a merry chase, running toward the crowd that had got inside the track fence and scattered the people right and left. Two of the steers were hard to lasso and after going up to the grand stand [and being shooed away by a lady with an umbrella] went down toward the north end of the grounds again closely followed by a cowboy. One of the steers by this time had got considerably riled and took after Arthur Parry who showed sprinting qualities that entitles him to be classed as a 10 second man. The steer showed the most, however, and caught Parry just in time to hunt him down on his knees and Parry kept travelling right along and escaped by crawling under the fence onto the track. Parry says he was awfully scared, but not enough so as to cause his hair to stand on end.
>
> Jack Yore, seeing the predicament that Parry was in, started after the steer intending to "tail" him, but stumbled just as he reached him and the steer not caring to follow Parry under the fence turned and made for Yore. Here was another exciting sprint with the

steer gaining at every jump and Yore, seeing he had no show of escaping, pulled his gun and fired a little over the animal's head twice in quick succession and succeeded in scaring the steer so he turned and went in another direction, and was caught and tied.[34]

Cowboy Everett Brisendine remembered of such events, "There was usually a lot of whisky back behind the chutes," a nuisance for rodeo organizations for decades to come.[35] Drunken cowboys who chased and roped steers, firing their guns within striking distance of the audience, enacted Wild West clichés as license for displays of "bravado largely for the entertainment of spectators," another witness remembered.[36]

Although during the 1880s early tournament organizers, along with Buffalo Bill Cody's Wild West publicists, would work to reform the cowboy's public image, steer roping exhibitions continued to celebrate old tropes of the uncivilized cowboy. Exhibitions were dangerous and chaotic performances in which "riders were unhorsed, the milling steers crashed against each other, . . . and horses were injured," as one report from San Diego explained with some delight.[37] Since on the range cowboys did not employ gunfire to calm cattle, only to kill them in case of serious stampede or other emergency, by such "genuine" cowboy performances poked fun at any spectator who believed this kind of match had any resemblance to actual cowboy work.[38] Range cowboys also embellished themselves as "genuine wild cowboys" by disorienting their roping steers "with a yell such as only cowboys can give," designed to entertain their own spirit as much as the crowds' expectations. Here cowboys were disruptive western agents of misrule who invaded town at tournament time, in the spirit of Daniel Boone and other "wild man" characters in American history, who challenged the forces of civilization that town boosters counterintuitively sought to promote with a cowboy contest.[39]

In roping exhibitions there was no judge, no timer nor rules, no prize saddle or other respectable reward for the cowhands who cut loose to get their metaphorical comeuppance against the stockmen who paid them so little and the cattle who made their work so difficult.[40] The working cowboys and other ropers who participated in busting competitions and exhibitions arguably had limited stakes in cattle that belonged to their employers and other cattlemen in any event, including those at the rodeo ground. Although they depended on stock owners for seasonal work, many cowboys resented cattlemen as "illegal monopolists of the public domain," who fenced off communal grasses and dominated local governments. Such highly capitalized ranchers made fortunes while suppressing wages and occasionally replacing American cowboys with Mexican cowboys, who were even more poorly paid. Texas cowboys in the Panhandle had even resorted to strikes during the collapse of the Beef Bonanza in the mid-1880s, exposing this point of view.[41] Steer busting reenacted the moment a head of cattle became someone's capital (the boss's capital, cowboys would have said) when captured for branding or shipping to market, but also cowboys' willingness to waste the boss's stock.

Many of these cattle owners had ignored a whole host of voices explaining the dangerous environmental changes underway as the number of acres required to support one head of cattle spiralled upward that decade.[42] When settler steer busting contests were proliferating north and west, ranching was less the seeming bonanza of the unregulated beef boom of the 1870s and early 1880s, and more a business requiring suppression of expense and risk wherever possible. The cattle investors who restocked and carried on after the Big Die-Up catastrophe of the mid-1880s put smaller herds on smaller ranges, fed them stored hay over the winter, and then sold them via Kansas cattle markets to corn feedlots in Illinois.[43] Suddenly, extensive ranching under this "midwestern system" required range workers—the famed free-spirited cowboys of lore—to spend their time putting up hay.[44] The storied cattle drives of the post–Civil War years were stripped down to twice-yearly roundups for branding and castrating, moving herds from one seasonal range to another, or the work of cutting out steers for transfer to the railhead.[45] In the late 1890s, while Arthur Parry and Jack Yore scrambled around an Aspen cattle pen with some frightened steers, Emerson Hough, a well-known writer of western stories, lamented what he saw as the degradation of cowboy work, saying, "Yearly it becomes more and more restricted, modified, and confined, less and less a wild gathering of the plains, more and more a mere barnyard fixture."[46]

Cowboys at a tournament were reenactors of the imagined old-time action and excitement of western life. Thus did steers unknowingly come to play a new western character: "the wild and untamed steer of the Texas prairies."[47] At tournaments, the promise of wild steer "outlaws" or "vicious fellers," especially longhorn cattle from Texas, was common in steer busting promotion for audiences everywhere. Tournament publicists routinely claimed to have the worst, largest, most dangerous steers anyone could find, whose very nature invited confrontation. These steers were "gathered up and brought, fighting, bellowing and protesting to the fair grounds and put in a pen," said one Wyoming newspaper in 1890.[48]

For a generation already, writers and romanticists had specifically venerated longhorn cattle from Texas and Mexico as representations of the supposedly untamed Southwest. Due to their lineage in "the blood [and] the instincts of Spanish cattle," and having "escaped and reverted to primordial nature," admirer Frank Dobie explained, the longhorns' apparent westernness stemmed from their self-sufficiency. They had become "fearsome opponents" of mankind after learning to defend themselves "in the wild lands of Texas before man fenced, watered and cleaned them of predatory animals," he said.[49] Cowboy lore expressed a fraught fascination for longhorns' "malevolent cleverness accumulated through years of vigilant freedom," as Edward Branch put it. "The Texan loved these cattle because they fought him."[50]

With their feral cultures and individual curiosity, these cattle passed survival skills from generation to generation through experience at large on the landscape. According to the travelers and soldiers who occasionally sought to kill and butcher them in Texas, in order to avoid contact with humans, longhorn cattle hid in dense thickets and brush, forging tunnel-like openings that a man on horseback could not navigate. When people still found ways to confront them, they revealed themselves to be "wilder and more apt to attack" than the bison or other ungulates.[51] It was a truism that one must remain on horseback to venture safely across the land in case unexpectedly encountering some of these creatures.[52] The longhorns' numbers rose and fell over the nineteenth century, largely in relation to the level of human predation. By the later 1880s, with the collapse of the Texas-based longhorn beef system, even in Texas itself, the few remaining pure longhorns increasingly appeared as rare relics. They evoked the easy abundance of the immediate post–Civil War Texas, when men returned from battle to find feral livestock abundant and harvestable, one that cowboy tournaments might resurrect.[53]

As rodeos appeared in more and more places in those years, cowboy tournaments came with standard promotional talk about how the contest would feature Texas longhorns or other "wild and vicious steers" for roping entertainment. This was just a distraction from the fact that, for over a decade already, continental beef production had actually been turning away from southwestern longhorn cattle. Cattlemen and absentee investors in cattle operations were favoring more energy-efficient, heavier meat-producing breeds that were more labor-intensive to manage but more profitable in the food system. Longhorns had been common enough in Texas for a time, but they bulked up slowly and provided limited flesh that was tough and increasingly unpalatable to eastern and foreign meat buyers.[54] In an attempt to capture hardiness and speedy meat growth in one animal, ranchers drove longhorns into the northern Great Plains and began favoring shorthorn and longhorn-shorthorn cross cattle. In time, fear of the tick-borne Texas fever (to which longhorns were immune, but shorthorn and dairy breeds devastatingly vulnerable) drove many states to limit or stop longhorn drives from Texas into their territories.[55]

Modern beef cattle, not least the mass-produced "market steer," proliferated in the 1880s as the "midwestern system" of beef production spread beyond its home in Illinois. The new cattle were somehow less western than the longhorns, some said. They were less capable of defending themselves from human and other predation or keeping themselves well-fed and watered on large ranges in difficult weather. Delicate meat cattle, made weak by human-engineered inbreeding and perhaps even dehorned, lived on fenced ranges where ranch laborers (cowboys themselves now domesticated by industrial beef) brought them hay or grain to eat in winter.[56] Many said that the new cattle submitted more easily to roundups and the trip to the slaughterhouse because they were "thoroughly domesticated" by "constant handling."[57] "The cowmen as a whole do not admire a muley [hornless cattle], because it reminds 'em of places where man and beast are confined in small enclosures," said cowboy memoirist Ray Ward some years later. Range cowboys had for decades interpreted their own identities through semi-wild, self-sufficient cattle and resisted the idea that purebred beef stock could survive on isolated ranges.[58]

Still, some shorthorn and longhorn cattle unwittingly contributed to the myth that honorably western cattle were strongly resistant to people. In close quarters, beef cattle of the era could be confounding and sometimes seemingly irrational villains, certainly not sympathetic characters. At work cowboys could be pulled off their horses and gored by a cow or bull, or fall under a stampede, or they might have digits or limbs twisted, broken, or severed by a taut rope pulled by a resistant steer. Word of mouth and the papers told of people killed or grievously injured by steers and other cattle, news that went beyond mere sensationalism. Especially in railhead towns where livestock routinely moved through business and residential districts, people had to trust transient drovers and vaqueros to contain in the streets cattle who sometimes "became unmanageable."[59] From small western main streets, to the lanes just off Market Street in San Francisco, to the stockyards of Chicago, disoriented

**RECEIVING A RAILROAD MAP.**
Teasing and goading cattle was a well-worn mode of mischief for kids.
"Receiving a Railroad Map." From Joseph G. McCoy, *Historic Sketches of the Cattle Trade of the West and Southwest* (1874).

steers periodically "tore through the streets" making "furious attack" and "causing much excitement." Cattle were also a legitimate public safety issue as they grazed on unfenced properties, and were known to charge and toss in the air or impale with their long horns passing pedestrians and horses. One "fractious steer" in Oregon, for instance, "defied all restraint and cavorted around the streets for an hour or more, terrifying all pedestrians. . . . and his antics were especially dangerous to children," said one incensed local.[60]

In the work-a-day West, whether on the range, in railhead towns, or in the rodeo arena, these steers seem to have been trapped by explanatory anthropomorphism, a confusion to which people have been prone in interpreting the behavior of many animals.[61] That is, like dogs, bears, and other creatures who express fear through behavior many humans perceive as aggression, cattle often acted out of fear but were interpreted as simply mean or capable of only the single emotion of anger. Western newspapers regularly characterized steers who escaped a drover's herd or corral not as lost, confused, or frightened, but as "maddened," "angry," or "infuriated," just as cowboy tournament promoters would do with the roping steers at the arena.

Steer ropers were drawn from the larger community of cowboys, and some of their memoirs tempered such portrayals of steers to mention the odd occasion when a particular cowboy traveled with and came to know one steer as an individual, learning his habits and thus how not to agitate him. By and large, however, as quasi-adventure stories, cowboy memoirs, too, told of steers who "showed fight" and "savagely charged" when provoked by pain, frustration, or some cause that was mystifying to people.[62] Of course, the draft animals used by overland migrants had been steers, namely oxen. Therefore, some argued that any given steer's aggression toward people was a product of the lack of extended exposure to humans or of having been "'on the prod' or 'riled'—a form of temporary insanity usually occurring after rough or strenuous handling."[63] Although their behavior varied according to breed, sex, and individual experiences, cowboy memoirists blamed cattle's dangerous behavior on their supposedly irrational and emotional minds, typecasting steers as merely "sullen with rage" or "fighting mad," especially older, more self-possessed ones.[64] Unknowingly, these creatures made the West more dangerous and also more exciting. By merely acting in their own interest to defend themselves, steers became vulnerable to a new kind of exploitation, not as food but as entertainment, since so many interpreted their behavior as consent to being toyed with.

Cowboy tournament producers and competitors masqueraded unwitting steers from these populations as living remnants of an imagined-bountiful and morally violent Old West while gradually purging—or claiming to purge— cowboy tournaments of apparently Hispanic practices.[65] Steers sometimes became unknowing proxies for that Hispanic heritage, described as "untamed natives of the Southwest," as the boostering talk went.[66] In practice, at cowboy tournaments, roping steers could be drawn from both "over-handled" shorthorns or Texas cattle, or from their crosses, as was convenient or desirable for any given competition promoter. Once in the arena surrounded by unfamiliar people and noise, many cattle displayed fear-based behaviors like running, pawing the ground with a hoof, or threatening a head butt that served the rodeo spectacle. Roping steers were also sometimes brought up to a tournament directly from Mexico, or drawn from local Texan stock, or neither, but falsely advertised to be "as wild as the plains of the southwest could produce," since people and cattle passed back and forth over the U.S.-Mexico border routinely.[67] To stockmen, supplying cowboy tournaments would soon represent

# BUSTING STEERS AT THE TURN OF THE CENTURY 31

Roping steer at Cowboy Park rodeo grounds, ca. 1910, Ciudad Juárez, Mexico. Juárez was a crossing point for many cattle driven north into the United States.
Courtesy of the El Paso Public Library, Otis A. Aultman Collection.

a way to wring a little bit more profit from a market steer before shipping him in a jam-packed railcar to an Illinois corn feedlot operation or to one of the animal slaughter monopolies in Chicago.

It is impossible to know the specific details of the lives of steers employed in steer busting since they were anonymous and interchangeable to rodeo people, who made no record of steers as individuals. We do know that before about 1910, roping steers were generally about four or five years old and enormous— "big as boxcars"—often weighing over 1000 pounds.[68] They appeared in coats of all colors with horns that might reach several feet across.[69] As bull calves, all of these steers had lived at-large for their first months of life with their cow and herd. Then, one day, each found himself chased down, roped, and tied out in the open someplace, with no analgesics or veterinary attention, or, perhaps, much sympathy from the exhausted men who did this dangerous, dirty work. As a man held him by placing a boot "on the critter's nose to hold its head still," a calf also felt the burn of a branding iron and a knife cutting out an identification notch from one ear or the skin of the neck.[70]

The four-year-old market steer was the most profitable animal to sell for slaughter. Although they bulked up less than bulls on the same forage, steers produced less-gamey meat containing more fat, which consumers preferred.[71] To produce steers from bull calves, range workers also "cut," or castrated them. A general practice was to cut the scrotum open with a sharp knife and manually pull apart and destroy, or "scrape off" with a knife, the spermatic cords leading to the testicles. This procedure guaranteed castration but also created an open wound vulnerable to screw-worms and infection.[72] Here was a process many must have understood to be painful and frightening to a calf barely familiar with humans, especially as he had to be stretched out between two ropers or straddled by multiple people to submit to the procedure. Afterward, newly minted steers might be seen "getting up and laying down" in discomfort, swollen, or bleeding heavily.[73] One cowboy recalled of the early twentieth-century practices, "Dehorning, castrating, branding, and vaccinating puts a lot of wear and tear on a calf. They can just die of shock."[74] Indeed, although there were no dehornings or vaccinations in the 1870s and 1880s, such rough handling—as necessary as it was to the production of market steers—often produced "a loss in flesh [that] . . . cut into profits," said another cowboy.[75]

In preparation for a cowboy tournament, a stock contractor located a dozen or so steers and drove them on foot or shipped them by rail to a stockyard near the performance venue. Drovers then moved those steers to the competition space, where they were marshalled into an unshaded corral until showtime. Once the busting competition was underway, often these same steers were run, thrown, and roped multiple times per day. Steer busting was a timed competition that rewarded haste and physical force on the part of ropers, so its speed and intensity made for an action-oriented performance in the arena that would have been entirely unsustainable at work all day with cattle on the land.[76] The roping pursuit functioned as it did specifically because of a steer's internal experience. And, indeed, the many storied and carefully practiced techniques of vaquero and cowboy sports existed only because many generations of frightened cattle and horses had run from a human being.[77]

At the unfenced rodeo grounds of the period, as quasi-wild beings having never visited such a noisy place before, steers stood together guarded by mounted pickup men, the riders who moved rodeo stock into place until they were cut out and driven toward the performance space at high speed. One rodeo reporter explained with unusual frankness how "untamed" western bovine behavior was elicited from steers confined in chutes to match the "wild steer" stereotype: "The steer is haled about with sticks, clubs, yells and whoops, until perfectly maddened, when the outer bars are suddenly withdrawn and he leaps out into the opening."[78] Thereafter, a steer would find himself chased, tripped, and roped while struggling to keep his legs free and to right himself. With the whites of his eyes prominent all the while, he would finally be unable to move, prone with the rope pulled taut at great pressure on his limbs and neck. This process could take sixty or ninety seconds with advanced ropers, three or five minutes more commonly, especially in competitions in which the steer was allowed a one-hundred-yard (rather than seventy-five or fifty) head start, which produced longer roping times.[79] Once tied, a steer might lie prone and bound on the ground until the judge decided the roping was a valid one. Or, sometimes, he stayed immobilized longer as, say, the roper posed before a photographer. Thereafter, at many competitions, steers were dragged from the arena while still bound, and only untied once offstage in a separate corral so they would not interrupt the next chase.[80]

The graphic trope of a resistant animal straining against a rope in the West was a familiar and persuasive one.[81] Since the 1840s, famed writers and illustrators, starting with George Catlin, had told of Mexican, Spanish, and Native American men who handled livestock with little compassion or patience, stories that collectively asserted that resistant, "terror-stricken" animals were integral to western life.[82] The Republic of Texas had issued a two-dollar banknote featuring a mounted Hispanic vaquero roping a longhorn at full gallop. Within another forty years, artists ranging from the famed Frederick Remington to anonymous pulp magazine illustrators to Buffalo Bill Cody's lithograph men created depictions of Western-styled action and adventure carrying documentary pretensions by way of dynamic-looking animal participants. As art historian Ron Tyler explains, such "noble and wild creature[s]" [were] representative of the best the Old West had to offer": galloping horses carrying whooping and shooting men or straining under the whip of a wagon driver; struggling animals of all sorts roped and thrown to the ground by cowboys or mountain men; horses or cattle with tongues extended from their open mouths, with the whites of their eyes showing, driven by cowboys across a rugged landscape.[83] In this abundant, exciting West, animals had no intrinsic value or moral significance, but they served as vehicles for romantic ideas about the power of heroic individuals who fought nature and won, although nature seemed increasingly tamed in the industrial age.[84]

Roping horse observing tied steer and roper. "Walter Glenn winner roping contest, time 45 seconds," 1911, Ontario, Oregon, Burrell Photo, Photographic Study Collection, National Cowboy & Western Heritage Museum, 2004.190.2, Museum purchase.

As cowboy tournaments followed the expanding cattle trade north and west, everywhere tournament organizers and the papers ignored or flippantly ridiculed the risks to steers. Papering over any uncertainty or diversity of local opinion over steer busting, they diverted attention from the immediate causes of rodeo livestock injury and death, taking it as an inevitable element of western life. Denver's 1887 tournament, for instance, was proclaimed "a howling success in every particular" by a paper in Temple, Texas, that had received news of it. "The tournament ... was taken part in by thirty-two cowboys, who thoroughly represented the plains fraternity ... rigged out in the most approved western garb [who] endeavoured to out-do their exploits on the range," the paper said plainly. "One wild broncho [sic] had his neck broken by a violent jerk of the lasso [during the bronc riding]. One steer resisted roping even after one of his legs was broken and another steer had one of his horns pulled out of his head. The people applauded, and the affair was voted such a happy event that it was repeated to-day."[85] Indeed, a sort of cowboy grotesquerie became popular in written descriptions of early cowboy tournaments. By this convention, authors seemed to relish the action and violence of cowboy contests, either noting animal injuries without comment or with approval,

The idea that resistant animals made westerners western was everywhere. Even a spool cotton trade card might present a vaquero and his horse "testing" and tripping a Texas longhorn. "Testing" Clark's O.N.T. Spool Cotton Thread on a Texas Longhorn, ca. 1875–1900. Library of Congress.

such that the injuries were present but also not present in the narrative at the same time, and thus carried no moral significance.[86]

The visual counterpart to this textual tradition was the image of a contorted, airborne steer at the moment before he hit the ground. Turn-of-the-century cowboy sports were central to the historical moment when photographers first sought to capture a visually striking "decisive moment" encapsulating an incredible athletic feat.[87] Like old lithographs and newspaper stories, they flattered spectators' expectations about the West as a place of natural abundance, frequent danger, and presumed-moral violence with and against animals.[88] The airborne steer was a preferred image among the standard shots photographers sought to capture at the rodeo grounds, and its replication and mass circulation on postcards, newspapers, and magazine pages only contributed to the catalogue of gratuitous depictions of violence against animals. By excluding any sense of those steers' full lives, the circulation of such snapshot representations normalized the use of cattle as a necessary and exciting element of Western life totally unrelated to larger systemic environmental or economic problems in the West. Steers were most frequently pictured not starving on the range, nor crowded in a stock car, nor hanging upside down in a slaughterhouse but artificially, spinning in the air at a sporting arena on a carnival day.

Alternatively, the graphic visual language of steer busting focused on the bound steer as newly captured capital, lying motionless at the end of a pony's taut rope. Many took the carefully trained horses used for steer roping to be the epitome of the cowboy's faithful horse, idealized in countless accounts of range work and western life, documentary and fictional. People praised cow ponies for understanding the danger of the steer during roping, which supplied "the prettiest picture in the whole panorama," said one admiring Wyomingite. "The sagacious little pony standing with his nose to the fallen adversary, straining at the line, and watching the steer with bright knowing eyes. He realizes that he's in a bad fix if the steer gets up, and he hasn't the least intention of letting him do so."[89] Ropers did expend extraordinary energy training their horses through day-to-day work, which many believed cultivated their "sagacity" and bravery in the face of the supposedly irrational, unsympathetic character of the steer.

Many westerners also took great pride in western equines because they were descended from Spanish and other stock deemed far superior to the effete Thoroughbreds championed by eastern horse aficionados, whose turf journals insulted western horses as "vast hordes" of discreditable beasts of unknowable lineage.[90] Even though cattle sometimes gored or otherwise injured the horses on the range, cowboys often said that because of "superb training" cow ponies were calm, uncomplaining, wise, and capable in the face of the dangers of the job. The talents of such horses, explained one cowboy's account, were especially "marvelous, considering the mongrel breed and rough handling he gets."[91] The cowpony in the steer-busting arena was a creature both of nature and human culture, once free but conquered by the cowboy, and now his helper in the symbolic ritual of keeping the Western struggle alive.[92]

For steers at the tournament grounds, beyond any mental and physiological stress produced by fear, inability to graze, lack of water, overheating, or physical exertion, a minority also suffered broken horns, damaged or broken limbs, and occasionally a broken neck. Many died right in the arena as the crowd looked on. How many died or suffered injury is impossible to know. The inevitability of it was plainly built into the regulation of the sport in many places, for instance, "Rule 6—If the steer is killed, that run and tie shall not be counted, and the party shall have [a] chance at another steer."[93]

Steer busting spread across the continent in a period when people regularly saw dead animals, whether a collapsed workhorse, a strangled coyote, or a pig carcass at the butcher's shop. Still, to many, steer busting produced egregious displays of violence toward animals that embarrassed the West, raising the question of how or whether to change the event to prevent injuries and public criticism. "The performances were most sickening and have wrapped up contests of this kind for Grand Junction because of the brutality exhibited," said one western Colorado newspaper after a steer busting competition had been included in Grand Junction's Peach Day festival. "The cowboys broke the necks of three of the steers, and one of them, after having its neck broken got up to move off. It was necessary to put the knife into his throat," to the horror of many spectators the paper said.[94] Steers were being injured so frequently at cowboy tournaments that no one bothered referring to such things as "accidents." That habit would catch on later, in the 1920s, as rodeos exploded in popularity and winced under critical scrutiny such that their promoters devised ways of publicly dismissing chronic problems as supposedly isolated incidents.

By 1900, with the popularity of steer busting came controversy that would challenge rodeo's early founders to find a way to adapt just enough to survive. Steer busting had spread from those early performances in southwestern places like Austin, following the expanding cattle trade north and west to dozens of county fairs and cowboy contests in the West. Animal advocates in California blamed the phenomenon on the economic success and "notorious cruelty" of Cheyenne Frontier Days. Wyoming's now-iconic rodeo was founded in 1897 and quickly became an enormous affair, drawing competitors from around the continent and Hawaii. Within a decade "every industrial exhibition or agricultural fair in California had its wild west performance as a necessary adjunct," one exasperated humane advocate said of the resulting entertainment fad.[95]

The interest in cowboy tournaments crossed the Mississippi and even in Chicago promoters tried out a (particularly badly managed) cowboy sports exhibition at Tattersalls Hall that rattled spectators. News of the debacle was reported as far away as Utah: "Some of the cowboys were the worse for liquor, and after teasing a big, long horned steer until it was nearly maddened, they turned it loose and tried to rope it. Before they succeeded the steer ripped up a pony in a shocking manner. Loud cries of indignation came from the spectators and many people left the building."[96] This event was halted abruptly by its

Probably dead steer at settler busting competition, Cowboy Park rodeo grounds, Ciudad Juárez, Mexico, ca. 1910.
Courtesy of the El Paso Public Library, Otis A. Aultman Collection.

organizers, the Chicago Hussars club. Yet, even in the Southwest, some among cowboy tournament audiences were known to "boo and hiss" at roping exhibitions in which the ropers were visibly drunk, their horses endangered, or steers suffered broken horns or limbs.[97] Within the humane community around the U.S., steer busting and other forms of roping had become a national issue.[98]

Anti-cruelty advocates had been established in the West for some time, accompanying the growth of churches, municipal government, and other forces of temperance and civil society. Stocked with white middle-class and elite Americans with the luxury of monitoring animal use and funding various temperance-style reform movements, humane groups represented progressive town and city people, in large part. Officers from city and state humane organizations (whether a Society for the Prevention of Cruelty to Animals, a Humane Society, or a Humane Association) had in many places been given police powers by government to surveil animal use, issue citations, recommend charges, and appeal to whoever was in charge at a given rodeo to have offending individuals ejected.[99] Frequent critics of cowboy tournaments early on, they and their donors actually represented a broad segment of the community, and they opposed more than just steer busting, especially targeting bronc riding, steer wrestling (bulldogging), and wild horse races.[100]

Humane associations challenged the myth of steers' consent to roping when they used terms like "brutality" and "cruelty" to describe steer busting. "Cruelty" was a complex term that such organizations had employed for at least fifty years already to identify animal suffering they deemed unnecessary, with predictable debates ensuing over what constituted "unnecessary."[101] For instance, many animal advocates agreed that animal suffering in the name of entertainment was usually "cruelty," but animal suffering that supported food production was not. Indeed, ranching and farming fell under the often-unspoken agricultural exemption that gave farmers and ranchers protection from scrutiny by humane organizations, government inspectors, and the meat-and-dairy-eating public. It was not that there was no concern for range cattle. Consider the empathy symbolized by Charles Russell's famous drawing "Waiting for a Chinook," depicting a starving cow during the Big Die-Up, who shivers in the snow as wolves draw near.[102] Still, ranchers expected respite from responsibility for injury or death to animals roaming largely unsupervised on vast ranges, and ideally for those on the rodeo grounds, too.

At the Capital State Fair in Austin, where settler-organized steer busting competitions appear to have debuted, a familiar pattern had emerged in this respect. A competition would be publicized in the local papers, then citizens or humane officers would decry the event and the injuries, mental and physical, to steers—hopefully with friendly journalists listening there or in a nearby city. Thereafter tournament organizers or their allies would ridicule those critics in other newspapers. In Austin, people had stepped forward the second year busting appeared to argue against it and also a whole host of activities at the fair that might encourage bad behavior on the part of the community: liquor sales, gambling, the "deer chasing" spectacle, and the cockfights, which in 1883 included an advertised "battle royal, in which it is expected to turn 75 heeled game cocks in the pit at the same time."[103] In part, this critique was aimed at purging from settler-organized fairs and town fiesta days the pastimes of Spanish or Mexican origin that were deadly for animals, like chicken pulls, Spanish or Mexican-style bull fights, bear baiting, and cockfights. In succeeding decades, this process contributed to the apparent Americanization of settler cowboy sports, and the popular canard that the classic cowboys of the free-grass era had uniformly been white. Although increasingly unwelcome at settler-sponsored events, the Mexican American animal sports community and their Euro-settler allies continued at other venues with cockfights, horse tripping, and other traditional southwest animal contests that reflected a denial or misunderstanding of those animals' experiences.[104]

In Austin, when critics had appeared, newspapermen had initially responded by singling out doubters for public shaming, naming them as church people, "ladies [who] faint," and delicate eastern tenderfoot visitors. "The growlers, who fail to do anything for the benefit of the capital city, continue to oppose the fair," one writer argued. These people were merely "self-constituted moral guardians, . . . soured against the world" and motivated by "fanatical and puritanical opposition."[105] These kinds of ad hominem attacks against detractors would become as routine as the accusations of cruelty circulating around cowboy sports.

In many places thereafter, steer roping additionally revealed a growing urban-rural divide, apparent in the city rivalries and newspaper wars of the period. In one typical flare-up, an editor from Athena, Oregon, a tiny community situated on the road connecting the cowboy tournament towns of Pendleton and Walla Walla, Washington, raised the alarm. Another small town further east, Sumpter, had held a steer busting competition as part of a community holiday. A number of Portlanders had caught wind of the steer busting there and, Athena's newspaper editor said, "threw a moral spasm" in a "righteously indignant manner" by claiming that a steer had been teased, then injured, by the cowboys. "The *Portland Telegram*, ever on the alert for a 'story' from Eastern Oregon that may be colored to suit the fancy of some dude space writer on its staff, is struck in the solar plexus by the *Sumpter Miner*," he joked, dismissing the concerns of urban critics:

> A potato race or a pie eating contest would probably be more in line with the agricultural ideas of Portland. . . . But the smack of the real West, with its turbulent pastimes and its manly diversions is a bit too swift for a community of farmers. Linger among your wine presses, O Portland, yank the lacteal from the bosoms of your kine, plant your prunes and garner your hay crop! But if a vigorous community like Sumpter sees fit to manifest its wild western ways by roping the festive steer, pray don't be too severe.[106]

The reference to "the festive steer" revealed the myth of animal consent woven into this defense of busting, implying that the steer's mental experience or injuries were no damper on his "festive" attitude, too.

Rural and small-town westerners in many places would rely upon these foundational stereotypes in debates over rodeo sports for decades to come: self-righteous, ignorant, delicate urbanites luxuriating in a more diversified economy had no right to criticize real westerners, people shaped by their labors as stewards of animals and the land, which they rightly expressed by their enthusiasm for rugged, unsentimental entertainment. These kinds of disagreements over rodeo sports, between residents of large western cities like Seattle, Denver, Vancouver, San Francisco, and further afield in Chicago, Boston, and New York, would become common thereafter. Still today that is an important story that waits to be told more fully across the twentieth century.

Meanwhile, Sumpter, Oregon, the location of the offending steer busting contest, was a small resource town situated close to a gold strike near the Idaho border, with lumbering and ranching nearby. The region was still recovering from the Modoc War of the 1870s, which had displaced people and wildlife, and killed millions of trees, and was followed by a destructive snowfall in 1889 that temporarily destroyed Oregon's cattle business. By 1903, the place was on the mend, but continued economic development and in-migration in Oregon had required recasting the recent past and the near future, not as one of warfare and predictable environmental disasters, but as a bonanza story with settlers as the rightful heroes.[107] The town of Sumpter was, like Athena and countless other rural communities, seeking to make something of itself by appropriating southwestern cowboy competitions and the ideal of easy western abundance as their own local heritage. To other observers, the artificiality of an eastern Oregon town claiming Texas-style steer busting as local tradition was impossible to ignore.

The claim to historical accuracy of steer busting was a tricky issue that would see the event temporarily banned at a number of prominent rodeos after about 1905. To save roping, in many states and territories unions of stockmen and local humane advocates proposed that range work practices had actually changed, so tournament roping should, too. Wyoming Humane Society officers lobbied Cheyenne Frontier Days officials to adopt "the practice in cattle land today, the most humane method yet devised, [which] requires two ropers to each animal. One throws a rope over the steer's head while the other skillfully lands the snake-like lariat over a hind foot. Both ropes are then drawn tight as bowstrings by the trained saddle horses, and the animal is stretched out at full length—helpless, but uninjured. Equal skill is required, but the brutality is absent."[108] Here was the origin of the modern rodeo sport of team roping, which was sanctioned by the Rodeo Association of America (the precursor to the Professional Rodeo Cowboys Association) only in 1942. It was not so fast-paced or violent as busting, instead rewarding ropers who were accurate enough to capture a steer quickly and gracefully, ideally without strangling or pulling him to the ground.[109] Teams of men had captured cattle in this safer, more energy-efficient way for many years, so cowboy tournaments had reached a fork in the road. Steer busting celebrated waste and carelessness in an abundant environment from the cowboy's point of view; the new team-roping techniques urged cowboys to be careful with their employer's stock as valuable, finite property.

The controversy over whether to keep steer busting or replace it with either team roping or nontripping steer roping (enforced by judges by way of time penalties or disqualifications for ropers who busted a steer), spread throughout western states. Even in Arizona and New Mexico, both early locations of competitive settler-oriented steer busting contests, arguments broke out. In reference to the "necessary suffering" standard of the period, supporters of steer busting insisted that the rough treatment and injuries steers experienced at tournaments were not cruel since they served an economic function and—importantly—a unifying cultural function in the community.[110]

To protect the cattle trade and the Wild West civic brand, state-by-state, legislatures began passing vaguely worded bills that appeared to prohibit competitive busting, although usually naming it in the legislation simply as "roping." In Texas, for instance, among the various events popular in the "mushrooming rodeo sport," that "had broken out over Texas" by the 1890s, steer busting was a favorite: "one of the most colorful events for many a fan," remembered rodeo folklorist Chuck Walters. Texas state steer busting champion Clay McGonigal was so admired that "teen age cowboys aspired to outdo the master of the loop, and they practiced all over the countryside, sometimes on their own stock, more often on stock belonging to prominent ranchers." Colloquially, throughout the 1890s people spoke of the quick tripping and tying of a steer as "doing a McGonigal." Prominent ranchers, far more politically powerful in Texas than cowboy tournament promoters, cowboys, or their teenage admirers, simply ordered their allies in the state legislature to pass a bill outlawing tripping, which they did unanimously. Walters lamented, "rodeo took a body blow from which it was a long time recovering."[111]

In Texas, as would be the case in other jurisdictions that decade, rodeo was at the mercy not of humane organizations but of cattlemen who controlled which bills were passed in state and territorial legislatures. At this rough-and-ready early stage in rodeo history, ranching and cowboy tournaments had a sometimes-adversarial relationship, even though the two would become closely aligned after World War I. In the meantime, at their 1903 convention, Texan cattlemen expressed support for legislation banning tripping at tournaments in order to discourage their employees from doing so on the range. In 1905, Texas designated steer busting a misdemeanor with a fine between one and five hundred dollars (an enormous sum at the time) for "Any person who shall engage in a roping contest with other persons or alone, in which cattle or other animals are roped as a test or trial of the skill of the person or persons engaged in such roping contest, for money or prize of any character, or for any championships, for anything of value, or upon the result of which any money or anything of value is bet or wagered."[112] The wording of the law potentially gave humane officers, who were licensed with police authority regarding animal protection laws, the power to crack down on all sorts of entertainment, and even range work.[113] Of course, they did no such thing. Instead, humane officers appeared at some cowboy tournaments only to supervise the show and shoot any animals injured on site. Still, one animal advocate noted with regret that the laws "were insufficient to cover the many diversified abuses at such exhibitions."[114]

By 1907, Cheyenne Frontier Days was the final marquee show that decade to still openly feature steer busting, even though the Wyoming Humane Society (WHS) insisted it was a "disgustingly brutal practice."[115] Cheyenne, just northwest of Denver, was the Wyoming state capital, founded in the 1860s where the Union Pacific railroad crossed the Crow River. The Cheyenne area was dominated politically by a trio of "mustachioed Republicans," and by 1906 boosters spoke of the region as a limitless storehouse of natural resources—"coal, oil, iron, copper, gold, silver and countless other minerals [that] await capital and enterprise" including an (impossibly) "inexhaustible quantity of water for irrigation."[116] The state suffered through a series of cattle booms and busts, although Cheyenne and the state would weather the 1907 financial panic, which struck in the fall just after the Frontier Days rodeo, since the economy there was grounded mostly in agriculture.

Still, for ranchers coping with a state where eighty-three percent of the land was government owned, due to the loss of access to Forest Service lands in 1907 and the expense of leasing federal ranges, "it took much scheming, scrambling, and perjury to assemble the acreage needed for a sound ranch operation."[117] In fact, the largest political cleavages in the state were between cattle and sheep raisers, and between monied interests, settlers, and ranchers who competed over scant water rights.[118] There were no sheep events at Cheyenne Frontier Days, so the sheepmen were not symbolically linked to Cheyenne's or Wyoming's civic and promotional brand, while the cowboy tournament events distracted spectators from political inequalities in the state. Many in the humane community were more concerned that busting fostered a tolerance for cruelty on the part of citizens, especially children. Thus did it tarnish the supposed reputation of what one activist called "The State of Wyoming, that Western commonwealth vehemently protesting against the epithet of 'wild and wooly' attached to it by the average Easterner, and proudly boasting of its advanced civilization."[119]

For many detractors, this was precisely the point. The WHS called busting "a relic of barbarism ... entertainment belong[ing] to a dead period of western life."[120] For Wyoming to come across as a modern place, settled and regulated, citizens had to shake their stubborn love for steer busting and other cowboy sports that terrorized and injured or killed livestock. They needed to wrangle with the difficult question of how to represent their engagement with their environment among themselves, to tourists, and to investors in an authentic but disciplined way. Why should Wyoming be branded and sold with a paradox? Either it would be represented symbolically by violent engagement with animals, the myth that steers and others asked for such treatment, and that Wyomingites relished watching such brutality, or it would be a modern state of the United States ready for sensible investment and respectable society.

Thereafter, opponents of steer busting in Wyoming sought to adapt Texan legislation banning "steer roping contests" to cultivate an economic argument that would hopefully achieve anti-cruelty goals. Wyoming stockmen, who held the balance of power in the state, noted in those years that each spring and summer they would find "many steers on the ranges with broken legs and horns, and occasionally one with back or neck broken." They blamed these injuries and deaths on their cowboy employees, who practiced their roping skills in the weeks leading up to each July's Frontier Days by singling out "a lone steer on the range" for multiple practice ropes.[121] Many cattlemen had explicitly forbidden their cowboys from busting company stock when roping them legitimately for doctoring. Thus, busting steers was unsanctioned and "is not now a 'characteristically Western act of the cattle range,'" one WHS officer insisted, speaking for concerned cattlemen who generally chose not to speak directly to the papers.¹²² At Cheyenne's Frontier Days, another officer said, "The steers are thrown so hard that they are frightfully bruised, sometimes the whole side of an animal being rendered unfit for market purposes after it is butchered, owing to the tremendous shock with which it is brought to the ground. Horns are broken off, legs are broken."¹²³ Even if not killed or visibly injured, busting produced additional wastage since once busted, a steer gained no weight thereafter.¹²⁴ Perhaps this cattlemen's complaint was the origin of the claim (or hope), employed by Clifford Westermeier in the early twentieth century and countless of rodeo's supporters thereafter, that rodeo people would be kind to their animals because of those animals' monetary value.¹²⁵

Steer busting was consequently plagued by problems: for stockmen, steers killed and injured on ranges by practicing cowboys; for some community members and humane groups witnessing steers killed or injured in the arena, animal suffering and damage to society as citizens became desensitized to such violence or were encouraged to enjoy it. By the summer of 1907, after one steer lost a horn and another was grievously injured in the shoulder at Frontier Days, rumors circulated "to the consternation of punchers" that busting would finally be banned.¹²⁶ One agent of the WHS was so confident of a ban that he warned cowboys in a newspaper editorial, "Let this notice be a warning to all that would show their prowess at the expense of suffering to the helpless cattle."¹²⁷ Gone was the Wild West character of the wild and angry Texas steer whose very nature tempted cowboys to prove themselves. Humane advocates sought to recast the steers as "helpless cattle," an idea upon which rodeo's critics still rely. Thereafter, some public talk about cowboy sports included empathy for steers in riding, roping, or tailing competitions as "poor thing" or "victim" of human "tormentors," for instance.¹²⁸ In 1909 after animals again died at Frontier Days, the Wyoming legislature did finally pass a roping law.

The steer busting crisis of 1903–1909 did not resolve the longer-term disputes over the practice. Across the West, legislation prohibiting "roping" went unevenly or entirely unenforced at small-town, dirt-road, and private-ranch roping competitions where there was usually a zero percent chance that a state humane official would be on hand and inclined to hold rodeo participants accountable. At marquee cowboy tournaments, humane officers endeavoured to keep steer busting off the program. Many rodeo committees kept it, simply

Still busting at Frontier Days. "Clark McIntyre steer roping," July 31, 1954, Cheyenne, Wyoming, Devere Helfrich, Devere Helfrich Rodeo Photographic Collection, National Cowboy & Western Heritage Museum, 81.023.09343, Museum purchase.

noting it in their show program with a wink as "steer roping" or "steer tying," or relegating it to early-morning slack competitions that took place before spectators arrived. Equally, in the following decades, many ropers turned to calf roping and team roping, in which animal injuries and death were less obvious to spectators.[129]

Meanwhile, local and state humane societies either gave up the fight or lost interest in challenging individual rodeos over steer busting. After working with cattlemen to support legislation banning steer busting, as early as the 1910s, even the Wyoming Humane Society had refocused on other issues: small animal well-being (cats, dogs), the unlawful killing of some wild birds, overwork of equines, failure to supply food or water to confined livestock, cockfighting, and dog fighting. Essentially, they gave rodeos a pass.[130] Despite the laws on the books, many western animal advocacy groups like the WHS developed partnerships with local rodeos wherein they were on hand nominally to supervise but not to impede what went on, reflecting the values of the broader community in which they worked and raised funds.[131] No image of steers as helpless cattle could dislodge the myth of vicious western steer, which legitimized open violence against rodeo animals as central to Wyoming identity. Today it is important that we fight any rodeo nostalgia that ignores such things because the open, enthusiastic brutality of early cowboy sports is the truth of it.

Regulation and elimination of the worst abuses, primarily at the big marquee shows that cooperated, did in fact help cowboy tournaments transform into the modern institution of rodeo after World War I. So did rodeo people ensure that their sport was linked to a nostalgic past but also modern and adaptable, replacing the "wild" cowboys of that early generation with modern cowboy sportsmen and women who followed the rules, were individually accountable, and respected fair play. When disagreements and criticism cropped up thereafter, rodeo people could always point to local laws and tournament regulations (no matter how vaguely worded or seldom enforced) to deflect critics. Culturally, steer busting and early cowboy tournaments figuratively regenerated the old West through violence, as cultural critic Richard Slotkin might explain it. Each tripped steer retold the story that western animals showed resistance as a kind of invitation or consent to be roped, ridden, wrestled, or tied. As more and more of the land came to be controlled by moneyed interests and, by the 1910s, the federal government, rodeos would also economically regenerate the West by founding an entertainment that celebrated rural beef production and supported community development no matter what the future held.

CHAPTER 2

# Steamboat and Other Early Buckers

Imagine the stock pens at the rail yard in Cheyenne, Wyoming, in the autumn of 1914. Four men stand around the body of a dead horse, a black gelding with three white socks. Some minutes earlier one of the men had discharged a weapon into the horse's skull, killing perhaps the most famous bucker in rodeo history, Steamboat. We do not know with certainty which of the four men pulled the trigger. It may have been Floyd Irwin, rodeo competitor and son of famous stock contractor and rodeo producer Charlie Irwin. Or perhaps Johnny Rick or Bob Lee, hired hands and exhibition riders for Steamboat's owner, the Irwin Brothers Wild West Show, out of Cheyenne. Or it may have been Paul Hansen, Irwin Brothers bronc rider and later sheriff of Laramie County, Wyoming.[1] "Ashamed to tell it," said another Wyoming bronc rider of the aftermath, "but . . . a rope was tied to the great horse and [he] was dragged to the city dump."[2]

The night before, Irwin, Rick, Lee, and Hansen had shipped Steamboat by rail from the Utah State Fair in Salt Lake. There he had been billed as the worst among Irwin's string of "real outlaw horses of the West . . . a meaner or more vicious collection of stock would probably be impossible!"[3] The Irwin Brothers' traveling Western show filled out the fair's program of agricultural and industrial exhibits, with a circus tacked on for variety.[4] After having bucked in a muddy arena in a rainstorm during the show, Steamboat had found himself crowded into an unsafe pen with skittish, unknown horses as lightening and thunder filled the sky.[5] Squeezed and jostled, or perhaps spooked so he ran up against rusty wire in the corral fencing, Steamboat was later found by Charlie Irwin's men to be "badly scratched and torn up."[6] With the fair over and the men eager to leave town, Steamboat and dozens of other animals rolled out of town on a Saturday with the sun low in the sky. As the train sped through the dark of night toward Cheyenne, the horse was "terribly swollen and dying," Paul Hansen later admitted.[7] Blood poisoning quickly set in. Once the show was back in Wyoming, a Cheyenne veterinarian duly confirmed what Irwin's men suspected of the fifteen-year-old horse: they should "put him away."[8]

Within days, news of Steamboat's death had reached every corner of Wyoming and beyond in "Famous Horse Dead" stories in countless western newspapers. In those stories the death of a middle-aged horse became not an opportunity for reflection or second-guessing but an opportunity for celebrating all the cowboys with a lot of try who had attempted a ride on the "King of Buckers."[9] Here was an inglorious if predictable end to what rodeo people would celebrate as an extraordinary equine "career." Bud Gillespie, one of Steamboat's early handlers, gushed, "Steamboat bucked in more arenas, threw more riders, traveled more miles in many states in the United States and provinces in Canada than any other horse."[10] Still, Steamboat ended up at Cheyenne's livestock dump, a horse like any other.

In the 1910s, Cheyenne's dump was to the south of town on a hill with a view of Crow Creek, old Highway 85 (today I-80), and the rolling yellow and green hills beyond. This was and is beautiful country with a periodically dark history. "The bullet that ended [Steamboat's] life," claimed the *Wyoming Tribune*, "was fired from the rifle of the late Tom Horn, Wyoming's most famous murderer."[11] Horn was a notorious soldier, scout, and livestock investigator of the 1880s and 1890s. Hanged in 1903 for killing the teenage son of a Wyoming sheepman, Horn was feared in his day but later viewed with great nostalgia by some. Charlie Irwin and his brother Frank were said to be friends who "sang in harmony at the hanging of the range detective."[12] Still, why raise the issue upon the death of this horse? Possibly, Steamboat's tenuous connections to glamorously violent moments in Wyoming history absolved his human handlers of any responsibility for his death. By this imagining, Steamboat was himself an "outlaw" linked directly to the drama and violence of the Old West in Wyoming—vigilantes, cattle rustling, fence cutters, and, now, whatever the horse had lived through.

Here was one of the more stubborn fantasies people held then and since about the horse: "Steamboat may rightfully be considered to have chosen his career, for he did not submit to being broken as other horses did and did not become everybody's nag. If he had, he eventually would have stiffened up, and would have been put on the plow, and when unfit for the plow would have been sent to the rendering plant or ground up for fox feed."[13] As had been the case with the steer spun in mid-air and busted, many people seemed to relish

"We loved yuh fer yer very orneryness!" Poem and imagined monument to Steamboat in entertainment trade journal, *The Billboard*, 1915. Steamboat was widely believed to be interred at Frontier Park in Cheyenne but was ignominiously buried in the town's livestock dump.

bronc riding as an honorable contest. They imagined those horses' attempts at escape as a desire to "perform" for an audience of rodeo spectators and thus become the imagined aggressor in rodeo's drama of the western struggle.

Steamboat's particular posture while bucking, with his arched back and head bowed low in preparation for a kick and twist to dislodge a rider, was described as a "sunfisher" pose, and the image became ubiquitous in western culture.[14] To explain this phenomenon, this chapter tells the story of Steamboat and the nature of bronc riding between the 1890s and 1910s. In those years, Wild West shows still flourished, but they shared cowgirls and cowboys, producers, and animals with the growing network of community rodeos. Some of those were produced from scratch by local rodeo committees, and some were put on by hired production companies who delivered exhibition rides or entire rodeos. This chapter explains how bronc riding as sporting entertainment evolved from the work of the West's famed horse breakers and became entertainment by the turn of the century, when Steamboat first was famous. The wild and feral horses supplied to Wild West shows and rodeos were animals of harvest—like a gold strike. People applied a kind of bonanza psychology to them, finding them where they could, using them up as fast as need be, and making the most of them with the least expense. In mining western herds for horses who could be made to buck, rodeo became a new way to monetize horses and to ask of them what people demanded of themselves, often recklessly. This undertaking was an expression of rural westerners' own quarrel with the land and faith, or hopes, in its continued abundance.

After the steer busting conflagration of 1905–1909, the vicious "outlaw" bucker became the dominant animal character in rodeo sports and its iconography. The public was fascinated, or at least persuaded enough to humor the gambit. The horse outlaw epitomized how an independent western animal supposedly behaved and thus mirrored stubborn western ideas about the need for determined independence. Bronc riding with its bounding, kicking horses, "wrecks," and cowboy and cowgirl injuries defined early rodeo as what today we would call an adrenalin sport. The West imagined by bronc riding was riddled with violence yet somehow free of animal suffering and human weakness, and one in which nature eagerly participated in its own exploitation. Famous and much-loved artists replicated the ideal in graphic and plastic arts depicting quirt- and-spur-driven horse riding. Frederick Remington, Will James, Ross Santee, Walt LaRue, Charles Russell, Alexander Phimister Proctor, Mary Bonner, and others employed the sunfisher pose to represent a moment of infinite potential. Later, the sunfisher became the mascot for the state of Wyoming, stamped out on thousands of licence plates, tourist brochures, folky souvenirs, the uniforms of sports teams at the University of Wyoming in Laramie—everywhere.[15]

Deaths of famous buckers like Steamboat were regrettable, of course, yet any neglect of these horses only mirrored people's neglect of themselves. The Wild West show world of the 1890s to 1940s was a harsh environment, utterly man-made, in which people tested the limits of their bodies and health with seemingly little consideration for the future and, often, limited financial compensation. Wild West shows featured paid performers, sometimes billed as just demonstrating cowboy sports, sometimes billed as competing in cowboy contests although the results were scripted. Simultaneously, community rodeos proliferated as stationary events put on by paid and volunteer staff and a rodeo committee, or by a production company promising genuine competitions featuring local competitors. Cowboys and cowgirls paid entry fees and, if they won, took away cash, silver belt buckles, saddles, and other trophies. Some of these men and women also took usually better-paid work in vaudeville, early cinema productions, larger Wild West traveling shows, or the big circus companies (which routinely offered Wild West features by then), supplementing that with competitive rodeo winnings or contracts when possible.[16] For many rodeo fans, the era is remembered as a golden one, when rodeo cowboys and cowgirls were rural, working-class westerners from cattle and sheep country, rarely high school educated, but often exceptionally talented and very hard working.[17]

Steamboat and thousands of other horses traveled the Wild West show and community rodeo network in years when rodeo was becoming institutionalized as a sensational magnification of ranch labor and western life. The original and most famous traveling show, Bill Cody's Wild West, was on its last legs financially by 1900. Various community groups, livestock breeders, agricultural fair committees, and others had sought to limit less prestigious Wild West shows that many perceived as fraudulent. In Washington, for instance, legislation prohibited "Wild West shows in connection with county or State fairs."[18] Public interest in western shows persisted and the entertainment industry paper *The Billboard* admitted they offered "everything from the very creditable presentations of Buffalo Bill, the 101 Ranch and so on down to the mere blood and thunder Diamond Dick, bad man and 'Injun' killing stuff that also went under the name of 'Wild West Shows.'"[19] Owen Wister's iconic novel *The Virginian* (1902) and the important film *The Great Train Robbery* (1903) bolstered interest in Westerns, but offered competing narratives about cowboys as both villains and heroes.[20]

The fame of Bill Cody's outfit, the 101 Ranch, and the broader Wild West show sector of the tent show trade inspired "copy" Wild West shows.[21] Founded by entrepreneurial ranch people adept at trick riding, horse breaking, and the newly popular rodeo events, many were family-run shoestring ventures. Booger Red's Wild West Wagon Show "consisted of little more than ["Booger Red"] Privett [and his wife Mollie], a wagon, a few horses, and a helper or two."[22] Traveling winding roads sometimes traveled by speeding logging trucks, the Hall-Studnick Wild West Show toured small towns in Washington, Oregon, and California to perform in communities who invited them, bringing all the stock, wagons, and other supplies. One of the troupe's bronc riders doubled as camp cook.[23] The small-show trade served smaller towns and rural areas that the big-budget shows might not, and so coexisted with them. In the first two decades of the century, a handful of particularly entrepreneurial competitors, and a few vaudevillians working the Wild West show trade, founded and ran rodeo production companies foundational to the broader rodeo sports industry, with Lucille Mulhall, Tex Austin, and Guy Weadick among them.[24] Although a number of these ventures were started by moderately famous riders with some film work to their names, like "Booger Red" or Buck Jones, they regularly "went busted" in weeks or months.[25] *The Billboard* chronicled many such failures, too numerous to count, in their "The Corral" column on the Wild West show and rodeo trade.

Still, here was a new and entrepreneurial lifestyle for rural people, compelling because it offered travel, personal liberty, and freedom from ill-paid labor in mining, agricultural stoop work, or the assembly line. Interwar bulldogger and bronc rider Loyce Creed traveled the circuit with his partner, trick rider Mary Creed, the two of them bouncing from Texas to Colorado to South Dakota month after month. "Rodeo was a business to us," he explained. "We went out and won what we could, then save[d] our money and went back to work on the ranch."[26] Many rodeo people and rodeo families, children in tow, led this transient life with a ranch property as a base camp, or not, taking up hand-to-mouth jobs putting up hay a few weeks here, trapping wild horses or tending sheep for a few months there. Ranch living, when possible, was a lifestyle as much as a business and it required subsidizing with side jobs as many ranches failed in those years due to economic downturns, animal disease outbreaks, and debt leveraged with untenably high interest rates.[27] Some romantically described these rodeo people as a mobile community resembling the transient cowboys of the storied free-grass cattle era before 1890. Camping at the fairgrounds, public parks, and empty lots, or rooming in cheap hotels near the rodeo grounds, they would perform in one town, then disperse and disappear, only to materialize at the next venue a few days later.

Even though she had small children, Alice Holder rode broncs by trading baby-sitting favors with other female competitors and cowboys' wives. "I did it five or six years . . . I was 18 when I started," she later recalled of her time on the circuit. "I finally got so mashed up it wasn't fun anymore. . . . I wouldn't trade those days for anything in the world. . . . We thought we were in heaven, but we've all got arthritis now, so it isn't so funny now."[28] Competitors like Holder rode broncs, wrestled steers, and roped and rode with no safety equipment and no health insurance. Injuries were endemic, a product of the nature of the event itself plus cheaply prepared rodeo venues. Muddy grounds and racetracks with dangerously sharp curves downed many horses, who slipped and fell on their riders or were otherwise hobbled by "slippery ground, which would engulf [a horse's] feet up to the ankles with every jump."[29] In 1925, Roy Kivett, the adopted son of one of Steamboat's owners, stock contractor Charlie Irwin, died while steer roping in Salt Lake City "when his horse turned a somersault over him and crushed him to death. It was a very sad time for the Irwin family and sad for all who attended the show," one industry publicist remembered.[30] Still, people were not deterred. The injuries offered bragging rights. Bronc rider Frank Studnick reported, "I had bad luck with my left shoulder which I threw out of place twenty-six times in my ten years of rodeo . . . , and the right one once."[31] Interviewed later in life, many said they would not change a thing, and that the injuries and uncertainties had all been worth whatever consequences people endured at the time or later in life.[32] Rodeo people imposed those values and expectations on their animals, too.

Where, then, should we set the story of Steamboat and the other famous bucking horses of the period? Windswept in the back of an open-top trailer on a dirt highway, the various alternately dusty and muddy paddocks of the continent's rodeo grounds, munching hay at a railway livestock depot, or dozing in a stock car while the landscape passed by outside the window? Instead,

"Old Steamboat," location, date, and photographer unknown. "Horses in a Corral, Center Horse Is Old Steamboat," Wyoming Photograph Collection, ROD57, Wyoming State Archives, Department of State Parks and Cultural Resources.

picture Steamboat in a corral, date and location unknown. A compact horse bearing a rough coat from outdoor living, he stands with one of his famous white-socked hooves just lifting off the ground. Ready to bolt if need be, he looks at a photographer who leans through the fencing to capture his image.

Here is one of just a handful of photographs in existence showing Steamboat at ease, not bucking, not sunfishing, nor making his "long crooked jumps" around a rodeo ground.[33] This is how Steamboat spent most of his time and, in many ways Steamboat's life story was typical of many thousands of western equines, although people imagined him very differently. Born in Wyoming in 1896, he was a Percheron and "Mexican hot blood" cross, and he lived at large on a range near Chugwater that was leased or owned by a Wyoming man named Frank Foss. Left to breed and live unsupervised for months or years at a time, Steamboat and his kin were one of countless bands that seemed to accumulate on every ranch property of any size, as well as public lands, reservation lands, and large private ranges.[34] Young horses traveled with a dominant stallion and his harem of several to two dozen mares in a highly sociable band, with "tag-along geldings" keeping their distance in a loosely organized herd of their own. Cowboys and landowners would often attempt to manipulate the reproduction of these herds, shooting or gelding most of the stallions, and adding intact draft stallions into a herd to increase the size of offspring.[35] Such men employed hands-off management techniques, letting such horses overwinter without aid, and rounding up "survivors in the spring." Many suffered severe weight loss after months pawing the ground to find frozen grass under the snow.[36] Like cattle, they were caught and branded while young, then rounded up at age three or four years to be pressed into somebody's service. They might be Quarter Horses, Thoroughbred crosses, or mustangs of unknowable lineage.

Horses left to themselves on a range or pasture and not ridden frequently are known to evade capture when a person with a halter approaches since, as the wisdom goes, the horse has decided he does not want to go to work. We might see them as wild animals who by their behavior reject the human ideal of an "ancient contract" and seek autonomy. For horses in private-range bands, this was especially so because they were only seasonally exploited as temporary saddle horses, and thus had no chance to develop trusting or pain-free relationships with individual people. Instead, captured and saddled by force by strangers, then often driven with spurs and quirt, these horses had experiences in captivity that could lead to psychological trauma (balkiness or unpredictability, as cowboys knew it) and physical injuries. Cowboy memoirist Charles Siringo wrote of "sore-backed Spanish ponies" with saddle sores and chafing from ill-fitting saddles and dirty blankets that added pain to the exhaustion and fear these horses experienced.[37]

Older horses trained new foals to avoid humans, and they were famously difficult to capture. People called them "wily," "crafty," "trickish," and generally exasperating. Lead stallions or sometimes a dominant mare would spy humans on the horizon and charge off with mares and their young in tow at a gallop, stopping after some distance to see whether they were being still being pursued. At times stallions would start mares and their young galloping away, then suddenly turn to run toward human stalkers, violently challenging them with kicks, stomps, and bites. Men tasked with capturing such horses might labor for days, following a band as it travelled from watering hole to watering hole, skittish and alert to any sign of people or other predators. Openly chasing wild or free-roaming owned horses was exhausting, dangerous work for men and their mounts, themselves burdened with galloping with saddle and rider. Many horses and plenty of men died doing it.[38] Pursuit was safest if people exercised patience, waiting for an opportunity to guide resistant bands into a portable corral or a canyon. Others employed tamed horses, allowing them to mingle with wild ones and calm them, driving the whole group to a collection site on hoof over a period of hours or days.[39]

The men who searched wild herds, ranch pastures, and local stockyards for useful horses to supply to the military or rodeos were simply adding a new element to the centuries-old continental horse trade that had begun in the South and Midwest back in Spanish days. Those wild herds had been descended from the compact horses, with coats of any color, who walked or ran away from Spanish, Mexican, Comanche, and Cheyenne herds.[40] Human contemporaries frequently noted them as beautiful and intelligent but wary of people.[41] Their numbers in those years are difficult to know, but by the eighteenth and early nineteenth century certainly they numbered in the millions and outnumbered cattle in many places. Californio cattle ranchers perceived feral horses to be a nuisance already by the 1820s, capturing and killing large numbers each year to protect the carrying capacity of their ranges.[42] In Texas, feral horses were abundant enough that century that men captured and drove them for sale into the eastern U.S.[43]

Indigenous Peoples on the Plains effectively "created the western horse trade," says historian Dan Flores, when they captured these animals using old means of herding them into enclosures and holding "horse fairs," where buying and selling took place. This was a politically important economy that Spanish, Mexican, Native American, and visiting American traders all sought to control.[44] After the American Civil War, the anchors of the horse trade were Wyoming, Montana, and the Dakotas, where wild and feral-but-owned horses flourished. In this, the development of the horse trade mirrored the cattle trade to a degree, spreading north and west from Texas and the Southwest. Indeed, for all the talk of cattle kingdoms and beef bonanzas, horse ranching or harvesting was equally central to the resource-extraction economies of the West and the transformation of the landscape from bison ecology to precariously managed commercial range.

Three years after the first capture and release of Steamboat, cowboys collected the famous horse on Frank Foss's range and sold him to the Swan Land and Cattle Company. Swan Land was the famous Scottish corporation that owned large tracts of land and possibly more cattle in Wyoming than any other company or individual. Like the legend of Tom Horn's gun, here Steamboat was linked to Wyoming's Beef Bonanza and range-war era, as well as the vigilante justice employed by large cattle operations to monopolize land, water, and animals. Later, a broad swath of the public nonetheless romanticized that difficult period in the state's history, although it had been people like them—small-time homesteaders, ranchers, and working cowboys—who had suffered at the hands of entities like the Swan company.[45] Wild horses captured and tried out for rodeo work bucked as early as age two, far too young contractors will tell you now. Upon capture, many had never worn shoes or a hackamore, and often carried plenty of parasites.[46] However, nor did they know the boredom and loneliness of life as a cart horse, no irritating check rein, or plodding in endless circles running a sweep or treadmill.[47]

"When he was three we branded and castrated him," remembered Wyoming cowboy Jimmy Danks of those early days. "At that stage, I feel sure Steamboat could have been broken. Probably would have become a good cow horse." The young horse became known as Steamboat because he "whistled" when he breathed. In his feral days on the Foss range he was remembered as "wild even in his youth." Horses cannot see directly behind, and have only monocular vision with little depth perception, except for a sixty-five-degree range directly in front. Thus, to see someone or something properly, horses must often raise, lower, or turn their heads to avoid being spooked and, when head movement is restricted by a halter lead pulled taut, they may feel disorientation and alarm. Roped for castration and marking, Steamboat experienced that plus the sensation of men climbing upon him. The young horse had fought with his attackers when they sought to brand him, "and in doing, struck his nose, breaking a small piece of the bone."[48]

Horses like Steamboat facilitated a lifestyle and also entrepreneurial opportunities for a subset of the Wild West show and rodeo community, a small group of men just then inventing careers for themselves as rodeo producers and stock contractors. Although the cowboy may have served as the human face of Wild West shows and rodeo sports, the rodeo producer controlled the necessary stock, and so held enormous power and was already a dominant force behind "the show." Charlie Irwin of Cheyenne, Wyoming, the final owner of Steamboat, was one of the most successful among these early entrepreneurs, who scouted horses "that liked to buck and could not be ridden" for Wild West shows and community rodeos.[49] Irwin's business prospered and his Y-6 Rodeo Livestock Company eventually held stock at properties in Meriden, Wyoming, and San Ysidro, California, while Charlie and his daughter-assistant Pauline Irwin Sawyer were a fixture at rodeos around the continent for several decades.

By then, ticket sales, arena talk, and press chatter seemed to indicate that spectators wanted to see rodeo sports that featured dramatic, explosive action. Wild horses drawn from western rangelands had the responsibility of reproducing the ideal of the vicious outlaw horse invented by rodeo committee publicists, travel writers, illustrators, journalists, and a hundred bragging cowboys. Many of these horses were captured, like Steamboat, living wild on private ranges, public land, or reservations. People put together small strings of bucking stock from those herds, or pieced them together from local livestock auctions, which they offered seasonally to one or more rodeos. One retired rider remembered the sense of expectation cowboys had, arriving in town on rodeo day and heading back of the chutes to find these odd horses assembled, "every kind of locoed ole cayuse you ever saw, blind in one eye, anything nobody in town could ride."[50] People suspended empathy for these animals in the search for opportunity and value.

Before a rodeo used permanent fenced arenas or bucking chutes, bronc riding took place in a clearing surrounded by riders, people on foot, wagons, and, later, automobiles. There was considerable variation from place to place and over time in how these competitions proceeded, although they all employed a saddle. Bareback bronc riding would not appear at most rodeos for another decade or so.[51] Generally, the ride involved roping, snubbing (tying) to a post, blindfolding, saddling, and mounting an unbroken horse. In some ways, the event resembled the twentieth-century wild horse race rodeo event. Upon a signal from the timekeeper, a mounted cowboy would approach the group of horses, who were often extremely agitated by that point. One early account has it that the horses, "maddened and trembling," "scented danger, and [were] off like the wind crowding each other to the fence and making vain attempts to escape the rider's eye." The rider chose one horse and roped him or her by the neck, which might take several minutes as the horse dashed back and forth avoiding the lariat.[52]

Employing his roping horse, rope, and saddle horn as steer ropers did, the cowboy wrapped the free end of the rope holding his chosen horse around the horse's rear legs to pull them out from under the horse and throw, or bust, him or her "down with a 'dull thud.'"[53] After a cue from the judge, the roper would then attempt the very dangerous job of applying a hackamore and blindfold, allowing the horse to stand up, and strapping on a saddle. That could take a further several minutes as the prostrate horse struggled and kicked to escape. Once in the saddle, and the blindfold was removed, the cowboy would ride until thrown or until the horse ceased bucking, kicking, and jumping, a process that was painful for rider and horse, and could take up to fifteen minutes.

Popularly, accounts of bronc riding constituted a parallel to the cowboy grotesquerie depicting steer busting as an artistic tradition that seemed to relish equine distress and resistance in the face of cowboy captors. The *Rocky Mountain News* joked of one cowboy, "Had 'Broncho' Jim been allowed five minutes more time the horse he was handling would have been carried away in sections. As it was, the animal was taken out of the corral with a neck resembling that of a giraffe."[54] People delighted in and made light of what these horses withstood, imagining them as heroes, not victims. "Buck isn't a name for it," said one account in *Northwestern Live Stock Journal*, marvelling at the desperate energy of one horse:

> Up in the air and down with all four legs bunched stiff as an antelope's, and back arched like a hostile wildcat's, went the animal. But the rider was there, and deep into the rowels he sank the spurs while he lashed shoulders and neck with the keen stinging quirt. It was brute force against human nerve. Nerve won. A few more jumps and the horse submitted and carried the man around the corral on a swinging lope. It had all been done in seven and a half minutes. The crowd cheered.[55]

These severe exhibitions passed muster since many seemed to see horses as inherently resilient, which is what they wished to believe about themselves as rural westerners, too.

Bronc riding was a stylized, invented performance designed for a paying audience, depicting the work of the West's famous horse breakers, but distorted as a kind of reversal of the taming process wherein cowboys sought to make captive horses appear wilder.[56] Western life and industry, not least the business of ranching in particular, were only possible due to the service of equines, including mules, donkeys, and millions of horses who experienced breaking. Stories of late spring and summer horse roundups told how newly corralled horses huddled together as far from approaching men as possible. The lead breaker would select one horse, who then found him or herself roped and pulled away by the neck. Thereafter, horse breakers pulled on the rope until the struggling horse was choked out or perhaps just "downed," that is, repeatedly pulled onto his or her side while kicking and struggling, eyes wide and nostrils flaring in fear and filling with dirt until he or she learned not to struggle once roped.[57] Thereafter, once a horse was prone and bound, men would apply to the horse's head a hackamore and often a calming handkerchief blindfold or old sack, which, once removed, triggered a horse to fight. Horse breakers thereafter might encourage a horse to resist until exhausted or until the bronc buster ceased goading the animal at the instant the horse realized that relief came from ceasing to struggle.

The next step was often to slowly approach, speak gently to, then saddle a new horse by first binding up one leg, since on three legs horses were less likely to jump and kick, perhaps also twisting an ear "to distract him."[58] Others would trip a horse, whereafter a group of men would set upon the hapless animal with hackamore, blindfold, blanket, and saddle all at once. Once saddled, a horse would be unbound and left to kick, run, and roll on the ground in resistance to the sensation of the saddle and cinch strap. Finally, a brave (or foolhardy) man got into the saddle and hung on, raking the horse's ribs with his boot spurs and whipping the horse with a quirt as punishment for resisting, ceasing only when the horse became exhausted. This procedure trained horses to associate calm behavior with relief from the whipping and spurring. Everyone seemed to take for granted that in the breaking process "horses showed fear and fought" by "plunging, kicking, stamping, biting, snorting, twisting and whirling."[59]

Many horse people reasoned that a violent breaking process void of compassion for horses made horses calm since they came to respect and seek out human control once they recognized their captor's superiority and their rightful "duties" owed humankind.[60] Other observers found the western way of breaking a horse to the saddle to be "cruel" because it could result in terminal equine injuries like broken legs or mental trauma that prevented utility to humans. Clifford Westermeier believed hurried, fear-based breaking to be a false economy because it was an "ordeal [that], more often than not, left the horse with a hatred for and eternal grudge against his master."[61] In more contemporary terms, a growing body of research is beginning to show that horses can learn in various ways, and that methods employing fear and pain may work in the short term but cause mental trauma and welfare issues in horses that are "responsible for the alarmingly high wastage of horses euthanized due

Detail from Charles Russell's portrayal of the stages of horse breaking.
*Frank Leslie's Illustrated Magazine*, 1889.

to behavioral problems."[62] Still, early in the century such training worked as a form of operant conditioning. Force-broken horses became "broke" when they came to understand and accept that the easiest way to avoid pain and fear was to obey instruction and stay calm. The process frequently had to be repeated over a series of days or weeks to break some horses.

It was not that people did not know how to train a horse "by easy degrees, gentling [them] in ways that seldom involved pitched battles," or by breaking them to lead first, then the saddle; such means are as old as time.[63] As a kind of dominance training taken as a contest between man and animal, early western techniques emphasized speed over a more patient, "thinking," non-fear-based approach to training. This was especially so as horse breakers, or "bronc busters," were paid by the head, and so profited by haste.[64] Financial motivations were interlinked with cultural license and the unsentimentally masculine, "tough" persona of the bronc buster. These cowboys were transient rural workers who, much of the time, were bound to piecework and hopefully some winnings on rodeo day in order to scrape by. They were "prepared to conquer their mounts by direct assault, pitting strength and skill against the wildest efforts of the untamed horse," one westerner remembered of his boyhood awe for such men. "Many aspired . . . , but few attained."[65]

Californio and Mexican horse breakers dominated the trade in California after statehood and in Texas well into the twentieth century. They were said to employ old, harsh traditions of horse breaking from the Spanish era of simply spurring and tripping horses to the point of exhaustion, giving those methods "a certain reputation for cruelty" since horses were easily injured or killed.[66] These self-interested accusations on the part of settler communities held a small grain of truth. Hispanic traditions dated from earlier periods when wild horses had been abundant in some regions, and although horses suffered injuries "it was a matter of little importance given the abundance of animals," as Richard Slatta explains this kind of plain instrumentalism.[67] Other racialized gossip talked of "how the Indians 'broke' their horses" by confining a horse without food for some days "until it got so weak that it could hardly stand up—much less pitch a rider," which some said was dishonorable.[68]

It is unclear which, if any, Indigenous horsemen used such tactics, and plenty did not. Blackfoot horsemen, for instance, left the horse breaking to teenage boys. Lighter than adult men, they broke two- and three-year-old horses without saddling them by leading them into shoulder-depth water that triggered a horse to stay calm and walk out with a rider on board. Or they jumped on horses standing in swampy or "boggy" ground, which made bucking and jumping too difficult. They also blindfolded horses and rode them to exhaustion, just like Hispanic and settler horse breakers.[69] Settler communities operated in some denial, to be sure, hiring horse breakers or purchasing horses previously broken by such boys yet insisting that settlers had relatively more empathy for horses than nonwhite westerners—despite whatever cheering they might do for the bronc riders they saw at a Wild West show or the local Pioneer Days cowboy tournament.

"We had more fun than anybody," said Everett Brisendine, who busted horses for five dollars each in the 1910s. "Didn't have a worry in the world, you know. In them days there was lots of horses and . . . why you'd go to work anywhere. . . . You're not overburdened with intelligence but you could handle them rank horses."[70] With such youthful bravado and determination in the face of dangerously frightened horses could come serious injuries. Men had reason to keep back from a jumping, rolling, or kicking horse and to minimize the amount of time a horse would spend fighting the saddle and the unfamiliar people who brought it. Many rode "'roughstring,' which meant to ride 'all the mean horses,'" horse breaker Ed Strickland said, or the "broncs and old out-law horses that the average cowpuncher can't ride," which Ross Santee said accumulated on ranches, simply taking the risks and injuries in stride.[71] One Idahoan listed what horse breakers endured for the "prestige" and "distinction" they earned by being kicked, chased, bitten, and otherwise challenged by a frightened feral horse: "Inguinal rupture, severe bruises and abrasions," as well as "sprained joints, broken bones, twisted backs, floating kidneys, and multiple bruises and scars commemorating violent contacts with corral poles, rocks on the ground, or the vindictive hooves of ornery cayuses."[72] Agreed another, "There was no whistle in ten seconds, no pick-up men and no Boy Scouts to run out and help him if he got his wind knocked out" in the corral.[73]

Horse breakers, many of whom competed as bronc riders when they could get to a rodeo, and took busting work or dude ranch work when necessary, operated in an economy of paternalistic violence against working animals like horses.[74] By turns, they recalled loving some horses very much while routinely resorting to kicking, whipping, or beating green horses, or chasing them down, roping, and dragging them.[75] Some forced saddles on previously broken but periodically resistant horses since, in one interpretation, the horse simply had "forgot that he was supposed to be broke and gentle. . . . [H]e would rear back and plunge and kick sideways at you when you tried to tighten up the cinch, and for the first little bit after you got on him he would dance and kick up and try to get his head down so he could buck and throw you off."[76] Horses who accepted the saddle one day, then later changed their minds, were to these men both angering and funny equine scoundrels just asking for a showdown. Some people simply continued to ride a known-difficult horse even when he or she threw them repeatedly, while other riders gave up on "fractious" horses, letting them loose indefinitely on their range or employing them as pack animals.[77] Some were sold to the Army remount depot or tried out for bucking with a rodeo producer.

At the Wild West show or rodeo ground, these men and the many women who rode broncs performed for paying audiences and rodeo producers who wanted an exciting show that could be translated into breathless newspaper copy, exciting graphics for souvenirs and programs, and thus further ticket sales. There, unlike at private ranches where feral horses came in to be broken, bronc riders had no boss to answer to if the horse he or she fought was injured or traumatized to become permanently balky, unpredictable, or prone to biting, kicking, or rearing. To the contrary, the goal in a bucking contest was not to help a wild or feral horse learn to stay calm, but rather to cause a horse simply unfamiliar with or resistant to human contact to display the behavior of a frantic horse being attacked by a predator.

So was the work-a-day western horse turned inside out and transformed into the popular western character of outlaw bucker, supposedly eager to face off against a human rider. Most of the horses employed in bronc riding were wild and unaccustomed to being ridden, but not necessarily prone specifically to producing the arched sunfishing posture that people were suddenly taking as normative. Champion rider Jimmy Danks said of Steamboat, "He would lead nice to hand; he just wanted to buck. Well he wouldn't fight you, 'til you went to riding. Kinda wanted to buck. I guess he thought bucking was his business."[78] Indeed, people took the display of a particular behavior on the part of a horse as an endorsement of various human constructs—"sport," "roughstock," "rodeo," "Wild West"—which gave the horse a persona as "outlaw."

When Steamboat worked for the Irwin Brothers, the company billed him as "Worst Outlaw in the World—the Horse Which Threw the Best of Them"[79] The outlaw bronc was a parallel and equally Western character to the Texas longhorn or the wild steer: clever, energetic, and determined to remain free and resistant to "the thrall of human will" on animals.[80] "The Irwin show will visualize the scenes familiar so many years ago to early westerners, when a man's ability to stick on the back of a wild horse meant his means of livelihood," said some of Irwin's promotion in those days, directly linking domination over livestock with western prosperity.[81] The bronc outlaw ideal normalized the belief that a struggling, resistant, pitching horse was an inevitable and necessary aspect of western life, and an agent in his own harassment by cowboys. Horses like Steamboat would unknowingly make the character of the determined cowboy bronc buster possible, too.

One of the most sustained but unsuccessful western efforts to bend and shape the West to settler goals was the centuries-long campaign of extermination against gophers, among other creatures who insisted on making their own uses of western lands simply because they always had. Bisulphate of carbon was one tool ranchers, farmers, and gardeners employed, pouring it down the gopher holes they found. The holes led to gopher colonies' complex tunnel networks but tripped and lamed horses while the gophers observed and chirped their alarm noisily nearby. Bisulphate of carbon produced heavier-than-air hydrocyanic gas, which was dangerous for people to breathe. Warned one contemporary advisor, "It is a deadly poison and must never be inhaled. The bottle containing it should be kept tightly corked until the moment it is to be used."[82] In Montana, journalist and local historian Joseph Howard remembered it as "a foul-smelling sulphide compound obtained from a druggist" in small glass bottles. It was harmless to bare skin, but melted and burned hair. "A few drops flung on a horse's rump were certain to cause unscheduled and highly diverting incidents," he said of those who caused mischief in small-town festival parades "celebrating something so the cowpokes could ride up the street and back and show off their outfits." Colloquially, to burn a horse with the compound was called "hokey-pokeying," which a horse took "like a red-hot poker at the base of the tail, [and so] reached for the sky with his hind feet."[83]

In the Wild West show trade people called bisulphate of carbon "highlife" and, in the decades before widespread availability of cattle prods that delivered an agitating electrical shock, highlife was used to cause a burning sensation that compelled horses to struggle and fight a rider. In 1911, M. F. Hennessey, officer for the California State Humane Association, found a whole gallon container of the stuff stashed back of the chutes near the roughstock at the State Fair Rodeo in Sacramento. He confiscated it.[84] Thereafter, Hennessy and some colleagues appeared at Rodeo Salinas. Organizers knew he was coming, yet "even then he found them attempting to use 'high-life' on the horses and steers, making the animals frantic with fright and pain, so that they would produce the much desired 'thrill,'" reported an incredulous supporter in San Francisco. Bisulphate of carbon, applied even sparingly on an animal, "produces a freezing sensation for a short time and causes the animal to become furious with fright," he reported.[85]

Hennessey and his colleagues also found people at Salinas resorting to brads, the workaday nail employed for building all sorts of structures. At one point, the "particular wildness and agility" of a bucking horse ridden by a woman competitor caught their attention: "Watching closely they saw the woman frequently place her hand back of the saddle. Each time she did so the horse would jump and kick furiously. Going over, they found spots of blood on the horse and several holes where they skin had been punctured by a nail or other sharp object," he reported. "The woman refused to give up the instrument or admit that she had prodded the horse. But she was severely reprimanded and ordered at once from the grounds," said Hennessey. Humane officers had seen this before. Cowboys sometimes resorted to a "sharp, nail-pointed brad to poke [a bucking horse] should he show an inclination to be docile."[86] Riders admitted equally to "slowing down a fiery horse by placing [a] block of wood under the cinch on his ventral vein," although Clifford Westermeier insisted this was an "old timers'" habit long abandoned by the early 1940s.[87]

Highlife, brads, chunks of wood—here were strange connection points between settler transformation of the West, its environment and animals, and the cowboy sports that romanticized that transformation. It is not clear exactly how widespread and frequent were the use of highlife, brads, or other artificial means of inducing pain and fear to extract or inhibit practiced bucking behaviors from horses. However, it is safe to say that these practices were widespread within the rodeo circuit. Rodeo people travelled from show to show everywhere, after all. To some rodeo competitors and spectators, such tactics reeked of "fake" rodeos and old-time circus and museum scams. Primitive means of artificially drawing particular behaviors out of animals have been a part of show business since at least the 1840s, when P. T. Barnum doped small animals with laudanum as a Happy Family display purporting to show normally antagonistic creatures living in harmony in a small enclosure. Wild West show and early rodeo people resorted to circus-style tactics since many horses just did not measure up. Most bucking broncs were simply drawn from ranges, and were thus unaccustomed to human interaction, certainly, but not necessarily prone to the athletic bucking, kicking, jumping, and spinning that rodeos needed for bronc riding. A dependable bucker was not necessarily wild, and vice versa. So, brads and high-life would often inspire a horse to fake it, so to speak.

In spite of the scandal over steer busting during the previous decade, by 1910 humane advocates in California, Wyoming, Colorado, and other states had either witnessed or been told of serious animal cruelty problems (or, at least some defined them as problems) at Wild West shows and competitive rodeos. Through the word-of-mouth and letter-writing networks of humane activists and their supporters they received many reports: people employing lame or otherwise injured animals in competitions; wild horse races routed along a too-long racetrack, thus producing "animals, nervous, excited and frightened, sweating and ready to drop at the finish"; wild horses roped and choked "until their tongues loll and their eyes pop out"; bulldogging steers killed or "subjected to the most excruciating agony" by competitors; steer busting that broke limbs and horns; the sight of crippled animals desperately attempting to drag themselves to safety in such settings; cowboys and local kids "teasing and tormenting the animals in the corrals and roping the steers for sport when not in the exhibitions," as well as animals corralled for hours with no water.[88]

Even after the steer busting controversy at the turn of the century, in the 1910s many citizens still appear to have been taken aback by the continued and ballooning popularity of cowboy tournaments and the treatment of livestock they witnessed there.[89] Some had been complaining to local humane associations for perhaps two decades by this point. They provided a steady supply of gossip and whistleblower information and asked to what degree rodeo events resembled actual ranching or cowboy work and, even if they did, why such "brutalities" should be repeated just for public amusement.

Nonetheless, even some local humane advocates internalized the special myth of consent reserved for outlaw buckers—that is, prey animals taken as western aggressors. Mrs. F. W. Swanton, Oregon Humane Society inspector at the Pendleton Round-Up, told the papers that steer busting employed animals who were merely "chased about and frightened," which constituted cruelty that would drive away spectators. Yet, in the next breath she insisted that the bronc busting was different: "As a matter of fact, most of the horses enjoy the bucking contests more than do the riders. I have seen some of the so-called outlaw horses actually smile after they have unseated a cowboy."[90] State Humane Association operatives in California claimed to have stopped steer busting and bulldogging in the state by 1920, but not "bronco-busting" as it was "a little beyond our reach at present, as the breaking of wild horses for the saddle is looked upon as a legitimate enterprise; but the cruel methods heretofore involved are forbidden, as spurs must be wrapped with tape or taken off."[91]

Spurs? As was often the case in Wild West shows and early cowboy tournaments, it was not the extremes, the worst cases, and most embarrassing "accidents" that revealed the true nature of rodeo, but the commonly accepted practices that persisted in plain view. Looking back on the era before the common use of chutes for readying bucking stock and riders, Wild West show performer and rodeo competitor Goldie Cameron explained that bronc riding was an entirely different affair from the mid-twentieth-century variant, not least because women were frequent and celebrated competitors in her day. "There weren't any 10-second rules and you learned to ride your spurs," she said. "Horses bucked more naturally without these new-fangled flank straps."[92] (A flank rope wraps around the horse before the hips and encourages a horse to kick up and back; by the 1960s, the rope was often replaced by a flank strap, a wide leather belt covered in sheepskin.) To Cameron, "natural" bucking indicated a horse who struggled in varying ways as if resisting the saddle and horse breaker, head low and sunfishing. The "new-fangled" flank ropes (and they were bare ropes that rubbed horses raw, not the fleece wrapped straps used today) in front of the hips triggered a horse's instinct to resist a predator as well as the urge to kick up and into the visual blind spot that horses have directly behind.[93]

Flank ropes would not come into widespread use until the 1920s. In the meantime, cowboys and girls rode their spurs, and were admired for it. "The good riders never flank-cinched to make their horses buck, nor did they ride trained 'buckers,'" explained one later romanticist. "As often as not, they rode horses that had never been ridden before, or never ridden successfully."[94] Essentially, these were simply frightened horses, who would run as much as they might jump, spin, kick, or buck, and often required severe spurrings to produce any kind of crowd-pleasing action, especially the sunfisher ideal. At many rodeos, event judges actually *required* heavy spurring for a qualifying ride.

Spurred riding coerced apparent consent from bucking horses just as people beat or twisted the tails of roping steers so they ran from the chute at good speed, ostensibly inviting chase. Cowboys also commonly employed rawhide whips, or quirts, to produce more dramatic bucking. Many are visible in early bronc-riding photographs, flourished in the air by the rider in order "to larrup [them] unmercifully."[95] Cowboys and their supporters equally boasted of riders who "cut the pony to bits" or "spurred him to ribbons."[96] So said Sam Brownell, a rider associated with the famous bucker Tipperary. Riding another horse, Tanglefoot, in 1917 at the rodeo in Cheyenne, Brownell claimed, "When we got ready for the final ride the judges said: 'We want to see blood on those horses' sides. Not too much pulling on the heads.' I had the long-shank, spoke rowel spurs that would bring the 'claret' out if you put them to work." Brownell won the competition.[97] Some horses were unable or unwilling to buck, jump, or spin. Said a biographer of one famous rider, "The horse hardly moved a muscle. Booger Red finally got a ride out of the bronc by striking it over the ears and spurring its flanks."[98] Yet, even with famous buckers, for riders to expose the supposed natural wildness of these imagined outlaws required plenty of goading. "When Tipperary was cut loose Sam hit him with both spurs as hard as he could drive them. He kept spurring. The horse went insane," reported a biographer of Sam Brownell with some awe. "Tipperary bucked at least 400 yards before he finished."[99]

Rodeo's detractors were horrified by the brutality of bronc riding. Some especially looked for the "long, sharp rowels of the Spanish type, or of spurs that have locked rowels or rowels which will lock," explained Clifford Westermeier in the 1940s, alluding to the common belief that cowboy cruelty had links to Hispanic horse cultures.[100] Advocates had long called spurs a form of cruelty, "quite one of the worst" and "abominable" for injuring and traumatizing horses, which "spoils their tempers, and in time galls them to such an extent that they become vicious animals."[101] By this argument, mild horses could be turned into violent buckers with repeated spurring and whipping. One animal advocate explained,

> The rider mounts the animal forearmed with a specially sharpened pair of spurs. As the animal commences its frantic lunges or "bucks" to unseat the rider, he sinks these spurs into the animal's flanks and "sticks on." The spur rowels penetrate half to three-fourths of an inch. Another form of cruelty consists of "roweling" the animal. This is done by moving the legs back and forth from the knee; the spurs being on the heels of the rider, the flanks of the horse are cut and slashed until the blood fairly runs from the wounds.[102]

This was graphic detail, but detail that matched what cowboys and newspaper men of the period bragged about themselves. In 1908, the Wyoming Humane Society briefly got spurs suspended at Cheyenne Frontier Days (although not the dozens of other smaller community and ranch rodeos in the state), a rule the competitors simply rejected after two years. By 1911, spurs were back.[103]

Rodeo subculture cultivated many euphemisms that deflected attention from horses' nature as prey animals, instead conveying a sense that horses were the real predator. People variously called horses "man-killer," the "worst horses," "the most vicious outlaws the West can produce," "a mean sun-fisher," "whirlwind bucker," and "anarchists," among dozens of other colloquialisms imaging them as aggressors in any contest.[104] Certainly, there was some hyperbole here, enriched with the passage of time as retired riders built their reputations in the close-knit rodeo community through bragging about long-remembered rides on an infamous horse.[105] And, it was also true that horses inexpertly or violently broken for hands-on human contact, or simply unwilling to submit to it, could be very dangerous or unpredictable.

This was Steamboat's world. Yet he was such a revered and valuable bucker, celebrated for his energy and style when resisting a rider. Was he perhaps spared such terrible treatment by cowboys, so many of whom later spoke at length of their love for Steamboat? No, he was not. Many dozens of men tried to ride him and several claimed to have ridden him to a standstill, and many for far longer than the regulation eight seconds that constitutes a points-winning ride today.[106] In the 1950s, Steamboat's handler Bud Gillespie would tell of these men and of his experiences shuttling the horse from show to show for exhibition rides around the northern Great Plains between 1902 and 1914. His recollections, even if embellished or foggy with nostalgia in some specific detail, convey that Steamboat was, in essence, asked to travel and endure periodic abuse in exchange for being remembered by westerners as a great horse. Gillespie conveyed these stories with great pride and openness about what went on. Today, rodeo people are far more guarded with their public comments about rodeo animals and the complexities of the sport's past and present.

Gillespie's account revealed that Steamboat was often mismanaged, although Gillespie did not see it that way. The horse was bucked repeatedly in short periods of time, shut up in a box stall between rides, emerging for the next ride with legs "stove up," swollen, weak, and at times "seemed to be suffering physical discomfort." He was put out on a range to overwinter each year, found each spring in a "weakened state" because he had been surviving on frozen grass all winter and was underweight. Cowboys spoke openly about earing Steamboat down "by grabbing an ear in each hand and twisting and pulling down on them simultaneously" in order to mount him.[107] His owners also allowed riders to use their spurs without restraint until "tracks were distinct and deep" or with spurs "screwed into the horse until they were solid." In 1904, Steamboat's owners encouraged William Craver, aka Pecos Craver, a Buffalo Bill Show roper and rider, to ride Steamboat at the Albany County Fair in Laramie where "Pecos went into action with his quirt and surely hit Steamboat hard, as the wallops could be heard all over the fairgrounds." The next year, they allowed Otto Plaga from Sibylle, Wyoming, a try. Gillespie remembered with respect, "He rode with perfect balance and worked his feet as though he was riding a bicycle while a horse was bucking; in so doing he always left his trade mark on the horse's shoulder and along his flanks in the form of a spur trail."[108]

People were not embarrassed about this display. They boasted about how hard this rider or that had whipped Steamboat with a quirt, or spurred the horse with all his strength, seeming to take the violence of the ride and the horse's response as an indication of the power and manliness of the rider. Indeed, riders who did not enact such violence in their ride were taken to be dishonorable. "Clayton Danks Awarded the Prize to Everyone's Disgust," announced the *Denver Post* in relation to the 1909 Cheyenne Frontier Days show in which the audience hissed and yelled out "Fake!" "Rotten!" and

Steamboat enduring a spur-and-quirt rider, Ed Carver, in 1907. "Old Steamboat in Action," Stimson Collection, STIM/4025, Wyoming State Archives, Department of State Parks and Cultural Resources.

"Robbery!" at Danks and the arena officials after the Wyoming cowboy rode Steamboat *without* spurring him. Even Clifford Westermeier agreed, "'Old Steamboat' without spurs is about as active as an extinct volcano."[109] In Wyoming, where cowboy tournaments were proudly brutal to animals, the audience expected riders to be as coarse to a horse as possible to make the horse as violent as possible and to increase the difficulty of the ride. Anything less was too easy, at least on the cowboy. This was an idea residing in old range-cowboy ethics that "in an argument with a pitching pony," men should not impede or fail to encourage bucking and kicking, but rather encourage it and "ride him fair," as Emerson Hough, writer of western stories, had explained in the late 1890s.[110]

For about fourteen years Steamboat was mounted by such men and shipped back and forth between Cheyenne Frontier Days and a variety of smaller community rodeos around the northern Great Plains—Wyoming, Colorado, South Dakota. After about 1910, Steamboat was struggling and riders knew it. The middle-aged Steamboat, even when harassed, was less energetic in his bucking. Yet people rode "the old horse" nonetheless.[111] His managers reserved him for pass-the-hat exhibition rides since he was losing his power and would buck for shorter periods and with fewer acrobatics before giving up underneath a rider. In 1914, the year Steamboat died, the horse was shipped with the Irwin Brothers show for many dates throughout California, around Nevada, and to a number of small towns in Idaho, Oregon, Wyoming, and finally Utah.

During the years Steamboat was traveling, talk of fraud in the industry created plenty of audience confusion over exactly what people were seeing when they watched bronc riding at a Wild West show or a local competitive cowboy event.[112] As the cowboy sport craze spread around the West, transient promoters might appear in town to put on a show billed as a "genuine cowboy tournament" that was really a Wild West show, shipped in like a circus to present scripted demonstrations of cowboy sports. There were also scoundrels who produced competitive cowboy tournaments that invited local men and women to compete but were scams, which everyone realized only when the impresario was seen driving out of town with all the prize money and entry fees just as the last rider was being thrown to the ground by a kicking bronc.[113] Rodeo people went to great effort to shut down such "fake" shows and distinguish regulated, competitive community rodeos from scripted Wild West shows and fraudulent productions. Yet, in all these cases, many of the buckers who appeared there were entirely artificial in their own way, a fake sunfisher created by spurring and whipping a live horse before an audience.

Just after Steamboat's death, people came forward asking that the famous horse be disinterred from the livestock dump and buried with a monument at Frontier Park, the rodeo grounds in Cheyenne. Initial newspaper reports in 1914 explained, "Old Steamboat has been buried near the old dump grounds adjoining the stock yards. There is no marker over his grave and it is held that unless action is soon taken, the great bucking horse who could not be subdued will have vanished from sight forever."[114] Thereafter, the story that Steamboat's grave was indeed at Frontier Park circulated everywhere, although the money had never actually come together to find his body and move it there. The magazines and papers that wrote about the horse perpetuated these false impressions, even though people in Cheyenne could see there was no monument to Steamboat in place. For several decades, cowboys were even said to have believed that Steamboat "slept" at Frontier Park, and discussed it when they visited Cheyenne to compete.[15] Then in 1955, about forty years after Steamboat's death, a *Wyoming State Tribune* investigation produced "the flat statement today of an eyewitness at the destruction of the great horse," Paul Hansen, who insisted that Steamboat had been shot, dragged to, and deposited into the livestock dump, and left there.[116]

There was renewed attention to Steamboat just then because in 1951 the University of Wyoming had taken an image of him sunfishing as a model for their campus monument showing a resistant bucker and cowboy rider. By the logic of the period, the sculpture was meant to honor horses for their "important role . . . in the development of the West, and particularly Wyoming."[117] Two of the officials involved in the project praised the long-dead horse: "The swelling muscles and determined look in Steamboat's eyes . . . indicate the strong, independent nature of the pioneer West."[118] The sunfisher is now the icon for Wyoming and the University of Wyoming, although it denies what Wyomingites did to horses to create it.

By mid-century, the legend of Steamboat was that he had only been ridden by two men, Dick Stanley and Clayton Danks. So said Danks to more than one journalist. Danks would appear as an "old timer" in a number of Western-lifestyle magazine articles, as late as age eighty years, posed in Western attire as "Conqueror of Steamboat." Riders like Jimmy and Clayton Danks, Dick Stanley, Pecos Craver, and Otto Plaga derived their identities and modest notoriety from interactions with famous horses. This kind of cowboy nostalgia offered an imagined western animal who defiantly resisted but was somehow complicit in his own captivity and commodification—that is, a consumer-friendly animal with no needs except to please his audience.

Steamboat's legend had by then proliferated in print at the hands of community boosters, old timers, and tourism magazine journalists. Cheyenne veterinarian and rodeo historian Joseph Palen assembled extensive scrapbooks documenting rodeo sports and his association with Cheyenne Frontier Days in those decades. He had an entire folio devoted to Steamboat, all of it published after the horse's death. From the 1930s to the 1990s, Palen found dozens of stories about Steamboat in *Western Horseman* (many times), *Westerner, Horse Tales Annual, Horse Lovers Magazine, Frontier Times, The Cattleman, Canadian Cattleman, Hoofs & Horns, Rodeo News, Wyoming Stockman &*

*Farmer, True West,* and *Old Timers Wild West,* as well as dozens of small-town newspapers across the West and further afield.[119]

These many accounts told a similar story. The bucker had risen from humble beginnings to stardom, they said, and only one rider (or maybe two, depending on the storyteller) had ridden him, gaining their own fame from Steamboat's unique bucking style and "determination to win."[120] The horse had humbled many cowboy champions and had displayed the "true spirit" of the West in his love of competition and resistance to control. Steamboat had helped make rodeo a viable element of the western economy (especially in Cheyenne). He will never be matched, and he stands as one of the most venerated personalities in rodeo history. Many also faithfully reported that the horse had been honorably interred and memorialized at Frontier Park in Cheyenne.

These popular pro-rodeo accounts overwhelmingly made no mention of how Steamboat had declined in his later years, or how cowboys and show officials encouraged riders to spur and whip the horse regardless, nor how he died. Equally, rodeo's historians have perpetuated these misunderstandings by ignoring the role of spur-and-quirt bucking in the production of many famous early broncs, and the relish with which people employed these tools or watched them employed. They have forgotten about the dangerous rodeo grounds and long hours of travel in the early days of the sport, and what people asked of horses in order to put on a show, exposing instead how embedded the myth of consent has been in the sport's history. Both for westerners and for those who read about the West in magazines and newspapers, Steamboat's public memory was defined solely by his arena performances and the implication that he chose his life as a bucking horse. "Steamboat left a fine heritage of the art of bucking," said Gillespie and Burns upon the crafting of the sunfisher icon for the University of Wyoming. "In his prime he was without peer in the art of cracking off riders."[121]

CHAPTER 3

# Interwar Broncs and Wastage

In 1912, the secretary of the Montana State Fair in Helena, a fellow named James Shoemaker, opened an envelope bearing exotic Canadian postage. Inside was news of a new rodeo, the Calgary Stampede. "For the bucking contest here," the letter boasted, "I would say to you, that we are going to have [the] buckinest bucking horses that ever bucked a buck."[1] It was Guy Weadick, trick roper, vaudevillian, Wild West show promoter, and now the charismatic founding personality of what would become one of the continent's original big shows. Weadick was out to boost the Stampede and to persuade Shoemaker to spread the word among local cowboys that it was worth their while to take a chance on a rodeo in Canada. Believing he could make Calgary famous, Weadick and his assistants invited attention for the rodeo from filmmakers and sent marketing materials and letters as far away as New York City, including that boasting note to Shoemaker in Helena. Calgary and the Canadian West were about to be integrated into the popular conceptions of the Wild West as the rodeo industry boomed in the early twentieth century.

Calgary was a well-meaning little city on the banks of the Glenbow River just east of the Rocky Mountains. Its annual July rodeo and city festival, the Stampede, would become part of an early twentieth-century trend whereby community rodeos began to take on the pretensions of western heritage festivals, displacing Wild West shows as the premier venue for cowboy sports. Weadick would be one of many promoters to tell the press and the public that his show would preserve old cowboy and pioneer ways that modern Canadians and Americans seemed to be forgetting in their rush forward into the future.[2] In the press and at the show, these claims to historical truth came across by way of costumed "Old Timers and Indians" featured in Stampede parades and pageants, editorials promising "Ranch and range scenes . . . depicted faithfully to the last detail," and assertions that during Stampede Calgary would indeed turn back the clock to "Rough and Ready Frontier Days."[3] As

Weadick promoted the Stampede, these claims also came by way of bucking horses. Many believed that a horse resisting a rider encapsulated the "spirit of Calgary," or the idea that the city was ruggedly determined and a place of infinite possibility for the future.

Whose frontier the Stampede would portray was an open question. Many Calgarians thought the idea of a cowboy tournament as a civic event for their city was patently absurd. Calgary had a thriving annual agricultural exhibition to convey a business-friendly personality for the city, they said. That fair already publicized regional opportunities for oil extraction, land speculation, and tourism. Calgary did not need an American-styled Wild West show with a few Mounties tacked on to create a unique promotional brand for the city, they grumbled.[4] Undeterred, Weadick knew he had the political and financial support of key local officials and influential ranchers nearby. Once the show debuted, he suspected correctly, a critical mass of Calgarians would make this American import their own.

By the 1950s, Calgary and its Stampede would become known by the white cowboy hat, which people wore during Stampede week as a sign of community hospitality and industriousness. Before that, it was the sunfishing bronc that was the most prominent symbol of the city's reputation. The Calgary Stampede was born just as the gasoline engine was displacing work horses in the daily life of many people on the continent. The horse population would peak in the 1910s, then begin a steady decline in the 1920s.[5] Among the horse owners who remained, there was a steady trend away from employing horses primarily for labor and power and toward leisure, show, or entertainment uses.[6] It was no accident that people embraced the ideal of the bucking horse in those years since the animal seemed suddenly exotic and nostalgic, even though, in many ways, the rodeo bronc was really a feature of the modern entertainment business.

To produce the sunfisher ideal, the Stampede would draw stock from local ranches or from men with a few horses to lease or sell. Before the mid-century advent of born-to-buck programs, in which people purpose rodeo broncs, there was a shortage of dependable buckers in the business. Hence, people talked about the few stars for decades: Midnight, Gravedigger, Cyclone, and "Old Steamboat," among them. To understand what went on behind the scenes as rodeos and their stock suppliers labored to provide living horses who could similarly produce the sunfisher ideal, consider the story of a horse no one remembers, a grey mare people called Greasy Sal. We know of her life only in the barest terms from the business records of the Stampede. Although most rodeos' business records have been lost or are held in private collections stored in attics and basements, the Stampede's records are carefully preserved at the Glenbow Museum in Calgary.[7]

Greasy Sal bucked at the Stampede just when many small-time ranchmen and horse sellers were working out how to turn horses they believed to be "bad ones," unsuited to farm or ranch work, into something useful and profitable. In Calgary, promoting and improving bronc riding as a marquee event in the show required, in effect, extracting and promoting the horse "buck" as authentic and necessary western horse behavior. Such an undertaking could not be achieved without significant inefficiencies. Many horses were drawn into the Stampede, and rodeo more generally, in order to supply the volume and quality of bucking that modern riders and audiences expected. Those trends produced great wastage, that is, the phenomenon of horses being drawn in, tried out, and quickly discarded in the drive to find and supply dependable levels of bucking at the show. At the same time, the history of the early Calgary Stampede shows us that interwar rodeo producers were working to temper the brutal nature of rodeo sports—in the arena at least. Those refinements helped modernize bronc riding so that cowboy sports would be appealing and useful to communities like Calgary looking for entertainment, revenue, and western-themed branding opportunities.

People who have never been to Calgary may have a difficult time understanding the strange and serious reverence many in the city have for the Calgary Stampede. It is not to be criticized or lampooned in any way, especially by the press, local or national. Since the mid-twentieth century, Canadians have often called Calgary "Cowtown" in reference to Alberta's beef ranching economy, and the Stampede truly is "Cowtown's sacred cow."[8] Armies of local people, those famous white-cowboy-hat-clad rodeo volunteers, will tell you today about how mysterious Stampede is. They will explain how in the 1950s or 1970s or 1990s when they helped out, for months there would be no obvious sign of activity downtown. Then suddenly, at the Stampede grounds next to the Saddledome, the rodeo, its people, vendors, buildings, livestock, competitors, and fans would magically materialize, seemingly from nowhere, every year, right on schedule. Yet it was not always so. When Guy Weadick founded the

Calgary Stampede in 1912, and when it became a regular feature of the city's summer calendar in 1919, the Canadian cattle trade had a different center of gravity. To the east it was Ontario that held a lucrative, century-old cattle trade based in meaty British shorthorn breeds. Ontario's stockmen had business and trade relationships mostly reaching down into the U.S. Midwest.[9] To the west of Calgary, British Columbia had a more modest but respectable and more diversified rural trade in horses, cattle, and dude ranch vacations, which were bolstered by provincial and federal land leasing legislation dating back to the 1880s.

Compared to Ontario and British Columbia, Alberta's ranching industry was relatively underdeveloped. There had been in-migration by Americans and a corresponding cattle boom in the 1880s, similar to the beef bonanza in the U.S. West in those years. Large investors leased land and raised cattle, beef prices rose, and railways appeared. But then, settlers—sodbusters—soon appeared at the rail depots and fenced-in subsistence operations on Alberta's rolling prairies. These new immigrants, plus the terrible winter and economic downturn of 1905–1906, broke up many of the larger, absentee-investor ranching operations in the decade before Guy Weadick appeared in Calgary. The cattlemen who rebuilt their herds would suffer another grievous collapse in 1919.[10] Hence, just as rodeo had been an optimistic work of fiction in the American towns that took it up in the 1890s and 1900s, in Calgary the Stampede was troublingly artificial since ranching was no guarantee of happiness or wealth in Calgary or rural Alberta.

As community leaders had done in Oregon or Wyoming in the last two decades of the nineteenth century, rodeo committees and chamber of commerce publicists in western Canada equally spent the 1910s and 1920s adopting the cowboy tournament as a local "tradition" and calling it "rodeo." Plenty of people were opportunistically ignoring the Canada-U.S. border in those days in any event, especially the many Americans who made their way north to settle. Inevitably perhaps, similar rodeo traditions developed in the two nations in a common network that competitors, contract acts, fans, and others relied upon as a whole.[11] In the early days of the Stampede, although it was primarily Albertans who competed, men and a few women from Wyoming, Montana, New Mexico, and Arizona appeared there as well.[12]

Community rodeos across the continent tended to follow a common format by this time. Beginning with a parade in town, at the arena there would be an opening procession and announcements. Next came competitive roughstock or timed roping events for women and men, interspersed with contract acts like fancy roping performers and comedy teams who, like the rodeo announcer, cracked jokes that lampooned the bravery/foolhardiness of the rodeo competitors and the human condition more broadly. Outside "the show," the Stampede featured an "Indian Village," parties and dances, and a small carnival. Such community festivals usually still had links to agricultural fairs and other modes of exhibiting local crops, livestock, and manufactured products to locals and visitors.

The Stampede would become part of a network of community rodeos run by local committees and volunteers linked by 1929 in the Rodeo Association of America (RAA), a precursor to the Professional Rodeo Cowboys Association (PRCA) and the Canadian Professional Rodeo Association (CPRA), although the Stampede and the majority of tiny town rodeos existed outside the syndicate. A core group of what would become the big marquee shows of the twentieth century, in Prescott, Cheyenne, Pendleton, and Salinas, dominated and were probably the most lucrative.[13] Of the dozens of smaller-scale events, plenty were badly run and operated at a loss. Some failed to pay winning cowboys and cowgirls the promised cash prizes even after accepting their entrance fees. Still, this network of rodeo committee groups refined the management of for-profit competitive rodeos, learning to craft events that visitors seemed to enjoy and that the city and business class found promotional and profitable.[14]

Many rodeo people sought standardization and reductions in regional variation to strengthen the whole network, in part, by forcing out the remaining "fake" rodeo operators. Those productions looked like a competitive rodeo but traveled town to town with competition results scripted in advance. Wild West shows also still circulated and offered only demonstrations of cowboy skills, not actual competitions, along with dramatic performances of stagecoach attacks or simulated bison hunts. Unlike the cowgirls and cowboys contracted to perform in Wild West shows or fake rodeos, competitors at local community rodeos were often local ranch workers or travelling amateur competitors, and they did not get paid unless they won their event. This lent a spirit of authenticity to community rodeos that spectators seemed to prefer.[15]

Every RAA rodeo would feature saddle bronc riding, steer bulldogging, steer roping, and calf roping as the core events. The Calgary Stampede was unusual in that, from the beginning, it also offered bareback riding competitions, a more dangerous version of bronc riding that featured horses with less patterned bucking, jumping, and spinning.[16] There, Guy Weadick would pioneer the quantitative approach to rodeo management, developing early systems and materials for the grading and comparison of human competitors and roughstock by Stampede judges, as a way to measure and improve performances year over year.[17]

After World War I and experimentation with cowboys sports of the previous decades, rodeo committees developed more compact programs that often left out controversial events like steer roping, especially in major cities and east of the Mississippi.[18] The Calgary Stampede followed these trends in some ways by, for instance, refusing steer roping of any kind in favor of a Canadian variant called steer decorating. Competitors jumped off a running horse to tackle a steer merely to "decorate" one horn with an elastic band bearing a small flag.[19] Local critics argued early on that the Stampede should present an ideal of western life free of animal suffering or displays of obvious cruelty, although the Stampede still featured wild cow milking and a wild horse race.[20] At the same time, Guy Weadick founded the Stampede's chuckwagon races beginning in 1923. This event was an exceedingly dangerous one for men and horses and is still unique to the Canadian prairies but highly controversial among animal advocates and the public due to the number of horses injured and killed in such races.[21]

The RAA made possible a universal point system to aggregate competition results and provide a way to name top competitors as champions, rather than having rival rodeos each claim to do so every weekend.[22] In this way, community rodeos participated in broader trends on the continent in reforming and standardizing sports of all kinds to better serve audiences, especially urbanites with plenty of disposable income. Officials moderated the violence in many sports, especially football, while financially dominant leagues, teams, and owners emerged to create more uniformity across competitions or performances.[23] In rodeo, the violence would be tempered, or more correctly camouflaged, as, for bronc riding, most rodeos abandoned blindfolding and tying a horse by the head tightly to a wooden post, that is, snubbing. They also phased out the most brutal spur-and-quirt riding while adopting side-release bucking chutes and flank straps (more on that transition below).[24]

In spite of persistent rural poverty, increased media attention and consumer spending on entertainment drove growth in rodeo through the interwar period. Automobiles and nascent middle-class tourism gave rodeo-based city festivals more customers and a certain vogue, which rodeos always have in economic boom times. Ambitious producers founded mainstreamed events as far away as New York, Boston, and Chicago in which rodeo people and animals came into town lock, stock, and barrel to compete, rather than asking locals to give riding or roping a try. "Promoter-producers" like Tex Austin, Fred Beebe, and Guy Weadick developed new, more lucrative contests that drew better competitors, female and male, some of whom moonlighted as stunt riders or actors in Hollywood.[25] This was rodeo as a ranching heritage show in the abstract, not as a reflection of local identity, with Tex Austin's Madison Square Garden show appearing in 1929 as the centerpiece.

By the mid-1920s, in Calgary the festivities and the boost to local business during the Stampede had won over important newspapers, tourist magazines, the railways, and hotel owners. Increasingly, a critical mass of Calgarians also saw their own opportunities in the fictions the Stampede offered about the rural Canadian West and their city, or at least in the parades, carnival, and unbridled drinking that would take place during the week.[26] As for those fictions, Calgarians who endorsed the rodeo would labor diligently to define themselves recognizably *as* westerners. The Stampede's competitive events would convey these usually unspoken values, which one could find only vaguely encapsulated as the "cowboy spirit" or "real spirit of Calgary" in local papers, rodeo publicity, and Calgary tourism office promotions. The graphic representation of this concept came in the form of the rider and "sunfisher" bronc image, airborne with arched back and head pointed down, symbolizing a moment of infinite possibility and ambition.

In Calgary, the sunfisher icon quickly became useful to a broad sector of the business community. Newspapers initially encouraged the habit by accepting advertising for the Stampede that might, for instance, feature a full-page image of a sunfishing bronc with his head simply pointed down. Or, perhaps the horse displayed more acrobatic twisting, appearing airborne while dislodging a rider, who flails in mid-air or lies crumpled on the ground. With such images came charged patter that told spectators that their ultimate goal at the rodeo should be to:

—SEE—
The Bucking Horses
The Bucking Steers
The Bucking Bulls
The Bucking Mules .[27]

"Let 'Er Buck." The dynamic image of bucking bronc with rider was always an icon of the Stampede. Calgary Stampede Pennant, 1912. Glenbow Archives, C-7753, Calgary, AB.

Stampede iconography often featured the bronc "buck." Detail from 1930 Calgary Stampede daily program sheet. Weadick Fonds, Glenbow Archives, Calgary, AB.

Readers might also fold over a page in the *Calgary Herald* to find a used car lot employing the image of a rearing horse and cowboy waving his hat in optimistic greeting. Or, perhaps, it was a local brewery that employed the bronc-buster image to claim that their business was "Ridin' Pretty" and "On Top To Stay."[28] The Stampede's roughstock events also supplied captivating, dynamic illustrations in the form of early rodeo photography, which would also circulate as postcards. The cards commonly featured broncs embellished as, for instance, a "Stampede Twister" who produced "precipitous trajectories" with "a gale of dust . . . [and] pounding hooves" to challenge the continent's best riders.[29]

Living horses had the responsibility of bringing that equine fantasy to life. Among them was Greasy Sal. As a work-a-day Stampede bronc, she left only scant traces on the historical record, but in that she was far more typical than the few "outlaw" celebrities of the thousands of horses passed around the rodeo world at the time. No one celebrated Greasy Sal with photograph postcards or "old-timer" stories in which this fellow or that had ridden her to a championship win. Instead we can begin her story with the basic facts that, for several years in the late 1920s, the Stampede employed her in the

Canadian saddle bronc competition, then briefly as a bareback riding horse, until she disappeared around 1931.

Greasy Sal was among the twenty or so broncs owned by the Calgary Industrial Exhibition Company and held at a property known simply as the Stampede Ranch. Before the rodeo purchased their current rural property two hours to the northeast of the city in 1961, Stampede staff managed a cache of horses on a property that Guy Weadick and his wife, fancy roper Flores LaDue, had bought in 1920. Four years earlier, Weadick had produced the ill-fated Sheepshead Bay Speedway rodeo in Brooklyn ("In No Manner or Method a 'Wild West' Show, but a Fair, Square, Clean CONTEST. Without Rehearsal, Sham, Make-Believe or Misrepresentation!"), which went broke before the cowgirls and cowboys were paid in full.[30] That event, although a financial failure, brought rodeo to audiences outside the West, driving continental interest in the sport. Weadick had returned to Calgary in 1919 to become a fixture in the city as the main producer, arena director, and booster for the Calgary Stampede annual rodeo and city festival.

Located in the rolling hills southwest of Calgary at Longview, just where the prairies come to an abrupt end against the base of the towering, snow-capped Rocky Mountains, the Stampede Ranch was and still is a spectacular and imposing little corner of Canada. Weadick and LaDue ran and publicized it as a working ranch to capitalize on newly built Canadian roads and a fad for dude ranches in the West, which complemented the growing wilderness park system and the interest in automobile camping. Many guests were hosted at frequent parties there, livened up by Weadick's gregarious and entertaining personality as "a tremendous drinker who crashed automobiles with alarming frequency" but whom many people found charming.[31] He had many interesting stories to tell. LaDue and Weadick, for example, were proud to alert visitors "Did you know? That neighboring outfit over there, the E. P. Ranch, is owned by the Prince of Wales."

That pocket of the prairies was also decent country for horses. In Canada, horse ranching was often several times more profitable than the cattle trade, although some said it required more land per head of livestock because horses were relatively inefficient digesters of their forage.[32] On Weadick and LaDue's property, staff let the horses breed and picked out buckers for the Stampede, sometimes also renting them out to other rodeos.[33] They were the "small tough horses of complex heritage" that were critical to ranching in western Canada.[34]

More broadly, solo cowboys frequently travelled on a saddle horse to compete at a rodeo with a bucker in tow, in hopes of renting or selling the horse to the rodeo.[35] A few rodeos actually insisted that bronc riders supply a bucker to the competition string in order to ride themselves. This was an old tradition from the 1880s, newly relevant as a way to keep the professional stock contractors, like the much-resented Irwin Brothers, from monopolizing a given rodeo, and to help local riders access prize money.[36] Stampede stock managers also rented horses for the rodeo from private individuals, often a chuckwagon driver, a roper, or a riding competitor offering a couple of "bad ones" to the show. Such individuals wrote frank letters to Guy Weadick: "Steve and I are taking a chuckwagon into Calgary, and I would like very much to contract five bucking horses, and get some jobs for my men, as we are all BROKE" (emphasis in original).[37] A few appeared every year at rodeo time at the Stampede grounds with their contracted horses, plus perhaps a few others on the side, hoping to "try their best to collect on the excess." On one occasion, Guy Weadick alerted one colleague, "This has always been and I guess always will. Bert Long [and] Lawrence Bruce are offenders in this particular line. But the thing to do is pay them for what we contract and no more."[38]

Local ranchers and other rural men who supplied the bulk of the Stampede's horses generally contracted for five or ten head, or less.[39] A small group of Alberta men sought instead to make a serious business of stock contracting by finding proven buckers for the growing number of community rodeos in western Canada. In doing so they also demonstrated the developing relationships between stockmen, rodeo producers, and competitors who were reshaping city rodeos such that they required a supply of buckers, not just one or two at a time, but in large numbers from a handful of powerful suppliers. Greasy Sal had thusly been purchased in 1927 from Jim McNab of Macleod (now Fort Macleod), Alberta, through the Stampede's stockman, retired rodeo champion Clem Gardiner. She had apparently been owned by a stockman named O. Jardine the year before when leased to the Stampede for bucking with a dozen other horses. There was a lot of horse trading going on as these men weighed their finances and business plans season by season.[40] Typically, Greasy Sal performed for two or three of the seven days of the show along with dozens of other horses, all indicated with a brand and a show name in the Stampede's horse lists.

Greasy Sal received a name that indicated riders would have a difficult time staying in the saddle. Generally, horse naming practices drew from old cowboy and ranch traditions of naming horses in a remuda ("all the saddle horses of an outfit thrown together") according to their coloring, shape, distinguishing characteristic, or some inside joke among the cowboys.[41] Rodeo horses were in show business, however, so their names enhanced and added entertainment value to the broncs. Some names endorsed audience knowledge of contemporary popular culture and trends, cinema, celebrities, or Wild West clichés: Alberta Kid, Sox (baseball), The Sheik (in 1927 in reference to the famous Valentino films), King Tut (whose relics had recently been discovered in Egypt), Lindbergh (celebrity aviator), or Dirty Dora (to lampoon the "Dumb Dora" comic strip popular in the 1920s and 1930s). Some show names drew attention to the acrobatics or supposed effects of preferred horses: Elevator, Jim Stink, Corkscrew, Zig Zag, Earthquake, Cyclone, Explosion, Flying Devil, Night Mare, Funeral Wagon, Calamity Ann.[42] Such bronc titles roasted the cowboys who attempted to ride them, distracting from or diminishing these horses' experiences of intolerable pain, fear, or frustration when a rider got on board. Such names also branded broncs with an identity that implied it was their nature to buck—that they consented to be in a rodeo by bucking—and so rodeo was only helping them live up to their potential. These horses were consumer-oriented creatures, marketed to rodeo audiences solely by their few minutes in the chute, and the ten or twenty seconds in the arena.[43]

Meanwhile, Guy Weadick and his office managers produced plenty of paperwork—letters, invoices, inventories, competition records, notes and messages scribbled on the back of envelopes, and scorecards. All of it comprised a mundane bureaucratic record of the work necessary before everyone materialized at the Stampede grounds each July, as well as to measure and manage the results at the show in preparation for the next year. Modern rodeo required proper record keeping, as well as standardized time keeping and scorecards for evaluating rider and animal alike in order to shake off charges of rigged results or of presenting a substandard rodeo that would repel competitors and ticket-buyers.[44] Duly collected, sorted, and stored carefully in Calgary Exhibition Company filing cabinets, many of them are today still marked with ink that bled in the rain, or which became creased and brown with grit from the desk in the judge's shack and the dusty hands of the men who handled them, folded them up, or put them in a shirt pocket. Among these records are many dozens of ledger-size inventories that people in the office called "horse lists," some detailing the origin of each horse, some their brands or names and coat color, and still others with bucking results that

Weathered 1926 "Horse List," featuring Greasy Sal and famous buckers, the "original" Gravedigger and Tipperary, "not halter broke." Stampede Fonds, Glenbow Archives, Calgary, AB.

measured and managed buckers systematically. Only some horses were ridden for ten seconds, generating scores marked in the columns on the right side of the sheet. From them we learn that in 1927 Greasy Sal was one of one hundred ninety-five broncs employed at Stampede. Two years later she was among two hundred sixty-seven bucked over the Stampede week.[45]

As arena director, Guy Weadick labored to produce the kind of bucking performances riders and audiences demanded. In essence, the process required a sort of mass production of bucking. For any rodeo, the most damning complaints that competitors, business sponsors, and fans could level were that events moved too slowly, transitions between events were awkward and lengthy, or the bucking stock were too placid, something the Stampede's producers assiduously avoided. Still people criticized and scrutinized the stock and their movements. More consistent buckers were beginning to circulate, but so too were more cowboys with more practice and focus, especially at lucrative rodeos like the Stampede. Weadick would explain in 1929, "This year I contracted more horses than the year before. This was absolutely necessary, owing to the fact that ... the quality of the riders [was] better." The previous year, the Stampede had made the risky investment of contracting enough to put together a bucking string of one hundred and fifty horses. "Out of the bunch there are always duds, regardless of what those you contract from tell you. ... To give a show worth while, I think the opinion of all this year was that we had the best bunch of bucking horses we have ever had, but in order to get them we had to contract more."[46] By the early 1930s, everyone saw that by bringing in more horses and keeping detailed records of average scores awarded by judges to each horse, the consistency and quality of the bucking were improved.[47] The escalating numbers of horses necessary to supply the rodeo indicate the growing wastage in the trade, as rising numbers of horses were tried out, used briefly or not at all, and then discarded in the search for enough quality buckers.

By that time, "old-timers," who as young people had actually performed the rural labor rodeo and Wild West performances were purported to demonstrate, had begun retiring from the business. Forgetting how brutal early cowboy tournaments could be, some grumbled in the trade papers that the modern cowboy had become a showbiz desperado character that one got over with fancy dress and provocative, reckless behavior.[48] Less sensational roping or riding events no longer appealed to audiences, one old hand lamented, because cowboy skills had been "burlesqued so much" by rodeo sports, especially in gruesome novelties like steer busting or spur-and-quirt driven bucking contests that were a reversal of the real breaking process.[49]

Still, the old-timers had a point. The industry was changing quickly to adapt to modern ticket buyers' expectations for rodeo as a maturing sport trade premised, not simply on informal wagering and whiskey, but on guaranteed action. They were expensive investments, but fenced arenas and permanent bleachers, shaded if possible, focused performances around spectators' viewing needs. More ticket buyers in turn attracted food and souvenir vendors, and perhaps a fellow selling seat cushions from his car in the parking lot. Bucking chutes had appeared at Stampede already in 1919.[50] In the later 1920s, Greasy Sal bucked in newly constructed fenced arenas that preventing bucking horses or other stock from running out of sight.

A new generation of competitors was attuned to the new procedures as rodeos elsewhere that could afford to do so installed fencing and side-release bucking chutes, which were standard equipment by 1930. (A side-release enables the horse to exit the chute without dragging the cowboy against the chute.) Directly across from the grandstands Greasy Sal waited in a bucking chute without a blindfold but in hackamore and saddle as her rider lowered himself down and prepared a strong grip on the lead rope attached to her halter.[51] The opening of the bucking chute gate (and perhaps a kick with the spurs or a boot heel from a chute man) triggered Greasy Sal to begin resisting her rider, and many horses learned to save their energy for that moment.

To the horses scouted and reserved for rodeo use, the process of bucking was one in which they were no longer ridden to a standstill but successfully freed themselves of a rider every time, and they learned how to do so as quickly as possible. Recall Goldie Cameron's disapproval of "new-fangled" flank straps that focused horses on kicking up and back into their blind spot, and so reduced variability in bucking behaviors. Although the sunfisher was the graphic ideal, flank straps trained the new horses that it was the strap that was intolerable, not the rider. The modern bucking process essentially displayed the effects of operant conditioning on a horse, which rodeo people colloquially described as an innate "love" of bucking off a rider. In fact, the raw ingredient for the outlaw bronc was simply a horse who tended toward fighting and kicking (rather than running), was unaccustomed to riders, and was flanked in a chute. Greasy Sal and other broncs were rewarded for the bucking behavior with freedom from the rider and the flank strap. During the ride, with a spurring rider hanging on in large part by gripping the lead rope attached to Greasy Sal's head harness, each pull restricted her head and her ability to see the rider and to look at and evaluate the noisy chaos around her. Whether by immediate fear or uncontrollable instinct, she—like all bucking horses—spun, jumped, and kicked at what she could not properly see but which must have felt to her like a predator attack.

Rodeos had also begun limiting roughstock rides to a maximum of ten seconds (in later years that would be reduced to eight seconds to increase the chance of a successful ride), evaluating horse and rider by a points system for the quality of the performance. This innovation sped up the bucking go-rounds so spectators saw new action every few minutes, while also preserving the stock since many horses ridden to a standstill were essentially broken and would cease bucking thereafter.[52] A points system and grading sheets marked by hand by a judge in the arena facilitated standardization in evaluating horse performances and rewarded those that reproduced the outlaw character by offering the most spinning, kicks, jumps, and bucks.[53] The judging was not always dependable or fair because judges could be biased, inattentive, or inexpert. Still, it provided a basic way of quantifying and monetizing bucking. The innovations of the 1920s in Calgary and at many other rodeos in those years sought to shape and measure a bucking horse's behavior to the entertainment and managerial needs of the rodeo and its audience. Even in these early days, the wildness that audiences witnessed on the part of Greasy Sal and other buckers was a carefully crafted one.

Instead of painful spur-and-quirt bucking, or cowboys spurring and waving their hats to frighten and disorient a horse, the flank rope encouraged horses to kick back and up since it triggered the sensation of being attacked by a predator on the haunches. Certainly less bloody or visually violent to spectators, the flank rope was perhaps just masking or sanitizing a horse's experience for audiences since the use of it did not require a rider to whip a horse harshly or draw blood on his hide to extract the necessary behavior. For several decades, flank ropes were just that: ropes or bare leather straps. It would be some years before people began applying a wide, leather flank strap with a wool fleece sheath that eliminated the skin abrasions that bare flank ropes caused as horses bucked and kicked.[54]

Although sceptics were quiet in Calgary—as they would be for decades in that loyal city—some of rodeo's critics further afield were unconvinced that flank ropes were as humane a way to produce bucking as rodeo people claimed. "Onlookers do not always realize that what is merely an exciting exhibition to

This is not Greasy Sal, but she may have looked like this horse, Steele Grey, with whom she labored as "outlaw" at the Calgary Stampede. Souvenir postcard, 1928. Glenbow Archives, Calgary, AB.

them is intense suffering to the animals," said Mrs. Edward Weld, director of the New York Women's League for Animals after the yearly Madison Square Garden rodeo. "The torturing cinches which are used to make ponies and steers buck and plunge . . . make of the rodeo a thing of cruelty which should be barred by law from arena and screen."⁵⁵ Indeed, the Hollywood "running W" scandal was in the news when Greasy Sal was working at the Stampede. Animal advocates and film industry insiders exposed how Hollywood animal wranglers used wire devices known as a "running W" to trip horses in dramatic fashion for chase and shoot-out scenes in the many Western or epic drama films of the period. Notoriously, a reported one hundred horses had been tripped and killed to film the 1925 biblical epic *Ben Hur,* for instance.⁵⁶ To rodeo's critics, similarly, bucking behavior produced with a flank strap or spurs was not natural but artificial, extracted by a cruel device from unwitting horses, and in a self-serving way that produced a higher kick that drove the interest in bronc riding. Said Mary Cavanaugh of the Anti-Rodeo League in Chicago to the *New York Times* of the social damage caused by rodeo, "We are back in the arena of ancient Rome, except that in Nero's day the Christians were sacrificed to animals, and now animals are sacrificed for the amusement of Christians."[57]

The 1920s were an especially active period for rodeo's critics, who had been watching the sport grow for several decades and were worried that the violence children saw in the arena might cause them to abuse animals or might desensitize the public to obvious displays of animal suffering. Indeed, animal advocacy pamphlets and magazines from the period accurately depicted and explained rodeo activities (more so than some that circulated after 1960). Further, animal advocates continued to question rodeo's myth of animal consent—imagining broncs as brave western beasts just asking for a fight—by explaining their behavior as that of frightened prey animals injured and traumatized by the sport.[58] Although there may have been a few careerists among them, by and large the members of these groups were people with sincere empathy for livestock, which blared out from every page of their publications decrying "cruelty" in rodeo and countless other settings.[59] Some advocates called for the outright abolition of rodeo, and some lobbied for laws banning them in their state, province, city, or county. Others worked with rodeos to eliminate particular events like steer busting, chicken pulls, or the wild horse race, while tolerating or even praising other rodeo events as an inevitable outgrowth of the ranching industry and thus acceptable as entertainment.

Rodeos responded by formulating basic statements forbidding "mistreatment" and "cruelty" to animals or "abusing stock."[60] Those statements served publicity purposes primarily, offering a way for rodeo spokespeople to talk in generalities about the policies and intentions of rodeo people, rather than animals injured and killed during the show. In my survey of the Calgary Stampede's records, I have seen no evidence that rodeo managers there set aside money in their budgets for compliance monitoring or other enforcement of their rules in those years.

Behind the scenes, rodeos dealt with animals killed and injured on rodeo day or in transport by compensating stock contractors financially. Bucking horses died or were injured at Stampede due to impact injuries from bucking, badly assembled chute systems, or reasons no one could pin down. In the Stampede's June 1930 horse lists and accounts of stock on hand, for instance, a bucker called Lady Luck was simply marked "dead," with no further information. Sid Bannermann of Kew, Alberta, rented seventy-five wild horses to the Stampede at ten dollars each the previous year, when Greasy Sal was bucking in the show. After the rodeo concluded, the Stampede compensated Bannerman forty dollars each for "one killed, one crippled" among his horses.[61] It is not clear today how many rodeos could afford to compensate contractors in that way, although those that did certainly must have attracted better contractors with the more consistent stock. Rather than bow out of the business when their animals were injured or killed, contractors and exhibitors took it for granted that some animals would inevitably be destroyed in any rodeo, as was the case in the day-to-day functioning at a ranch.

In 1930, the Stampede employed two hundred and thirty-five bucking horses. About fifteen percent were owned by the Stampede, Clem Gardiner, or Dick Cosgrove, and the rest were contracted from a dozen men, five or ten head at a time for fifteen or twenty dollars each. Numbers 203 and 204 on the horse list that year were the famous Midnight and Black Diamond, broncs from Medicine Hat owned by Russ Greenwood.[62] People remembered famous buckers like Midnight and Black Diamond for many years, including great detail on the specific patterns of movement they would display, the money they earned for their owners, and the cowboys who rode them, measuring all other broncs against them.[63]

Another famous bucker who appeared at the Calgary Stampede with Greasy Sal was the "infamous" Cyclone. One cowboy said he had "ridden worse buckers, but never one with Cyclone's unique back motion which unhinged the saltiest of bronc busters in quick order."[64] Like Steamboat, a number of these well-known horses died in inglorious ways: Tipperary, a celebrated top-earning "vicious outlaw bucking horse" of the 1920s, died in February of 1934 in "a howling blizzard . . . his bones picked clean by coyotes" at the Jump Off Ranch near Belle Fourche, South Dakota. He had been turned out for the winter with another exhausted bucker called Tip Top. In 1931 the two had been stolen from the same property and driven to Montana and nearly died until they were found starving in a remote barn three years later.[65] Another champion bucking horse, named Coon, "vaulted a fence, ramming a board through his chest, and had to be killed."[66] Hell's Angel, from a Montana ranch, "the greatest bucking horse in history," owned by influential but despised-by-cowboys rodeo producer Colonel W. T. Johnson, died of lockjaw about age fifteen in a railcar while traveling west after being bucked at a rodeo in New York.[67]

As in previous decades, living horses continued to unknowingly play the outlaw bronc in a broader graphic and storytelling context in which Western stories featured shootouts, chases, and other dramatic action. A generation of dime novels and Wild West shows, as well as popular accounts like Charles Wellington Furlong's *Let 'Er Buck* (1921) and John Barrow's *Ubet* (1934), celebrated the bucking horse as a wily character who challenged and exasperated cowboys, but also added action and humor to western life. The outlaw bronc separated the cowboy from an audience of "blasé, effete, lily-livered youths" in "the East" who knew not the outdoor life, as Furlong put it.[68] All these stories verified the rodeo's performances of the myth of consent around western horses, the fighting outlaws whose struggles invited the cowboy to prove his toughness.

In contrast, the new and abundant movie westerns celebrated horses' supposed desire to serve humanity by starring cooperative characters like Tom Mix's Tony the Wonder Horse. He was a primordial example who would set the stage for Trigger, Champion, Silver, Buttermilk, and other western horse characters so supposedly sagacious that they understood and wanted to support human endeavors. It was a fantasy alright, one that obscured the self-interest in human use of horses and the variability of actual living horses.[69] Local rodeos and the remaining Wild West shows instead told people that resistant horses were *the* classic western animal and that they were best viewed live.[70] The outlaw bronc and cowboy ideal was so recognizable that it was reproduced and elaborated on by artists, cartoonists, writers, newspapermen, and manufacturers of souvenirs and Western bric-a-brac. The western bucker was a true stereotype, as journalist Walter Lippmann would explain it in those days—that is, a fantasy or misrepresentation replicated so often that people began to take it as an unexamined truth about how western horses looked and behaved.[71]

The horses who could produce the stereotyped "buck" unknowingly contributed to the rodeo-wide convention for depicting horses as sunfishing or kicking outlaw buckers in flight. Every rodeo had to have the icon on display in programs, in advertising, or on the colourful illustrated letterhead used for business correspondence. We should not take this visual convention and its relation to horse behavior for granted. As with early cowboy tournaments tacked onto a local Peach Day festival or some other civic holiday, rodeo committees and graphic artists used trial and error to find the precise mix of violence and humor to which audiences responded and which rodeo people in turn seem to have internalized as normative. Broncs were presented not grazing on a remote hillside, or waiting in a paddock behind the arena, or being petted by a young woman dressed in fancy western attire but at their most explosively violent. As a result, the horse who did not jump and buck in expected ways appeared to rodeo judges, riders, and audiences as substandard and deserving of a low score or generating a re-ride for the cowboy or cowgirl in question. Many failed to perform consistently and were weeded out of the bucking strings supplied to the Stampede.

Rodeo horses had a public life as well as a life that took place backstage, behind the scenes of the show in the private marshalling and management zones that the Calgary Stampede and every rodeo had. Greasy Sal performed at Stampede each year between 1926 and 1930. Audiences may have noticed her as the arena announcer called out her name to the crowds each time she was ridden. The newspapers and countless photo-postcards also noted the names of Stampede's buckers for fans to learn, although Greasy Sal does not appear to have been among them. In 1927 the Stampede also leased Greasy Sal to another, unnamed rodeo in the care of stock manager, contractor, and competitor Clem Gardiner. That year, Gardiner nonetheless marked her on the back of a horse delivery list as out of the running for that unnamed rodeo: "X in foal."[72] This was decidedly backstage information.

What happened to Greasy Sal's foal is not apparent in Stampede records. Three years later she was being managed by Dick Cosgrove. A winning chuckwagon driver, saddle bronc rider, stock manager, and now arena director for Guy Weadick, Cosgrove would become a much-loved fixture at the Stampede and in Calgary until at least the late 1950s. In 1930, Greasy Sal foaled again at the Stampede Ranch. In late May that year Dick Cosgrove wrote to Weadick about the birth, "Gray Mare branded D2 I think she is called Grizley Sal [sic] she had a colt two weeks ago and I killed it."[73] Two other proven buckers, Baby Doll and Red Head, were also about to give birth but bucked again at Stampede later that year with no foals in tow bawling for their mothers and distracting these mares from the arena performance. Cosgrove had promised Weadick that the three would "be dry and in shape in time for the show."[74]

From a rodeo point of view, Greasy Sal and other mares were modern performers with a job to do, more valuable to the Stampede bucking than doing anything else. In this scenario, foals were wastage—or hopefully a lesson not to turn the mares out with the stallions at the ranch in the fall. Greasy Sal as mare (rather than outlaw bronc, as she was presented to the public) would have grieved the loss of her foal, spent a period of days or weeks calling and pacing the paddock fence lines or pasture looking for him or her. That aspect of her existence is an element we must consider if we are to have a more holistic

Dick Cosgrove and unidentified horse, ca. 1924–27.
Glenbow Archives, Calgary, Alberta.

understanding of her as a historical being with concerns beyond the bucking chute. That aspect of her life exposes the degree to which westerners created the animals' public reputations by allowing outsiders only limited knowledge about their full lives. Many locals and tourists would have taken a wild foal as symbolic of innocence, beauty, and optimism for the future, or, maybe, of the purity of nature in the West. Did Dick Cosgrove think about how his act of dispatching a newborn horse defied the claims Stampede participants made to have unique insight into and the authority over the West and its animals?

By 1930, Greasy Sal was nearing the end of her tenure at the Stampede. She was noted on one horse list in a group marked "These horses not very good," soon to be weeded out of the saddle bronc string and tried out for bareback as a last attempt to make her pay.[75] Other horses like Alberta Kid, Sliptivity, Santa Claus, Honorable Patches, Tennessee, Big Smoke, and Dirty Dora all seemed to still be bucking from that original group in which Greasy Sal had started in 1926. All the rest of the string were of more recent vintage.[76] It appears that for most horses the average number of years at Stampede that decade was perhaps four or five. Despite the industry lore about how bucking horses all lived to be very old, the majority of the Stampede's outlaw broncs disappeared far sooner, returning to their independent owners, or to the Stampede Ranch to breed more potential buckers, or to some other fate as a pack horse or slaughterhouse canner.

Calgary's civic identity and that of its Stampede were grounded in a fantasy about cowboy living that was a generation in the past by the time Greasy Sal disappeared. As a living horse, she was saddled with the responsibility of bringing the idealized western bronc to life. The bucking bronc ideal and the Stampede's presentations of buckers obscured the full lives of the many hundreds of horses drawn into the rodeo world, telling the public that they certainly were not disposable but rather enthusiastic partners in the adventure that was the interwar Canadian West. The symbol was ubiquitous in the American West, as well, not least in Wyoming. Today, countless small cities and towns feature a statue of a bronc rider at the rodeo ground or downtown at the main square.

Guy Weadick and his managers made some elements of their horses' lives public; others they kept confidential. Those decisions reveal that they well understood that they traded in polished stereotypes. There was no public sign of the wastage or human self-interest involved in the mass production of bucking at the Stampede, which still required older agricultural attitudes toward uses of the land and of horses to get the job done. Although audiences did not know it, in the production of western-styled entertainment, bucking broncs came to be through their handlers' pragmatic daily decisions about costs and entertainment value. Several decades ago, historian Keith Thomas described this phenomenon as a function of modern life wherein many people found themselves in a "confused state of mind" as they struggled to reconcile protective desires toward animals and the environment with humankind's accelerating and clearly self-enriching manipulation and consumption of the natural world. Wild West shows and community rodeos consumed many horses to produce a western horse ideal that provided, Thomas explained, the "mixture of compromise and concealment [that] has so far prevented this conflict from having to be fully resolved."[77] The myth of consent was encapsulated in the modern rodeo bronc, who came to the arena bearing a show-business name and for only a few explosive seconds a day, so audiences would not need to consider the larger costs involved in their consumer experiences of "the buck."

In 2012, Calgary was struck by a minor media conflagration when the head veterinarian for the Stampede, Greg Evans, told a local news station "for the first time" that "horses that don't make the cut to compete in the famous rodeo are sent to an Alberta slaughterhouse for meat." Staff at the Stampede Ranch had been breeding roughstock for almost one hundred years, producing many thousands of horses to find the minority who could "become the top bucking horses in the world," as Stampede publicists claimed. Evans explained that, while many Stampede Ranch horses appeared at Stampede, some were leased or sold to other stock contractors. But those weeded out of the Stampede Ranch bucking string had for years gone to the abattoir in Fort Macleod. This was the same town from which Greasy Sal had come when Clem Gardiner and the Stampede Ranch purchased her back in 1926, revealing the continuities in the horse, rodeo, and slaughter industries in Alberta for over a century.

Animal advocacy organizations asked why the surplus Stampede Ranch horses could not be sent to rescues or otherwise adopted out. "They are semiferal, . . . wilder than the average horse and for a lot of them it's a temperament problem, where they're not going to be comfortable in confinement of any kind," Evans explained. Purpose-bred for a single function, they would be too dangerous to live a conventional life.[78] Numerous horse advocates pointed out that the slaughterhouse was a lazy, cheap solution. The Stampede was shirking its responsibility because, said one, "completely feral horses can be domesticated. This is how the west was won."[79] That might have been true in decades past, in Greasy Sal's era, when buckers were found among wild herds simply unaccustomed to human contact. Yet, over the century, businesses like the Stampede Ranch had begun specifically cultivating horses unable to tolerate a rider and flank strap, and cultivated in a feral context in which training for any other life would be expensive and difficult when there were already so many unwanted horses in the province. Thus, perhaps the most notable aspect of the debate over the Calgary Stampede's contribution to that problem in North America was that the broad public was still unaware that there was any wastage in rodeo, but believed that every bucking horse naturally becomes a star.

CHAPTER 4

# Mid-century: Bucking Horse of the Year

One of the most influential and novel celebrities of rodeo at mid-century was War Paint, a Quarter Horse–Pinto cross saddle bronc. Like most of the famous broncs of rodeo, War Paint was male. People believed that mares might buck between age two and five or six, but eventually they would always quit. War Paint bucked for twenty years. Also, he was reputed to be a biter. Even today War Paint's stuffed skin poses at the Pendleton Round-Up and Happy Canyon Hall of Fame in Pendleton, Oregon, in the horse's famous dive posture with mouth open to remind us of his impatience with people. Or perhaps that was just a legend and people remembered him as more ornery than he really was behind the chutes. What we do know is that War Paint was a template for what modern rodeo needed from a bucker: photogenic, capable of challenging but patterned bucking, consistent in performance, and strong enough to cope with the travel that the expanding continental rodeo network required. Whether from War Paint alone or due to a broader trend in bucking stock, the era of the sunfisher had begun to pass, replaced by the diving bronc, of which War Paint was a classic example. He was a professional bucker for professional rodeo, some said.

In the postwar years, rodeo people did not invent any major new events or otherwise refine the sport in the dramatic ways they had in the early decades of the century. Everything was simply intensified. For one, there was more money afoot. Not until the mid-1960s would attendance at baseball and basketball games surpass that at rodeos in the U.S., for example.[1] Much of this new capital was won and earned by a small rodeo elite of male competitors and stock contractors, and many people noticed that women were being marginalized from the most lucrative events after World War II, just when the broader culture celebrated women primarily as homemakers and mothers. As the rodeo network grew, it also created chronic shortages of roughstock, especially bucking horses. Purpose-breeding broncs for the trade would in

War Paint diving at the 1955 Pendleton Round-Up, with photographers close at hand, bottom right. George Myren off War Paint, September 15, 1955, Devere Helfrich, Devere Helfrich Rodeo Photographic Collection, National Cowboy & Western Heritage Museum, 81.023.10516, Museum purchase.

time begin to solve that problem, as well as the cultural issue of consent. Born-to-buck horses were crafted to "just love to buck" and thus they became prey animals reinvented as sporting professionals who might be award-winners, just like the cowboys. In the professional era, the Rodeo Cowboys Association (RCA), later the Professional Rodeo Cowboys Association (PRCA), and the Canadian Professional Cowboys Association (CPRA), instituted Bucking Horse of the Year awards for saddle broncs and, in time, bareback bronc horses. These were rewards for stock contractors, not for finding explosive, dangerous horses at random in wild herds, but for crafting manageable and consistent buckers from proven stock.

Just when War Paint became famous, the RCA and its new publicity arm, the Rodeo Information Committee, were also talking nonstop of the professionalization of rodeo. To industry publicists, the professional rodeo man was no longer a working-class fellow from the West but an "athlete" who competed year-round, across the continent, and earned his income from winnings in "the most highly competitive sport in the world." This was a world wherein one had to "survive," as an RCA-sponsored, pro-industry book explained in 1956: "For the rodeo cowboy there are no salaries, no contracts or guarantees—not even an expense allowance. Each man must make his way through his ability and his luck [and] fierce competitive spirit."[2] The ethos of the sport mirrored old ideals that portrayed westerners as individualists who acted with complete independence and sole personal responsibility. In practice, of course, the rodeo community was far more cooperative and supportive. Rodeo competitors engaged in all sorts of cost and risk-sharing arrangements like prize splitting, money lending, and ride sharing, worked out in bars and countless rodeo arena parking lots. At the same time, American cowboys had balked for six years, until 1951, at the idea of RCA-sponsored group health insurance.[3] Professionalization meant supporting fellow competitors—within limits— and imposing these expectations on one's animals, including bucking horses.

Rodeo had become "big business," everyone said. So, if rodeo cowboys' authority no longer came from labor on the land, as industry publicists were insisting to every journalist who would listen, that idea ignored the fact that rodeo was still entirely dependent upon ranches and rural labor. Both were undergoing continued crisis. Ranching was still a financial loss for many of the families who carried on with it. Of the way rodeos functioned to help people cope in those days, Joan Burbick said, "The simple, primitive labor of the cowboy working with horse, cattle, and bulls became a pastoral image of a time before the taking of Western lands by syndicates, corporations, and banks. The conflicts over who had the right to land were forgotten once the rodeo cowboy danced."[4] The cowboys did dance, but at significant personal cost. Rodeo people spent hundreds or thousands of hours on the road. There was plenty of exhaustion, heavy drinking, and untold sacrifices by wives and kids asked to follow men from rodeo to rodeo, plus the car accidents, the arena injuries, and (often) stubborn refusal to go to the hospital, which led to more drinking.

The horses of rodeo did all that traveling, too. They were animals of the land but alienated from it much of the time, like rodeo people. In the golden age of the North American car culture when automobiles were abundant status symbols, cowboys drove the most expensive sedans they could afford, the powerful V8 engines hauling horse trailers if necessary.[5] Rodeo still traded on the ideal of western self-sufficiency and intimate knowledge of the land and its animals, although these relationships were increasingly defined by pavement. Hence, this chapter relates the story of rodeo's bucking horses in the years that led up to that moment at mid-century. It explains the sourcing of buckers from the 1930s to the 1960s, and the studiously ignored link between rodeo and the horse slaughter trade. It explores how the industry began the transition to born-to-buck breeding programs in the hands of a few powerful male-dominated stock contracting and rodeo production companies. The goal was the mass production of "double-tempered" broncs who bucked dependably, were safe to manage behind the scenes, and also could be featured in rodeo as horsey equivalents to the new camera-friendly cowboy athletes, like Casey Tibbs. Explosive but predictable buckers when the chute gate opened, like War Paint, the new broncs were capable of enduring the exhausting travel that professional rodeo required. Top riders wanted those horses for high-point rides and they sought out contractors who developed horses who displayed the new style of bucking that earned all those points—that is by diving instead of sunfishing. The transition to the diving bronc and the new modes of cultivating that kind of horse in born-to-buck breeding programs did not overturn the idea among rodeo people that some horses "just love to buck." Instead, the idea that the cultivated bucker was somehow still found in nature, despite any human influence, persisted and kept alive the myth that those horses were native to rodeo and central to the challenges it offered human competitors.

Just when Greasy Sal was being weeded out of the Calgary Stampede bucking string in 1931, wild horses on the continent were about to live through a tragedy of the commons event wherein people captured, then killed or sold horses without limits until the population collapsed. The tragic near-extinction of wild horses at human hands would ultimately inspire rodeo people to purpose-breed bucking broncs to guarantee their own supply. Back in the 1920s, the gasoline engine had begun to reduce horses' utility. Then, with the economic collapse of the 1930s, countless westerners set their animals loose to fend for themselves. Relieved of work, horses gathered where they could and began having babies. Montana in particular was said to be "black with horses" that decade.[6] In some places, government-sanctioned and -financed horse eradication programs had already begun in the late 1920s. Many ranchers hated free-roaming mustangs and had for decades. They complained that their own working horses, if left unattended in the wrong place, were sometimes lured away by wild herds and could not be retrained if captured again. Ranchers in Canada and the U.S. believed that wild or feral horses consumed forage that rightly belonged to cattle. After the Taylor Grazing Act of 1934 limited ranchers' access to public lands for low-cost cattle grazing in the U.S., wild horses seemed to complicate the work of the federal government to manage range health by ensuring that only leaseholders' cattle consumed the available forage.[7]

To others, free-roaming horses were the last of the West's free animals of harvest, a population that multiplied on the landscape with no human management and could be captured and sold. The most famous horsemeat-packing operation in these years was the Chappel Brothers Company. During World War I, the operation had prospered by buying workhorses or trapping feral horses for sale to Allied forces, exporting to Europe a claimed 117,000 horses, most of whom died in battle or from disease.[8] As much as people deeply regretted the Great War and the fate of horses in it, two decades later many westerners equally regretted Chappel Brothers' cultivation of the horsemeat trade. Under the Ken-L Ration brand and a subsidiary called the CBC Corporation based in Miles City, Montana (not incidentally, later home to the famous Miles City Bucking Horse Sale and Rodeo), the company canned horse carcasses to serve a growing consumer pet food market. The company bought or raised horses any way they could, moving beyond dog food to turn horse bodies into any product that had a market at any given moment, from fertilizer to glue. Many young men worked for the CBC in the 1930s, or the "Cornbeef and Cabbage outfit," as Montanans joked about it.[9]

Some called the 1930s the "great removal" because horses were so systematically captured and destroyed by Chappel Brothers agents and others.[10] There were various means by which a fellow or team of men might collect wild horses for Chappel Brothers or the West's auction stockyards. The most labor-intensive methods involved snaring, running to exhaustion, or trapping horses in a canyon or other geographic feature that prevented escape, methods that were extremely dangerous to prey and hunter and his horse alike. Others employed several riders on saddle horses, plus a small herd of tamed horses, allowing the calm horses to mingle with and relieve the wild horses of their fear. This method took some patience and time, but it allowed men to drive the whole group safely into a corral without any risky confrontations with dominant stallions or experienced mares fiercely determined to defend their band.[11]

Don Bell was a rodeo cowboy who sometimes worked scouting rodeo broncs from the thousands of horses that the Chappel Brothers transited through Denver before sending them to slaughter. "During those depression years . . . many of us young riders hung out at the yards and we all rode what we then called Try Out Broncs and we received one dollar a head and if we rode several that made us a lot of money back then," Bell remembered of years when road work or construction labor paid only $3.00 a day.[12] The work of testing horses to find those who would buck, rather than freezing or simply running, was lucrative but stressful. At the chaotic horse pens, terrified mustangs were impossible to approach safely or could be found fighting since they were packed into close quarters.[13] Still, it was true, as rodeo people said in those days, that many broncs unknowingly had their trip to the slaughterhouse postponed or cancelled altogether through scouting by men like Bell. Rodeo and the canning trade were simply two arms of the horse flesh business.[14]

The Chappel Brothers company was a large contender in the modern horse sourcing and slaughter business, but not the only one. Many western men tried their hand at mustanging (harvesting wild horses from public lands) or horse ranching. Ed Strickland, nephew of rodeo champions Hugo and Mabel Strickland, explained to a family biographer that his grandfather had been an important horse rancher. He had held many thousands of animals, some of whom he supplied to the military, some more carefully cultivated for use as polo ponies and sent by rail to the Northeast, and some crossed to produce mules for cotton plantations in the Southeast. "The remainder of Grandpa's horses went to Butte, Montana, where they were canned and shipped to Japan for human use," he said.[15] For families like the Stricklands, each horse had value of some kind; one just had to discover it. During the Depression, Strickland would turn to trucking or pick up some ranch or rodeo work, but when those opportunities fell through, he resorted, like many men, to "running horses" for sale to ranches or livestock auctions.[16]

It was said thereafter that the size of the wild horse population was directly proportional to men's bank accounts. "When times were hard, men preyed on the mustangs; when everyone was employed, the mustangs roamed freely." Many men became addicted to the hunt—mustanging was a "disease," some wives said—and the entrepreneurial income it generated.[17] Frank Dobie explained the allure similarly: "Mustanging on the pristine prairies was like fishing in the Pacific Ocean. The mustanger never knew what he might catch on his rope."[18] Once captured, the lucky among those horses might be sold to farmers. Others were auctioned off in groups, driven on hoof many miles to a stockyard, then shipped by train to their ultimate destination. The horses might cross the border, or perhaps land at the enormous horse sales in Miles City, a beacon of capitalism rooted in the exceptional horse country of the northern plains.[19]

The scale of human poverty in the West guaranteed that there was enormous economic pressure bearing down on western horses. The mustangers and canners, the ranchers who continued to fence land to keep cattle in and horses out, and government restrictions that made horses unwelcome on public grazing lands all caused the U.S. horse population to decline from an early peak estimated at twenty million in 1910 to about five million by 1954.[20] On the Canadian prairies, free-roaming horse numbers similarly declined throughout the 1940s. Believing they ate too much and were a nuisance on land suited to cattle or to plant agriculture, ranchers captured or killed them, sending 250,000 to the canners through the Western Horse Marketing Co-Operative up to 1951.[21] As rodeo people still relied on free-roaming and feral-but-owned herds to find bucking stock, the scale of human poverty in the West in turn produced a shortage of rodeo broncs.[22]

What was a wild horse at that moment, in any event? From a rodeo point of view, the status of "wild" was a function of a horse's individual nature and experience, not his or her status as an owned or unowned being. Westerners often referred to any unbroken horse as "wild," even a modern bucking horse shut up in a trailer and being driven down the highway, utterly unfree. Essentially, "wild" meant unbroken and perhaps so unaccustomed to hands-on human management that it was necessary to force such a horse into a restraint chute even just to fit a halter on him or her. Such naive wild horses resisted riders, not with patterned bucking but "wildly and dangerously because there is fury in them." So explained well-known rodeo journalist Gene Lamb of these horses' attempts to fend off human contact, probably more from fear than anger. Lamb admitted, "They are not used to enclosures, particularly enclosures surrounded by thousands of people."[23] Indeed, to some, horses were essentially wild animals, not domesticated, unless forcibly confronted and controlled by man.[24]

In captivity, these horses could be exceptionally dangerous, kicking, rearing and stomping on or biting anyone who came too close. At the rodeo arena, it was the job of pickup men to help dismounting roughstock riders get to safety and to direct stock of all kinds to the exit gate to keep the show moving. These men were (and are) expert ropers, riding strong and "broncy" (assertive) horses trained to approach bucking broncs without hesitation. At times, even pickup men found it impossible to direct wild horses employed as broncs into or out of chutes. One such horse circulating on the rodeo network in the 1950s was called North of Yellowstone. In a short essay about the bronc, "The Devil Horse," cowboy Don Bell joked that North of Yellowstone was more popular in Wyoming than President Eisenhower, but (or because) he was notorious for biting riders while bucking by twisting his neck around to snap at their feet as they spurred him. Sometimes people resorted to forcing muzzles on such horses to prevent bites and other defensive assaults back of the chutes or in the arena.[25]

The wild horse race was a more obvious way to employ these kinds of dangerous mustangs in a rodeo. Yet the growing sport increasingly required buckers for saddle bronc riding and more elite bareback bronc competitions, while only a minority of rodeos held wild horse races. Just as the industry's publicists were striving to produce more consistent entertainment and sell rodeo as a professional sport, bronc rider Deb Copenhaver remembered how cowboys resented the entrepreneurial men who trafficked in rough, frightened wild horses for bronc riding contests. In 1954, he accompanied cowboys Casey Tibbs and Bill Linderman to a bucking exhibition in Bridger, Montana, that attracted seven thousand spectators from around Montana and Wyoming.[26] Known as "matched rides," such exhibitions occurred irregularly as individual producers could hold them, but they had great promotional value for the sport. Featuring star cowboys in streamlined contests of bronc riding, without any other rodeo events, they presaged the bull-riding-only event boom that would begin in the 1970s by showcasing only a few rodeo stars, human and equine. The dominant stock contractors, rodeo producers, and promoters in rodeo tended to be risk-averse and competitive, carving out regions of influence where they monopolized the rodeo work. Matched rides offered a way for those seeking to grow the sport to temper such politics and territorialism in rodeo. For example, a stockman might be asked to provide his well-known bronc to a matched-ride event featuring well-known riders but held in a region in which he did not normally contract and with an event producer with whom he had no regular business relationship and viewed suspiciously as a competitor.[27]

One particular matched ride in Bridger, Montana, was innovative enough to be photographed for a piece in *Life* magazine. Deb Copenhaver explained in the piece what he found at the arena and how rural land use, the horse flesh trade, and bronc riding intersected:

> Shirley Hussy was the bucking horse man for Leo Cremer, and he brought the horses for the matched bronc riding. He'd gotten them from a man called Lawyer Rankin. Rankin had one claim to fame: he owned more land in Montana at one time than anybody else. Well, when Rankin bought out some of those ranches. . . . This one ranch had a bunch of palomino horses that were six to eight years old. They were wild and had never even had a halter on them, and that's what Hussey brought for the matched bronc ridin'. . . . They were big, tall horses. . . . Casey and Bill rode six head apiece that day. . . . The horses had no pattern and they were just wild. They'd climb up out of the chutes and there was no way of knowin' what they'd do next. They'd fall down and fight the chute—it was just a horrible day.[28]

The *Life* magazine spread from the Bridger event showed Tibbs and Linderman riding large, heavy horses in an arena floor crowded with men and ringed by a fence with boys and men sitting shoulder to shoulder. This was a noisy and probably terrifying context for mature horses having their first introduction to human contact.

In fact, dangerous horses had always been a problem in rodeo. Back in Greasy Sal's day, next to the name of the famous Tipperary, one Stampede stock manager had carefully marked the rodeo's horse inventories with the phrase "not halter broke" to alert chute men to the danger the horse presented because he was untrained to cope with hands-on management. Horses without such basic skills for coping with human contact raised the stress level for equine and man alike. From a showman's point of view, they also created chaos more dependably than the high-point rides that top riders, like Copenhaver, Tibbs, and Linderman, were beginning to demand as their notoriety began to shift the balance of power in the industry.[29]

Instead, riders and the more respected stock contractors in the business increasingly sought practiced, halter-broken horses who bucked dependably in patterns cowboys could learn, were not dangerous chute fighters, and had the stamina to cope with life on the road.[30] Here was a crucial conceptual leap that had a practical component, certainly, but which also set about creating horses who displayed the myth that true western broncs were outlaws who just loved to buck and were creatures born to the industry. The ideal had been around as long as riders and chutemen had complained about stock contractors who brought in frightened wild horses as buckers on-the-cheap. Famously, the men around Steamboat had claimed he would "lead nice to hand" and bucked because he "just thought it was his job."[31] Later popular memory about Steamboat and also Midnight said they were "known the country over as the sunfishingest, buckingest, orneriest broncs that any man ever tried to ride," but, as the story went, "were as docile as lambs until they felt the touch of leather on their backs. Children used to pet both horses, feed them sugar and pull their ears—while every cowboy from Mexico to Calgary aspired to ride the double-tempered devil horses."[32] Double-tempered horses jumped from the chute, bucked, spun, and kicked, then headed for the exit chute, where they became manageable again.

The main push for such professional buckers came in the context of the professionalization of rodeo and an important shift in the origin of competitors and fans. Already in 1952, the RCA All-Around Cowboy had been a kid from upstate New York. An aggregate winner of a series of rodeo events held around the continent, his name was Harry Tompkins. After he made his debut at the famous Madison Square Garden rodeo, he worked the circuit, eventually becoming so successful that he traveled between rodeos by plane. After just a few years competing, Tompkins collected his winnings and purchased a Texas ranch, where he and his new wife invested in some Hereford stock and set about being westerners. Tompkins was a dude in the spirit of Teddy Roosevelt and countless other men and women who went west seeking their fortune and a new identity. Although he was a native of Peekskill, New York, *Rodeo Sports News* nonetheless identified him in photos with the caption "Harry Tompkins, Dublin, Texas."[33]

These developments must have irked many longer-term rodeo people, especially working-class competitors from around the West who were not top champions but relied on smaller rodeos and local circuits. They had paid their dues. Many did the day-to-day labor at ranches and camped out on sheep ranges. They picked up odd jobs from rodeos by finding and transporting the stock, putting out the hay, or working for ten dollars a day as a chute man or stock pusher after being bucked off some horse or bull, simply to pay the way between one rodeo and the next. In between they drove thousands of miles in a sedan or truck.

Yet, suddenly, rodeo had become a "professional sport." So said the RCA on practically every page of their new trade journal, *Rodeo Sports News*. "Say Sport, Not Show," editors reminded readers for a decade. In their feature on Harry

Tompkins, *Time* magazine made much of his nonwestern, non-working-class origins. The unexpected often makes the best headline. *Rodeo Sports News* editors were delighted. Not only was a major news publication with international readership featuring rodeo as professional sport, the story exploded the stereotype of rodeo competitors as hard-drinking, rich-then-broke rural ranch hands, namely, rounders. So agreed celebrated rodeo announcer Cy Taillon, who praised the new rodeo cowboys: "They have developed such skill with rampaging livestock... that the average ranch hand would be licked hands down in competition with them."[34] Taillon dismissed working cowboys while forgetting his own working-class origins and how he had himself spent the 1930s living hand-to-mouth out of an automobile with his wife and daughter, driving show-to-show to find work, drinking heavily and letting cowboys sleep on the floor of the family's motel rooms. Still the heavy publicity given to rodeo in the postwar years by national news and lifestyle magazines attracted more competitors, even from outside the West, like Harry Tompkins. Many of them were better athletes and able to make a full-time living off the sport's expanding number of competition opportunities, such that the typical cowboy featured in the press was "less and less an apostate ranch hand," although still usually a white man.[35]

The primordial personality in this new trend of professional cowboy as media-friendly celebrity was Casey Tibbs, and he would be the public face of the transition from dramatic wild horse bucker to dependable crafted bucker. Tibbs was a champion rider, playboy, Hollywood personality, and famous drinker and gambler, although with a dark side to his personality of which the public was happily unaware.[36] In 1951, when rodeo was reaping more mainstream media attention, *Life* had printed a feature on then-twenty-two year old Tibbs and his "rip-roaring time on the broncs and off." In a series of candid photographs Tibbs rides a bronc, chats up "another admirer" in a hotel lobby, doctors his injuries, mounts a chute-fighting bronc, and is pulled over for speeding in rural Washington state. "Casey usually travels from rodeo to rodeo in a $4,000 Cadillac which he drives on the highway at 95 mph. He likes to drink and stay up late," *Life* said cheerfully before discussing Tibbs's many injuries, earnings, and dates. "In Copacabana Casey has a date with a New York model," explained the caption of one shot of Tibbs at dinner with a well-dressed young woman. "He thought she was 'real delicious'."[37] Portraying the top cowboy as a fellow who did little real work, earned plenty of money and female attention, and led an exciting life, the article was a turning point for the media profile of the sport.³⁸ One RCA publication promised in those days, "The cowboys who ride the broncs are as nonconformist as their mounts. . . . To these men the order of the day is broken bones and torn ligaments. Many are the stories told of these gritty characters. . . . It's enough to keep a good man busy, riding within the rules while he keeps his seat on the hurricane deck of a high-kicking, sky-jumping, end-swapping saddle bronc with a bellyful of bedsprings!"³⁹ Bronc riders were postwar playboy heroes suddenly, glamorous daredevils who represented all of rodeo in the public sphere.

Tibbs was an energetic promoter of the sport in those days, who took the spirit of this kind of publicity to heart. Younger and more charismatic than the older men who produced and managed the big rodeos and rodeo stock companies, he was perfect for this kind of glossy, image-heavy rodeo publicity. Tibbs was always looking for an opportunity to boost rodeo and its profile as a professional sport, especially when he became vice president of the RCA. Later in life he said that it was not easy persuading the powerful men who controlled the RCA at the time that the industry needed a National Finals Rodeo (NFR). Key people in the RCA did finally come around after Tibbs relentlessly asked them about it at board meetings and chased them down in hotels at various rodeos. Surpassing all the regional rodeos that crowned champions in various events, the NFR, first held in Dallas in 1959, determined "true world champions" once per year for competitors from the U.S., Canada, Australia, and beyond who competed in the RCA circuit.⁴⁰

Professionalization of rodeo in these years also meant marginalizing women into the roles of rodeo queen, dandy rider and other ceremonial functions, barrel racer, and, as always, the logistical and emotional labor of wife or daughter to a constantly traveling rodeo man. Up to the war years, women had participated in all the various riding and roping events at regular circuit rodeos, which is where the money was. The 1929 death of bronc rider Bonnie McCarroll during a ride at the Pendleton Round-Up gave some pause, but women's events persisted in most places. Still, a push was underway by some in the sport to monopolize the most lucrative purses and contracting opportunities. During the Depression, the Cowboy Turtles Association (later to be the Rodeo Cowboys Association), a union of rodeo competitors, and the Rodeo Association of America (RAA), an association of rodeo producers, cooperated to ensure that the management of the sport was all-male. Previously, women, notably performer and rodeo producer Lucille Mulhall, had held leadership and company ownership positions in the business.⁴¹ During the war years,

Gene Autry's Flying A Rodeo Company came to control a majority of the big-city rodeos and pointedly included no women's competitions, thereby setting a standard that other PRCA events would follow. Thus did a small group of men come to dominate the most profitable aspects of the industry, whether competitor, producer, or stock contractor, mirroring larger trends in the sports world.[42]

Gene Autry, Mary Lou LeCompte argues, was an actor known for films in which women were "mere props": "not only vapid, they were virtually anonymous, and portrayed by actresses who could neither rope nor ride."[43] Although Autry never said as much publicly, like his films, his rodeo productions were by and about white male cowboys, judges, and rodeo producers. Audiences appear to have accepted this since the whole culture was rebounding from the prominence of women in the workplace during the war years by imagining that women belonged at home raising children and leaving the public spheres of politics, business, and professional sports to men. In the rural West, women did all the same work on ranches as the menfolk and had long prided themselves on their ability to carry the double burden of caring for the household and the ranch. So, the exclusion of women from elite rodeo competition was certainly artificial. At the same time, many ranch women noted with regret that, despite what labor they provided, the masculinist rural cultures of the West saw far too many families put only male members on the titles of ranch properties and stock companies. Women rodeo competitors would soldier on, especially dominating perhaps the most widely practiced rodeo event, barrel racing, which evolved from the work of women relay racers employed by late-nineteenth-century Wild West shows.[44] Women rodeo competitors organized under the auspices of the Girl's Rodeo Association, established in 1948 and renamed the Women's Professional Rodeo Association only in 1981. Meanwhile the new professional rodeo reflected the strident masculinism of the period with cowboys and male-led rodeo production companies as the public face of the sport.

A parallel trend in the purging of diversity in the professionalization of the top ranks of rodeo was the marginalization of competitive trick riding and of human-animal comedy teams. The old Wild West shows, and circuses before them, had employed plenty of these kinds of trick riding and comedic acts. Some rodeos had held competitive, judged events for trick riding, although many complained that they slowed down the pace of the program and strained audience patience because so many inexpert contestants inevitably turned up to compete.⁴⁵ Thereafter, many rodeos had featured a few trick riding or trick and fancy roping competitions in which men and women competed together. By the 1950s, these competitions were phased out along with many women's events and replaced with contractors displaying the same skills. Especially during the Depression, when many productions scaled back their impossibly long programs, simplifying to seven or just five main competitive events, contract acts were employed mostly to entertain and distract the audience as chutemen moved animals around to transition from one competitive event to the next.⁴⁶

Participation in these arts declined when trick riding and trick and fancy roping shifted away from competitions to contracts, although audiences still admired the horses these performers trained and showed. Such work required "well-trained, calm and steady gaited horses that will tolerate a rider's movements around the neck, belly and hind quarters" as well as "gentleness, and a blissful state of indifference to his immediate surroundings," explain curators at the National Cowboy and Western Heritage Museum.⁴⁷ These acts made cultural sense at mid-century since there were similar horse characters afoot who spoke of the equine-human partnership ideal in rodeo: the wisecracking Mr. Ed, a suburban television horse who did no ranch work, or Trigger, a western horse from Hollywood, who also really did no heavy labor.

Trick riders and horse-comedy act performers celebrated the ideal of rodeo horse as practiced partner as much as roping horse events or the new more disciplined bucking horses would. Elizabeth Lawrence has explained that rodeo contained a spectrum of horse archetypes ranging from the frightened horses employed in the wild horse race, to halter-trained buckers, to the carefully trained hazing horses (who directed steers on a straight path for ropers and steer wrestlers to chase), and the roping and pickup horses who followed training exercised by a person through reins, saddles, spurs, and bits. At the far end of the spectrum were the most "tamed" horses employed in "high school" comedy acts that required no tools of enforcement or direction.⁴⁸ In the circus business, such performances of free horses were known as a "liberty act," and, as in rodeo, they represented the height of human-horse cooperation, and so were based in comedic logic rather than violent action and struggle.

Rodeo could have gone in this direction as a whole, transitioning toward judged events of trick riding or other human-horse performances focused on finesse through patient training of unflappable horses. It did not, however, because people still craved the action and violence they imagined to be central

Another kind of western rodeo equine: "High School Horse and His Trainer," comedy act. San Angelo Fat Stock Show, 1940. Russell Lee, photographer. Farm Security Administration—Office of War Information Photograph Collection.

to western rural identity. It was still true that the myth of western fortitude and uniqueness relied on contests with resistant animals and the myth of their consent to western violence, like broncs that people told themselves "just love to buck." Still, some of the industry's buckers were becoming well-trained in their own way, and the line dividing the contract act or roping event horse from the bucker was steadily evaporating at rodeos that could afford the top roughstock contractors.

All these horses—the terrified wild mustangs, the famous buckers, roping, trick riding, and comedy act horses—shared one exhausting and potentially deadly welfare issue that would have everything to do with changes in the sourcing of roughstock: transport. Professional rodeo was a creature of the highway system, and had been since the late 1920s when the automobile tempted countless people to give rodeo life a try as a career. Small-time players competed for "day money," dropping in on one rodeo one day, driving overnight, then competing at a second rodeo the next day, perhaps hundreds of miles away. Automobile camping was a popular middle-class novelty in the 1920s, but rodeo folks spent much of the year in vehicles and stock trailers that were functional but not comfortable.[49] In the 1930s, roads improved.

There was more pavement, more motor lodge hotels, and a few covered stock trailers. Rodeo regulars Gene and Shorty Creed remembered that in the 1930s they carried cargo boxes on the sides of their car, "to carry clothing, kitchen utensils, and gear, so that they could use the trunk as a manger to feed the stock" riding behind in a trailer.[50] People kept things simple to save money.

Before seat belts, air bags, or modern stock trailers that reduced stress and fatigue by allowing horses to ride sideways or diagonally in an enclosed heated or air-conditioned trailer with interior lighting for the nights, life on the road was dangerous and tiring. This was a problem that had persisted since the days when horses traveled mostly by rail, suffering from exposure, lack of ventilation, and injuries from falls or fights with other horses in confined, stressful conditions.[51] In retirement, bronc rider, stockman, and rodeo columnist Don Bell remembered the bare-bones nature of animal transport in the 1930s and 1940s as a fact of life. Crossing into Canada to attend a competition one time, he said inspectors from the local Humane Society appeared to scrutinize his stock trucks "loaded with bucking horses." The inspectors demanded the horses be unloaded, a difficult and stressful event for human and horse alike, and not reloaded until Bell and his crew had had a canvas cover made for the tops of trailers to keep rain, wind, and sun off the horses. Bell was particularly exasperated to thereafter be asked that "all exhaust pipes on [our trucks] . . . be made longer so the exhaust fumes went clear to the rear of [the] trucks." He later heard at the rodeo that other Americans crossing north for the show with a car and horse trailer had been ordered to have extensions connected to their vehicles' tailpipes, to prevent exhaust from choking their stock. After personally being delayed by a day at the border by all this, Bell concluded, "No, rodeo folks and animal rights are not allies."[52] In Bell's mind, such incidents made for bittersweet tall tales that excused the trials rodeo people put themselves and their animals through.

Still living a financially precarious existence with little opportunity for major investments in equipment, most rodeo people after World War II carried on by hauling horses in open trailers or trailers ineffectively employed or perhaps in bad repair. Accidents were common and people gossiped about their human and animal cost. Two noted roping horses of the period, V H and Streak, were killed after being severely injured in a trailer that overturned through careless driving in bad weather. Another famous horse, Baldy, was permanently injured while travelling back from a Canadian date when his horse trailer caught fire and he was permanently and visibly burned, although

Common open-top horse trailer, 1940, San Angelo Fat Stock Show and Rodeo, Texas, 1940. Russell Lee, photographer. photographer. Farm Security Administration—Office of War Information Photograph Collection.

not killed, before the men driving up front noticed. Well-known roping horse Benny Clegg died when the trailer he was riding in "came loose and smashed into a tree."[53]

Rodeo people wore their cumulative mileages like a badge of honor, reporting to one another or bragging to suitably astonished journalists about how they had driven 50,000, 75,000, or even 100,000 miles in a year. Top competitors, contract acts, judges and announcers, stock contractors, and other dedicated rodeo people attempted to make a living from the circuit, traveling back and forth across the continent according to the generally uncoordinated schedules of dozens of rodeos. As with the more successful rodeo people, the more talented, dependable, and famous a horse, the more he or she travelled. Rarely grazing undisturbed on a remote pasture, as rodeo expanded into a twelve-month schedule, much of the time—especially the nights—horses spent trying to doze standing up in a rattling horse trailer flying down some state or interstate highway at seventy miles per hour.

In 1957, Casey Tibbs had had an argument with stock contractor Vern Elliot about the quality of the bucking stock that decade. Older men like Elliot venerated old-time buckers like Midnight ("You loved them so much

Closed-top horse trailer. "Harley May with horse by trailer, July 18, 1958," Salinas, California, Devere Helfrich, Devere Helfrich Rodeo Photographic Collection, National Cowboy & Western Heritage Museum, 81.023.13628–01, Museum purchase.

you nearly choked up every time you talked about them," Tibbs ribbed Elliot). Tibbs advised that they stop complaining that contemporary horses were not nearly as challenging as the unpredictable, storied buckers from the first decades of the century. Modern horses like War Paint needed to be taken in context as purpose-bred animals who bucked more consistently. Importantly, as rodeo networks had grown several times in size and demanded more and more bucking horses all the time, they should also be appreciated for their ability to handle what rodeo as big business asked of them.[54]

While Tibbs's disagreement with Elliot was an element of generational change in the industry, Tibbs was also pointing out that transport was a significant welfare issue for mid-century buckers, and all rodeo horses. "Let's take into consideration how many times the bucking horse of today is used. A lot of them are used around fifty times a year. The old horses were never exposed to cowboys more than fifteen times in actual competition in one year," he said.[55] Today, rodeo's top contractors and veterinarians will tell you that travel is a major welfare concern for rodeo horses. If transported without

Rigging of an affluent cowboy. "Kelly Corbin with car and trailer, September 18, 1964," Pendleton, Oregon, Devere Helfrich, Devere Helfrich Rodeo Photographic Collection, National Cowboy & Western Heritage Museum, 81.023.2541l–10, Museum purchase.

exercise and rest periods, they may arrive exhausted from standing in a stock trailer for many hours or several days, possibly off feed or skittish in new surroundings.[56] Since the 1950s, some contractors have bred and prepared stock to tolerate travel, even bringing mares with foal along on short trips (without bucking the mare) simply to expose foals to the routine sounds, sensations, and fatigue of the road.[57] Still, horses often traveled with undoctored injuries, as Steamboat did in 1914, due to rodeo competitors' demanding schedules. Livestock welfare scientist Temple Grandin told one veterinarian in the late 1990s, "Transport injuries and fighting are major causes of injuries in horses. Rodeo horses are constantly in transit."[58]

As the rodeo network grew geographically and came to number over two hundred rodeos per year, plus the National Finals Rodeo, the puzzle of finding enough buckers prepared for the work raised the issue in the industry of what kind of horses the industry really needed.[59] Not everyone believed the search for more double-tempered broncs was good for rodeo. Even if the horses were manageable back of the chutes, their performances were too tame. Some folks were still nostalgic for the more dramatic horses of the spur-and-quirt bucking of the old days, which was still common at small rodeos that could not afford top stock from expensive stock contractors and thus leaned on wild horse suppliers. In his argument with Vern Elliot, Casey Tibbs decried the old-time bronc suppliers who "seldom had a horse that was halter broken or that wouldn't tear the chutes down." This kind of terrified wild bronc was increasingly alarming and regrettable to many riders, although admittedly such horses often were "crowd pleasers" because they reared on two legs, fell over backward, and performed other dramatic and desperate maneuvers. "The wild horse is an explosion horse and doesn't have the power or strength to throw it at you like a horse that has been bucked a lot. Also, an old bucker learns a few nasty tricks now and then," Tibbs explained of more disciplined buckers. They were accustomed to human handling and were practiced in patiently standing in the chute, then bucking, spinning, and jumping once the bucking chute opened. Such horses created opportunities for a better sporting performances and more prize money, rather than a crazy Wild West show wreck that had the potential to kill riders.[60]

A regrettable case in point was Miss Klamath, the Christensen Brothers Rodeo Company's "undisputed queen of saddle broncs" in the early 1950s. Miss Klamath was unusual in being a mare who bucked later in life, and was revered for her "unique style of kicking, perpendicular and higher with each jump," says the ProRodeo Hall of Fame.[61] She was also a dangerous chute fighter who in 1954 broke both rear legs while bucking in that explosive style that many old-timers missed in the new broncs, dying at age fourteen.[62] Her death was the lead story on the front page of *Rodeo Sports News*, which exclaimed, "Miss Klamath is Dead!"[63] Still, in an age when rodeo was trying to get on television and take advantage of industry trends to grow in profitability, not through gate receipts but through commercial sponsorships and as a venue for national advertising, images of "freakish" horses and "freak accidents" like this were not something a professional sport could weather.[64] Ideally, the professional double-tempered bucker was deemed to be calm in the chute, "not afraid of anything, they just concentrate on bucking you off," another cowboy explained to Elizabeth Lawrence of the shift to a more practiced bronc.[65]

Dependability in a bucking horse was also a vexing and mysterious question to many rodeo people who saw that even well-practiced broncs could be enigmas. "Very strange things happen to the bucking horse," explained Clifford Westermeier. At the Denver Stock Show, he had seen the revered Five Minutes to Midnight buck one day with a cowboy riding him past the ten-second mark (riders rode for ten or twelve seconds in those days). Then on a subsequent trip, the revered black horse "quit bucking during the last performance of the show, at least five seconds before the time was up.... Was the eighteen-year-old horse, world-famous as one of the toughest bucking animals in rodeo, finished? Would he buck again or had he seen his day?"[66] Plenty of rodeo people had also seen fierce horses buck with energy, then slow down until just before the bell, look over one shoulder at the rider to unnerve him, then throw him off, appearing to weigh their options during a ride.[67] Others said they knew of buckers who one day simply quit bucking and were put to draft work. A few years went by and those horses showed willingness to buck again—as though they had simply changed their minds.[68] Stock contractors noted that a new environment, fights with other horses in a bucking string, or some other reason no one could identify might turn a promising bucker into a nonbucker. Everyone knew that stock contracting and scouting horses was a risky speculation.

Horses like War Paint would become preeminent because riding styles were changing, in part due to the stardom of Tibbs. He and other riders studied horses and rodeo audiences to produce a riding style that was "an exhibition of exaggerated and graceful 'lick.'" Such riding required a rider to settle into a rhythm on a horse, with his free arm waving in a controlled way above his head, mirroring the movements of the horse. Tibbs mastered the style and the talent of "making the average horse look good," and, as his contemporary Sam Savitt said, "He was never wasting the good draws."[69] Those unpredictable, explosive buckers who threw a fellow off with erratic moves were popular with spectators, but they earned relatively low marks from judges. Champion riders like Tibbs sought horses who would buck in interesting ways that riders could study and learn, and thus ride to the bell while appearing to be in graceful control of the ride.[70]

This kind of riding was a very difficult skill to develop and perform in a visually pleasing way. Savitt explained saddle-bronc riding just so:

The things that would seem to help the bronc rider—the stirrups, the saddle, and the rein denied to bareback riders—may make the business of sticking on the horse a little easier. But they also make it considerably more complicated. Take the rein, for example. It's tied to a plain halter and is of absolutely no use in controlling the horse. The cowboy uses it for balance and it can be more of a liability than an asset. Broncs buck with their heads down, requiring the rider to take an average rein. But some broncs bury their heads way down between their knees, requiring a rein much longer than average. If the rein is taken too long, however, the slack will throw the rider badly off balance and the horse will do the rest. And if it's taken too short, the cowboy will be jerked over the horse's head like a yo-yo on a short string.[71]

Cowboys often asked one another for advice on "where to take the rein" on particular horses, and they generally shared this advice with one another, or so said Savitt and rodeo's other publicists. Stirrups, saddle, and spurs added other complications. It required great coordination not to lose a stirrup and not to be injured by the saddle horn if "caught under a rolling bronc." Many cowboys cut the saddle horn off their saddles. "The saddle-bronc rider can't touch the horse with his free hand, can't change hands on the rein or wrap it around his riding hand, can't touch the saddle or the horn. And if he expects to win anything, he has to spur the horse every jump of the way, raking his rowels in full half circles from shoulder to flank." On this style, riders were graded from 1 to 20, and the horse was marked from 65 to 85 points on the speed, height, and variation of bucking and jumping, though today both horse and rider are each graded out of 50 points.[72]

With cowboys beginning to have a larger voice in the business about how performances would look and what kind of animals they sought to achieve those goals, stock contracting and rodeo producing remained a hardscrabble business for all but a few. Many men operated as small-time stock contractors and lost money most years, combing through slaughter stockyards and horse auctions looking for buckers. They did it simply for the love of rodeo and its like-minded people, crazy about horses and adrenaline or addicted to life on the road. Yet, this information stayed behind the scenes and the public would be exposed instead to more triumphant stories about the sourcing of bucking broncs.

In 1966, Casey Tibbs made a film that portrayed stock contracting in the most extraordinary light and papered over its reality for most men in the trade. Entitled *Born to Buck*, the production had the western myth of horses' consent to their use in rodeo built right into the title. The premise of the film was this: Famous cowboy Casey Tibbs has been raising up real buckers for the rodeo in South Dakota, but after six years they've outgrown the land. Friends Rex Allen, a rodeo announcer, and Henry Fonda, Hollywood actor, provide folksy narration for a movie documenting Casey's old-time roundup and drive to get his wild herd of four hundred head to Montana. On this picturesque overland journey on horseback, Casey Tibbs leads a crew of classic Western characters: the gun-slinging but tenderfoot dude, the chuckwagon cook, various dyed-in-the-wool cowboys with excellent roping skills, as well as an ancient cowboy who frugally uses magazine pages as toilet paper. Says narrator Fonda in a warm voice, "This is a celebration of the true spirit of the West and of the ranchers and cowboys who know it best." Then, a long shot: as far as the camera can see to the horizon are fenceless, interstate-free rolling grasslands. The group encounters elk, bison, prairie dogs, mule deer, and wild turkeys in this Eden of the Great Plains ecology, with not a sign of DDT, mines, oil rigs, roads, or cities anywhere. In shot after shot, rough manes and long grasses blow in the wind and wild horses gallop together, headed west to a new adventure in the rodeo. Tibbs's film was a response, in part, to his irritation with the television Westerns that became so ubiquitous in the 1950s and 1960s. Shot on mundane sets in and around Los Angeles, usually in black and white, TV Westerns were utterly divorced from the landscapes, animals, and cowboy labors of the rural West.[73]

Tibbs's film was equally a persuasive vehicle for his philosophy on the cultivation of modern broncs and an important articulation of the myth of consent with respect to mid-century bucking horses. In it, Henry Fonda related Tibbs's ideas and their relation to the famous wild horses of the West:

> It's Casey's theory that really good bucking horses are born, not made. Oh, you can make a horse mean by mistreating it, but that doesn't mean he'll buck. The early mustangs had the fighting instincts he's after. Many of 'em were tamed and ridden, but some never were. They've been known to pretend to be broken, then wait until they came to a high cliff, and jump off carrying the

rider with 'em. Many bands of wild horses in California ran into the sea and drowned rather than be captured.[74]

This philosophy was almost identical to the old lore about wild cattle, especially the longhorns, animals whose westernness came from their inborn distrust of mankind. Tibbs asserted that these western horses also yearned to be free and so invited testing by cowboys. The balance one had to strike was between a wild horse in this old style who was unmanageable and one who was just wild enough to be trained to stay calm in the trailer and the chute, while still exploding into predictable bucking and kicking once the chute was opened. Hence, the film also provided an oft-repeated defense of bronc riding employing flank straps, specifically that no horse could be "trained" to buck but had to have "outlawry" in him. Born-to-buck programs simply increased the likelihood of finding such horses by reproducing proven buckers, large and agile, that top riders favored.[75]

The film related that after many years on the circuit and nine rodeo championships, Tibbs had come to believe that bucking stock were too inconsistent and (in the narration of Henry Fonda) "decided to breed his own line of ornery tornados. Broncs that are really born to buck." On land belonging to the Teton Sioux, who had agreed that Tibbs could graze one hundred head, Tibbs "got together a tough string and let them breed wild on the Lower Brule Indian Reservation." Tibbs had been rodeoing and working in Hollywood films and advertising for four years until the Lower Brule Indians contacted him to say that "the reservation is busting at the seams with about four hundred head and the word is: Move 'em!"[76] This was a foreshadowing of later debates over the size and sustainability of wild herds on private and public lands as autonomous horses found ways to prosper on "survival rations of grass and brush," as Fonda's narration termed the forage they found.[77] The viewer could decide if Casey Tibbs was reviving the true spirit of the West with his born-to-buck horse band, or simply making excuses as a neglectful horse owner who allowed his herd to multiply on someone else's land until they became a nuisance.

Reservation land had for many years been leased by agents of the Bureau of Indian Affairs and various Indigenous Nations themselves as grazing lands where sometimes there could be confusion over who owned what horse.[78] Many settlers imagined reservation lands as akin to national forests in the U.S. and Crown land in Canada, trespassing with the intent that whatever plants or animals they found there were free for the taking.[79] They were not. Although the old stereotype had it that it was Indians and white criminals who stole horses, often it was Indigenous Peoples in the twentieth century who had horses stolen from their lands. Horse theft was a problem in the rodeo business as well, others said. More than a few cowboy competitors had temporarily contracted horses with travelling stock contractors, only to never see them again or sold them with a handshake without ever being paid.[80] For many years, it was said that War Paint was himself poached from the Klamath Indian Reservation in central Oregon, although others claimed he'd been purchased from a member of that nation, fair and square.[81] Indigenous horsemen with access to wild herds struggled to gain access to the lucrative rodeo stock contracting trade, which was monopolized by a handful of dominant settler-led companies. In fact, only a few years before Tibbs's film was shot on the Lower Brule lands, just to the northwest and southwest a series of All-Indian rodeos had been born. Members of the Northern Cheyenne and Lakota Sioux Nations had formalized the ad hoc rodeos and gatherings they had held for several decades into the Cheyenne, Pine Ridge, and Rosebud Rodeos. These events built on those peoples' history as skilled horse breeders and made manifest the Indigenous politics of self-sufficiency that were gaining a larger public profile at that moment.[82] In his film Tibbs did not mention that trend among rodeo people; he chose rather to portray settler men as he viewed himself, as the true caretakers and cultivators of bucking horses.

Although rodeo lifeways were tied to the pavement, in his film Tibbs opted to drive his horses on hoof the one hundred and twenty miles they had to go. Trucking them would have made for a very un-Western looking film, to be sure. Still, Tibbs seemed to have welfare concerns in mind, acknowledging that horses often suffered in transit. The film explained that trucking his mustangs could be dangerous because "the new colts might get trampled, and the wild horses might hurt themselves. Most of them have never seen a man, never mind a fire-breathing diesel. Nope, Casey would do it the old-time way, the best way for the horses, he would drive them overland." The film's finale was a rain-soaked bucking competition and auction in Fort Pierre, South Dakota, in which "it rained cowboys," and the horses were auctioned to stock contractors and speculators.[83]

Tibbs was a little older and less photogenic than in his rodeo heyday when he made *Born to Buck* in the mid-1960s. The movie won praise and a few film awards, and was particularly brave in that, as a first-time filmmaker,

Tibbs produced, directed, and personally funded principle photography, only later finding distribution for the project independently.[84] The film captured the philosophies of cowboys and stock contractors, at the elite levels at least, who sought to breed and practice horses to buck dependably for the industry, investing in their welfare more than the old-time rodeo producers had.[85] Essentially, the ideal played out in Tibbs's film relieved viewers and rodeo fans of any responsibility for the experiences of the horses drawn into wild horse race or bucking events because it presented a best-case scenario as normative. Certainly, it distracted the public from the origins of many rodeo horses, scouted and sold as low-cost buckers for small-town and ranch rodeos by men still trolling public lands and slaughterhouse stockyards for "bad ones."

*Born to Buck* appeared not long after the public outcry over government-sponsored wild horse round-ups for slaughter. Beginning in 1958, just when War Paint would pose for his photo shoot for *Life* magazine, what many saw as damning images taken by photographer Gus Bundy were a scandal. Two 1950 gallery showings, then *Reno Pace Magazine*, and later the *Sacramento Bee* newspaper and *True: The Man's Magazine* first featured the images. During 1958 and 1959, they had been reproduced in a number of national publications aimed at middle-class readers and tourists to the West.[86] They depicted mustangers chasing down wild horses in Nevada, roping them to old tires until exhausted, tying them, and dragging them onto trucks to be sent to slaughter. The photographs and other news of these roundups of wild horses exposed that the killing took place at the behest of ranchers and government land managers. The men who did the mustanging did so seasonally or when they needed quick cash. They were not the storied cattlemen or working cowboys of the West, many discovered, but rather transient, opportunistic harvesters of free horses whom they sought to exploit, possibly to extinction.

Animal welfare groups, wild horse advocate Velma "Annie" Johnson, and thousands of concerned citizens pressured legislators to act. In Nevada, the negotiations over the right of unowned horses to live on public lands became especially contentious. Beginning in 1959, the resulting Wild Horse Annie Act (named colloquially after Johnson) outlawed "mechanized roundups" of horses on U.S. federal lands—on paper at least.[87] Their supporters viewed wild horses as deserving of protection like the bison or antelope, and symbolic of the spirit of the West in their persistence, self-sufficiency, and history of labor and companionship (at times) with people.[88] The larger idea, which rodeo celebrated in its own way by relying upon wild or feral-but-owned herds both materially and culturally, was that horses were native to the West. Specifically because they were resistant to humans, they had a right to life at large on the land, even if stock contractors would capture and exploit a minority among them at the rodeo arena.

Gus Bundy's beautiful but disturbing black-and-white photographs of the controversial Nevada round-ups would inspire the now-classic scenes in the 1961 Arthur Miller–John Huston film *The Misfits* of men hunting wild horse "strays" for the canners in Nevada. These years were the golden era of the Hollywood film and television Western, most of which burst with pride over American exceptionalism and masculinist stature at the height of the Cold War. *The Misfits* was one of a number of western stories in those years that reflected the New West more accurately—in some ways—by challenging those narratives. It depicted westerners as people seeking an independent, self-sufficient existence on the land but coping with chronic poverty, a harsh environment, self-destructive habits, and depressing contradictions by which they destroyed and consumed that which and those who defined the West as a place of hardy independence—like wild horses.[89] Many rodeo people were misfits of a sort, travelers who rejected conventional work and settling down, living on their own terms on the rodeo circuit, perhaps outside the middle-class nuclear family structure. Some expressed identification with wild horses who resisted capture as fellow "outlaws" who were unsuited for conventional working life.[90]

In the context of continued crisis for wild horses and the precariousness of ranching, the old-time overland horse drive portrayed in Casey Tibbs's *Born to Buck* offered rodeo fans a fantasy about the sourcing and development of bucking stock. The reality of bucking horse contracting since World War II in the rodeo business was more mundane. Imagine stock contractor Harry Vold directing assistants to load horses onto a tractor-trailer stock hauler at the Montana ranch of Earnest Tooke, then hit the highway, no time to waste, with a long drive ahead. In the 1950s, with so much money, publicity, and so many new people circulating in rodeo, a number of male-centered stock contracting companies built dynasties on their animals and their political savvy in winning and holding lucrative contracts with key rodeos. They prospered because they had the capital to purchase equipment, hire staff, and exploit the growing highway system to take animals anywhere. These contractors included Harry Vold in Colorado, Ernest Tooke in Montana, Cotton Rosser in

Alberta, Henry and Bobby Christensen in Oregon, and the Beutler Brothers in Oklahoma, among others.[91] The bulk of their horses were not the products of born-to-buck programs just yet, but rather horses that were tried out or inappropriately trained as saddle horses, for leisure or ranch work, with behavioral problems that made them unworkable and dangerous when they learned they could buck riders off.[92] The men running rodeo stock companies became so influential that they drove rule changes, incremental though they might have been, to refine judging and performance standards in the CPRA and PRCA. To protect their horses from injury, many of the rules sought to spare horses from the most damaging spurring or equipment that injured or gave cowboys an unfair advantage by restricting a horse's movements.[93]

In public, the patrilineal family ranch cultures of the Cold War years crosspollinated with the heavy publicity around rodeo and other western lifestyles to draw more attention to stock contractors as key players in the sport. In a pricey promotional coffee table book sponsored by the Professional Rodeo Stock Contractors Association, actor and rodeo producer Gene Autry praised these businesses:

> Many of the stock contractors gave their ranches, their lives, their livelihood, everything they had, for the cowboy. These people had sweat, grit, and determination. From family to family, generation to generation, with fiber and resolve—and a dedication that, more often than not, transcended any personal financial gain—they have strived to provide the American cowboy and cowgirl with the best American livestock to challenge their skills. . . . [The] American stock contractors of the past, and those of the current day, . . . have given an entire nation access to the romance and mystique of the cowboy, the color and legend of rodeo, and a continuation of the Western way of life.[94]

Autry was central to major changes in the industry after World War II (including the marginalization of rodeo women), so he was hardly a Luddite. Still, in talking about these modern, newly prominent rodeo stock supply businesses, he coated them with a patina of tradition and altruism that gave them familiar meanings as icons of male-led family businesses in the West. They were the ultimate settlers of the real West, providing all of us a great service. Really, such talk was a reflection of the ways the rodeo elite would help each other out by creating a sense that the politics and power imbalances in the business were only natural and markers of tradition and virtue.

It was a truism among stock men that good buckers were in short supply just when rodeo needed so many, as the number of rodeos had tripled since the Depression.[95] In 1955, former competitor and now RCA official and rodeo producer, Lex Connelly, explained the dilemma of the suddenly booming rodeo business: "To a livestock contractor, rodeo represents a large investment which must be kept in use to return a dividend. Such men have three constant problems—to get, by one means or another, more or better contracts; to cut down their own costs on the ones they already have; and to find more bucking horses."[96] Connelly knew that many tried their hand at stock contracting, but found the business more difficult and expensive than conventional extensive cattle ranching. Structured like cow and calf ranching operations, these ventures required patience and plenty of land to produce the herds from which a minority would become the kind of roughstock rodeo needed. The culture of the business was to let horses live wild until age four before trying them as buckers, with each horse requiring at least eighty acres of land on which to roam and forage.[97] Generally, only established stock contractors could afford to invest in their own breeding programs, while also, in order to guarantee a steady supply, scouting buckers at auctions or in the strings of rival companies willing to sell. They prospered also by systematically studying their stock to find opportunities for improvement or publicity.

Modern stock contractors constituted a niche business within the larger livestock trades, some of which prospered while rural Americans and Canadians considered the continued decline of the family ranch more generally. Beef consumption nearly doubled between 1950 and 1972 as the middle-classes tucked in, while the "suburban mythology of ranching" circulated in popular culture to idealize that life as honorable and sustainable. Meanwhile, independent ranches supposedly at the root of western identity and continental beef sales suffered with low beef prices, which crashed in 1951 and took a decade to recover.[98] Tourist and retiree in-migration also drove up the cost of living in rural parts, as did neighbors who sold out to developers of "ranchette" properties that weakened the inter-reliance between small operations and made other ranches vulnerable to corporate beef operations that bought them up and put waged workers on site.[99] For the families who developed successful stock supply and rodeo production businesses at mid-century, this was a risky trade and certainly many apparently large and successful companies failed suddenly, selling stock off at a loss to exit the industry. Notices of their auctions—"Complete Disposal Sale" or "To Dissolve Partnership"—could be found regularly in *Rodeo Sports News* alongside advertising for upcoming rodeos produced by famous stock contractors.[100]

So to produce more predictable and dependable, if less spectacular, bucking horses, contractors began acting consciously with their breeding herds. Earnest Tooke famously set to work on his family's ranch where his father, Feeke Tooke, had been cultivating and keeping bucking stock since the 1930s. Ernest began his own experiments with breeding and, as the story goes, began with Prince, and later Snowflake, the primordial Tooke bucking string stallions. By crossbreeding them with some mares whose names are lost to history (although they are remembered as good buckers, too), and the offspring bred to one another, Tooke essentially bred the two stallions to one another. Of the resultant offspring about one-third were buckers, which was an unusually high proportion. The descendants of those horses were sturdy, heavy-coated horses that people said they could recognize on sight.[101] Soon, business was very good. Tooke's horses found themselves sold and spirited around the continent to dozens of different rodeos and rodeo production companies.[102]

Breeding was important, but so was proper preparation of horses through bucking practice in which at a ranch property they would be introduced to corrals, chutes, and trial bucking. They might be brought in from overwintering, then bucked just once in a week, then twice, then with increasing frequency until, ideally, they learned to be calm in the chute and provide a rider with a high-earning ride, with the reward of losing both rider and flank strap after no more than ten or fifteen seconds.[103] At the same time, the concept of "born-to-buck" horse development was central to the publicity goals of professional rodeo. Founded in the early 1950s, the PRCA's Rodeo Information Commission was tasked with dispelling "old misconceptions that were published so blandly in the past: the 'trained' bucking horse, the 'paid' cowboy, the 'rodeo' that travelled around the countryside like a carnival or circus."[104] The preparation of horses for bucking, rodeo people insisted, was not "training" but simply the cultivation of an innate desire on the part of the horse.

The makeup of Casey Tibbs's herd in the mid-1960s would actually be typical of the born-to-buck herds people had been putting together for some years by then. Many in rodeo believed good buckers often had "a combination of high and low blood—one aristocratic parent for high spirits and one common-stock parent for stamina," as Sam Savitt explained it.[105] In his film,

Tibbs claimed that his herd was descended from "a tough string" that Tibbs had scouted years earlier. At its origin was "an outlaw strawberry roan stallion and some mares of the right caliber," he said evoking the famous 1930s cowboy song about a horse—"The Strawberry Roan"—who defeats an overconfident horsebreaker. "Wild horses tend to breed down in size. To make sure his broncs kept their size as well as spirit, he added many different kinds, Kentucky Thoroughbreds, Spanish bloods, and even one Clydesdale stallion to keep the bone and body in the herd," his film, *Born to Buck*, had explained in the voice of Henry Fonda. "By God they're beuts! Now, if they'll just buck like they look, rodeo's in for some new explosions."[106]

It was true that many westerners believed that, due to the social and power dynamics of stallion harems among wild horses, when one stallion became dominant, he would breed with mares, then his own daughters and granddaughters from those mares. As a result, often wild horses tended to become less vigorous and suffer more from genetic disease that reduced overall herd health. Of course, there was a hot debate about whether this was biologically true or just a settler prejudice against the wild horses living on the lands of Hispanic or Indigenous westerners.[107] Either way, adding draft stallions to a wild herd, as Tibbs did with his Clydesdale, along with extracting and killing wild stallions, were routine ways horsemen increased the genetic diversity and health of wild herds on many ranches.[108] Equally, many saddle bronc riders preferred to ride larger, heavier horses who jumped higher and provided cowboys an opportunity for more graceful form as they got into a rhythm with the bucking. "Little rats" was what Tibbs was known to call smaller bucking horses who seldom seemed to earn riders high-point rides.[109]

War Paint was not the product of a modern born-to-buck program nor fully double-tempered behind the chutes. Still, in many ways he offered a model for the professional bucker upon which stock contractors might build a reputation: capable of challenging but patterned bucking; consistent and strong enough to cope with the travel; highly photogenic. War Paint was the property of the powerful Christensen Brothers company started by siblings Babe, Henry, and Robert Christensen in the 1930s. Eventually the men struck out on their own just before World War II, driving animals to rodeos overland on hoof. In time, they came to utterly dominate rodeo in Oregon, holding contracts well beyond the state as well as a fifteen-thousand-acre property where they raised all nature of rodeo stock, including many famous horses. The industry remembers the Christensen Brothers as an admirable story of

Christensen Brothers invested in large tractor-trailer stock haulers that helped them dominate the northwestern rodeo circuit.
Courtesy of the Ellensburg Rodeo Hall of Fame, Ellensburg, WA.

small ranching businesses that helped to build up rodeo through sheer effort and pluck. "For more than 50 years, Christensen Brothers trucks and trailers kept intact the dirt arenas of the Pacific Northwest and Western circuit," explains a ProRodeo Hall of Fame history.[110] The Christensens were in fact talented marketers, advertising regularly in the rodeo press to brand the shows for which they contracted in an era when stock contractors had begun to seek publicity for their companies so as to hold on to key contracts.

The old debates about whether this bronc or that bucker was as good as the classic pre-war horse celebrities led some in the industry to worry that the public was getting the impression that contemporary broncs were lackluster by comparison. As is often the case in rodeo, there was a sense of belatedness to such talk since those early horses were ultimately used up in the 1930s when wild horses were captured by the canner trade, buckers were identified and extracted from those herds, and then were bucked to exhaustion. As a remedy, Casey Tibbs had plans for an annual Bucking Horse of the Year award that would provide media exposure, excuses for pseudo-events like award ceremonies, and special challenge rides. (The award was formally Saddle Bronc of the Year, but people remembered it as "Bucking Horse.") It also served to motivate, reward, and endorse the political clout of stock contractors, always looking for ways to make their brand more visible and their stock more valuable. "There

"PICTURES of 'The Bucking Horse of the Year,' WAR PAINT, are available from Christensen Bros. free." Advertisement for Christensen Brothers-Rex Allen rodeo production company partnership. *Rodeo Sports News*, 1957.

were good buckin' horses around, just as there were in the days of Midnight and Tipperary," Tibbs said in the mid-1950s. "The difference was, they were just not getting the credit they should."[111] Over time, the RCA, later PRCA, and other stock-of-the-year awards for various cattle and horse events would come to reward stock contractors, not for finding unpredictable, dangerous horses, bulls, or steers at random in wild or feral herds, but for crafting high-earning animals from closely managed stock.

Popular media was giving increasing coverage to rodeo and its horses in the fifties, especially glossy photo magazines like *Life* that could feature cowboy picturesque and rodeo sports action photography in such grand and appealing ways. They also featured full-page color advertisements for cigarettes and other then-glamorous products endorsed by well-known rodeo cowboys in fancy garb or pictured on the back of a bucking bronc.[112] Bucking Horse of the Year awards would provide an excuse for more such coverage, marked by press releases, arena ceremonies, a gala at the Hall of Fame, and other pseudo-events the media could cover. Other livestock awards and inductions into various rodeo halls of fame around the continent would follow in the succeeding decades and supplied a major tool for pretending consent on the part of all these animals—as though they had chosen a career and worked diligently to master their craft to win the awards.

War Paint was voted by top cowboys to be the first Bucking Horse of the Year winner in 1956, and again in 1957 and 1958, sharing the award that last year with another horse, Joker. Stock contractor Ernest Tooke remembered War Paint fondly as "a bronc that had every desirable trait: size, power, ability, desire, and plenty of color."[113] Others said that War Paint was not the most intelligent or ingenious in finding ways to "unseat rider after rider by their flailing contortions and with their crow-hopping twists and turns," as did other formidable broncs.[114] His owners, the Christensen brothers, agreed, "He has no distinctive or unusual bucking style. He just keeps trying."[115] War Paint was a "Good, Honest Bucker," *Rodeo Sports News* said, adding another layer to all the descriptions of the horse as a perhaps bland bucker, but also a point generator for the cowboys who could ride to the bell in perfect form and were mostly focused on their earnings.[116] Still, other cowboys said that War Paint knew enough to make "his traditional high jump out of the chute" then go into "his furious buck," so that many cowboys were ejected in the first seconds of their ride.[117] Consider again that image of War Paint, early in this chapter, diving at the Pendleton Round-Up in 1955. Look closely at his face and see that he bucks with mouth open and the whites of his eyes showing—veterinarians would call it "ventral tilting of the eye." That detail reveals how hard he was working at that moment to free himself from the intolerable flank strap. This was his experience with every trip out of the chute.

In January 1958, War Paint was sent to Denver where the Christensen Brothers accepted the 1957 Bucking Horse of the Year award before an audience in the arena. His handlers took the award, then War Paint was "paraded around the arena wearing the 1956 bridle" he had previously won. Then, they put him directly in a bucking chute for a matched ride with then–Saddle Bronc Champion Alvin Nelson in a promotional ritual that built excitement

War Paint wearing the Bucking Horse of the Year prize silver bridle. "War Paint at Hog Lake for *Life* magazine article," April 18, 1958, Red Bluff, California, Devere Helfrich, Devere Helfrich Rodeo Photographic Collection, National Cowboy & Western Heritage Museum, 81.023.13310, Museum purchase.

War Paint interacting with the media, backstage. "War Paint and Dallas reporter," September 17, 1959, Pendleton, Oregon, Devere Helfrich, Devere Helfrich Rodeo Photographic Collection, National Cowboy & Western Heritage Museum, 81.023.15153, Museum purchase.

and awareness around the sport's stars, human and equine. Alvin Nelson failed twice to ride the horse that day, saying only of War Paint, "I guess he'll be really famous now."[118]

After War Paint defeated Nelson in Denver, Tibbs came back from an injury to "have a try at riding the 'Saddle Bronc of the Year,' War Paint," the publicity promised. In the exhibition, Tibbs was offered one hundred dollars "mount money" and a further four hundred dollars for a successful ride. "Casey went up against the same proposition on the famous 'Miss Klamath,'" said one story, wedging in a plug for another famous (although dead) Christensen Brothers

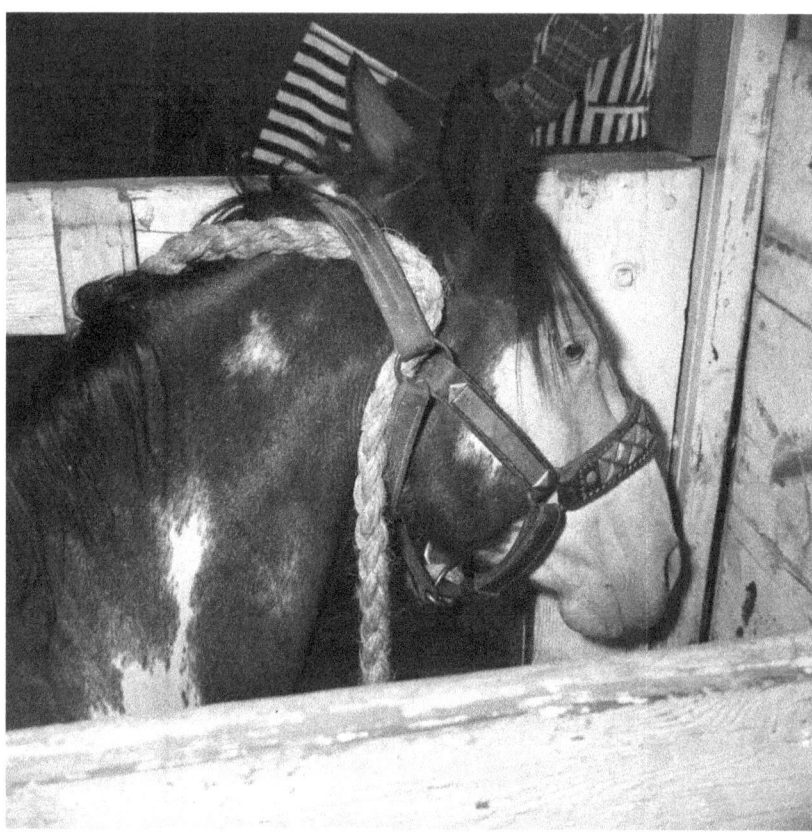

War Paint looking serious in wooden bucking chute. "War Paint," September 13, 1958, Pendleton, Oregon, Devere Helfrich, Devere Helfrich Rodeo Photographic Collection, National Cowboy & Western Heritage Museum, 81.023.14122-A, Museum purchase.

horse.[119] The RCA said the Tibbs–War Paint exhibition ride would communicate to the public that "there still are mighty good bucking horses."[120] It seemed to work. "The Denver arena was never so full of photographers and reporters. The three television networks covered the ride, releases went out over all wire services, photographs were carried by wire-photo and several magazines had assigned photographers," *Rodeo Sports News* reported.[121] Rumor had it that Christensen Brothers had insured War Paint with the Lloyds of London company for $10,000, a first in the world of rodeo, and that they received fan mail for him at their Oregon ranch.[122] These kinds of appearances were lucrative and became a routine aspect of War Paint's life. He made another glamorous appearance at the first National Finals Rodeo in Dallas in 1959, for instance.

Christensen stock unloading from wood-sided stock truck back of the chutes at the National Finals Rodeo. Gabby Hayes, Try Me, War Paint, Steamboat, Smokey, Mighty Mouse, and Off Truck, 1959, Dallas, Texas, Devere Helfrich, Devere Helfrich Rodeo Photographic Collection, National Cowboy & Western Heritage Museum, 81.023.15327, Museum purchase.

Behind the scenes, things were a little less glamorous, and War Paint was photographed being unloaded from the stock trailer, considering hay offered by a *Dallas Daily News* reporter back of the chutes, and later looking pensive in the bucking chute.[123]

Unlike Steamboat, who was bucked even as his age advanced, Christensen Brothers retired War Paint from bucking in 1966, before most rodeo fans and cowboys got any sense that he might be declining. Still, some said they could see a perceptible limp in War Paint's gait that *Western Horseman* magazine explained away as an aspect of the horse's career and "just the inevitable result of the hard, jarring jumps that made him famous."[124] As born-to-buck breeding became more common, buckers became too valuable to buck into old age with the risks of fatal injury. War Paint was still a famous horse, and his owners drove him to rodeo appearances without bucking, to be seen and photographed.[125] One rodeo historian marveled of the horse's labors, "He had traveled 540,000 miles across the United States and Canada."¹²⁶ War Paint died in 1975 at about thirty years of age, whereafter his body was put on display in the Pendleton Round-Up Hall of Fame.

Magazines and old-timers' stories have made much about how, beginning in the 1950s, wealthier cowboys flew on airplanes between big rodeos. Landing on little airstrips—Billings to Red Lodge, Prescott to Salinas—since much of the West was still a land of small towns and cities, certainly made the lives of rodeo's elite competitors seem glamorous.¹²⁷ But it was also evidence of how dedicated some rodeo people had become about trying to erase the land. The vast landscapes that made the continental West western and drew in people attracted to its silence, solitude, and fresh air actually made striving for a livelihood on the rodeo circuit time-consuming, fatiguing, and financially

Cartoon by Pete Dixon [Peter Passeri] poking fun at rodeo people and their contradictions. *Rodeo Sports News*, 1954.

ruinous for many. Rodeoing was a "lifestyle" essentially "consumptive," as Paul Starrs says of ranching. Both industries were expanded after the war with the help of government-funded highway and road-building projects that divided up the landscape. Publicly, rodeo people avoided talking about their connections to all that.

Yet War Paint lived at the nexus of these trends in the 1950s and 1960s. Rodeo became a professional sport, and people sought to make bucking horses famous as a way to keep the audience's attention. As he became famous for a more disciplined bucking performance and the high-earning rides he gave to politically astute, media-friendly competitors of the era, War Paint also obscured rodeo's continued links to other horses on the continent and the ways they were consumed. Rodeo lore and publicity made no mention of the canners, the slaughter auctions, the "glue factory," dog food, and foreign-menu fate of so many rodeo and ranch horses, favoring instead talk of the few stars who lived long lives in the sport.

CHAPTER 5

# Bulls and Men of the Late Twentieth Century

The story of bull rider Lane Frost and the bull Red Rock is one of the most famous and broadly inspirational in rodeo history. It has been retold many times by people who knew Frost or Red Rock personally, by many who did not, and certainly by a few who falsely claim to have known them. Frost grew up in Utah and Oklahoma in the 1960s and 1970s as the son of a dairying family. A gifted athlete, he was irresistibly drawn to roughstock riding while still in elementary school. Once he was competing professionally as a bull rider, people admired Frost's graceful riding style, extraordinary win record, avowed Christian faith, and generous, media-friendly personality.[1] Famously, in the seven-ride "Challenge of Champions" series in venues across California, Oregon, and Utah, Frost rode to a finish four times the top bucking bull of the period, Red Rock.

A red brindle-coated Brahma-Hereford cross himself raised by a family dairy cow in Prineville, Oregon, Red Rock was a double-tempered bull. Safe to approach on foot and pet in the stock pen, in the arena he was a wily bucker. As a rider would ready himself in the chute, Red Rock had learned to imperceptibly lower his entire body. Then, when he felt the rider leaning forward over his rope hand (and nodding for the gate to be opened), Red Rock would spring out in a powerful, impossibly high jump such that riders simply could not hold on. In three hundred and nine tries, Red Rock had never been successfully ridden for eight seconds, until Lane Frost did. Legend has it that Frost won by tricking Red Rock, nodding for the bucking chute gate to be opened while still leaning back, away from his rope hand. When the gate swung open, Red Rock paused for a split second, confused and looking out into the arena, then began to buck, but without his explosive advantage. Four times Frost used this trick and Red Rock could not throw him.[2] To rodeo people, this was an epic moment in the sport and a promotional boon as bull riding was receiving national sports and lifestyle news coverage as never before. Red Rock's owner and promoter, John Growney, and the event's photographer, Sue Rosoff, said that as they, Red Rock, and Frost drove from venue to venue for the series, they thought they saw the future of the sport materializing before their eyes. After the first few rides Growney noticed that at the sold-out Challenge of Champion shows half the audience was cheering not for Frost, but for Red Rock.[3]

Two years later, a bull named Takin' Care of Business gored Lane Frost as he lay on the ground after a hurried get-off, ending a routine eight-second ride at Cheyenne Frontier Days. Frost quickly bled to death on the arena floor as one of his broken ribs had punctured an artery. Many in the rodeo community were devastated and the effort to keep Frost's memory alive began. In 1994, New Line Cinema made Frost's and Red Rock's story into a much-loved movie, *8 Seconds*, starring then-heartthrob actors Luke Perry and Stephen Baldwin. The tenth, twentieth, and twenty-fifth anniversaries of Frost's death inspired memorial competitions, memorial belt buckles, newspaper stories, and various ceremonies at which his parents and fellow cowboys appeared and talked about Frost's legacy as a perpetually youthful and inspirational western athlete. Although Steamboat is not interred at Frontier Park, the Cheyenne Frontier Days rodeo grounds, the facility does feature a statue memorializing Lane Frost riding Red Rock. The monument speaks to Frost's continued status in the community many years after his death, as well as the industry's promotion of bulls like Red Rock as central personalities of the sport.

The lesson some took from Frost's and Red Rock's story was that they, too, should become bull riders. Young boys about six or seven years old were interviewed in 2013 at the Oklahoma rodeo school founded by Frost and were asked why they sought to ride bulls. They answered simply, "Lane."[4] Frost's biopic and old videos of his rides circulate in many households along with other memorabilia that keeps Frost current with boys and young men. In partnership with Frost's educational charity, Big Country Toys has for some years produced a figurine celebrating the Challenge of Champions rides, depicting Red Rock and Frost in action together. Packaging for the toy gives us some clues about the meaning people ascribe to their legend. "If people remember one thing about Lane we want it to be that he was a kind person and knew Jesus," the packaging quotes of Elsie Frost, Lane's mother. "Don't be afraid to go after what you want to do, and what you want to be. But don't be afraid to be willing to pay the price," it quotes the late Lane Frost ominously urging youngsters. Finally, suggesting further meaning to Frost's death, the

"Lane Frost & Red Rock" by Big Country Toys. Author's collection.

box recites the New Testament passage John 3:16: "For God so loved the world that he gave his one and only son, so that whoever shall believe in Him shall have eternal life."

Red Rock was inducted into the ProRodeo Hall of Fame in 1990 and died five years later of a reported stroke on the California ranch of his owner, Growney Brothers Rodeo Company. His Wikipedia page is lengthy. By contrast, we know little about Takin' Care of Business, the bull who gored Lane Frost—or martyred, some might say—except that he was a work-a-day bull owned and bucked by the Bad Company Rodeo stock contracting company, and that, when he felt Lane Frost fall from his back, he spun around and attacked the famous bull rider on purpose.[5] Takin' Care of Business received no statue, is not in any Hall of Fame, and as of this writing has no Wikipedia page. As a way to preserve the central beliefs of the sport celebrating individual responsibility and bravery, rodeo people have chosen to remember the triumphs and hopeful moments, like the famous rides Red Rock gave to Lane Frost.

This chapter is about bull riding since the 1960s and the bulls, stock contractors, promoters, and riders who transformed bull riding into a lucrative independent industry—something other rodeo events still struggle to achieve. The event spawned countless exhibition events, including the Challenge of Champions series and in 1992 an entirely new league, the Professional Bull Riders (PBR). The new bulls and many celebrated riders came along at a paradoxical moment in rodeo history, when the sport was at its apogee but so was animal activism and public criticism. Many rodeo people felt completely under siege. At the same time, popular culture favored assertive male personas aligned especially with rural and suburban conservatism, exemplified by Ronald Reagan portrayed as a cowboy rancher. Those cultural politics manifested in rodeo in the magnified masculinization of the sport at the elite levels, the rise of the bull rider as the iconic competitor, and the bucking bull as the sport's premier animal. Seemingly macho, enormous, and made of solid muscle, yet agile and athletic, the new bulls were only to be ridden by the toughest, most fearless cowboys willing to risk their lives and potentially "pay the price," as Lane Frost warned.

For stock contractors and investors, there seemed to be great opportunity. The business of breeding and cultivating bulls appeared to offer an alternative route to the goal of founding a money-making family ranch. In time, they would produce many famous bulls: V61, Tornado, Oscar, Red Rock, Bodacious, Mr. T, Dillinger, Little Yellow Jacket, and Mudslinger, among many others. Yet, there was immense wastage in the industry as contractors sought the few bulls who could provide the behaviors the sport required, both in competition and at rodeo schools needing practice stock.

Bull riding is a timed and judged event, with both rider and bull earning points for the style of their bucking, with rides of eight seconds earning the rider a qualified score from both his and the bull's performance. The new bulls were the Thoroughbreds of rodeo. Said to be safe to handle back of the chutes and in transit (often just a hope, more than a reality), once the bucking chute gate opened, the new bulls produced explosive, acrobatic performances that many took for knowing showmanship. Many of the more experienced bulls learned how to throw riders in just a few jumps, then quickly trot directly out the exit gate to the stripping chute where someone would remove their flank rope and usher them out back, away from the noise of the arena.

(Bulls wear a plain rope, unlike broncs who wear a leather strap covered in sheep's skin, although rodeo people often colloquially call the bull's flank rope a "flank strap.") In a way, these bulls had the myth of consent bred right into them. As a result, bull riding became much more difficult for the riders who could survive it, but it was ideal for television and the visually rich media landscape of the turn of the twenty-first century. The celebrity of famous bulls, their buck-off statistics, rider gossip about their individual bucking styles, and the grievous injury rates among riders like Lane Frost largely deflected criticism from animal advocates, who focused their efforts on other rodeo events as bull riding became a mainstream adrenalin sport.

As with many rodeo events, the origins of bull riding are difficult to locate and many people have gone looking for the "first." As the story goes, in the latter decades of the nineteenth century, initially it was on days off or holidays like July 4th that drunken range cowboys challenged one another to ride this bull or that cow, and maybe wagered a little.[6] By the early twentieth century, some Wild West shows and community rodeos featured steer riding with horned beef cattle just a few years old. Men and women rode them bareback as a humorous exhibition or as a competition. The film star Tom Mix famously won the steer riding event in Prescott, Arizona, in 1913.[7] People rode "any kind of bovine that was expected to buck—cows, steers, or bulls," explains rodeo historian Gail Woerner. To produce the desired behavior, some of those cattle suffered application of high-life, she relates, including one bull at a Texas rodeo managed by famed competitor and producer Lucille Mulhall. Her father, helping out back of the chutes, employed an old Wild West show tactic when he "practically saturated a steer with the stuff, so much so that the rider, Calgary Red, got a good share of it."[8]

In this context, rodeo publicity and journalism portrayed bull riding as exceptionally dangerous, "almost as mad and violent" as the wild horse race, said a report from the 1912 Rodeo Salinas, a particularly brutal and notorious rodeo that decade:

> The bull is driven out of the paddock into a narrow pen. When he is cornered there is a noose slipped over his horns, and if he be a

particularly savage animal, over his feet as well. Then a cowboy slips into the narrow pen with the bull and proceeds to put on a surcingle with straps affixed to which the rider can cling when the beast starts on the rampage. Of course the bull does not like the society of man in such close quarters. He endeavors to turn, to kick, to horn his wary companion in the pen. When the surcingle is adjusted, the cowboy primed for the job springs on the back of the beast, the gates of the pen are opened and the creature springs out on the track, with a bullish desire to send into eternity, or near there, the adhesive cowboy."[9]

There was no empathy for bulls in bull riding, nor for the steers in steer riding, both of which openly made sport of teasing cattle who, like the roping steers of that time, had their efforts at self-defense interpreted as aggression.

By the 1920s, descendants of Brahma cattle from the Southwest would transform the event.[10] Hump-backed, floppy-eared, pointy-horned, and exceptionally strong, the Brahma was a breed developed by American ranchers from various kinds of cattle from India, which investors had been importing since the mid-nineteenth century to crossbreed with Spanish and Northern European cattle. Brahmas and their crosses had loose skin that helped them stay cooler in the southwestern heat, and they proved themselves hardy and fecund in spite of high temperatures and long treks to find forage.[11] Rodeo producers had discovered that Brahma and their crosses were also more naturally suspicious of people (like Spanish cattle), well-muscled, and prone to agile bucking that especially challenged riders.

In rodeo, these cattle appeared throughout the twentieth century in bucking events. Mid-century stock contractors like Verne Elliot bred them on his own property and purchased them ad hoc, as he could. Cowboys found them more difficult to ride since they were wider in the body and had looser hide that "rolled" around under riders.[12] So, PRCA rules insisted that their horns be "tipped," that is, have the sharp point sawed off to reduce potential for fatal goring. Almost immediately, rodeo clowns (today known as bullfighters) and the ever-present safety barrel became, not just a comedic novelty, but a necessity on the arena floor in order to distract these "rank" bulls, who often attempted to attack fallen riders to the delighted horror of spectators.[13] Unlike broncs, who jumped with stiff legs and arched backs, Brahmas and their crosses kicked and twisted high in the air during jumps, especially with the application of a flank rope that triggered these prey animals to kick back and up acrobatically. Many bulls also learned to throw their heads back to injure riders who smashed face-first into their horns or skulls.

With Brahmas afoot, bull riding soon became one of the five core events in rodeo, along with bareback and saddle bronc riding, calf roping, and steer wrestling. Riders mounted a bull in a gated chute and applied a bull rope bearing a bell around the chest of the animal to grip on the ride, while one of the many men clustered around the chute applied a flank rope behind the ribs. Once out of the chute, both bull and rider were graded on style and performance, although only rides of eight seconds in which a cowboy stayed mounted and did not touch the bull with his free hand received a score calculated from the combined performance of bull and cowboy. For most of the century, riders wore spurs to help grip the bull and to keep their balance, and certainly to harass the bull into bucking harder, but officially not meant to cut and draw blood as with early bronc riding.[14] The bucking of these bulls was so explosive that cowboys had to tie their boots on. Incredibly, riders also performed in chaps, jeans, shirt, gloves, and hat, but no protective equipment.

Bull riding was perhaps the most dangerous rodeo event, along with bareback bronc riding, and particularly difficult bulls gained notoriety beginning at mid-century. One of the first nationally famous bulls was Tornado. On the first night of the 1967 National Finals Rodeo in Oklahoma City, well-known cowboy Freckles Brown (later mentor to Lane Frost, a relationship about which much would be made in Frost's day) made a qualifying ride on the bull. The *RCA Annual* praised Tornado and his "unblemished seven-year record against riders" as a knowing performer in the opening-night drama, which resulted in a five-minute standing ovation after Tornado bucked, twisted and jumped, but failed to eject Brown.[15] Tornado was "born sickly and skinny . . . a lot of people had had no hope of his ever turning out to be much more than potential hamburger," explains one popular biography. "But not his owner, Jim Shoulders . . . [who] patiently built Tornado up to an eighteen-hundred-pound bucking wonder, which he then set loose to wreak havoc on the pro rodeo circuit."[16] Tornado's biography, like those of other famous bulls thereafter, often came as a boot-strapping story of an undervalued bull cultivated into a winner by a wise stockman.

Jim Shoulders led an extraordinary life in rodeo. An Oklahoman, he won sixteen world championships in the late 1940s and 1950s, then spent the next decade as a stock contractor. He was the purveyor of Tornado and three other

Promotional material for V61 (top right), PRCA Bucking Bull of the Year in 1970. Sloan Williams, stock contractor, ca. 1968. Author's collection.

bulls named after weather events (Twister, Cyclone, and Hurricane), and he must have inspired many competitors too old or injured to compete to try their hand at stock contracting, too. Today, Tornado, the most feared bull of the 1960s, is interred with a monument on the grounds of the National Cowboy and Western Heritage Museum in Oklahoma City (formerly the National Cowboy Hall of Fame) to remind people of these stories. The monument does not note that Tornado died of "hardware disease," that is, from ingesting wire or some other metal object that "lodged in one of his stomachs."[17]

Around the same time, many people were also talking about V61, a Brahma-Jersey cross who so inspired dread that he could make no money. Cowboys who drew him refused the ride. Afraid rodeos would soon turn the bull away entirely, his owner, Sloan Williams, sold V61 to the Harry Knight Rodeo Company.[18] V61 soon became "world famous," claimed *ProRodeo Sports News*, after Harry Knight's men persisted and drove the bull from rodeo to rodeo where he threw cowboy after cowboy for a claimed five hundred outs (releases from the bucking chute) over six years. As the buck-offs mounted, the stakes grew higher and finally rider John Quintana won $708.00 by riding V61 to the bell for an exceptionally high score of ninety-four points, the highest recorded PRCA score to that point.[19] "The better they buck, the bigger their heart is," said one stock contractor of bulls like V61, who could cope with the travel schedule and still perform.[20] In rodeo terms, "heart" meant gameness, that is, the apparent willingness to consistently display the behaviors that the industry required, which many people took as a sort of consent and a desire to compete.

Stock contractors' work to get the right riders on their bulls at the right moment built plenty of excitement around the sport, and the nonrodeo media began showing some interest in the new bulls—as public individuals. In 1970, *Life* featured V61 in "Bull of the Year," an almost full-page action photo of V61 throwing cowboy Charlie Winters from his back in Cheyenne. In the image, V61 stands frozen on two front hooves, almost completely vertical in a huge kick toward the sky. This was the "droppy bull" posture much sought after by sports photographers and reminiscent of War Paint's dive. *Life* followed the increasingly common convention of portraying bull riding as bizarrely extreme (recall how steer busting and the icon of the sunfishing bronc had previously portrayed the West as a land of the strange and incredible). Rudy Vela, said the photo caption, was "the Texas rancher who bought [V61] for 22 cents a pound at a sale of canners and cutters five years ago," employing rodeo bonanza talk to imagine winning bulls as gambles that paid out enormous dividends. "Unregistered and thus unacceptable for breeding, V-61 tested out higher for bucking than for baloney, perhaps because he never outgrew the 'funny quirks' Vela associates with all orphan calves," said the piece of the bull's personality.[21] This kind of mainstream exposure individualized and exoticized bucking bulls as privileged stars of the West who were done a favor by rodeo because they escaped the beef market.

Although famous, V61 was not known by a promotional name, just a number to indicate his individuality to cowboys who studied his bucking and fans who read about him in the rodeo press. Promotional naming of bulls, as with the "weather" bulls Tornado, Cyclone, Twister, and Hurricane, was sporadic at this point but would become more common and help promote bull riding by articulating the idea that bulls were individuals one could come to know, as well as the fiction that they consciously desired to conquer cowboys in competition.[22] This naming was an interesting departure from traditional ranching and farming cultures that discouraged the naming of cattle, an idea conveyed to children to prepare them for the emotional distancing necessary come auction time (more on this in chapter 6).[23]

Bull riding would grow in popularity and revenue in the 1970s and 1980s. The sport made perfect cultural sense in the post-Vietnam War—Reagan—Rambo era when media culture and politics were populated by a bounty of virtuous, individualist, risk-taking heroes.[24] There was an element of victim-hood in this ideal as well, a sense of being under siege in a changing world. For instance, the film *Urban Cowboy* (1980) became a sensation just then. It starred John Travolta as a Texan oil patch worker hoping to buy his own ranch but believing himself unfairly constrained by social and economic realities challenging the "breadwinner conservatism" many white men still adhered to: women who will not do as they are told, alienation from the land, and a modernizing society in which tough, stoic men seemed less necessary to society. The barroom mechanical bull featured in the film became a country-bar fad thereafter, as did politically informed western attire. At the 1980 Republican National Convention, people wore cowboy hats as a symbol of reinvigorated masculinity associated with rural and suburban conservatism.[25]

The visually rich universe of professional sports marketing exhibited these trends by way of a "hypermasculinization" of athleticism that portrayed male sports stars as warriors who reassured the public that men still had "vigor and ambition, industriousness and will."[26] The white male bull rider was stoic, tough, determined to compete, and politically conservative. Along with the powerful, explosive modern bucking bull, he appears to have been an antidote to the sense of male victimhood some voiced in those days. Although they defied the physical "enlargement of men" one found in football, professional wrestling, or body building, bull riders nonetheless offered rodeo people a vehicle for the old myths that "women are built for birth and men for violence and death," and that some of those men, like Lane Frost, would sacrifice themselves in the arena to keep the dream of an independent West alive.[27] Western lifestyle magazines and advertisers found all this very compelling. Along with rodeo publicists, they employed a tourism-magazine picturesque style portraying rodeo competitors and ranch cowboys as Marlboro-man types, weathered and pensively silent. Just then, sponsorships were also becoming more lucrative and available for individual competitors, rodeo committees, and industry organizations.[28] Commercial sponsors like Lee, Wrangler, Crown Royal, Skoal, and Dodge juxtaposed their advertisements in that style in the pages of *ProRodeo Sports News* with images of roughstock riders and gossip about competitors' injuries, winnings, and "try."

The ultra-masculinization of rodeo after 1970 papered over the actual diversity of the rodeo community. For several generations by then, rodeo had been fed by networks of children's, high school, college, and other regional amateur competitions, with elite professional circuits administered by the CPRA and PRCA. At the same time, the growth of the sport overall, peaking in the 1990s, allowed others to form parallel rodeo networks like the Bill Pickett Invitational Rodeo, established by black rodeo producer Lu Vason in 1977, and the International Gay Rodeo Association, founded in 1985.

Women were still largely excluded from those elite levels. Behind the scenes, the elected executive councils and other leading administrators of the sport still reflected the male-led communities of the rural West, consisting only of men, with women serving in clerical or publicity positions. It was precisely in these years that barrel racer Charmayne James Rodman became one of the most winning athletes in rodeo or any sport. Employing her roping horse, Scamper, she won 1.3 million dollars in competition over her career. In 1988 she had been the single top earner, male or female, in rodeo since she so completely dominated her event. Still, the previous year there had been only three Women's Pro Rodeo Association rodeos, although typically a dozen or so occurred per year. Some believed that women's events suffered from "lack of visibility," minimal sponsorships, and participation. To some degree it was due to an unwillingness on the part of competitors and leadership to promote events dominated by women athletes by way of the image-centered sports media culture of the era, something male rodeo organization officials, stock contractors, and competitors did systematically.[29] For instance, especially after 1980, save the very occasional story on a famous woman barrel racer or contract trick rider, the pages of *ProRodeo Sports News* featured only men.[30] Increasingly, the public face of rodeo was politically conservative and hypermasculine, visually dominated by white men and purpose-bred bucking bulls.

At the same time, rodeo's promoters were devising various ways of describing incredible bulls as the expression of white male stock contractors. "We need cowboy heroes, but we also need animal heroes," John Growney would say some years later of the trend. Due to Growney's promotional savvy, Red Rock had become a template for how to cultivate and promote a bucking bull as an individual athlete and rodeo star who could promote and monetize the sport in new ways.[31] These animals were as much creatures of the media as of the ranch. After they "retired" Red Rock from competition, his owners, Don Kish and John Growney, developed a plan to create a born-to-buck program that capitalized on the famous bull's "genetics," with his spectacular buck-off record and his association with the venerated Lane Frost. "When Red Rock became famous, I would take the bull to fifty rodeos and promote the bull aggressively,"[32] said Growney of his strategy to generate excitement around a given bull and add value to the bull's later semen sales and descendants. They would breed him with cows descended from Oscar, the only other bucking bull (other than Red Rock and Tornado) to end up in the Pro Rodeo Hall of Fame. "The result is a line of bucking bulls with pedigrees that go back to two of the three most celebrated bulls in rodeo history," said Growney. Rodeo bulls with "pedigrees"? Suddenly, yes. Bulls initially found at random served as starting points for born-to-buck dynasties, and there are many of them now, churning out "animal athletes" by the hundreds.

Even with born-to-buck programs, bucking bull ranching was essentially a speculation. "You are lucky to get more than one out of ten bulls to buck that you buy at a sale, said Growney. Because of our breeding program, we're now getting 70 percent to buck." Growney's record was exceptional.[33] Decorated cowboy and PBR founder Ty Murray would claim a decade later that his uncle had ventured into the bucking bull business. "He bought five hundred head, and zero—zeee-ro—were PBR quality."[34] Perhaps there was some hyperbole here in order to emphasize PBR bulls as the elite of the elite. Still, the scarcity of Brahma and Brahma-cross bulls who exhibited the high-kicking, spinning,

Stock contractor John Growney (rear), Red Rock, and Lane Frost. San Jose, California, 1988. Sue Rosoff, photographer.

twisting behavior that bull riding came to require by the second half of the twentieth century was much talked about.[35] Few seemed to regret the scale of wastage in the industry and how many hundreds of bulls—like those owned by Ty Murray's uncle or bred on spec by dozens of other entrepreneurs—failed their tryouts and had nowhere to go but the slaughterhouse. I have yet to find a rodeo book, article, or any material that discusses the day the truck pulls up on the ranch to take used-up or unacceptable bucking bulls away to the abattoir.

Instead, in the 1980s and 1990s it became routine for bull breeders to talk of their sincere love for their animals—at least the winners. And it was routine for journalists and sympathetic writers to quote those breeders explaining how winning bulls were pampered "family" members, humanely "retired" from competition, mourned when they died, and provided special ranch burial sites.[36] Many stock contractors were doing more publicity, both within the industry and in the mainstream sports, tourism, and entertainment media. In the late nineteenth and early twentieth century, ranchers had not been folk heroes, but rather the villains of print and film Westerns.[37] Now magazines like

*Western Horseman, The Cattleman, ProRodeo Sports News, Canadian Cowboy Country,* and *American Cowboy,* as well as bull breeding magazines that emerged later, such as *American Bucking Bull* and *Bull Pen,* regularly featured interviews with stock contractors as salt-of-the-earth entrepreneurs, animal lovers, and preservers of the traditional family-owned ranch in the West. Pictured at their properties wearing western attire—a cowboy hat instead of a ball cap, at the very least—many came across as family men running breeding operations with adult sons and daughters preparing to eventually take over the family business themselves. As beacons of the western lifestyle, said the publicity, these specialty ranchers started with nothing but a dream and a bit of good luck, working closely with the animals to produce value from the land.

This was important public outreach in the volatile political context created by animal advocates of the era. Bull riders, stock contractors, and rodeo managers and publicists managed to weather this challenge, proving the sport more resilient and lucrative than other rodeo events. For several decades rodeo people had noted that outside the arena the sport was being dogged by what retired cowboy and RCA official and spokesman Gene Pruett in 1968 called "a well-financed effort on the part of various radical humane associations to bring about anti-rodeo legislation in ten states."[38] Most of this legislation would fail; still, the industry was looking for ways to protect itself from criticism and keep growing. Rodeo publications would spend the 1960s, 1970s, and 1980s reporting matter-of-factly on the odd city or municipal bylaw threatening rodeo competitions in whole or in part.[39] They reported on periodic harassment by the Humane Society of the United States (HSUS). They printed letters from members that asked the community to present a united front by becoming more skilled at talking to journalists in ways that refuted what rodeo people believed to be misinformation and misunderstandings spread by critics. Chief among these was the already-old canard, emanating either mistakenly or disingenuously from 1960s-era HSUS materials, that bulls bucked because they had ropes or other painful things attached to their "genitalia."[40] This idea irritated rodeo people and their fans to no end.

By 1991, the PRCA had formed a watchdog committee to monitor the new animal advocacy groups seeming to threaten the future of the sport. Its chairman, Myron "Doc" Etienne, explained in *ProRodeo Sports News* that PETA, HSUS, and others were now pushing not just for the refinement of animal use in rodeo (the old Humane Association or SPCA industry-positive, animal welfare approach) but for the elimination of animal use in rodeo entirely (the animal rights approach).⁴¹ Even top rodeo leadership seemed to understand that some reforms to individual events and more active challenges to critics were necessary. These issues had been discussed for decades but in a self-regulated industry the pace of change was glacial. "If those in the rodeo world think this is a nonexistent problem, they should just consider that there are 7,000 humane groups in the U.S. with a combined annual budget of $50 million," said PRCA board member Bob Thain in the summer of 1991.⁴² Earlier that spring, he had begged rodeo people not to ignore "the humane issue." "Everybody has their ideas on how to solve it. If we cannot resolve the humane issue within the PRCA, outside forces such as legislation and humane organizations might resolve the issue for us."⁴³

Although calf roping was still the most vulnerable event, even bull riding was at stake as rodeo people struggled to keep control of the public narrative about the sport. This was the age of the hand-held video camera, a consumer technology that would help invent reality television. The first sting came from a short-lived NBC found-footage video clip show called *I Witness Video*. In the fall of 1992, the show featured footage of a bucking bull breaking his leg at a rodeo in Pittsburgh. Rodeo supporters took it as a sensational hit job on bull riding that portrayed one "accident" as the norm in the sport. Rodeo fans were encouraged to write or call NBC to complain, and some did, marking a moment when rodeo fans newly began to imagine themselves as having a responsibility to advocate actively for the sport.⁴⁴

One threat averted in 1992 was House Resolution 3252, the Kostmeyer bill, a somewhat vaguely worded amendment to the U.S. Animal Welfare Act. As written, it could have been interpreted to close down zoos, aquariums, circuses with animals, horse racing, agricultural fairs, and rodeos. Referring to then-volatile environmental controversies, *ProRodeo Sports News* told readers to never mind Yellowstone's wolves or the spotted owls holding up logging in Washington state, the Kostmeyer amendment showed that it was ranch families and the rodeo cowboy who were the real "endangered species."⁴⁵

The Kostmeyer legislation was not passed. Instead, in the final months of the George H. W. Bush administration, Congress passed a mirror image of the Kostmeyer bill, the Animal Enterprise Act, which criminalized engaging in any kind of active obstruction or sabotage of businesses employing animals. The act included explicit protection for rodeos only due to direct lobbying by PRCA representatives, or at least the PRCA claimed.⁴⁶ Then, just before the Clinton presidential inauguration, PRCA columnist Terri Greer for the first time called the new post-1960s animal advocacy groups "extremists," noting that PETA and HSUS members had demonstrated at the recent Democratic National Convention.[47] To raise the alarm, Greer and others in the rodeo world would also rightly point out cynical fund-raising tactics by HSUS that drew public attention to rodeo sports in order to draw emotion and donations from the public.[48] These abolitionist animal advocacy organizations, rodeo people realized, were not persuaded by the older humane society or SPCA models that allowed for some animal suffering if it was deemed "necessary" to human endeavors.

The political climate around animal and environmental issues was so heated that a "siege mentality" had set in in ranch country.[49] The politics around rodeos were less intense in Canada, but similar resentments existed between urban and rural people there, which manifested in the increasingly common demonstrations against community rodeos and editorial page debates over whether rodeo was a wholesome, unifying element of Canadian culture. In both countries, industry-funded "citizens'" groups like the Center for Consumer Freedom (which also lobbied against anti-smoking legislation, for instance), the Animal Agriculture Alliance, and, later, Protect the Harvest, advocated in favor of animal agriculture and rodeo. They commonly demonized critics as radicals and extremists in order to counter the media outreach by animal advocacy groups now circulating graphic video and images of injures to rodeo animals.[50]

In 1993, in her *ProRodeo Sports News* column on animal activism, "Animal Welfare Issues," Terri Greer declared that cattlemen were "under siege." She warned that there was an "anti-beef movement" challenging ranching, and by extension rodeo. The movement was led by prominent liberal environmentalists like public intellectual and strategist Jeremy Rifkin, "a member of the radical community in the United States who feels his opinion on what Americans can or cannot eat is gospel and has turned the cause into financial gain." Greer charged that Rifkin and his allies were opportunists who made a living by attacking industries that employed animals.[51] Vice-President Al Gore had recently told journalists he had given up eating red meat, while in Canada, Albertan country singer k. d. lang received death threats after appearing in a TV spot saying "Meat Stinks" to alert people to the ethical, health, and environmental costs of meat consumption. Rodeo people, now largely grounded in the Republican party in the U.S. and the Progressive Conservative and Reform parties in Canada, distrusted federal bureaucracies and "big government" and had a love-hate relationship with federal officials and funding that, in many cases, subsidized the rural living that fiercely independent people insisted upon.[52] Social scientists of the rural West have called this late twentieth-century bundle of values and politics "ranch fundamentalism."[53]

Not until 1998 would an Earth Liberation Front cell infamously burn down a ski resort condominium under construction at Vail, Colorado, to cap off that volatile decade. By then the FBI, RCMP, journalists, and ranchers had begun to talk of "eco-terrorism."[54] Many rodeo people would give a knowing nod because they had long been immersed in conflicts over rural land use. Ominously, intruders lit on fire a barn on the northern California ranch of champion cowboy and former PRCA President Jack Roddy.[55] At rodeos near large urban centers, protesters became a routine aspect of rodeo weekends—a part of the show, even.[56] In time, industry media, such as *Beef* magazine, reported that environmental group Earth First!—"an unseen enemy, the radical fringe of the environmental movement"—was advising people how to cut fences and disperse cattle. It was a worrying scenario: "In this war, environmental terrorists strike isolated ranches on the western range with the goal of driving ranching from public grazing land. . . . Cattle have been shot, water tanks destroyed, corrals and buildings burned, and fences cut."[57] Many believed it was all part of a larger project to destroy the western economy—ranching, mining, oil, logging and tourism—as well as the rural, male-led family-business lifestyles this economy made possible.[58]

The 1990s transformed rodeo and its political atmosphere. Even academic studies of rodeo from the 1980s, 1990s, and early 2000s come branded with evidence of interaction with rodeo people suddenly suspicious of outsiders and raw from criticism. Historian Kristine Fredriksson insisted that anti-rodeo activists were mostly opportunists "exploiting the cruelty angle" to shut down rodeos with sensational, emotionally rich appeals directed at urbanites resentful of rural people.[59] In her project to interview former rodeo queens, biographer Joan Burbick reported, "I have been scrutinized by paranoid rodeo organizers who suspected I was a covert animal-rights activist or another type of potential troublemaker."[60] Jane and Michael Stern, writing about bull riding for the *New Yorker* in 1992 reported of the issue, "Mere mention of it is enough to end conversations with cowboys on the spot, or to provoke outraged diatribes against outsiders who simply do not understand Western ways."[61]

In the face of this, bull riding had nonetheless grown since mid-century to become a financially viable stand-alone event even while PRCA board members said out loud there was not enough money in rodeo more generally to reward the athletes properly.[62] Although CPRA and PRCA events were lucrative for some, by 1990 only three male cowboys had achieved $1 million in career earnings. Bronc rider Lewis Field did so between 1980 and 1990 but only by competing at an estimated one thousand rodeos. His earnings, he said, allowed him the modest investments of a piece of land in Utah and college savings accounts for his three kids.[63] Most kept at it out of a love for the lifestyle. The industry would capitalize on, or (some said), exploit reckless young men who admired classic riders like Larry Mahan and Lane Frost. Women were still riding bulls at smaller, regional rodeos but not at elite levels, since the CPRA and PRCA provided no women-only ranking and points system to encourage them in this reckless, macho endeavor. With their winnings increasingly eaten into by the higher registration fees of the decade, riders who achieved enough notoriety made more income on the side from sponsorship deals and rodeo school instructing.

Meanwhile there was money to be won at Bullmania, Bull Riders Only, Bull Bash, Bullnanza, and Super Bull Tour events. There seemed to be no end to the bull-riding-only competitions one could enter by the early 1990s. Many of these would be absorbed into the PBR after 1992, which began speaking to broad audiences in the U.S., Canada, Mexico, Brazil, and Australia. Bull riding offered a smaller cast of characters than an aggregate rodeo, and only a single event for which the public needed to learn rules and standards for appreciating top rides. To those unfamiliar with Canadian and American rodeo, or unsure about its ties to western rural conservatism and the old Wild West cowboy mythology, or wary of controversial events like calf roping, the PBR offered a simpler story: bull riding as adrenaline sport. Man versus bull. "Two great athletes in every ride," competing in the "Toughest Sport on Dirt."[64] At performances, show announcers proclaimed, "This ain't no rodeo. This is the one and only PBR!" Along with some intelligent deal making with sponsors by CEO Randy Bernard, the strategy to de-westernize bull riding to a degree so as to surpass the limitations of CPRA and PRCA structures was a raging success.[65] The PBR's Bull Riders Only tour had landed a paying television broadcast deal by 1995, while the PRCA was still compensating ESPN for putting their television show, *Rodeo Road*, on the air.[66] Soon top bull riders had yearly earnings in the hundreds of thousands or even millions of dollars.[67]

Bull-riding rodeo schools facilitated an influx of new riders from suburbs and cities across the continent. Gone were the days when teenage boys entered rodeos after simply a little experience fooling with livestock at home or on an employer's ranch. Bull riders increasingly came from urban areas and also Australia and Latin America. Many had never worked on a ranch and might not even know how to ride a horse particularly. "Justin McBride don't know if bulls sleep on the ground or roost in the trees," joked rodeo television commentator Donnie Gay of one such rider, successful though McBride was.[68] Butch Kirby's rodeo school advertised to such aspiring riders with only a fan's knowledge of the sport. In just a day, Kirby promised, "You will learn: Selecting the right equipment . . . Mental attitude . . . Proper exercises . . . How to get out on a chute fighting bull . . . The technique I used to win the World Championship. . . . Must have proof of Insurance." The ad ominously advised family members of young student riders: "Dear Parents. Yes, Bull Riding is dangerous, don't let anyone fool you. But, if your son is determined to ride bulls, do him a favor, make him learn the proper way. It does make the sport of riding bulls safer. Minors must be accompanied by Legal Guardian."[69]

Whether in the PBR or at PRCA, CPRA, regional or college events, those who performed their way into the upper ranks did so by competing in multiple circuits and on every possible ride. The most successful riders were below average height, lean, exceptionally strong, and capable of coping with the psychological challenges of such an injurious sport. Journalists marveled while family members worried, knowing that these men routinely competed with acute or chronic health problems. More than other rodeo competitors, bull riders are venerated for competing with "thigh/groin and knee injuries. . . . strained ligaments, pulled muscles, hyperextensions and bone chips in the elbow as a result of the tremendous forces transmitted through the arm and shoulder," as various sports medicine studies enumerate.[70] Riders frequently also suffer broken bones, dislocations, and concussions. Then and now, all bull riders cope with chronic pain and travel fatigue that increases the possibility of more injuries and contributes to heavy use of legal and illegal pain-killing drugs.[71]

Bull riders shared an ethic of bravery, tolerance for pain, and financial exigency—they only got paid if they rode—that drove them to compete with severe and chronic injuries that would sideline most professional athletes. One study on bull riders noted, "The term 'wreck' frequently employed by rodeo cowboys to downplay or minimize the physical, emotional and psychological trauma associated with a severe accident is indicative of this phenomenon."[72] Many stoically refused to see doctors or to quit riding to save their health—a phenomenon as old as rodeo and minimized with folksy talk like, "I tell you what, that cowboy's sure got a lotta try in 'im!" Lane Frost had ridden wearing only boots, jeans, shirt and hat. Still, the protective vests invented after his death by his contemporary, Cody Lambert, and the advanced helmets riders took up beginning in the late 1990s (although unregulated for minimum safety standards by the PBR or any other rodeo governing body) would not change the basic logic of the sport: engaging unnecessarily in self-destructive behavior for a psychological and financial reward, and some fame.[73] The bull rider's ethic could be seen as an extreme articulation of the broader western myth of resilience, bravery, and individual responsibility by and for young men irresistibly drawn to what one observer called "the most dangerous and violent legal sport in America."[74]

For bull riders in particular, the essence of a competitor's task was to be "tough" and solely responsible for the outcome of his efforts in the face of a terrifyingly powerful animal and the injuries that inevitably ensued. Larry Mahan was an early icon of this kind of bravely addicted bull rider. Readying his rope before an early 1970s exhibition ride on Oscar, he explained:

> The adrenalin that flows through your veins when you have to get on an animal like this, it's probably an all time high; it would be to me what the alcohol is to the alcoholic or what the dope would be to the dude selling the drugs. . . . . And it's something that you yourself have to do if you ride a tough animal. If I can ride a tough bull like Oscar, if I ride Oscar, then I've done it. I haven't had the help of any teammates or anybody else. It's just old Larry.[75]

Bull riders' toughness was a quarrel with oneself in a "conquest of fear and pain" that mirrored rodeo's older meanings as a quarrel with the land.[76] And the rewards? Larry Mahan systematically studied and documented the roughstock he rode, pioneered the cowboy practice of referring to oneself as a "professional athlete," and translated his notoriety into a marketing brand, which he licensed for product promotions, a rodeo school, a music career, and other ventures.[77]

It is impossible to count how many thousands of times rodeo people would exploit the recklessness of such riders to defend any or all of rodeo's events with the "what about the cowboys?" argument made possible by them: "Never mind the bulls (broncs, steers, etc.)—what about the injuries to the cowboys!" Bulls are enormous, powerful animals who, with each ride, had the opportunity to attack the rider. Their physical power inspired more awe than sympathy. And it facilitated a kind of rodeo whataboutism for discounting any fear, injury, or other stresses on the part of bulls when discussing the sport with outsiders who questioned whether these cattle were really so eager to be "athletes" in the business.

Many bulls were needed to train aspiring riders, and the human dangers of the sport obscured their trials. To see them more clearly requires that we go back to the ranches of the West where the new bulls were bred and prepared for rodeo, both the famous operations of the Growney Brothers and other, less-prestigious companies. Just as bull riding was bursting into mainstream culture in the early 1990s, the *New Yorker* thusly profiled the sport and revealed the mismanagement at some of these businesses, where neither USDA inspectors nor representatives from the PRCA, CPRA, or PBR were present to police how often bulls were bucked, whether they received regular veterinary care, were suffering chronic impact or strain injuries, or experienced mental trauma. First the reporters, Jane and Michael Stern, viewed a PRCA video, *Animals in Rodeo: A Closer Look*, that the publicity team had been handing out to journalists of all kinds hoping to counter complaints about flank straps and cattle prod use in rodeo. Then they ventured out to Cheyenne Frontier Days, where they found robust, relaxed-looking cattle and horses in "roomy pens with big tubs of water, salt licks, and plenty of feed." So far, so good.

Next, they encountered a bull rider who told them of his experiences at unsanctioned rodeos in Texas where "he'd witnessed chute men pressing steel burrs underneath animals' tails and sticking their testicles with pins." Said the cowboy, "Whatever it takes. The point is to get the animals in pain. They are in this little box and they cannot get out. It's no wonder they jump." While the idea that the flank rope is tied to the genitalia is a false one, it may have begun as reference to sharp objects and later cattle prods, or "hot shots," applied to the testicles to coerce tired, painful, or lackluster bulls to buck again as the chute opened. So, the story was partly true, but like a game of telephone, the details became confused with many retellings.[78]

Seeking more information, the reporters traveled to a rodeo school where they found inexperienced, older bulls put in chutes for bucking by "untrained wranglers [who] were trying to maneuver a dozen frenzied bulls from their holding pens into the chutes by applying prods countless times to their noses, ears, eyes, and testicles." They saw bulls desperately trying to climb out of bucking chutes, injuring themselves, with legs caught in chute bars, or becoming stuck in transfer chutes that connected holding pens in the rear to bucking chutes, unwilling or unable to move. "One of them [the stock pushers] hoisted a long two-by-four with nails protruding from the tip and bashed the bull on the head so hard and so many times that the board began to splinter. Stunned, and bleeding from his nose and mouth, the animal staggered and retreated. In the pen, many of the bulls had open wounds on their backs, and the torn flesh was clotted with flies," the Sterns wrote with dismay. A number of these animals appeared bruised from being confined in close quarters with unfamiliar bulls.[79] Many hundreds of bulls were being bred for bucking, most existing in non-PRCA or CPRA-regulated or utterly unsupervised lower-level competitive circuits, rodeo schools, or private ranches. They represented the wastage in the industry and they might suffer injury, overwork, and abuse from improperly trained staff, along with the corresponding mental strain, until graded out into the food system and forgotten forever.

By the 1990s, although the cowboys were only as capable as they had been in the past, the bulls had changed. The new goal for stock contractors was to produce a heavier, stronger, but more agile bull who could jump and buck acrobatically, generating opportunities for riders to earn qualified rides over ninety points—but without intentionally injuring riders. Bull riding needed more Red Rock, not Takin' Care of Business, and certainly not Bodacious. That bull would become a lesson to the industry of how the agency of bucking stock had to be carefully controlled and shaped. For our purposes, his story is also a crucial case exposing how bulls were created in those days in order to bolster the myth of bulls' consent to their use in rodeo.

Bodacious carried a familiar rodeo-style rags-to-riches biography. Born in Oklahoma in 1988, after three years to himself on cattle ranges scattered with cacti and mesquite trees, he emerged "ribby and raw boned" with a blonde coat and horns turned slightly downward.[80] He was a Charbray cross, descended from Mexican longhorn, Brahma, and Charolais beef cattle.[81] Bought and sold twice, he finally landed with the Andrews Rodeo Company of Texas in 1991, going by the stock number J-31. Renamed "Bodacious," he grew to 1,850 pounds and his owners promoted him as "World's Most Dangerous Bull." Andrews made him a valuable carrier of corporate endorsements and, in time, father to a rodeo bull-breeding program worth millions of dollars.[82]

At the Andrews Rodeo training arena, stockman Phil Sumner put young bulls through brief three- or four-second test rides with a remote-controlled dummy on their backs designed to link resistant behavior with quick relief from the aggravation of a simulated rider. When his turn came, J-31 "jumped high, but could not seem to figure out the point," an Andrews company history explains.[83] Men working with such bulls watched them buck very carefully, releasing the dummy at the exact moment they displayed the specific moves the industry sought, which they imagined as "an advantage for the bull" since tending to throw riders. Later, stockmen also bucked young bulls with amateur riders before judges and potential investors at private ranches and futurity, derby, and classic events in which unproven bulls are tried out to establish basic rankings before entering PRCA, CPRA, or PBR networks. Hence, with Bodacious, Sumner and his assistants were using a kind of operant conditioning to introduce their young bulls to the process of being bucked while hopefully giving them the idea that they had power over the riding situation. As with bucking broncs, rodeo people insisted that bulls are thus not "trained" to buck by humans, but simply found as animals driven by instinct to resist, and encouraged to develop that behavior to serve the bull riding performance.[84] Unlike broncs, for whom the flank strap and spurring was generally intolerable, for bulls it was the sensation of a human rider or bucking dummy on the back that was intolerable. Here was a context in which bulls could decide for themselves what "the point" of bull riding was, and respond to the triggers of rider and the open bucking chute gate by bucking, spinning, and twisting in resistance.[85]

It seemed to the people around him that the turning point for J-31 came with his fourth "trip," or exit from the bucking chute in competition. That time, the cowboy riding J-31 got his hand stuck in his bull rope while trying to dismount. Such "hang ups" are a common occurrence since the bull rope is always wrapped very tightly. "Frantic to escape the flopping man at his side, J-31 flung himself higher and higher," his company biographer explained.[86] His handlers surmised that this experience gave J-31 a particular dislike (or was it fear?) of being bucked thereafter. With each successive ride he continued to dislodge cowboys, his work rewarded each time since he would either throw the rider or find the rider had jumped off after the regulation eight seconds required for a points-winning ride had expired. A trip down the exit chute to be stripped of the flank rope and relief from the noise of the arena would always follow as a reward.

Late in 1991, J-31, still not full grown, traveled to a rodeo in Oklahoma where he was paired up with bull rider Terry Don West. West recalled, "A friend of mine come up to me and he says, 'Terry, you got J-31, it's a bad cat. I mean, he's *bad.*' Shoot, I thought. I went and looked at him, a 1,250 pounder. I thought, how bad could he be?" Run into the bucking chutes that day, J-31 kicked and climbed the walls, especially as West came to have his bull rope wrapped around the bull's ribs. West swore J-31 tried to kick him as he mounted the bull: "He acted just demon possessed, just a wild, wild bull. I get on him, and he won't stand still for me." Then the gate of the bucking chute opened. "Gosh he blew out of that box," West remembered.[87]

Soon word-of-mouth describing J-31's behavior in and out of the bucking chutes was being carried through the rodeo community and told enthusiastically to journalists. J-31 seemed to be learning by trial and error how to become quicker at ejecting riders, while riders watched him and developed a body of knowledge around his unique responses to the context of the bucking chutes.[88] One rodeo promoter warned cowboys, "Bulls are not dumb.... They're very intelligent, they have their own personality and distinct way of doing things."[89] That informal wisdom plus a bull's buck-off statistics created his individual reputation, which in turn could mentally predispose a rider to fail. In 1992, J-31 also received the show name Bodacious from Sammy Andrews, an important component in the creation of a commercial brand identity for the bull and his increasingly profitable behaviors, a brand which would later represent various breeding and merchandising ventures.

Certainly Bodacious was developing the powerful habits most bucking bulls displayed. Inside the bucking chute, looking out toward the arena, Bodacious was known sometimes to move around restlessly as the rider prepared his rope. Once the gate opened, he would jump and kick with such energy that all four hooves left the ground at once, his outstretched body almost vertical or twisting in the air in a movement known as a "body roll." He also discovered that he could spin in one direction, then, when he felt the rider losing his balance and falling into the center of the spin—"the well," it is sometimes called—suddenly pull away in the opposite direction, causing the cowboy to land on his shoulder or head in the dirt below. The financial value of these behaviors is considerable since the bull's performance creates the rider's "competitive opportunity," as the judges say, since the rider and bull each receive a score from the judges, which is combined to determine the points the rider achieves.[90]

During the 1995 season Bodacious began routinely displaying a newly dangerous move to follow those bounds from the chute.[91] The behavior was a

J-31 imagined and marketed as "Bodacious! The Master of Disaster."
*ProRodeo Sports News*, 1996.

"sort of stutter hop on his front legs, followed by a faster, more powerful lift with his head," the Andrews Rodeo Company explained.[92] Terry Don West had already experienced this move at the 1994 Houston Livestock Show and Rodeo. "Houston was a nightmare," he admitted later. During that ride, the bull hit him in the chest so hard with his head—intentionally, West was sure of it—that he suffered six broken ribs and a collapsed lung. He crawled to the edge of the arena thinking, "I'm dying today, this is the day, it's going to be right here in Houston from a bull called Bodacious." Later, West would recall his original 1991 ride on the bull: "The first thing he tried to do was jerk me down. He almost, with his head, hit me right in the jaw."[93]

Bull rider Tuff Hedeman was not initially intimidated by Bodacious. He had earned an astronomical ninety-five-point score (out of a possible one hundred) in 1994 on the bull.[94] In October 1995, Hedeman again attempted to ride Bodacious, who exhibited "the patented Bodacious head butt," smashing Hedeman directly in the face with his skull.[95] Hedeman somehow dismounted, then stumbled out of the arena and went directly to the hospital.[96] "I couldn't begin to tell you which bones were broken—everything from here to here was crushed," he said demonstrating from one cheek to the other. "They peeled down my face and just had to piece it together [with] five titanium plates and a number of screws."[97]

Later that fall, at the National Finals Rodeo, Hedeman again drew Bodacious in the daily lottery that matched bulls with riders. He refused the ride, winning a standing ovation from the crowd, later explaining that Bodacious was no longer a legitimate adversary because "he did something bulls are not supposed to do [to mounted riders]."[98] A vocal group of veteran bull riders agreed, and many seemed to take the bull's behavior personally. "The worst part of him is you could be making a perfect ride on him and he'd knock your head off. . . . He was an absolute monster," bull rider Cody Snyder complained.[99] This was an elaboration of the myth of consent. It came built into cowboy ethics insisting that in a ride, both rider and bull should have an opportunity to dominate the other, the cowboy when riding, the bull after the "get off," when the cowboy left his back, either intentionally or unintentionally. Bodacious's skill at injuring riders *before* they dismounted defied these ethics because he could hold the balance of power for the entire struggle. This was the myth of consent taken to an unfair extreme, it seemed.

A few days after Hedeman declined to ride Bodacious, the bull used his famous move to shatter the left eye socket of cowboy Scott Breding. The next night bull riders named Bodacious "National Finals Rodeo Champion Bucking Bull," perhaps in an effort to urge Sammy Andrews to "retire" the bull, which he did immediately.[100] "I didn't want to see Bodacious waste away unridden in some back pen," Andrews said of the possibility that if he defied the riders, he might in future ship Bodacious to rodeos only to find riders blacklisting him.[101] Thereafter, "Old Bo" died of kidney failure at the Andrews' Addielou, Texas, ranch on May 16, 2000.[102]

The publicity value of Bodacious's behavior and the macabre tale of Tuff Hedeman's facial injury, plus the continued interest in the legend of Red Rock and Lane Frost, drove public interest in bull riding, an expanding bucking bull breeding industry, and the funding of the Professional Bull Riders.[103] The PBR would become very lucrative by escaping the old financial treadmill of just scraping by, by way of cowboy entrance fees and modest sponsorships. In 1992 a group of bull riders competing on the PRCA circuit each invested $1,000 to found an independent competitive tour focused solely on bull riding, some years later accepting further venture capital from Spire Capital Partners. "If [the founding riders] could form a united front and stick together, they could stop getting nickel-and-dimed by small-time rodeos [and present] the best riders in the world on the best bulls in the world," an official history explains.[104] Successfully rebranded as an extreme sport aimed at audiences with more money, bull riding could prosper in the sports marketplace on its own.[105]

The PBR proudly distanced bull riding from the perceived parochialism and animal welfare controversies of traditional rodeo events with the taglines "This Is Not A Rodeo" and "Toughest Sport on Dirt." While other rodeo people publicly called animal advocates "extremists" and "radicals," PBR marketing and publicity astutely deflected the attention of animal advocacy groups by responding with patience and a modicum of frankness about the mechanics of the sport. Although they would develop a recruitment-sponsorship deal with GOARMY.COM and carried vaguely patriotic overtones in the U.S., the PBR became successful by avoiding explicit discussion of rural politics or the era's culture wars. Their disciplined marketing and fan outreach focused instead on human and bovine stars as equal competitors for a diverse base of dedicated fans, rural, suburban, and urban.

Throughout the 2000s, the PBR was frequently described as "one of the fastest growing sports on television," and contracted for weekly cable television broadcasts, with a purported one hundred million viewers by 2009.[106] The league cultivated a broad media profile, a critical positioning strategy in professional sports since the 1970s, in various city newspapers, *Sports Illustrated*, ranching magazines, *ProRodeo Sports News*, pbr.com (with separate sites for Brazil, Mexico, Canada, Australia and the U.S.), and various websites run by fans, participants, governing bodies, and stock contractors. Prize money grew from $250,000 in 1994 to over $15 million by 2010.

At its heart, the PBR was from the beginning about masculine athletic celebrity, with respect to both bulls and cowboys. Ty Murray is probably the best-known cowboy associated with bull riding. He is one of the most successful competitors in rodeo history, competing in all three roughstock events at both PRCA and PBR competitions, and winning the All-Around Cowboy aggregate award seven times. Like other sports stars, he reached beyond hardcore rodeo fans into mainstream media and popular culture, sometimes bolstering his own brand, sometimes serving as a celebrity representative for rodeo or the PBR.[107] After its founding, he became president of and broadcast commentator for the PBR and also tried his hand at acting, appearing on various scripted and reality television shows, most famously *Dancing with the Stars* in 2009.[108]

Previous cowboys had been stars and translated rodeo notoriety into sponsorship deals, careers in Hollywood, books, movies, and other for-profit branding opportunities. What was new was the bucking bull industry made the wily move of portraying their bulls as equal celebrities and athletes. This tactic went beyond simply telling friendly journalists "These bulls just love to buck!" Marketing from ranch magazines to rodeo websites and television broadcasts described PBR bucking bulls as partners, celebrities, and athletes with fans, "merch," and social media profiles. VHS tapes, then DVDs, then online video made these bulls, their bucking highlights, and "behind the scenes" content all the more accessible.[109] PBR performances and television broadcasts promised cowboy and bull as "two great athletes in every ride."[110] This marketing tactic had begun during Red Rock and Frost's day, but the PBR employed it systematically such that it seemed to reconcile the contradictions of an industry that asked people and animals to suffer injury without complaint.[111]

The promotion of rodeo bulls as celebrity athletes covered over the wastage in the business. As bull breeding and the PBR became more lucrative, many more bulls were bred, tried out, then weeded out and sent to the slaughterhouse at a young age. Many minor league buckers languished at rodeo schools and the lower levels of the rodeo circuits where less experienced animals required more hot-shotting, more roping, were more likely to get choked out by a pickup man (suffocated to the point of collapse by a rope pulled around the neck), or injured in the stock trailer or while desperately trying to climb out of a chute. Bucking bull celebrities also distanced the PBR from industrial agriculture, including pet food and other manufacturing employing animal byproducts like bones and hides.

168 CHAPTER 5

PBR branded plush toy of Slingblade, portrayed as a "droppy" bull, diving down to throw a rider. The toy's ear tag displays the bull's buck-off record. Author's collection.

Industry talk around these bulls employed subtle slights of hand to imply consent on the part of the bull and, somehow, a knowledge of how professional rodeo sports delayed the trip to the slaughterhouse. Bucking bulls were large and powerful but also agile and intelligent. When they bucked, they opposed the bull rider but not the sport of bull riding, to which they were presumed to be native since they were purpose-bred for the sport. This was a way of thinking internalized by PBR publicists, journalists, stock contractors, and fans as the appropriate way to speak publicly about buckers, and it drew from older CPRA and PRCA traditions of speaking of "talented" buckers.[12] Although everyone knew bulls could have no actual cognition of abstract human concepts like publicity, bull rankings, or the business model underlying the PBR, the implication of this thinking was that top bulls had a responsibility to bull riding.

The PBR portrayed its bulls as "dedicated athletes and competitors" who somehow chose "careers" in bucking and so rejected life as an anonymous commodity suffered by most beef cattle.[113] Little Yellow Jacket was one of the most spectacular and celebrated buckers of the early 2000s, earning the award of Bull of the Year in the PBR three times based on his scores and a vote by members. PBR publicity said, "He didn't just enjoy competing, he wanted to compete. If he was grazing in a 1,000-acre pasture and you pulled a trailer in and opened the gate, Little Yellow Jacket would come running and jump right in it on his own. It didn't matter how far he traveled to an event, what the weather was like, or how bright the lights were—he always came to the arena to put on a show."[114] One business magazine called Little Yellow Jacket "a great salesman for the circuit. Explosive out of the chute, he had an 85 per cent buck-off rate and was diabolically theatrical."[115] After dislodging the talented rider Chris Shivers on one occasion, PBR publicity claimed, "Little Yellow Jacket, as he always did, paraded in a small circle with his head held high before walking through the out gate.... He owned it." Framing the bull's bodily behavior as human-style showmanship, whether by willful or unintentional misinterpretation, industry culture came to see his behavior after a ride as triumphant, asserting he knew the meaning of his acts as humans did.[116]

Little Yellow Jacket was not the norm. Of the many bulls bred and tried out, the few who made it to elite levels in PRCA or CPRA competition or into PBR circuits generally had "careers" of just a few years. Many peaked around age four or five.[117] For the few high-earning bulls, animal welfare in rodeo had improved to a large degree. For instance, the PBR bull Western Wishes was made to perform one hundred outs between 1999 and 2006, while over the same number of years a decade earlier old Red Rock had been driven to three hundred and nine competitions. Between about 1965 and 1971, V61 was believed to have been bucked almost one thousand times.[118] From a business point of view, ideally one bucked a bull for fewer, better-paying gigs in order to reduce expense and the possibility of "career-ending" health problems, which occurred with great regularity.

Celebrity status did not protect these bulls from bucking and transport injuries, but the ways fans coped with that reality exposes how well the "bovine athlete" marketing worked to support the PBR, even when things went wrong. Major Payne was a red muley bull owned by a triad of investors—Steve and

Karlene Katich, the 2010 winner of PBR Stock Contractor of the Year, Jeff Robinson, and some investors known as Pinnacle Bull Group. Major Payne carried a sadly ironic name. The bull's publicity explained late in 2010, "One of the things that makes Major Payne special is how much he loves the game. He seems to get better the more he travels and the more he bucks. He is as tough as can be. Major Payne is excited to go.... [Back of the chutes] he's more calm now. He's relaxed and doesn't waste energy."[119] Here the bull was a professional who, somehow, coped with a fatiguing travel schedule that any stockman would understand to strain his health and, as with bull riders, predispose him to injury.[120]

Four months later, *Buckin' Stock* magazine reported that the bull (since renamed Super Duty in a sponsorship deal with a truck manufacturer) had been injured that spring while bucking at a PBR event in St. Louis. The "prior undiagnosed injury" was caused when "bone fragments in his right rear leg broke off during competition—causing his weight to shift—resulting in a sprained collateral ligament in his left stifle."[121] Stifle-joint injuries in cattle can be difficult to spot and to treat before they become severe, even in cattle not involved in rodeo.[122] More generally, impact injuries to legs or backs have always been common and have sidelined plenty of bulls or required euthanasia, as the "Ask Dr. Warner, DVM" veterinary column in *Bull Pen* attested in those years. A PBR press release later updated fans that Major Payne "appeared to get his left hind leg caught in the chute as he prepared to exit with Silvano Alves on board." One reader, "cactus-sue," exposed how the marketing of these bulls functioned to convey them as rodeo pets, of a sort, when she said in the comments widget on the press release, "Hoping and Praying Major Payne will have a speedy and complete recovery!!!! I've been heart broken over this, since seeing him on Sunday! ... Let's hope some rest and extra alfalfa will be good for Major Payne!! What a sweet and handsome picture of Major Payne [in the press release]! Please get better soon!!"[123] Major Payne, a.k.a. Super Duty, never returned to competition.

Fans, riders, and stock contractors cared about injuries to bulls, certainly, but not enough to abandon bull riding. Responding to online reports of severe lameness caused by bucking in champion bull Code Blue some years earlier, another fan had exposed how rodeo people and PBR fans imposed their values onto the sport's bulls by drawing on the myth of consent grounded in a sense of human stewardship: "Everyone that is concerned about the bulls getting injured has to put things in perspective.... You have to look at the bulls as being athletes. Football players are gonna blow out knees, baseball players shoulders and so on. Injuries are going to happen... More than likely Code Blue will retire and spend the rest of his life with the ladies. That is a better option than most bulls have."[124] Riders exhibited serious denial about their own injuries and the risks they took in the arena, and fans expected the same of the bulls, weighing the realities of the beef industry against an imagined retirement impregnating cows, ignoring or unaware of the role of artificial insemination in bucking bull breeding. Either way, the impression was that these bulls were bred to suffer these injuries, so people should not complain.

Constant pressure from riders looking to get an edge on these new bulls meant that welfare problems, old and new, required constant vigilance on the part of stock contractors, who struggled at times to motivate PBR management to police the sport. For instance, in the early 2000s some Brazilian riders on the PBR tour had begun tying bull ropes so tightly, with the help of several men all pulling together, and lingering in the bucking chute so long that bulls were seen "gasping for breath." Some collapsed and many gave logy rides because they fought for air while bucking. Valuable and celebrated bucker Dillinger broke his leg in one such incident. Rider Ednei Caminhas and a group of fellow riders "soaked" Dillinger by squeezing his chest with an impossibly tight rope for many minutes as people behind the chutes looked on, growing increasingly alarmed. Dillinger then fell inside the chute, extending a rear hock through the chute bars in his panic. Stock contractors also coped with the perennial problem of riders secretly employing sharp spurs, instead of the very dull, unlocked rowels they are permitted to use to hold on to a bull without causing visible injury.[125] Riders snuck onto these elite bulls wearing sharp spurs regardless, sometimes cutting them. PBR officials began holding ad hoc meetings to admonish riders and held unannounced inspections to tamp the problem down. Still, the majority of stock contractors said nothing publicly about unsanctioned "soaking" and sharp spurring of bulls. They complained privately and simply hoped for the best, wary of contradicting industry marketing that cowboys loved the bulls, which contractors relied upon as much as the riders.[126]

For several decades by then, these bulls had been purpose-bred on ranches and kept, not on remote ranges where they would be asked to fend for themselves over a harsh winter or blistering summer, but in pastures and barns where they were richly fed with grain for long periods of weight gain and growth. The industry had also become reliant on other technologies that focused labor and money on cultivating bulls who could display the specific behaviors elite bull riding required, similar to the speculative breeding and training of Thoroughbred race horses. Semen sales, artificial insemination (AI), and surrogacy all became important, for instance, in breeding one bull to one cow three or four times simultaneously by implanting fertilized embryos from the pair in multiple surrogate cows. AI and surrogacy had been widely practiced in the dairy industry since the 1960s, and rodeo stock contractors adopted it wholeheartedly in order to produce more "competitive" animals whose performances could be quantified in their offspring's buck-off statistics and pedigrees.[127]

The PBR gave new energy to the industry of selective breeding and conditioning of bucking bulls in Canada and the U.S. Central here was and is the American Bucking Bull Inc. (ABBI) and the National Bucking Bull Association (NBBA), the main registry organizations.[128] Bull riding and breeding media, like *Buckin' Stock*, *Hump N' Horns*, *Pro Bull Rider*, *Bull Penn*, and pbr.com grew, tempting new riders and investors to try their hand in the business. Although none of their animals sold for the price of a winning Thoroughbred horse, some were valued at $50,000, and the network of breeders and trainers functioned in similar fashion to produce proven buckers. The ABBI registry took guesswork and false claims out of the bucking bull trade and made more bucking bull ranch operations financially viable, for periods of time at least. No one could claim to be selling a descendant of Bodacious or Mudslinger without DNA records that demonstrated it to be true. In the trade, breeders made reference, not to pedigree or long lineages reaching back many generations to famous animals (as with horse and dog breeding), but to "genetics." Indeed, many breeders came to imagine themselves as managers of gene pools, as much as live cattle.

The new technologies did not produce docile, Holstein-like cattle easily managed back of the chutes by a person on foot. Dr. John Shull, a veterinary embryologist working at one bucking bull ranch, explained that bucking cattle actually had some unique welfare issues since they were bred to dislike people in some respects, and thus were "a high stressed animal. It's just like working with an antelope." Shull said that many breeding cows struggled to get past a "flight and fright" experience of their human handlers, which drove "hormonal imbalances and steroid release, and things like that get in the cow's system that are not good for fertility and reproduction." Artificial insemination procedures used dependably with dairy cattle became difficult and expensive with rodeo cattle. Bucking cows "mess up the transport of the semen through the oviduct, they mess up the egg transport down, the ovulations. All the hormones involved get skewed because of the stress level to the cow," Shull continued. "If you can get a calm bucking cow, she's of no value to you. So you're dealing with an animal that essentially needs to be as wild as possible to do her job. But then that's exactly the opposite of what I need."[129] Bucking cows were being bred for the specific tasks of demonstrably bucking in test events then reproducing and managing a calf, but not for their own welfare. They were not sent to any rodeo, so were entirely invisible to fans. In that regard, they shared a burden with other mass-produced, single-purpose animals like layers, broilers, or dairy cattle, who were productive of value for their owners but inherently dysfunctional within those industries, in some respects.

For bulls, ideally the contractor's goal was to find one or two proven buckers, earn them some notoriety, then found a breeding operation to replicate them. Stockmen disliked working with stock who balked at entering or exiting stock trailers, transfer chutes, or the stripping chute. More practiced bulls learned to burst from the chute as the gate opened, buck off a rider (or not), then head straight for the exit gate. The best bucking bulls ostensibly displayed "angry" behavior but without experiencing the emotions that normally correlated with it, like fear. People applied this perception to many bulls whose behavior exposed a different experience. No matter if they attacked a fallen rider and no matter how much drool they sprayed, or if they defecated in the chute from fear, people took bulls' ability to generate those movements and behaviors as a kind of endorsement of bull riding by these "bovine superstars."[130] In doing so, people made a common error in many animal industries by equating monetized productivity with "happiness" and consent to their use in the business.

For these reasons, talk in the industry fetishized the trope of the "bull you kin scritch" as evidence that these bovines endorsed bull riding and enjoyed competing against riders. Essentially, this ideal was a double-tempered bull, although people did not refer to them as such. Interviewed in 1992, Rudy E. Vela, PRCA contractor of Brahma bulls since 1958, explained how "gentling down" bulls actually helped to cultivate more consistent buckers. "We brush them all over with our hands to get them used to people, and we teach them how to stand still when they are in the chute. That takes days. Then we walk them into the arena and show them how to get out the gate when it's time to leave."[131] So said Sammy Andrews, owner of Bodacious, "You know in his environment, he's a gentle as a puppy, when he's penned with his partners or out on the ranch breeding cows for the future little Bo's of the world."[132] A monster during the brief moments after he was released from the bucking chute, these bulls were professionals, as the logic went, and even a family member to his owners who sometimes pet him as though he were a dog.[133] "That gate opens . . . you'll see one just blow out there and buck like hell, chase the clowns," said rider Gary Leffew of the ideal. "Yet he gets . . . in the back pens back there and you can go ahead and scratch him. [He's] just like, 'job's done,' you know?"[134]

It is one of those strange coincidences in rodeo history that in 2013 the unprecedented media savvy of PBR management, one of the organization's greatest strengths, intersected with its greatest vulnerability. On a Professional Bull Riders broadcast that year, retired cowboy and PBR announcer J. W. Hart demonstrated the nature, function, and application of the flank rope on a bull for a short segment called "PBR 101: Flank Strap." Shot live at the bull chutes in the arena as a PBR competition rumbled along noisily in the background, Hart showed the rope to the camera. He demonstrated how to throw the long end over the bull's flank, then pull it forward under the bull by reaching through the chute bars with a long wire "chute hook," then pull the rope through the ring on one end of the rope and secure it with a slip knot. Taking a matter-of-fact, nondefensive tone, PBR commentators thereafter explained that it was still an "urban legend" that the rope was attached to the bull's testicles or "male parts."

The short video was part of a series of "PBR 101" pieces broadcast live, then offered for a time on the PBR website, and later on Youtube.[135] From a business point of view, the flank strap item was typical of the PBR's smart marketing strategy. It was designed, not to ridicule or dismiss people who asked questions. Instead, the strategy was to use those questions as an opportunity to explain the sport and some of what goes on behind the scenes at events and on bull ranches, at least as a recruitment tool for ticket buyers, or city boys who might become the next Ty Murray.

Back to the television, as Hart tied the flank rope on the bull in the chute, in the upper right of the screen could be seen the boots and chaps of a rider simultaneously readying his bull rope. Of all the competitors in the PBR, it was Ty Pozzobon. A rider from Merritt, British Columbia, he grew up in the Nicola Valley, a region of high-altitude cattle country with conifer-dotted, suede-textured hills, and notoriously harsh winters. After five years of competing in PBR and CPRA events, and the Calgary Stampede, Pozzobon had defied the sport's extraordinary odds to get to that PBR broadcast. Then, three and a half years after Pozzobon appeared in the corner of that PBR 101 piece, he died by suicide. For a year by then, his wife, friends, and family had noticed he was in trouble, although they did not at first understand the cause of his depression and failing health. After multiple concussions, lack of proper medical care and recovery, Pozzobon was suffering from symptoms of chronic traumatic encephalopathy (CTE).

Despite the sport's openness in many ways, some say bull riding has "a quiet concussion crisis" and is ripe for a lawsuit by riders or their families. In spite of the new equipment developed after the death of Lane Frost, larger, more agile bulls buck with greater force, more quickly, and more acrobatically. Even though Bodacious is long dead, his progeny and that of the famous Oscar abound. The PBR admits that injuries to riders increased considerably after 2000, with injury rates believed to be ten times worse than in the NFL or NHL. After Pozzobon's high-profile death and, as with Lane Frost, sincere despair in the tight-knit Canadian rodeo and bull riding communities, in 2017 the Canadian arm of the Professional Bull Riders instituted new regulations giving on-site medical staff the power to prevent concussed riders from competing.[136] For many rodeo people, the what-about-the-cowboys argument has long glamorized the violence of the sport and exploited the terrible toll on young riders addicted to the sport's highs in order to deflect criticism of treatment of the bulls. In Lane Frost's day the habit was to memorialize the individual rider as a hero and martyr and avoid the larger questions about preventable injuries to people and bulls. After Ty Pozzobon's death, people said kind things about him, too, of course.[137] Still, a Canadian doctor who works with bull riders noted recently, "It seems like the rodeo world is afraid somebody is going to get mad if they do something. [But] the time for action is well past."[138]

Here was the inevitable endpoint of a trajectory in which rodeo people and fans took bull riders as martyrs of a sort, and encouraged or at least did not stand in the way of the risks they took and the damage they inflicted on themselves in competition. Certainly, they served to keep a certain kind of reckless western manhood alive, a symbol of the old western quarrel with the land and with oneself, acted out with resistant western animals. Yet, as breeders crafted and marketed bulls as bovine athletes, they created a construct that masked the actual balance of power between humans and cattle. Bulls suffer injuries and many, many die in service to the sport. But if rodeo people tolerate the sacrifice of men like Lane Frost and Ty Pozzobon as regrettable but not enough to stop, then there may be little hope for any respite for the bulls, who are so much stronger, after all.

CHAPTER 6

# Calves and Other Babies of Rodeo into the Twenty-First Century

Rodeo people have seldom managed to convey to the public their view of calf roping as a technically complex event requiring hundreds of hours to master. Also known as tie-down roping, the event requires one to train a roping horse, then act seamlessly with that horse to complete several dozen steps to comply with event rules and produce a timed performance in, ideally, less than fifteen seconds. Still, among rodeo's many contests, calf roping in particular suffers from a damaged reputation. Many see it as an abusive display of power, which it is when a human and a horse team up against a six- or eight-month-old calf. Calves are quite pathetic looking, cute even, with their loose joints and large doe eyes sporting long lashes. Certainly, critics of rodeo have long advocated for the bovine "babies" of rodeo, seeing calf roping as the sport's Achilles heel. The event is unique in rodeo in that there is no myth of consent here, not in the promotional sense nor in the ancient contractual sense. There is no arguing that calves are custom-bred to enjoy roping. There are no calf celebrities in rodeo who can be featured in the press or rodeo programs to help people understand the sport. No one in rodeo has ever seriously portrayed calves as ornery western brutes just hankering for a fight.

Hence, calf roping can conjure up an old western stereotype of the cowboy as reckless and unfeeling, one that challenges rural western portrayals of the cowboy as a skilled and kind steward of livestock. Because calf roping is a timed event requiring speed and dramatic action, there has been little motivation among competitors to make it more delicate. Monty Roberts, the famous trainer known as the "horse whisperer," explained the event as he experienced it as a young roper at mid-century:

> In the calf-roping event, a small, 200-pound bovine scatters from the gate, moving more nimbly than the bigger animals. . . . A cowboy races after him. As he builds his loop and closes in,

the calf knows he is there. He ducks his head and flattens his ears, expecting his pursuer—as a predator—to catch him on the back of the neck. The cowboy throws the loop around the calf's head, keeping the other end of the rope tied around the horn of his saddle. All in one motion, the horse stops hard, the roper dismounts, and the calf is jerked off its feet and lands with a thud on its side. The cowboy runs at him with a small length of rope [piggin string] in his teeth, waiting for the calf to rise to his feet. The roper's task is to throw the calf to the ground again and then wind the rope around any three of his legs. . . . The instant the cowboy completes the tie and throws his hands in the air, the field judge drops the flag and the clock stops.[1]

Roberts's perspective on rodeo is a complex one. For instance, although he is known as a compassionate trainer who avoids inflicting fear or pain on horses, he supports bronc riding as an "event in which the horse truly enjoys himself." Yet, even Roberts expresses ambivalence about tie-down roping. "Calf roping is not a pleasant event, and bears no comparison with what actually happens on a ranch," he says, before revealing that as a young man "I did more of it than I care to admit."[2]

Despite its controversial nature, calf roping is not routinely hidden away in the early-morning slack competitions or in dirt-road ranch rodeos like steer roping or busting, but rather remains a prominent event featured in the main competition at the rodeos that include it. Although it might seem that the rodeo community is united in support of calf roping, in fact rodeo people have had questions about it. Many enthusiastic rodeo competitors, fans, show producers, and stock contractors would be unconcerned if tie-down roping died out or was replaced with breakaway roping, which does not involve tripping calves or pulling them down by the neck. Many personally find the event too extreme or they worry about the negative attention it brings to rodeos striving to stay relevant in the twenty-first century.[3]

When Monty Roberts roped as a kid, ranchers concerned with reducing stress in calves during capture tended to let roped calves "run with the rope" for a few paces, as in competitive breakaway roping, instead of jerking them to a stop. Stock people also endeavored to approach calves slowly to avoid having to chase them, which helped prevent exhaustion to calves, horses, and people that always cut into the bottom line on a working ranch. At the rodeo grounds, meanwhile, roping often objectively injured and traumatized calves, preventing weight gain at the feedlot that could make them profitable as beef. By the later twentieth century—the age of more docile beef cattle and squeeze chutes—timed, competitive rodeo calf roping became as abstract and artificial as bull riding. (Squeeze chutes are barely larger than a head of cattle, allowing medical procedures to be performed without injury to animals or people.) Yet, the event has always been honest in that calves are anonymous and disposable in our world, and calf roping portrays them as such.

For roping calves, even when people argued about the bovine traumas and injuries in the sport, what has gone on behind the scenes has generally been ignored as people have debated what calves experienced in the rodeo arena. Roping calves have long linked rodeo directly to the continent's cow-calf operations, and to the growing and serious environmental consequences of industrial animal agriculture, especially the resource-guzzling beef industry. Calf roping is perhaps best understood as a drama of twentieth-century family ranches. In that light, perhaps there is a new reason to be unsettled by calf roping. It forces us to contemplate not simply the roping but also the calf and the systems of animal and environmental interaction that lie beyond the local rodeo, in which we are all implicated.

This chapter thus explores how calf roping replaced steer roping as the most prominent roping event in rodeo, but left many of the same animal welfare and publicity problems unresolved. It sets the stage with a discussion of how calf roping has been culturally connected to junior rodeo events for children. These events are rituals that symbolically purge any sign of vulnerability or weakness from rural communities while recruiting children into the sport. Thereafter, as a case study of sorts, the remainder of the chapter is bookended by two moments in the history of calf roping in British Columbia: Vancouver in 1949 and an adjacent suburb, Surrey, in 2007. Both moments were typical of the public debates and conflicts that have surrounded calf roping, showing us how some rodeo people have defended the event. The latter case of Surrey's Cloverdale Rodeo is also unusual in the sport's history because rodeo officials there voluntarily eliminated calf roping when animal injuries became too glaring. In between those two historical moments, I tell the story of beef calves employed in roping practice pens to explain their larger meaning and connection to cattle ranching. Like the roping steers discussed in chapter 1, roping calves have been anonymous, so this chapter carries no detailed story of a particular calf. Unfortunately, the historical sources we have—magazines and newspapers, rodeo business correspondence and periodicals, roping manuals, and even veterinary medicine studies of calf welfare in rodeo—equally treated calves as nameless and interchangeable, so an individual story is difficult to tell.

Regardless of the rodeo community's ambivalence about it, calf roping has always drawn large numbers of competitors. As steer roping and tying were formally banned at many of the better-paying shows by the 1910s, many ropers turned to calf roping.[4] Both women and men competed, and, before being marginalized during the public masculinization of rodeo at mid-century, women's competitions appeared at many rodeos until well into the 1940s.[5] In the 1970s, calf roping became so popular among men that the event could be a serious headache to arena directors coping with more competitors than spectators might have the patience to watch.[6] For ranching people, calf roping at the rodeo made sense as a metaphor of economic survival and rural solidarity because, as much a business chore, roundup and branding days had traditionally served as opportunities for community cohesion among neighbors.[7]

Many of these ropers tried their hand at calf roping specifically because the event seemed to produce fewer obvious physical injuries in the arena if calves were not tripped by the rope, that is, busted. There were no horns to be snapped off, for instance.[8] Additionally, over the first decades of the twentieth century, stock contractors supplied younger animals for the event, so there was no need to rope heavy four-year-old market steers anymore. By mid-century, the event generally employed weaned calves under two hundred and fifty pounds, less than one year old, very agile with loose joints, and so more challenging to lasso. Those smaller calves, along with larger roping horses, produced much faster roping times. A critical mass of competitors found the event appealing to take up and, for quite a few, relatively lucrative at rodeos across the continent.[9]

First a brief aside to think about how rodeo has culturally and practically addressed the vulnerability of the young, whether cattle or human, and in

Roping calves and horses, San Angelo Fat Stock Show, San Angelo, Texas, 1940. Russell Lee, photographer. Farm Security Administration—Office of War Information Photograph Collection.

turn the role of calf roping in the rodeo universe. For many rural people in Canada and the United States, to be a western or rural person meant doing difficult things others would or could not, without complaint, and demonstrating that ideal through particular interactions with animals. In rodeo, people were not weak or squeamish; they were strong, determined, and stoic. In ranching and animal agriculture more broadly, people learned to participate in animal husbandry by caring about and for livestock materially while also emotionally distancing themselves in order to cope with the sadness that came up at auction time. Rodeo and ranching people learned this as children, although it did not come naturally. Instead it was a skill one developed before puberty and an element of adulthood. Junior rodeo events became a way to communicate those requirements to participants and spectators, including children, and to metaphorically purge vulnerability from the community.[10]

Juvenile cattle, that is, calves, were subject to multiple uses in rodeo because they were generally not dangerous to people. They were also more accessible to compete with or against for those with small hands and little strength or athletic experience, especially young kids. Children's calf events of various kinds proliferated during the interwar years. They helped rodeo people clean up the sport's reputation to some degree, recasting rodeo as a wholesome family endeavor rather than the folly of drunken rounders. That in turn helped recruit more kids, who might grow up to be adult rodeo competitors or to introduce their own children to rodeo. At the Black Hills Roundup in Belle Fourche, North Dakota, for instance, child calf-riding events appeared in the 1930s and offered a prize of one dollar for successful rides of calves supplied by a local rancher.[11] Children from ranch families across the West participated in special kids' events at small-town Saturday and Sunday rodeos as well. Many had chores to do on horseback at very early ages, so they knew how to rope by the time they entered primary school. They might even attempt riding local stock for ad hoc winnings of loose change collected from spectators or small gifts donated by local businesses.[12]

Rodeo events for kids, such as calf roping, calf riding, and, later, goat tying and "mutton bustin'," also proliferated after World War II at county-fair rodeos and agricultural festivals near suburbs and cities that might not have a PRCA or CPRA rodeo attached. Such events were unsanctioned by the major rodeo organizations but exposed non-ranching audiences unfamiliar with rodeo to the sport as family entertainment.[13] "At the fair rodeos, a lot of the little kids with aspirations to be cowboys show up. They're the champions of the future; the people who prolong our sport," said one PRCA official of the recruiting power of such entry-level events.[14] Champion cowboy Larry Mahan was a particularly famous example of this pipeline into the sport. He was no ranch hand, just a kid from Salem, Oregon, who started out in junior rodeo calf-roping events and eventually became a revered bull rider.[15]

Calf roping and riding, and other junior rodeo events, powerfully conveyed to children ways of thinking about and making use of livestock that were grounded in common ranching and farming philosophies. These families believed that humans had dominion over animals and the land, and undoubtedly for some, that children must be tutored in the old western attitudes of self-reliance, toughness, and the rewards of hard work. "The cowboy knows, loves, and respects animals, or he would not be a cowboy in the first place," goes the well-worn platitude of the sport.[16] One Oklahoman explained how in the 1950s his family prepared him to reconcile such dominionist beliefs about "love" and "respect" for livestock with what he saw in calf roping, thus reassuring him: "I was always told as a kid that it doesn't hurt them. They're

Child rider falling from calf, June 15, 1947, Sisters, Oregon, Devere Helfrich, Devere Helfrich Rodeo Photographic Collection, National Cowboy & Western Heritage Museum, 81.023.02816, Museum purchase.

a lot tougher than we are."[17] Livestock should be tough like rural westerners, or even more so, the thinking went.

Then, beginning in the 1970s, parents in league with rodeo and agricultural fair organizers conveyed this combination of personal stoicism and dominionism to their four- to eight-year-olds through mutton bustin' competitions, also known as "wool riding." In this event, girls and boys age eight and under rode on the back of a running sheep to be shaken off and thrown to the ground. Sheep from western ranches had escaped the rodeo until organized mutton bustin' appeared at Denver's Stock Show that decade. Various promoters developed it thereafter as a contracted add-on event for rodeos and agricultural fairs. Parents encouraged their children to participate in such "confidence builder" exercises or expressed nostalgia for their own childhood rodeo experiences. Some children proved enthusiastic and delighted in the experience. Others were deeply reluctant but subject to immense parental pressure to participate. Injured or frightened from a fall and trampled by the sheep, they would be lifted to their feet from the dirt and assertively told to stop crying and wave to the crowd—"show them how brave you are, honey."[18] Only in the last decade or so have mutton bustin' organizers required child competitors to be clad in a helmet and protective vest.

In practice, mutton bustin' was serious training by parents to their children on how one should understand and engage with livestock. It was also a form of black humor, like the wild horse race or wild cow milking (in which two cowboys wrangle a lactating beef cow and milk her into an empty beer bottle). "Nothin' like strappin' your kids to farm animals and callin' it entertainment," joked the announcer during one competition in Kansas where kids were being tutored on the adrenalin-pumping aspects and physical injuries of the event.[19] One production company promoted it as a corollary to bull riding, as "The Toughest Sport on Wool."[20] The sport soon attracted critics, including animal advocacy organizations who called it "child abuse" and "endangerment" that encouraged kids to risk their health while learning to enjoy harassing sheep who would frantically bleat, trip, and sometimes fall in their attempts to get away.[21] Indeed, the event seemed to carry deep meaning for some—whole identities were at stake. Countered one commenter on a story decrying mutton bustin' in a magazine for urban pet owners: "Look, rodeo is a way of life. These kids want to do this. . . . We are the type of people that do all the dirty and tuff jobs that you office and city people are either to [sic] scared or weak to do. . . . These kids are braver than you apparently, because when you look at rodeo or mutton bustin' all you see is pain and fear, when they look at it they see a challenge and a chance to show how tuff they are and be proud of themselves."[22] If rodeo people encouraged their kids—their "babies"—to participate in rodeo as early as age four, who among them would argue that cattle babies should be exempted?

<hr />

The exposure of calves and human children to rodeo events that symbolically purged weakness and vulnerability from the rodeo community was not acceptable to humane groups, editorialists, and members of the public who spoke out against calf roping. Public controversies over the event have occurred regularly since at least the 1910s, beginning in Salinas and Sacramento, then in New York, Los Angeles, Phoenix, Tucson, and beyond.[23] One such conflagration in Vancouver in 1949 stands out because, in part, it effectively ended rodeo within the city limits. It demonstrated how precarious rodeo's support was in some western places, especially in larger cities, where a multitude of ticket buyers could be found yet might not represent the sport's core constituency.

We know almost nothing of the calf at the center of the spring 1949 scandal over calf roping in Vancouver. He had probably been eaten within the year. Still, a few people worried about him and the other animals assembled that May in the eastern part of the city. That week, *Vancouver Sun* writer Jack Scott opened his regular column with the heading "Fear for Fun." The Scott family had ventured out to the Marpole Rotary Club Stampede believing they would see some western-style trick riding and fancy roping. Instead, they witnessed rodeo events that left Scott's nine-year-old daughter "pale and angry at the scene of wanton brutality" that she saw. She was particularly hurt and shocked, Scott said, to discover stated plainly in the rodeo program that cowboys were awarded points for spurring bucking horses. The bronc riding had also employed bare rope flanks (with no wool cover) and he said horses were burned by them as they bucked. "In the corral below us the hands cursed and clouted the cattle, clubbing them with psychopathic viciousness across the muzzle and eyes to herd them into the chute," Scott continued with dismay.[24] While how many is difficult to say, Scott correctly noted that he was among a number of "earnest citizens who have written letters to the editor condemning the Marpole Rotary Club's Rodeo as sadistic cruelty to animals."[25] Scott here echoed several decades of rodeo's critics who had similarly come to believe that rodeos were not appropriate for children because they displayed violence against animals.

Although the Scott family might have been new to the sport, Vancouver was no stranger to rodeos. During the 1920s, the yearly Hastings Park rodeo had appeared at a nearby horse track. Later, at Callister Park, a gritty venue facing Renfrew Street across from the Pacific National Exhibition grounds, a local company called West Coast Rodeo had been holding the Callister Park Rodeo since the 1930s.[26] Vancouver was a working-class port city benefitting from extractive industries like lumber, fisheries, grain agriculture, and mining. Still rough around the edges, the city had industrial, residential, and recreational land packed side by side.[27] Home movies of the Callister Rodeo production from the mid-1940s show what appear to be oil derricks looming over the arena from just behind the south bleachers, and only a modest spectator turnout.[28] That rodeo offered lackluster roughstock, who mostly ran around the arena rather than jumping or kicking, and certainly displayed no twisting, spinning, or body rolls.[29]

SPCA officer (woman on left) visiting behind the chutes, Callister Park Rodeo, 1943. City of Vancouver Archives, Vancouver, BC.

The Marpole Rotary Club held their Stampede that May in Callister Park to raise money for (of all things) their children's charity. It was far larger and better publicized than the old Callister Park Rodeo, had drawn competitors from as far away as Texas and Oklahoma, including famous cowboys like Bill Linderman, and—notably—it newly featured calf roping. As though expecting trouble, in the two weeks of publicity for the event, a local paper, the *Province*, had reassured people there would be no cruelty. The paper was obviously in league with the show's promoter, much-loved Albertan "King of the Cowboys" Herman Linder (the newspaper called him "Hermie"), and now rodeo promoter. To the *Province* and anyone else who asked, Linder insisted that the cowboys would be "careful of the stock" and that "it is a rarity when any animal suffers any serious injury or even has its hair ruffled" at a Linder rodeo. Could rodeo people be "cruel, vicious persons?" proposed a friendly *Province* columnist, Ken McConnell. "That just does not happen," he insisted.[30]

In fact, in planning for the event, city officials had indeed raised questions about animal injury. Linder had chided them not to worry by marshaling a couple of already-routine deflections: (1) the rodeo would adopt SPCA animal protection rules used at the famous Madison Square Garden rodeo (i.e., we have regulations); and (2) cowboys are well-meaning and would never commit "deliberate cruelty" (i.e., accidents happen, but only rarely).[31] Using an early version of the what-about-the-cowboys argument, once the rodeo was in full swing the *Province* puffed, "There should be a society for prevention of cruelty to cowboys!" on a day in which three riders were sent to hospital but, "there were no reports of animals being harmed."[32]

The rodeo ran from Tuesday to Saturday, but the following Monday, Herman Linder faced charges of animal cruelty in Vancouver's police court. The prosecutor chose two representative cases to take action against the entire rodeo, specifically a bronc who had been scratch-spurred to the point of drawing blood on the shoulder, and the roping of a calf who had been landed on his head when roped and knocked out. For what took place, court filings declined to charge the stock contractors who supplied the event, nor any spectators who cheered it on, nor the Marpole Rotary Club, nor its politically prominent rodeo committee chair, White Spot restaurant chain founder Nat Bailey. Instead, they held four cowboy competitors and Linder responsible for "unnecessarily abusing domestic animals."[33] The case of the spurred bronc would drag on for some months with considerable media attention as people argued over whether the injuries to the horse were due to spurring at the rodeo or an altercation with another horse during transport before the rodeo.[34]

Stuck in the middle was the British Columbia SPCA, which coexisted with local rodeos and picked their battles to focus largely on dog and cat overpopulation. The Vancouver branch of the BC SPCA was tasked with sending officers to inspect rodeos and agricultural fairs in the city, and they had done so at previous Callister Park rodeos. This year, as with previous ones, they appeared and visited behind the chutes and initially appeared to have no complaints. In his account of the scandal, written two decades later with the participation of Herman Linder, Linder's biographer, Cliff Faulknor, reported that local SPCA inspectors at the time were "extra men working for wages" and had been "real nice guys." Previously SPCA officials had visited local rodeos personally, but in 1949 they employed hired inspectors, for reasons that are unclear. In any event, waiting until the rodeo had finished its run, Faulknor surmised, "They only brought it [animal injuries] up in the first place to show they were on the job. But the whole thing got out of hand." Lolling about back of the chutes, they had chewed the fat with rodeo people, then only recommended charges, Faulknor accused, because the SPCA was too weak to withstand the complaints from ignorant members of the public—or, more correctly, perhaps the urgent letters and phone calls to the SPCA office from incensed donors.[35] The Vancouver branch of the SPCA was just then devising ways of accommodating animal use in the city in order to facilitate access for inspections and some sort of oversight, however slight. That approach caused rifts with local donors and SPCA branches elsewhere in the province.[36]

All the while, one thing no one disputed during the eight-month scandal over the Marpole Rotary Club Stampede was what had occurred in the calf roping contest. Jack Scott and his family saw the rodeo's stock pushers "putting the high-heeled, spurred boot to calves to send them in terror out to the ring" to be chased, roped, and tied.[37] SPCA officer David Ricardo later testified in court that he had seen the roping performed as "calf busting" when cowboy Chuck Erwin, from Walla Walla, Washington, had roped the calf in question. The calf had been flung off his feet to hit his head so hard that he was knocked out on the arena floor. Everyone agreed they had seen several competitors rope a running calf, pull their horse to one side, and loop the rope around the saddle horn such that, when the roping horse suddenly stopped, the calf was jerked off his or her feet and was, essentially, busted like a steer. Neither the lawyers for the defense, nor the veterinarian they brought in to testify, nor Herman Linder himself denied this description of events. However, the calf busting was not unnecessary cruelty, they argued, since busting calves was against the rules and was "accidental" when it did occur.[38] Indeed, the debate in the courtroom became stuck in the old rut of whether the calves' suffering had been "necessary."[39] Magistrate William McInnis agreed that, if a roping competition was to take place for a money-making rodeo, any cruelty that occurred was necessary. So, he threw out the charge against Linder and the cowboys.[40]

Still, rodeo in general received so much negative publicity in Vancouver during the 1949 case that other promoters appear to have been deterred. The old Callister Park and Hastings Park rodeos did not reappear, nor did other promoters appear in their place. Linder attempted to resurrect rodeo in Vancouver in 1959 by staging one in league with the Pacific National Exhibition, the city's agricultural fair. The venture lost money due to heavy rainfall and, as in 1949, serious mismanagement of ticket sales and delivery that was unable to exploit the minority of Vancouverites who would attend a rodeo. Then again, in 1969, Linder attempted to mount a production in the city but lost money when he could not marshal a critical mass of locals to attend. "Vancouver is just not a rodeo town," griped Cliff Faulknor later, blaming local anti-rodeo opponents who made claims about cruelty in rodeo that were "hysterically exaggerated."[41] Such dismissive talk revealed the degree to which some rodeo people in Canada, as in the U.S., were still simply unwilling to hear from critics, and so cast them as uninformed or overly emotional city people who were easily upset by sensational newspaper reports.

The debate over calf roping and rodeo in Vancouver was just one of many that would dog the event in the following decades in Canada and the United States. One of the mysteries of calf roping is how the event nonetheless persisted as a prominent aspect of rodeo even while rodeo people realized—even as they were dismissive of critics—that the sport was developing a problematic reputation.[42] Certainly, in all those debates over calf roping and in the records that rodeos left behind, there is almost no information recorded about the calves at the center of the sport and its controversies.

To find rodeo's calves, we need to look beyond the rodeo arena to the practice pen and the cattle trade, where calves were anonymous, interchangeable parts in beef production for over a century. "Poor animal," said *Frank Leslie's Illustrated Newspaper* in the 1880s on their plight in extensive ranching operations, fending for themselves on large ranges in all weather. At roundup time young beef calves found themselves roped and led or dragged away from their cows, cast, held down, branded, then released "plunging off to rejoin the herd . . . marked for future sacrifice." The calf's life "thenceforward [was] hard as its end [was] tragic."[43] Such was the experience of calves, whether Texas longhorn, or later shorthorn, Angus, Hereford, an "odds and ends" cross of those breeds, possibly including some Brahma stock, or, in the later twentieth century, Corriente cattle, which were popular as roping stock. Calves were the raw material of the beef production system, which was often in plain view just beyond the rodeo arena where cattle foraged or waited for another hay bale delivery on a hillside, or sat in pieces under plastic wrap at the market. In the nineteenth century, North Americans had decided that meat eating was a sign of respectable economic status. In the twentieth century, people especially fetishized beef steaks.[44] These were choices without which there may have been no calf roping at the rodeo.

Half a century later, ranching was all over television in any number of cowboy and western shows, none of which encouraged much sympathy for cattle. North American consumer culture connected beef eating to the supposed inevitability of the settling of the West, in this way. In the early television boom of the immediate postwar years, the title sequence for CBS's iconic western *Rawhide* depicted a drive of "dogies" (orphaned calves) "through rain and wind and weather—Hell-bent for leather" to the tune of the show's famous theme song. Sung by Frankie Laine, who recorded many western-styled songs of the period, the theme's arrangement included the sounds of cowboys yelling "Ha!" at imagined cattle, accompanied by the vicious cracks of a "rawhide" whip, recycling the old idea that cowboys were unsentimental toward cattle:

> Keep movin,' movin,' movin'
> Though they're disapprovin'
> Keep them dogies movin'
> Rawhide!
> Don't try to understand 'em
> Just rope, and throw, and brand 'em
> Soon we'll be living high and wide.

The phrase "high and wide" is a very American one indicating, in this context, cowboys who arrive in town at the end of the drive, receive their pay, and go about town feeling confident and wealthy. The dogies, meanwhile, became capital deserving little empathy or consideration. Left to wait at the stockyards for their trip to the feedlot, the cattle benefitted from neither the cowboys' nor TV viewers' attempts to understand them, and their resistance was dismissed as pointless "disapprovin'."

That was just a television scenario, of course, albeit one that played week in, week out for almost eight years. Meanwhile, back at the working ranch in the 1950s and 1960s, operations employing the midwestern system of stock raising had been transitioning to less violent practices. Patient herding helped ranchers manage cows and calves without the rough treatment involved in roping and dragging cattle on open land. Referring to cattle by the generic term "cow," Joan Burbick explained the logic behind the transition, as told to her by a former rodeo queen from a ranching family in Washington, near the Idaho border: "No one wanted to run down a cow or spend much time roping one. Running makes the cow lose weight, and weight equals money."[45] The rodeo queen's family had always employed paddocks and squeeze chutes to round up and doctor cattle in order to minimize their fear of human handling. As was true for so many rodeo events, calf roping actually presented the inverse of actual ranch practices, a wasteful and reckless one.

At the rodeo ground, the clotheslined calf at the end of the cowboy's rope was a visual sensation, but that same calf distracted people from changes in ranch work. Over the course of the century, the number of cow-calf operations in Canada and the U.S. increased and came to outnumber beef-steer ranches (selling animals two or three years of age), which had predominated

A perennially problematic image for rodeo: the clotheslined calf. San Angelo Fat Stock Show, San Angelo, Texas, 1940. Russell Lee, photographer. Farm Security Administration—Office of War Information Photograph Collection.

at the turn of the twentieth century. "Calves are the major product today," said a 1968 agricultural economics textbook, *Ranch Economics*.[46] Born in the spring, calves nursed and might eat some supplementary "creep feed" to grow from less than one hundred to over four hundred pounds in seven months, thereafter left to graze or eat feed until reaching market weight of about five hundred pounds, and sold to a feedlot. In the 1960s, at age two and 1,200 pounds, he or she was sold to a meatpacker and slaughtered. Calves emerged into the environment through birthing and survival that could be particularly difficult, depending upon whether, one rancher explained, "someone helped the cow if necessary, and watched the calf for signs of sickness until it was six months old."[47] In extensive ranching, many calves died from the inattentiveness of ranch owners and cowboys unprepared for late spring blizzards that froze and stranded vulnerable new calves. Other dangers included a range of diseases, drowning by falling through ice on frozen bodies of water, and ranchers who exceeded the carrying capacity of the land, which forced newborn calves to travel too far with their cows to find forage.[48]

Although ranch hands and owners might grow fond of a particular cow, since she might be willing to interact with humans, live in the herd for many years, and provide income, calves seldom engendered such feelings. Ranchers consciously worked to keep it that way because calves were essentially a cash crop. Yet things were more complex than that because, even though many ranch people had been taught these lessons as children, they still felt a sense of responsibility to their cattle and very occasionally might adopt one as a ranch pet. *Ranch Economics* illustrated the emotional conundrum with a cartoon illustrating "Business Management." In it a rancher looks lovingly over a group of his animals. "Aren't they beauties, Curly? We're getting better cattle every year! Proud of them—they're . . ." he says to his ranch hand, Curly, who interrupts: "You don't git me into helpin' you fall any more in love with 'em! You're like a sick cat when we sell anything we raise!"[49] Calves were feedlot cattle in the making, a transient commodity that many imagined as unfeeling or unthinking so as not to live with a contradiction that would hamper the work. Again, the ability to distance oneself emotionally from one's cattle on auction day was a central element of rural western adulthood, even if it was not practiced with complete uniformity.[50]

In "next year country," as faithfully optimistic ranchers and farmers have imagined themselves, calves were transient and interchangeable but held out hope that one's lifestyle could be possible a little longer.[51] The transience of calves was captured in the agricultural economics concept of "calf-crop percentage," or the number of calves born and reaching market weight per one hundred cows age two or older. By the 1960s, few ranches were achieving eighty percent, which was generally the point at which all of one's operating expenses were paid.[52] Calf-crop percentages had been increasing since the nineteenth century, and "death losses" were decreasing to a few percent so that many ranches were more productive and efficient. However, so had those ranches' expenses been increasing over the century—dramatically: taxes, labor costs, feed and equipment costs, credit to ride out the lows in beef prices and one's own miscalculations about the land's carrying capacity.[53] At the rodeo, roping calves were disposable. On the ranch, they were not. Once one got over the eighty calf-crop percentage that marked the break-even point, every extra calf one could usher toward the stock trailer at auction time meant take-home pay, free and clear, for the resident family or absentee owner.[54]

Continuing concentration of wealth in the beef industry up to the 1990s would exacerbate these conditions, which were also made worse by the rise of high-capacity feedlots that increased profits and kept beef artificially inexpensive for consumers at the expense of animal welfare. South Dakota rancher

Linda Hasselstrom lamented the fate of such calves, sold off to feed distant people alienated from the land that produced them. After a year or more grazing and socializing in a herd, the calves were gathered and sent to auction and the feedlot, a regrettable process Hasselstrom contrasted with her own husbandry practices,

> A trucker crowded as many calves as possible into his truck and sped east several hundred miles to a feedlot in Iowa or Nebraska. There the calf was dumped into a lot where it may not even have had space to lie down. Shoulder to shoulder, hundreds of calves struggled to a feed bunk to eat corn protected by the latest agricultural herbicides, guaranteed, according to their advertising, "to kill everything." The biggest calves, like schoolyard bullies, always ate the most. Some of the weakest may have been injured, or died. When it wasn't eating, the calf stood idle, often knee-deep in mud for six months or more, until it was killed for your dinner.[55]

The regret Hasselstrom expressed was grounded in a sense that in handing her stock over she was betraying the ancient contract that justified human exploitation and sacrifice of cattle in exchange for good welfare (in the colloquial ranchers' sense). She did no fattening or slaughter of her own cattle, but handed them to parties with no long-term stake in their experiences.

Industry trends ignored any responsibility individual ranchers might feel toward their calves in the search for continued efficiencies that produced the most meat with the least inputs of time, space, and money. The modern feedlot was and still is reliant on environmentally taxing corn feed, antibiotics, and other drugs to suppress what Rhoda Wilkie chronicled as "a range of well-recognized animal-related problems—for example, digestive ailments, including liver abscesses, laminitis (i.e., inflammation of the hooves, which can cause acute or chronic lameness), heat-induced stress from prolonged exposure to intense sunlight, and behavioral abnormalities such as tongue rolling, bar sucking, and aggression."[56]

Just at the historical moment when Linda Hasselstrom and other ranchers spoke with regret about the horrors of the feedlot, although still sending her calves there, the *Washington Post* printed in 2001 a chilling front page exposé, "They Die Piece by Piece." Their investigation in the U.S. documented the ineffectiveness of industry and USDA monitoring of slaughter and how the Humane Slaughter Act (the only U.S. regulation pertaining to livestock, who lived most of their lives without protection due to the old agricultural exemption custom) was, essentially, meaningless. Many whistleblowers—from inspectors, to veterinarians, to slaughterhouse workers—described how privatization of the inspection process, relieving the overtaxed or disinterested USDA, had created a black hole of disassembly line speed-ups and abuses. They reported livestock insufficiently stunned at the beginning of the line, then conscious while being dismembered, eviscerated, or skinned. The story provided screenshots from undercover footage of an insufficiently stunned steer blinking his eyes while on the disassembly line.[57] Since most ranch activities and rodeos in the U.S. were exempted from state and federal animal cruelty and welfare laws, the Humane Slaughter Act was the only legislation that might apply to livestock, even if only for the last day of their lives. In this reality it was not easy being cattle.

For many decades, rodeo promotion and storytelling ignored all of this. It papered over the trials and miseries of people and cattle who lived with the uncertainty, labor, and emotional difficulties of ranching and industrial beef in favor of rodeo contests that celebrated individual winners who symbolically protected ranching families and rural life.[58] Since the 1950s, calf ropers had been among those heroic cowboys, and their relationships with roping calves mirrored those in the feedlot and slaughter industry more generally. Calves' vulnerability was not something to mind, but something to exploit; calves were all destined for slaughter in any event. Starting at mid-century, ropers needing to prepare for competition simply purchased calves from the local stockyard, neighbors, or ads in the paper advertising young cattle for "the practice pen," namely calves kept on hand specifically for roping practice. As calf roping at the elite levels became more lucrative, specialty stock breeders and dealers would begin to breed and supply roping calves in large numbers, creating another little niche in the continental cattle market supported by rodeo sports.[59] Far more calves supported rodeo roping in practice pens, rodeo schools, and local roping clubs, where a small herd as well as roping dummies were kept for members to rope, than at the arena on competition day.

Nonetheless, we can learn a little bit about the lives of these calves since they unknowingly left their mark on the historical record in instructional roping manuals produced by the event's champions. The revered Texan roper Toots Mansfield was a fixture in the sport throughout the 1930s and 1940s, winning at the prestigious Madison Square Garden rodeo seven times. He became a superior roper through expert training of his roping horses and consistent, error-free performances in competition.⁶⁰ In about 1961 he founded a rodeo school in Big Spring, Texas, that was the first to feature calf-roping instruction. Young men turned up there to practice on a small herd of one hundred and seventy-five calves that Mansfield kept on site, cycling them out when they grew too large, balky, or injured for roping. These calves were mostly Herefords with a few Brahmas mixed in for variety, between three and twelve months old and weighing about two hundred pounds each, and so somewhat smaller than one would find at a rodeo.

Mansfield's generously illustrated manual for aspiring calf ropers, *Calf Roping*, showed the school in session. Huddled together in a small pen or being handled by students, the calves spent teaching days with no apparent water or shade. Some of them stood patiently while Mansfield demonstrated all the various holds and poses involved in the ground work of roping, pulling on a leg here, tugging on the flank there, grasping a head into an instructive position and holding it in place while the photographer focused the shot. To train students, some among these calves endured repeatedly being hoisted in the air, turned on their sides, and landed on the ground, that is, flanked, by novice ropers practicing that move. These calves ran from a chute and took a rope to the neck multiple times per day. They lay prone in the dirt while students practiced binding three legs with a piggin string—over and over—with a spotter holding the calf's head against the ground with his boot. "When practicing tying, an assistant can help hold the calf down by putting slight foot pressure on the calf's neck. This eliminates struggling in early tying lessons. Calves are changed frequently in these practice sessions," Mansfield explained.⁶¹

Indeed, Mansfield more than once warned student ropers to think about ways to "conserve your calves," referring obliquely to the toll that roping took on them. For example, one could train one's horse to release the tension on the roped calf once the piggin string was secure. He also advised that, when roping repeatedly, one should drive calves back to the starting chute calmly and without haste. "This conserves the stock since the calves don't try to duck, dodge, and turn back." For practice sessions, Mansfield recommended a "non-choke loop" on roped calves and an assistant to hold them still as students practiced jumping from the horse to run down the rope line to the calf since "this saves a lot of wear and tear on the stock." Without referring to any of the sport's "no jerk down" rules, he offered tips on how to rope and spot calves so that they did not get jerked off their feet when being run from the chute up to four times in one day. How many aspiring champion ropers

Practice-pen calf, Mansfield, and students at Toots Mansfield's roping school in Big Spring, Texas. Mansfield, *Calf Roping* (1961).
Courtesy of *Western Horseman*.

could afford to keep a sufficient number of calves around in the practice pen for such luxuries, we cannot know. Certainly, calf roping had a reputation as "an expensive sport" because good roping horses could be pricey and because practice-pen stock needed replacing all the time.[62] Mansfield's *Calf Roping*, like any proscriptive literature, undoubtedly represented an ideal situation that was not normative. It also indicated that "soured" or exhausted stock was a chronic problem in practice-pen herds. Those calves resided on remote ranches with no dedicated veterinarian, humane officer, or USDA inspector present to advocate for their welfare.

A generation later, perhaps the most successful calf roper in rodeo history, Roy "Super Looper" Cooper, likewise published his own amply illustrated roping manual and held calf roping workshops. Cooper was from New Mexico and the son of calf roper Tuffy Dale Cooper, who had competed with Mansfield in the old days. Tuffy Cooper had ensured that Roy began practicing and competing in early childhood and he won often, eventually earning college scholarships in Texas and Oklahoma. Famously, in 1979, Roy almost completely severed his right hand with a taut rope. His quick recuperation and two decades of championships thereafter constitute, from a sports-history point of view, an incredible tale of athletic and mental perseverance.[63] By the year 2000, over an exceptionally long, thirty-year career in rodeo, Roy Cooper had become the first cowboy in any event to win over $2 million in competition. He developed innovative common techniques and ropes that cowboys used, and thereafter roping times became much faster among elite competitors everywhere. Often, Cooper could rope and tie a calf in only eight seconds.[64]

Like Mansfield, with a chapter in his manual entitled "Problems," Cooper offered advice to new ropers about the ways that calves complicated roping practice. It speaks volumes about the detailed knowledge ropers absorbed in order to quickly quash any resistance on the part of their prey. Some calves would kick their legs as a roper tried to bind three together. Cooper advised, "Sit down on him and tie close to the ground, because a lot of calves will show more willingness to kick if they are rolled on their backs with the feet high in the air." He also recommended grabbing a handful of "flank" to stop a calf from kicking in resistance while one was trying to apply the piggin string.[65]

In Cooper's era and in Mansfield's, roping regulations required that, after roping a running calf and pulling him over, then jumping to the ground to run down the rope line, competitors must "throw calf by hand and cross and tie any three feet."[66] Cooper warned that some calves simply collapsed at the end of the rope and refused to get up. This behavior put ropers in the absurd position of having to somehow get the calf (too frightened, or stunned, or stubborn to attempt jumping up and running away) up on his hooves again in order to thereafter complete the step of throwing the calf down by hand, or flanking him. Cooper recommended minimizing the damage to one's roping time by using the right hand (at the rear of the animal) to grab a handful of hide and pull the calf up. If that was unproductive, one would grab and pull up on the tail while holding the calf's head up with the left hand, hoping that the tension on the rope from one's horse would also pull the calf to his feet.[67] In Cooper's generously illustrated book, calves posed for this instruction, too, photographed lying in the dirt or spinning in mid-air in the various postures necessary to capture Cooper in every stage of the action. In some of the photo illustrations these calves look sleepy or indifferent. In others they are visibly strained and frightened, with the whites of their eyes obvious.

In 2004, rodeo journalist Gavin Ehringer let slip something about the practice pen that rodeo people usually kept to themselves; certainly, neither Mansfield or Cooper mentioned it directly. In a cowboy picturesque–style newspaper piece entitled "The Mud, the Blood & the Poop: A Rodeo Insider Takes You behind the Chutes of America's Cowboy Sport," Ehringer criticized the routinized attacks on rodeo from People for the Ethical Treatment of Animals (PETA) as "woefully uninformed." PETA continued to circulate the old myth that flank ropes were tied to bucking bulls' genitalia, he said. They held the PRCA responsible for the goings-on at amateur rodeos, "where abuses seem more common," and which represented eighty-five percent of all rodeos but over which the PRCA had no authority. He complained that they repeated hearsay about animals injured at rodeos without dependable data. "If PETA truly wanted the skinny on animal injuries, they'd have to post observers in the backyard practice lots of aspiring rodeo kids," Ehringer said of the open secret in the sport. "As a calf roper once confided to me, 'Yeah, I accidentally killed and injured lots of calves when I was learning. I mean, I plain roped their heads off till I really learned how to handle them and not hurt them.'"[68]

Since the early days, rodeo people had taken it for granted that even in competition such "accidents" would happen—chronically. The year before the 1949 controversy over the Marpole Rotary Stampede's calf roping in Vancouver, a contractor named Aleck Hartell had contracted forty-four pairs of cows with calf to the Calgary Stampede. As was standard practice there, Hartell received payment of $792.00, plus $50.00 for "2 damaged calves @ $25.00 each." Stampede stockman Dick Cosgrove approved the transaction by penciling across the voucher "O. K."[69] For many stockmen and ropers, calf losses were not actually "O. K." but rather an inevitability that may have been regrettable, although not enough to quit roping or leasing roping stock to the rodeo. With the influx of ropers and increasing investment in the sport in succeeding decades, a few rodeo people sought technical solutions to maximize the durability of roping-pen stock. One company in Nebraska sold by mail order collars for practice pen stock called "Calf Savers." They advertised many benefits, including "less calf time in sick pen, greater calf resale value, . . . reduces initial stop shock, practically eliminates choking down—calves recover quicker from stop and are 'throw ready' sooner . . . Practically eliminates swollen and stretched necks."[70] So, here it was in black and white, aside from any fear or other mental strain, colloquial knowledge among ropers of the physical stresses that put calves in the "sick pen" or to the slaughterhouse early because of "stretched necks" and other injuries sustained on private ranches.[71]

With respect to the steers employed in non-busting steer roping and team roping, horn wrap protectors would become standard practice by the 1990s in order to prevent ropes burning into ears, horns being snapped off, and other painful experiences that trained roping steers to duck the rope and otherwise resist.[72] Yet, rodeo officials and calf ropers seem not to have seriously considered protective collars for roping calves in competition, although they might have helped rehabilitate the event with some detractors. Calf roping competitors interviewed by anthropologist Elizabeth Lawrence in this era explained that "calves were just beef, and they never were perceived as possessing 'rights' or deserving sympathy."[73] Perhaps prominent rodeos and governing bodies never mandated collar use because calf welfare was never important enough to a critical mass of competitors, contractors, and rodeo officials. Such innovations would have silenced some critics, but perhaps they also slowed roping times.

Meanwhile, neither Toots Mansfield nor Roy Cooper discussed a long-attempted and more common refinement in calf roping, the "no jerk down" rule. Just a few years before Herman Linder and Chuck Erwin were charged with animal cruelty in Vancouver, Clifford Westermeier explained how the rule was designed to prevent calf busting, or "to jerk a calf off its feet," by penalizing ropers with a ten-second addition to their roping time. He noted that the rule's ultimate purpose was to protect the sport, rather than the stock: "This particular part of the calf roping rules applies only to those contests held in cities where the Humane Society objects to calf roping. The penalty of 10 seconds has the tendency to prevent contestants from being too much in a hurry to make time."[74] Westermeier admitted there was some variability in interpretation and application of no jerk down/anti-busting rules. At many rodeos, the rules might not be in effect at all, on the books only for publicity purposes, or in effect only at the discretion of judges in a sport notorious for inconsistent, inexpert, and biased judging.[75] By the mid-1970s, some believed the rule was ineffective in many locations because judges who dared enforce it were booed loudly by rodeo spectators. As the logic was at the time, the responsibility for calf injuries lay with stock contractors who delivered substandard stock. Calf roping was rightly a rough, unsentimental, timed event—one hundred percent representative of the spirit of the West. If calves employed at the rodeo were too weak to take it, this was not the cowboy's fault. In the arena, it was his job to demonstrate his own toughness and that of western animals so as to metaphorically banish vulnerability from the entire community.[76]

Ropers and their allies also avoided responsibility for damage to calves by blaming their horses. Roping horses employed in calf roping or steer roping have generally been Quarter Horses, bred and trained for this one rodeo event. They must charge from the starting chute, then chase the calf at an even distance, that is "rate cattle," in order to allow the rider to accurately lasso the calf. Thereafter, explains Clifford Westermeier,

> The horse is trained not to stop dead in his flight, while the rider dismounts and goes down the cord to the calf. Rather he must ease up gently, in order not to "bust" the calf, but he must keep the rope taut enough to prevent the struggling animals from running about and adding time to the score. After the calf has been thrown and tied, the horse continues to hold the rope taut enough to prevent the animals from floundering, but not taut to the extent of dragging the calf.[77]

This is certainly a complex task in which horses must size up individual calves and act with precision. Often, when calves were jerked off their hooves, it was not because they were tripped like steers by the roper pulling the rope behind their rear legs. Calves tripped because they were "dallied or tied to a saddle . . . [with a] half-hitch around the saddle horn with the rope after the catch has been made."[78] As a result, some convinced themselves that in fact it was the roping horse who violated the rule when a calf was knocked out or dragged while prone.[79] In this interpretation, horses who stopped too abruptly or pulled too strongly on the roped calf represented a failure of training and performance, giving roping competitors and supporters a way to discount every busted calf as an unwanted "accident."

As with other rodeo stock, well-trained and consistent roping horses have long been sought after, revered, remembered, leased, bought, and sold. If not animal athlete celebrities on par with famous bucking horses and bulls, many roping horses are remembered by name and talked about for years. The trials and tribulations of the roping horse are nonetheless a story that is yet to be told, and there is certainly some unsettling history there. For instance, people were stunned when officials kicked Tuf Cooper, son of Roy Cooper and a champion roper himself, out of the 2015 Calgary Stampede for openly whipping his roping horse and violating their recently strengthened "animal care protocols" after a failed attempt in the calf roping that week. The Stampede had never in its one hundred and five year history disqualified a competitor for animal abuse, even in the face of the dozens of horses killed or fatally injured in its iconic chuckwagon races and that event's historical problems with alcohol and animal abuse in the Stampede's barns.[80] On the live CBC broadcast of Cooper's run, even the TV commentators fumbled their banter for a split second at the sight of Cooper vigorously whipping his horse, Rio, who trotted toward the exit with ears turned back toward his master, clearly smarting from the rope.[81] The episode seemed to point to knowledge of the broader training context of the sport on the part of the Stampede's Animal Care Advisory Panel, a body formed in 2010 to manage some aspects of animal treatment and certainly serve the Stampede's publicity goals.[82]

Traditionally, rodeo's supporters have normalized such practices with euphemistic talk of "a stern lecture given the horse by the empty-pocketed cowboy" who finds himself disqualified or fined by inaccurate roping horse work.[83] Training of these horses was rigid, lengthy, and constant in order to guarantee absolute accuracy of their performances and limit horses' autonomy in the arena. By contrast, bucking horses were left half wild together in pens, pastures, and ranges when not traveling to or at a rodeo in order to preserve their sense of self-direction and their power to respond in their own way in the arena. Roping horses required confinement in tie stalls that formed a small enclosure for constraining the horse and heavy-handed dominance training that ropers used to prevent horses from innovating or adding behaviors to the task in the arena, instead convincing them to avoid punishment by following their training in every single respect.[84]

In the late 1970s, one roper frankly explained to anthropologist Elizabeth Lawrence, "You can't baby a calf-horse; he must listen and respond like a child. They have to fear you a little." Lawrence noted that many rodeo people described their relationship to a roping horse as parental, requiring care but also discipline because "perfection is demanded." At the Calgary Stampede, Lawrence had herself seen one roper who threw dirt at a horse who performed incorrectly. She recorded audience members who similarly blamed horses for imperfect roping performances and rejected the idea that the horse should have any individuality or "input of its own" into the elements of the calf roping process they are asked to complete.[85] In this understanding of roping horses, the properly trained horse is not a baby and, like human children in rodeo, is expected to compete without complaint or error. By this logic, the obedient horse is a team player who symbolically seems to consent to the competition against the calf by following his or her training.

By contrast, the fate of calves as vulnerable animals at rodeos was more obvious to the public and thus challenged claims made by rodeo people that they were enacting a caring stewardship over livestock as a reflection of rural western heritage. Increasingly, some said that rodeo stock contractors and cowboys could not be trusted to define what constituted injury or suffering on the part of roping stock. This was an accusation that exacerbated the broader political polarization around rodeo and other forms of animal agriculture and entertainment in the later 1980s and early 1990s. The PRCA at first responded with blanket statements that would only undermine their overall message by painting an impossibly rosy picture. One handout booklet claimed, "The PRCA's professional judging system produces the desired effect of preventing mistreatment and abuse. 'It's just about completely eliminated the problem.' . . . PRCA sanctioning is an absolute guarantee that a rodeo will be produced by people who truly care about the animals."[86]

Instead of answering specific questions politely and in detail, as PBR publicists would generally do, with respect to rodeo as a whole and calf roping in particular, at first spokespeople at rodeos small and large, like officials at the PRCA, appeared to have no obvious plan to communicate about specific cases of animal injury or death. Instead, they resorted to vague talking points in hundreds of television, newspaper, and magazine interviews, which followed a familiar pattern, which can be paraphrased as follows: We have the utmost respect for our animals; we have regulations; veterinarians are present at the NFR (and the other large elite shows); few calves are killed or suffer broken limbs in the arena before spectators; therefore there are no calf injuries and critics are ridiculous, disingenuous, or uninformed and should be ignored. In her 2007 history of roping sports, *Rope to Win*, Gail Woerner chronicled decade after decade of criticism of calf roping, including local laws banning rodeos in whole or in part, such as the much resented (but mostly symbolic) 1989 Rhode Island law outlawing non-breakaway calf roping. Yet, she coached fellow rodeo people to simply dismiss questions about roping with a folksy heading in one chapter that avoided any specifics: "Humane Issues, not hardly."[87] In an atmosphere in which, for half a century, rodeo people had derided their critics, how could anyone admit publicly that those opponents might be correct about anything? Instead, many in rodeo deflected questions and simply asked people not to believe their own eyes when they watched the show.

In particular, calf roping was chronically dogged by images of the clothes-lined calf, snapped at the instant the rope became taut, pulling a calf to a halt and to the ground. According to the industry, any apparent "humane problems associated with the calf roping event" were simply an issue of optics at city rodeos. "Calf ropers should come up with a modification that does away with jerking the animal over backwards," said Doc Etienne, a member of the PRCA animal advisory committee, "because it is that sight that is offensive to the urban population."[88] Clifford Westermeier had said the same thing fifty years earlier. Now, at the direction of the PRCA, for instance, ESPN sports station broadcast staff agreed that, at the instant just before the rope went taut around a roped calf's neck, they would cut away from the calf to show the roper descending from his horse.[89] True, fans of the sport might have found it more interesting to watch the roper and his technique at that instant. Yet rodeo people everywhere also knew how the image of a calf straining at the end of the rope had become symbolic of criticism of rodeo as a whole.

The two sides of the debate over appearances seemed to be talking past one another. Those who ran the governance organizations believed that the rough treatment of calves was not inhumane because rodeos aspired to reduce broken legs and necks by employing no stock that was "sore, lame, sick or injured, . . . or any animal with defective eyesight."[90] Of course, as Clifford Westermeier had said back in the 1940s, such rules were designed to protect the quality of the animal's performance and the cowboy's chances in competition, not to prevent injury to calves.[91]

Another tactic the larger rodeos and organizations marshalled was to find industry-friendly veterinarians who shared the perspective that in ranching, rodeo, or any animal agriculture, animal injuries were constituted only by physical injuries and were inevitable accidents when they occurred. The PRCA, for one, found friendly veterinarians to defend rodeo as a whole with generalized statements about the sport's dedication to animal welfare and PRCA rules relating to stock. They spoke of the high price of top stock (a category that did not include roping calves) and other vague, best-case-scenario-as-norm ideals that painted rodeo in an impossibly perfect light. One University of Tennessee veterinarian went on record to defend tie-down roping, saying simply, "It's a safe way of handling calves."[92]

In the late 1980s and 1990s, the PRCA told journalists and rodeo people that they had surveyed a number of events and found that less than one percent of roping calves in competition "sustained any injuries," mostly to the legs.[93] Rodeo spokesmen and the sport's allies regularly cited industry studies that claimed, for instance, "an injury rate of 0.00054" from almost 28,000 animals across all the sanctioned events who experienced a total of only fifteen injuries. They noted that for some years the PRCA had required a veterinarian to be on site or on call at their rodeos (although this requirement excluded the vast majority of smaller rodeos and the practice pen).[94] It is unclear how much veterinarian observers were expected to intervene to prevent injury, fear, or pain in the arena since they had no power to alter the nature of the competition nor to enforce any no-jerk-down rules, all of which were decided by rodeo governance bodies and event judges. Instead, they were present to look at roping calves as an inspector would at a stockyard: examining animals for lameness and communicable livestock diseases, such as Bovine TB or herpesvirus, and to protect, not disrupt, rodeo and the transcontinental circulation of animals it relied upon.[95]

Major rodeo governing bodies also appropriated the term "animal welfare" in place of older talk of "humane" concerns. They conflated improved welfare in terms of transport and handling, especially of the most lucrative roping horses and bucking stock, with the status of all animals involved in rodeos.[96] Veterinarian James Furman, speaking on behalf of the industry, lit a small firestorm in the *Journal of the American Veterinary Medical Association* (*JAVMA*) when he called roping calves "bovine athletes." In his article, he noted that the PRCA had in 1947 pioneered "the first rules for humane care and treatment of rodeo animals . . . seven years before the founding of the Humane Society of the United States"—a statement that ignored a half century of preceding animal advocacy by humane groups to rodeos, asking for events to be refined or eliminated, and for handling practices back of the chutes to be improved. Indeed, the piece was simply a retelling of PRCA talking points developed in the previous decade to deflect criticism by discussing rodeo in the most ideal terms. It cited no independent studies of rodeo calf welfare.[97]

Readers of the *JAVMA* were left to wonder how rigorously the PRCA animal welfare rules were practiced or enforced since the organization was self-regulating and did not make disciplinary matters public. Former rodeo competitor and veterinarian Peggy Larson responded in the *JAVMA*, not with broad or vague statements, but specific detail of how "stress kills" in calves, as well as the names of cattlemen and other large-animal veterinarians who had testified that rodeo stock contractors "lose calves from illness as well as roping injuries—some say as high as 50%."[98] Echoing a similar debate among Canadian veterinarians fifteen years earlier, Colorado veterinarian Mark Taylor responded similarly: "Animals [in rodeo] do not have to have overt injuries in order to feel pain. . . . We should work as a profession to stop this type of animal sport-torture."[99] Some years later, noted cattle welfare expert Temple Grandin drew from her own experiences as a person on the autism spectrum to argue that for cattle with limited ability to understand or control their surroundings, fear was far more damaging to an animal's health than pain. Not only did fear suppress the immune system and cause weight loss in the short term, but it created ongoing anxiety that stressed health long term because prey animals are designed to be "vigilant" and "on the lookout" for threats by continuing to be afraid that the frightening event might reoccur.[100]

Large-animal veterinarians, many of them rodeo people themselves, had been struggling with how to interact with rodeos for several decades. Their veterinary oath directed them to prevent and relieve animal suffering and to protect animal health, certainly. Yet the profession had always supported livestock use for meat production in the name of public health and economic growth.[101] Beyond her piece in the *JAVMA*, Peggy Larson spoke out often about the sport and named calf roping as the single rodeo event most dangerous to livestock. She recounted speaking with USDA meat inspection veterinarians in the 1990s, one of whom had observed rodeo animals arriving at slaughterhouses and remarked, "I have seen cattle so extensively bruised that the only areas in which the skin was attached was the head, neck, legs and belly. I have seen animals with six to eight ribs broken from the spine that at times puncture the lungs. I have seen as much as two to three gallons of free blood accumulated under the detached skin."[102] This passage has been repeatedly quoted by news outlets, as well as countless animal advocacy books, magazines, and websites ever since. Another veterinarian Larson spoke to reported finding cattle arriving direct from competition at Frontier Park in Cheyenne bearing "broken ribs, punctured lungs, hematomas, broken legs, [and] severed tracheas and the ligament nuchae were torn loose [broken neck]."[103]

The same year the *JAVMA* presented the Furman-Larson debate over rodeo animal welfare, changes were afoot in the veterinary profession, rodeo, stockyards, and slaughterhouses. Over the previous decade, more people had begun to speak openly of the need to include animals' mental experiences in evaluations of their welfare.[104] Temple Grandin advised in another *JAVMA* piece, "The sound of people yelling and screaming is stressful and aversive to cattle, and shouting at cattle is highly aversive . . . raising animals' heart rates more than the sound of a gate slamming," reiterating her contention that for cattle fear is often more dangerous than pain.[105] Here again was the age-old but usually ignored call to take the sentient experience of livestock seriously as a form of "injury," something rodeo people had been denying since the 1880s. Unlike powerful bulls and broncs whom many (mis)interpreted as vicious and just asking for a fight, calves running from the chute or bound, white-eyed and tongue-extended, always appeared obviously frightened and possibly in pain. A later study explained that frightened or painful calves did not make any sound during roping simply because "tightening the noose around the neck inhibits vocalization."[106]

Renaming the event "tie-down roping" had no impact on the calves who made calf roping possible. The new name originated in Australia in the 1990s and many rodeos and organizations in Canada and the U.S. had, one by one, adopted it by the early 2000s. One Texan fan interviewed at the Calgary Stampede complained to a journalist, "I'm not fond of it. It is calf roping and they're just trying to pacify the animal rights people."[107] It is doubtful that the new name fooled rodeo's opponents. Indeed, often animal advocates have been quick to offend rodeo people because they have refused to parrot the sport's euphemisms, including the reimagination of calf roping as tie-down roping. Such a tactic attempted to sanitize what critics considered to be painful, frightening, physically harmful, and completely unnecessary treatment of livestock. In truth, the renaming of the event perhaps functioned primarily to help rodeo participants, fans, and those just discovering rodeo to push aside any doubts and present a united front in a politically polarized context.

To illustrate this point, back in Vancouver calf roping remained a perennial political issue. Just south across the Fraser River in Surrey, the Cloverdale Rodeo and Exhibition Association had founded their own rodeo in 1947, just two years before the Marpole Rotary Club Stampede controversy. Surrey was then an agricultural delta, covered in scrubby deciduous forests and vegetable farms. The Cloverdale Rodeo found an audience and persisted to become one of Canada's largest and most prominent rodeos, and it did so in an agricultural region without significant beef cattle production. Cloverdale's rodeo was like many in Canada in which the stock, staff, competitors, and their families came in from out of town to perform for working-class folks and farm families. There, participation in or attendance at rodeos and the adoption of western styles—hats, boots, and other western gear—was a symbol of rural identity, in Canadian terms, of playing or performing as "country" rather than specifically western.

Sixty years later, the rodeo was in hot water. Surrey was no longer a predominantly agricultural town but a densely populated suburb of Vancouver noted for its large South Asian immigrant community. It was being quickly transformed by the region's booming development sector flush with global capital, and thus, some of the most expensive real estate in the world. Small but vocal advocacy groups like the Vancouver Humane Society (VHS), Animal Advocates, and Liberation BC were waging war on the Cloverdale rodeo by way of onsite protests and letters to the editor in the two main newspapers in Vancouver. They also received open support from local community papers, including *Coquitlam Now* and the *Surrey Leader*. Since the 1970s, neighborhood papers like these had periodically courted controversies that the main Vancouver papers avoided by publishing graphic accounts of animal abuse in labs at the University of British Columbia as well as the miseries of animals caught in leg-hold traps in the BC backcountry.[108]

In 2006, Debra Probert, director of the VHS, urged rodeo organizers to make some changes, noting that the city of Vancouver had the previous year (mostly symbolically) banned rodeos outright. "Surrey is growing and urbanizing rapidly.... With so many new citizens and with ethnic minorities already making up over a third of the city's population, how reflective will rodeo be of the community's culture and values?" she asked in reference to Surrey's marketing slogan, "City with a Heart."[109] Probert asked that the current CPRA-sanctioned tie-down calf roping be replaced with breakaway roping by which "when the calf hits the end of the rope, the rope will break, thus eliminating the most pain." The VHS also exposed whistleblower accounts of "tail-twisting, kicking and banging of the animals' heads against the bars" of stock chutes to guarantee calves would bolt into the arena.[110]

Public protests to discredit or interrupt Cloverdale Rodeo's competitions and sway public opinion had been going on for two decades already. They employed modern, media-savvy protest techniques. Drawn from social-reform traditions going back to the Yippies, certainly, and even suffrage and union activists before that, they sought to expose contradictions and hypocrisy in public life by impeding or embarrassing the powers-that-be. One Liberation BC activist had marched in the Cloverdale Rodeo Parade itself carrying a sign declaring the rodeo to be cruel.[111] More than once the VHS had also harassed the rodeo by hiring a plane to fly overhead pulling banners that asked, for instance, "Having Fun? Rodeo Animals Are Not."[112] They broadcast numerous radio spots asking people to boycott the rodeo, including one aimed at tearing down the myth that agricultural animals are somehow less sentient or capable of fear or pain. In the soundscape of the piece, a yipping cowboy riding a galloping horse lands his rope around the neck of a frightened dog, who yelps loudly, with a voiceover that asked listeners to consider if calf roping was any different. In 2006, the VHS even mounted a cheeky demonstration of "cruelty-free cowgirls ... scantily clad in daisy dukes, tied up blouses, cowboy hats and not much else" bearing a banner that read "No One Likes an 8 Second Ride."[113] Then, the next year, Pamela Anderson, the noted celebrity animal advocate originally from BC, made a public statement with the VHS against Cloverdale's roping of calves crafted to point out their vulnerability and lack of consent to their use: "A baby animal, frightened and agitated."[114]

The advocacy pressure and media attention for reform was sure and steady, year in and year out. Although they had sent inspectors to the Cloverdale rodeo every year (as required by provincial legislation), for six decades the BC SPCA had refrained from intervening in or publicly criticizing the event, even though the organization's own formal policy statements opposed rodeos. As had been the case in 1949, local branches of the SPCA tended to coexist with local animal industries, only gently urging them toward welfarist reforms in order to preserve their access to the animals in question. Other animal advocacy groups pointed out the contradiction to BC SPCA supporters, who in turn eventually motivated BC SPCA officials to join the groups asking that the Cloverdale rodeo be considerably reduced or replaced entirely by some other kind of public entertainment. This challenge came just as the site of the Cloverdale fair and rodeo was being evaluated by Surrey city council for potential redevelopment, which might put the rodeo out of its home. This would have been an alarming situation for any rodeo committee.

On May 8, 2006, just days before that year's rodeo was set to begin, representatives from the VHS were permitted to make a direct presentation to the Surrey city council, which had heard similarly from Animal Advocates several years earlier but had chosen not to act. In the presentation, executive director Debra Probert asked that calf roping, wild cow milking, and live animal acts in the half-time show be banned. The presentation featured images the VHS had commissioned from a professional photographer at a previous year's competition. Among them were images of a bucking horse bleeding from both nostrils, a bull futilely trying to climb out of a bucking chute, steers with heads twisted around one hundred and eighty degrees, and many calves photographed mid-flanked or clotheslined—precisely the type of images that had haunted calf roping continent-wide for so many years. One city council member told journalists that these "were not pretty pictures."[115] Still, the council took no action to outlaw calf roping or the rodeo. The rodeo board, supported by the CPRA, insisted that the Cloverdale show was sufficiently regulated and supervised. They did not comment on the accusation that stock pushers twisted roping calves' tails just as the chute opened, such that calves burst out because they were hurting and frightened.[116]

The following year, it was a single roping calf who tipped the balance for the Cloverdale Rodeo. As with the Marpole Rotary Club Stampede calf who was jerked down in 1949, we know little about the Cloverdale calf. He was supplied to the rodeo by the Kesler ranch of Magrath, on the Alberta prairie fifty miles north of the Montana border. In early May 2007, the calf had ridden to Surrey in a stock trailer crowded with other calves, and perhaps horses or bulls. Starting out over the plains, he travelled over the Rocky Mountains, then wound all day along the curves of an interior highway, through ski and snowmobile country, past ranches, hobby farms, vineyards, and auto malls until the trailer stopped at the Cloverdale arena, just a few miles from the Pacific Ocean. There the calf was directed into a pen at the rodeo grounds to wait, huddled with other calves, in possibly the noisiest place he had ever been. On Saturday night, while fleeing from the chute, he broke his leg and was soon after euthanized.

A hasty news conference followed the next day in which rodeo representatives announced something unique in rodeo history: with the support of

VHS photograph of Cloverdale Rodeo calf, mid-flanking, with taut choke rope and extended tongue, presented to Surrey City Council in 2006.
Courtesy of the Vancouver Humane Society.

Dianne Watts, the mayor of Surrey, the Cloverdale Rodeo was voluntarily abolishing calf roping of any kind permanently. Also to be discontinued were wild cow milking, steer wrestling (a steer had been killed in that event four years earlier), and team roping (the timed event in which one roper captures the head of a steer while a second roper catches one of the steer's rear legs, stopping a running steer ideally without knocking him down).[117] Cloverdale Rodeo spokesperson Laura Ballance explained that the CPRA refused to allow any modifications to the calf roping or steer wrestling, but that Cloverdale management felt strongly that it was time to either refine or cancel these events. They had listened to "feedback we've received from thousands of rodeo fans who attend our event here in Cloverdale" to make the decision, she said, making no reference to the bad publicity caused by years of criticism from local animal advocacy groups.[118] Still, the case showed that such challenges might actually offer an opportunity to rodeos to adapt and remain relevant in their communities, as the Cloverdale Rodeo would bravely do.

Today, over a decade later, the Cloverdale Rodeo and Country Fair is still going strong in Surrey, and local animal advocates have since turned their attention to rodeos in the BC interior, Vancouver Island, and Alberta. Cloverdale may have dispensed with calf roping, but there are still babies at the rodeo because it still features mutton bustin' for kids age three and up. The rodeo's website says about the event, "Parents will be asked to sign a release/waiver form prior to performance ... [and] provide proof of personal injury insurance for the contestant."[119] At Cloverdale, it is still unresolved how or whether rodeos train young people to have ostensibly western or "country" attitudes about livestock and about their own "toughness." More commonly, though, debate within the rodeo community about any of these issues remains private, and the show goes on.

The fiction of a unified rodeo community totally confident in their monopoly on knowledge of livestock put forward by rodeo marketing, histories, and sport associations does not mean people have had no doubts. Yet, this fiction has been useful because it seemed like a way to fend off rodeo's critics. Only anonymously would an informant tell authors Wayne Wooden and Gavin Ehringer in the early 1990s, "For a calf, being yanked backwards from a full run by a rope around its neck has got to be a nasty experience. How can we really justify this? And lumping everyone who might be worried about this under the umbrella of animal rights activist seems too easy and an oversimplification."[120] Plenty of rodeo people have variously dismissed those critics as a small group of "crazies, malcontents, radicals, extremists and vegans."[121] Recall the young woman I saw at Cheyenne Frontier Days wearing a "P.E.T.A. People Eating Tasty Animals" T-shirt with her cowboy hat. Bernie Rollin, a well-known Colorado State University researcher on rural human-animal relationships, recently warned rural North Americans against this alarmist stereotype because it hinders people in animal agriculture from adapting to new realities so as to survive: "As far back as 2004, polls found 70 percent of the American public wanted farm animal welfare legislated. That number is now well north of 90 percent," he said to a meeting of farmers and ranchers. "So when you dismiss people as extremists when they believe animals have rights, you're making serious tactical errors [which] can cost you customers, and more importantly, freedom."[122]

Indeed, calf roping represents both a problem and an opportunity for rodeo people these days. It has long navigated the same problems that were introduced into rodeo by steer busting over a century earlier. Calves suffered injuries and traumas, which many rodeo people wished were not part of the sport. Many members of the public found tie-down roping too violent and periodically laws were passed to ban the practice. Unlike steer busting, the industry did not formally discredit tie-down calf roping as it had steer busting, although many rodeos avoid trouble by featuring breakaway calf roping instead. Since rodeo people still use no myth of consent to explain calf roping, the vulnerability of the calves is really a vulnerability for the sport, itself designed to purge vulnerability and weakness from the rural West, symbolically at least.

# Epilogue

In the summer of 2014, I sat on some low bleachers at the outdoor arena of the Redstone Rodeo, Gymkhana, and Mountain Race, just off the highway reaching from Williams Lake, British Columbia (BC), out toward the coast at Bella Coola. Redstone belongs to the Alexis Creek First Nation, or Tŝideldel, and is part of the Tsilhqot'in Nation in the Cariboo Chilcotin region of British Columbia. It is spectacular and isolated country—a plateau of grasslands, forests, lakes, and steep river valleys that endure exceptionally hot, dry summers. From Redstone, people drive almost two hours to find a supermarket or a bank. The nineteenth-century ancestors of today's Tsilhqot'in majority in the region endeavored to keep out road building, miners, and settlers. They were largely successful.[1] At the Redstone Rodeo that summer, save for maybe a dozen tourists, everyone there was from a rural section or small town in southern BC.

Drivers on back roads here quite often come across local people's horses, standing around in little groups on this beautiful landscape with hooves unshod and their manes and tails untrimmed. These horses are tame and allow strange people to approach them and give their shoulders a pat, but they are autonomous. They manage themselves on the land and probably have never seen the inside of a box stall. People around here, Indigenous and settler, have raised horses and cattle since the nineteenth century. Just to the south on the Fraser River is the Gang Ranch, founded by two Virginians in 1863 and still in operation. For many years it was the largest ranch in the world. When founded, it started a process by which the provincial government confiscated unceded Indigenous territory, and corporate and proprietary ranching operations learned how to monopolize it in places by exploiting ineffective range laws.[2] In 1864, members of the Alexis Creek First Nation defended their territories from this kind of settler encroachment by violently turning back a road-building crew sent from Victoria by a gold prospector. The

Canadian government retaliated by inviting six Tsilhqot'in chiefs to promised peace negotiations, then arresting and hanging them.[3] The Tsilhqot'in people maintained a formidable reputation thereafter nonetheless.

Over the next half century, some Tsilhqot'in men revitalized that reputation by periodically harassing and killing outsiders who trespassed and ignored locals' authority. That discouraged all but a handful of homesteaders and ranchers. Those who ventured in and stayed understood that they inhabited plateau lands only at the convenience of Tsilhqot'in leaders. Many people here have pointed to the Chilcotin War as a reminder that the popular ideal of "conquest through benevolence" in the Canadian West is just a stubborn myth, that the conquest was never total, and that sometimes it involved violence on both sides.[4] Today, many traditional Tsilhqot'in sites for seasonal hunting, camping, and harvesting furs or fruit are still accessible and in use, but they are controlled by the Crown. Indeed, everyone here, whether Indigenous or settler, continues to contend with the power of the federal and provincial governments over the land.

While this colonial history produced persistent inequalities and political tensions in British Columbia, since the 1920s people have always gone to the rodeo together.[5] In much of Canada and the United States, Euro-Canadian and American settlers prevented nonwhites from participating in the mainstream of the sport in the twentieth century by discriminatory judging, by banning Indigenous competitors from restaurants and hotels near rodeos, and by other means.[6] In BC, however, interracial rodeo has been the norm, in both participation in and hosting of rodeos. Back in Redstone that summer day, I learned that the rodeo is part of the British Columbia Rodeo Association network. It has no elaborate budget for advertising or publicity, beyond a matter-of-fact listing on the British Columbia Rodeo Association website and schedule cards displayed with the tourist brochures at provincial visitor information outposts on the highway. Sponsored by regional construction and lumber companies, the Redstone event is one among a continental network of Indigenous-operated and "All-Indian" Indigenous-only rodeos where, as the saying goes, "the cowboys are Indians."[7] It is a confident assertion of Tsilhqot'in entrepreneurialism and the desire to be visible collectively as modern people with a love of horses and rural living.

To be frank, that day in 2014, the Redstone show was not the best-organized rodeo I had ever attended. I did not know the arena director, or anyone from the Alexis Creek First Nation, or the stock contractor hired for the event.

There were long delays between events. A number of times the announcer had to call participants in from the parking lot or wherever they were, telling them to hurry up since it was their turn to compete. After one bull rider made his get-off, the bull he had been riding refused to go to the exit chute. The pickup men roped him and pulled, and pulled, and pulled, until the bull was choked out and collapsed in the dirt. A middle-aged Caucasian man sporting a large cowboy hat appeared with a cattle prod and began zapping the bull with it, over and over, with the ropes still taut on the bull's thick neck. The bull did not move. A tourist in the crowd, possibly visiting one of the dude ranch resorts nearby, declared, "My God! Where is the owner of that bull? This man is abusing that bull!" Someone mumbled, "Actually, that guy's the stock contractor. That's his bull." Calling to the man with the hot shot now, the tourist shouted, "Stop that! Hey! Stop that! Leave him alone—can't you see he's hurt?" A couple of people snickered. Here again was that old urban-rural tension in rodeo history. The scene reminded me of the Denverites or Portlanders who worried about steer busting in small-town Wyoming and rural Oregon over a century earlier, and were ignored or told to mind their own business.

Then it was time for the mountain race. Sometimes promoted as a "suicide race," the event appears at a minority of outdoor rodeos where the venue allows and is exceedingly dangerous. In places like Omak, Salinas, Vale, Oglala, and Redstone, men, often fortified with liquid courage, race on horseback from a starting line at the crest of a steep mountainside or riverbank overlooking rodeo grounds down to a finish line in the arena, producing a noisy and dramatic show. In Redstone, it took a while to get the event going. Finally a group of men on horseback made their way up the steep hill dotted with a few conifers behind the arena and waited for the starting gun at the summit.

Seconds after the race began, several horses and riders went down and disappeared into a cloud of dust on the steepest part of the slope, just a few feet past the starting line. The race continued with some of the remaining riders charging into the arena. One horse arrived at the bottom of the hill with no rider and trotted off to the left toward a pasture nearby. Two riders arrived at the bottom of the hill on foot and walked into the arena to some applause. One rider did not come down at all, and we would later find out that he had fallen from his horse on the slope and was severely injured. His name was Jason Coutlee and he was from Merritt, that town just to the south that was also home to Ty Pozzobon, the well-known local bull rider who died from complications due to chronic traumatic encephalopathy (CTE).[8] Coutlee died in the helicopter air ambulance before he could be saved. In his memory, Redstone officials renamed this event the Annual Jason Coutlee Memorial Mountain Race and have carried on with it ever since.

Just after the race, at the bleachers and in the announcer's box, no one knew yet that Coutlee was fatally injured. As we all waited for the air ambulance to arrive to take him to the Alexis Creek clinic, then a hospital in Kelowna, it was also not clear whether the downed horses were alive or dead, how injured they were, or whether anyone was checking on them. People were talking about at least one having a broken leg—a fatal injury for a horse. Chatter in the crowd had it that one of the horses did not belong to the rider who had ridden him and fallen, but was just a loan from somebody else at the rodeo. What a shame, people said, to lose a good horse like that. As an outsider to that community and an academic researcher there simply to observe what took place, I was reluctant to intervene. Ashamed to tell it, but I did not drive out to the highway to find cell service and call the SPCA office in Williams Lake to send someone out to investigate, bring veterinary help, and perhaps timely euthanasia. Since that day, I have wondered how long those horses suffered on the side of that mountain and I second-guessed my choice not to act. In many ways, rodeo has tested and exposed people and their values for over a century, and now I was being challenged just so. As I wrote at the beginning of this book, we are all implicated in the history of rodeo and its contradictions.

Photographer Gabor Gasztonyi has for years produced picturesque photography of First Nations rodeos in the Cariboo-Chilcotin region, including Redstone. Regarding a recent show of this work, Gasztonyi endorsed his subjects by saying, "I was always impressed with the care taken with horses and bulls in all the events I attended. The people of the Chilcotin have a mysterious bond with animals."[9] This is sincere praise from a non-Indigenous person whose art requires considerable intrusion into a community that, although they welcome you to the rodeo and will chat politely out the truck window if they pass you at the lake, may not wish to be scrutinized too much by an outsider. Still, perhaps some outsiders have faith in the idea that Indigenous people have a particularly special relationship with their horses because, in a rodeo context, it conveys rodeo's myth of animal consent with a twist. Tsilhqot'in citizens do not claim to be quarrelling with the land, wishing to bend nature to human will. They do not insist on living in rural places because it needs to be civilized or made productive. They are not out to speculate in pure-bred bucking bulls or broncs who can be advertised as eager "animal athletes."

Instead, like other Americans and Canadians, for them rodeo is form of political and cultural activism supporting rural identities grounded in horses and, in this case, many centuries of living in the region. Here, the same rodeo tests in which a person struggles against or pushes an animal to his or her limits, which settler communities use to celebrate their appropriation of the West, convey an opposite message. Here it is about the work of the Tsilhqot'in to keep a firm grip on their autonomy and distinct culture grounded in over a century's work as ranchers and horsemen.[10] The calves, bulls, and broncs are provided by a regional settler-owned stock contracting company, and people bring their own saddle horses, drawn from the area's autonomous but tame bands. That people have a right to use animals in these ways goes without saying here. In spite of things that go wrong, many here might say that horses and cattle are better off with people than without.

Although First Nations communities have been central to rodeo in British Columbia since the beginning, the Redstone rodeo was only founded in 1998, in part to fund and build a new outdoor arena for local kids to use.[11] Rodeo is a living thing, and an event like Redstone's shows off rodeo's adaptability and continued relevance in helping communities imagine themselves and speak to others about who they are in an entrepreneurial way. Beyond Redstone, although for a century the institution has seemed fragile or, at times, under siege, no matter who opposed or supported rodeo, it was in no real danger of fading away. Today, when many other animal entertainments, like aquariums, circuses, roadside and city zoos, and television and film productions employing live animals, are winding down, rodeo is alive and well. It has always been and continues to be a way to aspire to fortitude and bravery by people who believe they can and should have power over animals and land in the West. The sport still wrestles with its contradictions and rodeo people still ask animals to take the same risks that they impose on themselves, but often without the rewards.

# Notes

### Introduction

1. Blunt, *Breaking Clean*, 272–73. Judy Blunt's classic memoir documents her life in an eastern Montana ranching family in the 1960s, 1970s, and 1980s. Along with her personal struggles as a woman and mother in a place and time rooted in male authority and land ownership, Blunt recounts how her family persevered in the face of blizzards, rainstorms, drought, brushfires, mud that made roads impassable, and limited access to veterinarians and doctors. Eventually she came to question her role in this tradition, and she gave up her marriage and ranch life to live in Missoula. See also Lawrence, *Rodeo*, 64.
2. In this book, I refer to this broad group as "rodeo people," an admittedly awkward lumping together of an exceedingly diverse array of people over space, time, and individual politics. Still, I take rodeo people to be unified in their active or political support for rodeo as a social, cultural, political, and economic tradition.
3. Starrs, *Let the Cowboy Ride*, 74–75.
4. Starrs, *Let the Cowboy Ride*, 18, 53, 67, 71–75.
5. Smith, *Virgin Land*.
6. Lawrence, *Rodeo*, 7–8. See also, for instance, Hoy, "From Folk Game to Professional Sport," 150; Penrose, "When All the Cowboys Are Indians," 687–705; Rollin, "Rodeo and Recollection," 1–2.
7. A very large number of books and articles about rodeo have been written for participants and fans, including profiles of famous competitors, organizers, and longtime rodeos, as well as memoirs and accounts by "old-timers," of which thousands have appeared in magazines and newspapers since the 1920s. The academic research on rodeo falls into two general camps, first pro-rodeo social science studies (see, for instance, Groves, *Ropes, Reins, and Rawhide*; Mellis, *Riding Buffaloes*; Wooden and Ehringer, *Rodeo in America*) and second, anthropological/historical works that acknowledge animals and the environment nominally but take their fate as a given (Lawrence's *Rodeo: Wild and the Tame* is an exception to this trend; see, for instance, Allen, *Rodeo Cowboys*; Fredriksson, *American Rodeo*; LeCompte, *Cowgirls of the Rodeo*; Stoeltje, "Power and Ritual Genres" and "Rodeo: From Custom to Ritual"; Westermeier, *Man, Beast, Dust*).
8. Laegreid, *Riding Pretty*, 4–6; Stoeltje, "Rodeo," 244–55.

9. Allen, "Real Cowboys?" 70; Allen, *Rodeo Cowboys*, 14; Boatright, "American Rodeo," 195–202.
10. Carr Childers, "National Finals Rodeo"; Hoy, "Origins and Originality of Rodeo," 16; LeCompte, "Wild West Frontier Days," 54–67; Stoeltje, "Power and the Ritual Genres," 135–56.
11. Burbick, *Rodeo Queens;* Hoy, "Origins and Originality of Rodeo," 16; Iverson, *Riders of the West*, 82–87; Kelm, "Riding into Place"; Kelm, *Wilder West*; Laegreid, *Riding Pretty*, 4–6; LeCompte, "Cowgirls at the Crossroads," 27–48; Mellis, *Riding Buffaloes*, 35–42; Penrose, "When All the Cowboys Are Indians," 687–705.
12. Worster writes of his work in *Under Western Skies*, "There are some historians who can ignore the role of nature in our past, some who cannot. These essays are the pleasures and pains of one who cannot." (Worster, *Under Western Skies*, viii.)
13. White, "Animals and Enterprise," 237–38.
14. See, for instance, Dobie, *Mustangs*, chapters 3, 4, 5; Harrod, *Animals Came Dancing*, 9; Iverson, *When Indians Became Cowboys;* Thistle, *Resettling the Range*, 14–69; Wise, *Producing Predators*, 47–67.
15. Nance, *Animal Modernity*.
16. White, "Animals and Enterprise," 237; see also Thomas, *Man and the Natural World*, 302–303.
17. Aron, "Lessons in Conquest," 128–29; see also Worster, *Under Western Skies*, 15
18. Hixson, *American Settler Colonialism*, 199; Lause, *Great Cowboy Strike*, x.
19. Patricia Limerick wrote some years ago that "the encounter of innocence with complexity is a recurrent theme in American culture, and Western history may well be the most dramatic and sustained case of high expectations and naïveté meeting a frustrating and intractable reality. Many American people have held to a strong faith that humans can master the world—of nature and of humans—around them, and Western America put that faith to one of its most revealing tests" (Limerick, *Legacy of Conquest*, 29). Regarding the "new" Western history see, for instance, Cronon, Miles, and Gitlin, eds., *Under an Open Sky;* Limerick, Milner, and Rankin, eds., *Trails*; Milner, O'Connor, and Sandweiss, eds., *Oxford History of the American West*; Robbins, *Colony and Empire*; Robinson, ed., *New Western History*; White, *"It's Your Misfortune"*; Worster, *Under Western Skies*. Frank J. Dobie's many articles and books provide an important foundation in western animal history. More recently, new Western histories of human-animal relationships tend toward documentaries of human predation, exploitation, and extinction, and provide an important context to this study. See Alagona, *After the Grizzly*; Barrow, *Nature's Ghosts;* Brown, *City Is More Than Human;* Coleman, *Vicious;* Colpitts, *Game in the Garden;* Fleharty, *Wild Animals and Settlers*; Flores, *American Serengeti;* Isenberg, *Destruction of the Bison;* Jacoby, *Crimes against Nature*; Jones, *Wolf Mountains;* Price, *Flight Maps;* Sayre, *Ranching;* Van Nuys, *Varmints and Victims*.
20. Over a decade ago, Jeff Williams called for more attention to the interactions and rituals outside the main rodeo events in the arena—"the show," as it is often

called by rodeo participants—although for him the "backstage events" excluded rodeo procurement, development, management, and disposition of rodeo animals (Williams, "Prolegomenon for a Field of Rodeo Studies," 4).

21. Paul H. Carlson, "Myth and the Modern Cowboy," in Carlson, ed., *Cowboy Way*, 2; Martha A. Sandweiss, "Interpretation," in Milner et al., *Oxford History of the American West*, 671.

22. Regarding the "Eastern" production of the mythical West, see, for instance, Murdoch, *American West*, 22. See also Bold, *Selling the Wild West*; Dippie, "The Visual West," in Milner et al., *Oxford History of the American West*, 675–80; Warren, *Buffalo Bill's Wild West*, 72–73.

23. On westerners' own exploitation of western myths see, for instance, Butler, "Selling the Popular Myth," in Milner et al., *Oxford History of the American West*, 771–79; Etulain, *Telling Western Stories*, 12–16.

24. Carlson, "Myth and the Modern Cowboy," in Carlson, ed., *Cowboy Way*, 206–7; Worster, *Under Western Skies*, 15. Certainly, the myths of the West are old analytical territory for scholars, who have produced a vast scholarly literature on this topic, although they are generally silent with respect to human-animal relationships. See, for instance, Bold, *Frontier Club*; Murdoch, *American West*, 12; Smith, *Virgin Land*; Marx, *Machine in the Garden*; Slotkin, *Gunfighter Nation*, 1–28; Slotkin, *Regeneration through Violence*, 5; Worster, *Under Western Skies*, 3–18.

25. Lawrence, *Rodeo*, 175. See also LeCompte, *Cowgirls*, 2–4.

26. Vern Kimball, quoted in Gordon Pitts, "Making the Rodeo Run," *Globe and Mail*, July 12, 2010, https://www.theglobeandmail.com/report-on-business/careers/careers-leadership/making-the-rodeo-run/article1368379/.

27. United Nations Environment Program International Panel for Sustainable Resource Management, *Assessing the Environmental Impacts of Production and Consumption*, http://www.unep.fr/shared/publications/pdf/dtix1262xpa-priorityproductsandmaterials_report.pdf; Food and Agriculture Organization of the United Nations, *Livestock's Long Shadow* (2006), http://www.fao.org/3/a0701e/a0701e00.htm; Rachel Premack, "Meat Is Horrible," *Washington Post*, July 30, 2016.

28. Inspiration for this point comes from Jonathan Safran Foer's discussion of the "myth of consent" within North Americans' cultural ideas about meat. "A common trope, ancient and modern, describes domestication as a process of coevolution between humans and other species. Basically, humans struck a deal with the animals we have named chickens, cows, pigs, and so forth: we'll protect you, arrange food for you, etc., and, in turn, your labor will be harnessed, your milk and eggs taken, and, at times, you will be killed and eaten. Life in the wild isn't a party, the logic goes—nature is cruel—so this is a good deal. . . . This is the . . . myth of animal consent. It is offered by ranchers in defense of the violence that is part of their profession, and makes appearances in agricultural school curricula. . . . The animals, in effect, want us to farm them. They prefer it this way. Some ranchers I met told me of times they'd accidentally left gates open, and

none of the animals fled.... The persistence of the story of animal consent into the contemporary era tells of a human appreciation of the stakes, and a desire to do the right thing." Foer, *Eating Animals*, 99–101.
29. Stephen Budiansky, "The Ancient Contract," *U.S. News & World Report* 106, no. 11 (March 20, 1989): 74. See also Foer's discussion of ranching and the myth of animal consent above.
30. Ritvo, *Animal Estate*, 25–26, 37.
31. Here I employ the term "dominionism" to describe broadly a philosophy that the interests of humankind always outweigh those of animals, and that people can and should exercise power over animals in self-interested ways. In the rural West, and beyond, these ideas are often grounded in particular readings of the Bible and providential forms of Christian belief. They hold that God wishes the planet to be a site of human supremacy, and that rural people are the enactors of this plan. This philosophy is so ever-present in the United States and Canada that many people barely notice that they are immersed in it, which explains why debates over the phasing out of this or that mode of animal use can make people extremely frightened and angry. Interrupting animal use can threaten a person's very identity, which explains why public debates over rodeo sports often become so heated. On dominion as a human ideology (and a critique of it), see, for instance, Ellis, "Boundary Labor," 107–8; Scully, *Dominion*, xii, 11–20; Thomas, *Man and the Natural World*, 17–40.
32. Starrs, *Let the Cowboy Ride*, 27–29. See also Nance, "A Star Is Born to Buck."
33. Hixson, *American Settler Colonialism*, 199.
34. Coleman, *Vicious*, 10–11, 229.
35. Cothran, *Remembering the Modoc War*, 131.
36. Coleman, *Vicious*, 10–11, 229; Colpitts, *Game in the Garden*; Cothran, *Remembering the Modoc War*, 18–19; Limerick, *Legacy of Conquest*, 311–12; Smalley, *Wild by Nature*, 199–200; Van Nuys, *Varmints and Victims*, 4; Wise, *Producing Predators*, 4.
37. Warren, *Buffalo Bill's Wild West*, 222–28; OK Corral & Historama, http://www.ok-corral.com/.
38. Bold, *Frontier Club*, 1.
39. Maher, *Mythic Frontiers*, 34.
40. Hoy, "From Folk Game to Professional Sport," 150; see also Etulain, *Telling Western Stories*, 15; Hoy, "Origins and Originality of Rodeo," 31–32.
41. Rodeo has been a bridge between two contradictory ideas born in the nineteenth century and still carried with us: first, the modern consumer ethic that emphasized guilt-free comfort and satisfaction, represented by movie and book Westerns as well as inexpensive supermarket steaks (among many other things); and second, a set of agricultural values and practices in the West that valorized the use of animals and the reshaping of the land, and upon which the consumer ethos was entirely dependent, although many consumers were unaware of or in denial about

this. Keith Thomas describes the roots of this "human dilemma" in early modern England: "On the one hand they saw an incalculable increase in the comfort and physical well-being or welfare of human beings; on the other they perceived a ruthless exploitation of other forms of animal life." Thomas, *Man and the Natural World*, 302. See also Starrs, *Let the Cowboy Ride*, 27–28.
42. Anderson, *Creatures of Empire*; Fischer, *Cattle Colonialism*, 5–7.
43. Fischer, *Cattle Colonialism*, 6–7; Iverson, *When Indians Became Cowboys*, 14; Wise, *Producing Predators*, 49–60.
44. Exceptions to this rule include Fredriksson, *American Rodeo*, 135–70.
45. Popular histories of rodeo abound. They include books and articles by and for rodeo people, which often bleed into the promotional writing in magazines, newspapers, and books, plus biographies and memoirs of famous rodeo promoters and competitors. There is a children's literature and countless "old timer" accounts that have for over a century appeared regularly in various self-published or regionally published books, western magazines, and newspapers. For a sampling, see for instance Darden, *Scrappy*; Knight, *Pete Knight*; Moulton and Moulton, *Steamboat*; Ringley, *Rodeo Time*; Woerner, *Cowboy Up*; Woerner, *Belly Full of Bed Springs*.
46. Baxter, *Cowboy Park*, xxvii. See also, for instance, Mahoney, *College Rodeo*; Westermeier, *Man, Beast, Dust*.
47. Johnson, *Biting the Dust*, 85; Rollin, "Rodeo and Recollection," 1–2.
48. The works on Mexican and Mexican American rodeo have so far addressed the phenomenon primarily from an ethnographic or anthropological perspective. See, for instance, Sands, *Charrería Mexicana*. With respect to barrel racing, there are many, many manuals, guides, and memoirs written by top coaches and competitors, but no history of the sport beyond some very brief summaries. See, for instance, LeCompte, *Cowgirls of the Rodeo*, 158–62; Woerner, "History of Barrel Racing." There appear to be no histories written yet of American Junior Rodeo Association, Little Britches, high school, or other children's rodeo events beyond Sylvia Gann Mahoney's *College Rodeo*.
49. Hixson, *American Settler Colonialism*, 5.
50. Conducted in earnest over the last fifty-five years or so, AWS research has produced findings that have revolutionized human understandings of the complexity of animal experience, culture, and biology, and of the future questions we must ask as research continues. Like all scientific work, ethological and AWS research are a product of particular political and cultural contexts that shape the kinds of questions researchers are interested in exploring and the methods they are prepared to employ in doing so. Research is premised on the assumption of nonhuman ability, an idea grounded in the fact that complex mental and social abilities are an evolutionary advantage in many species, not simply in humans. This approach assumes that since animals are products of evolution, they can be trusted to know what is best for them in responding to immediate

contexts. The scientific literatures on cattle and horse welfare are very large, constantly evolving, and exceed the space available here. See, for instance, Fraser, *Understanding Animal Welfare*; Ryder, "Measuring Animal Welfare"; or see the publications of the Universities Federation for Animal Welfare.

## Chapter 1

1. Lawrence, *Rodeo*, 177; see also Fredriksson, *American Rodeo*, 144–45; Westermeier, *Man, Beast, Dust*, 244–46. John O. Baxter's various books and articles present an exception to this rule: he discusses steer injury and death in each of his works on steer-roping competitions.
2. Later also known as "steer tripping" or, in the later twentieth century, "steer jerking," steer busting was distinct from the less dangerous "steer roping" that some rodeos present today, wherein ropers do not sweep the steer's legs from under him so as to spin him in the air. Lawrence, *Rodeo*, 36–37, 177.
3. "Rough Riders," *Heppner Gazette* (OR), September 8, 1896. See also Harding [Barrow], "Passing of 'Busting,'" 140; Westermeier, *Man, Beast, Dust*, 229.
4. Hixson, *American Settler Colonialism*, 113–44.
5. Sandweiss, *Print the Legend*, 332; Warren, *Buffalo Bill's America*, 69–74; Wrobel, *Global West*, 2–3.
6. Barker, ed. "History of the Strickland and Taylor Families," 3; Baxter, "Sport on the Rio Grande," 248–49; Hoy, "Origins and Originality of Rodeo," 23; Stanley, *Life and Adventures of the American Cow-boy*, 34; Stoeltje, "Rodeo," 247.
7. Hixson, *American Settler Colonialism*, 5.
8. "Austin Notes," *San Marcos Free Press*, November 2, 1882. The phrase "wild and untamed steers" appeared in advertising, newspaper stories, and other literature beginning at least in the 1870s, reflecting a certain romanticization of western cattle descended from Spanish stock.
9. The *San Antonio Times*, quoted in "Austin Notes," *San Marcos Free Press* (TX), November 2, 1882; "Ex-Confederates for McKinney," *Galveston Daily News* (TX), August 7, 1883; "From Austin," *The Weekly Democratic Statesman* (Austin, TX), December 29, 1883. Saloon owners and other members of the business community were prominent rodeo promoters in this period (Baxter, "Ropers and Rangers," 331). In the decades since those Beef Bonanza days, about as many authors went in search of "the first rodeo" as rodeo publicists claimed to represent that primordial show (LeCompte, "Hispanic Roots of American Rodeo," 57–59). For various communities' rival claims to having been first, see Boatright, "American Rodeo," 197; Hoy, "Origins and Originality of Rodeo," 16–17, 23; Reddin, *Wild West Shows*, 160; Westermeier, *Trailing the Cowboy*, 344–76.
10. The *San Antonio Times*, quoted in "Austin Notes," *San Marcos Free Press* (TX), November 2, 1882. See also, for example, "The Acme of Success," *The Weekly Democratic Statesman* (Austin, TX), November 2, 1882.

11. "The Acme of Success," *The Weekly Democratic Statesman* (Austin, TX), November 2, 1882.
12. Webb, *Great Plains*, 235–36.
13. "Cowboys' Work and Ways," *Frank Leslie's Illustrated Newspaper*, April 8, 1887, 118–19. See also Branch, *Cowboy and His Interpreters*, 95; Wilson, "'I Was a Pretty Proud Kid,'" 51–57. Already, the newspapers and dime novels had for some time described the clothing of drovers and vaqueros, both work-a-day and fancy versions for roundups, since readers might be shopping for gear themselves or just be feeling curious. Dary, *Cowboy Culture*, 202.
14. "The Acme of Success," *The Weekly Democratic Statesman* (Austin, TX), November 2, 1882.
15. Various authors have argued that rodeo was actually inspired by the Wild West shows, but my research seems to indicate more of a chicken and egg relationship, wherein community cowboy tournaments and the Wild West shows materialized at almost the same moment. See also Frederiksson, *American Rodeo*, 140.
16. Webb, *Great Plains*, 261.
17. Pomeroy, *In Search of the Golden West*, 174–75. See also Baxter, "Sport on the Rio Grande," 246; Brado, *Cattle Kingdom*, 15
18. Baxter, "Sport on the Rio Grande," 252; Baxter, "Ropers and Rangers," 320, 325; Davis, *Parades and Power*, 3–7; Glassberg, *Sense of History*, 68; Ryan, *Civic Wars*, 242; Sacks, "Charles Fletcher Lummis"; Thornton, "San Diego's First Cabrillo Celebration," 167–80; Worster, *Under Western Skies*, 227.
19. "Capital State Fair," *Austin Weekly Statesman*, September 13, 1883; "Austin Capital State Fair," *Bastrop Advertiser* (TX), September 29, 1883.
20. "Austin Notes," *San Marcos Free Press* (TX), November 2, 1882.
21. Baxter, "Sport on the Rio Grande," 247–48; Baxter, "Ropers and Rangers," 320, 325; Baxter, *Cowboy Park*, 135; Westermeier, *Man, Beast, Dust*, 32–37. Still, rodeos held by Spanish-speaking westerners were seldom chronicled in the Anglophone press. See LeCompte, "Hispanic Roots of American Rodeo," 61–64; Sacks, "Charles Fletcher Lummis," 162–63.
22. Starrs, *Let the Cowboy Ride*, 56–57; Smith, *Virgin Land*, 200, 208–212.
23. "The Acme of Success," *The Weekly Democratic Statesman* (Austin, TX), November 2, 1882; Baxter, "Ropers and Rangers," 317.
24. Sandweiss, *Print the Legend*, 332; see also Webb, *Great Plains*, 235–38.
25. Slatta, *Cowboys of the Americas*, 49–50.
26. Lawrence, *Rodeo*, 61–63. In many western memoirs, people tell of cowboys who teased cattle or horses and boasted about it. See, for example, Hough, *Cowboy*, 176.
27. Hoy, "Origins and Originality of Rodeo," 29; Park, "San Franciscans at Work and at Play," 46; Sacks, "Charles Fletcher Lummis," 163. Nineteenth-century travelers throughout the Southwest came across all these practices, finding that many were Hispanic in origin but intercultural in participation, before and after American acquisition of these territories. See Fischer, *Cattle Colonialism*, 133–35; LeCompte,

"Hispanic Roots of American Rodeo," 57–59; Premo, "Recreating Identity," 43–45; Westermeier, *Man, Beast, Dust*, 33–34.

28. Early nineteenth-century Californios, for example, held performances in which "selected steers would be chased on horseback by a vaquero with a special knife. At just the correct moment the rider would strike the neck between just the right vertebrae, and the steer would be killed instantly, its spinal cord severed." Hoy, "Origins and Originality of Rodeo," 29.
29. Sacks, "Charles Fletcher Lummis," 147, 165; Thornton, "San Diego's First Cabrillo Celebration," 172; Chuck Walters, "My Favorite Rodeo Story," *Rodeo Sports News*, February 15, 1957. See also Davis, *Gospel of Kindness*, 179–84.
30. Hoy, "Origins and Originality of Rodeo," 29; see also LeCompte, "Hispanic Roots of American Rodeo," 60; LeCompte, "Wild West Frontier Days, Roundups and Stampedes," 55; Myres, *Ranch in Spanish Texas*, 30.
31. Sacks, "Charles Fletcher Lummis," 166; Thornton, "San Diego's First Cabrillo Celebration," 172.
32. Stoeltje, "Power and the Ritual Genres," 143–47.
33. Slotkin, *Regeneration through Violence*, 22.
34. "Last Day of the Races," *Aspen Tribune* (CO), August 23, 1898. See also Sacks, "Charles Fletcher Lummis," 147.
35. Brisendine, *Old Cowboys Never Die*, 27; see also Kelm, *Wilder West*, 140.
36. Branch, *Cowboy and His Interpreters*, 95.
37. Sacks, "Charles Fletcher Lummis," 162. See also Smith, *Virgin Land*, 122–24.
38. Branch, *Cowboy and His Interpreters*, 95. See also Barrows, *Ubet*, 192; Jordan, "Pistol Packin' Cowboy," 76. See also Dobie, *Longhorns*, 87–106; Webb, *Great Plains*, 264–67.
39. "Rough Riders," *Heppner Gazette* (OR), September 8, 1896; LeCompte, "Hispanic Roots of American Rodeo," 63–64. See also Lawrence, *Rodeo*, 45–46; Smith, *Virgin Land*, 88–98.
40. Baxter, "Sport on the Rio Grande," 249; Hoy, "Origins and Originality of Rodeo," 31.
41. Lause, *Great Cowboy Strike*, 85–136; White, *It's Your Misfortune*, 345; White, "Animals of Enterprise," 262–65.
42. White, *It's Your Misfortune*, 345; White, "Animals of Enterprise," 262–65.
43. Howard, *Montana*, 158–65; Lause, *Great Cowboy Strike*, 162–63.
44. Cronon, *Nature's Metropolis*, 222; Igler, *Industrial Cowboys*, 122–74; Jordan, *North American Cattle-Ranching Frontiers*, 267–74; White, "Animals of Enterprise," 261–62.
45. Howard, *Montana*, 140–46.
46. Hough, *Cowboy*, 177.
47. "Roping Texas Steers," *Cheyenne Daily Leader*, June 26, 1890.
48. "Roping Texas Steers," *Cheyenne Daily Leader*, June 26, 1890.
49. Dobie, "First Cattle in Texas," 180, 183, 190. See also Worcester, *Texas Longhorn*, 66–80. In contrast, cattle producers favoring heavy beef breeds, such as those at

railroad feedlots in Illinois and Kansas, tended to dismiss longhorns and other southwestern cattle as cheap "Texan scrub cattle" due to their descent from old Spanish stock (Hoganson, "Meat in the Middle," 1031, 1042–44).
50. Branch, *Cowboy and His Interpreters*, 12. By contrast, shorthorn and heavy beef cattle breeders in the Midwest ridiculed Texan cattle as degenerate since they were descended from old Spanish stock and left for decades to manage their own reproduction. Hoganson, "Meat in the Middle," 1042.
51. Christiansen, "Extinction of Wild Cattle," 93; see also Brand, *Cowboy and His Interpreters*, 13; Dobie, "First Cattle in Texas," 186–89, 192.
52. Christiansen, "Extinction of Wild Cattle," 93–94. For the broader idea that beef cattle are calm around people on horseback but "mildly outraged by the spectacle of a man afoot," see Barrows, *Ubet*, 82–83.
53. Jordan, *North American Cattle-Ranching Frontiers*, 275; Slatta, *Cowboys of the Americas*, 19. In the next century, Frank Dobie would celebrate feral longhorns as "Bovine Pioneers in a Harsh Land!" who made a "conquest of the West." Indeed, popular veneration of the Texas longhorn seems to have been more intense during the twentieth century, verging into the realm of tall tale. Louis Kleber's 1972 *History Today* account embellished their reputation thusly: "The cowboy found the longhorn as independent as himself and possessed of a perverse nature that sharply contrasted with the docility of domestic cattle. In 1854, the *St Louis Intelligencer* declared that they had 'seen buffaloes that were more civilized.' The longhorn was as wild as the wild west." Dobie, "First Cattle in Texas," 173; Kleber, "Era of the American Cowboy," 340. See also the cover of the 1980 University of Texas Press edition of Dobie's *The Longhorns*, https://www.amazon.com/Longhorns-J-Frank-Dobie/dp/029274627X.
54. White, "It's Your Misfortune," 220–21.
55. Hoganson, "Meat in the Middle," 1028–31; Worcester, *Texas Longhorn*, 66; White, *It's Your Misfortune*, 221, 223.
56. Hoganson, "Meat in the Middle," 1029; Ward, *Cowboy at Work*, 62.
57. Jordan, *North American Cattle-Ranching Frontiers*, 232, 267. Specht, "Rise, Fall, and Rebirth of the Texas Longhorn," 350.
58. Ward, *Cowboy at Work*, 62; see also, Webb, *Great Plains*, 239.
59. *Chico Enterprise*, quoted in "A Very Narrow Escape," *Sacramento Daily Union*, July 26, 1875.
60. "A Dangerous Steer," *The Dalles Daily Chronicle* (OR), April 4, 1894.
61. Explanatory anthropomorphism is a common phenomenon in human-animal relations, especially before the later twentieth-century advent of ethology and animal welfare science research. Specifically, it was, and is, a way of coping with the limited means of communication between animals and people, whereby people tend to infer the motivation of animal behavior from its apparent function, results, or emotional effect on a human viewer. "With this approach," Randall Lockwood explains, "we are inclined to offer circular definitions and explanations of animal behavior, thinking that by naming a behavior we have explained its

basis." Lockwood, "Anthropomorphism Is Not a Four-letter Word," in Hoage, ed., *Perceptions of Animals*, 48–49. See also Fudge, *Animal*, 26–27.
62. See, for instance, Adams, *Log of a Cowboy*, 174–75; Brand, *Cowboy and His Interpreters*, 12–13; Stanley, *Life and Adventures of the American Cow-boy*, 31.
63. Jacobs, *Cattle and Us*, 38.
64. Adams, *Log of a Cowboy*, 166, 175; Hough, *Cowboy*, 65; Siringo, *Lone Star Cowboy*, 39; Stanley, *Life and Adventures of the American Cow-boy*, 14. For example, Hereford beef cattle and Holstein cows are generally very docile, and bred to be so, while Brahma or Angus cattle, especially bulls or cows with a calf in tow, can be very dangerous to people on foot. Jacobs, *Cattle and Us*, 38.
65. LeCompte, "Hispanic Roots of American Rodeo," 58–59.
66. "Busting Steers for Amusement," *Oregonian* (Portland), July 18, 1909; reprinted in part in various places, including "A Cruel Sport," *Rathdrum Tribune* (ID), July 22, 1910.
67. "Steer Roping Feat," *Daily East Oregonian* (Pendleton, OR), March 21, 1908; Hoganson, "Meat in the Middle," 1044; Sacks, "Charles Fletcher Lummis," 147.
68. Baxter, *Cowboy Park*, 118; Jordan, *Rodeo History and Legends*, 13.
69. White, *It's Your Misfortune*, 220–21.
70. Ward, *Cowboy at Work*, 60; see also Dary, *Cowboy Culture*, 145.
71. By the mid-twentieth century, cattlemen tended to sell steers at two years of age and it became unusual to see a four-year-old steer at the slaughterhouse any longer. Jacobs, *Cattle and Us*, 39.
72. Liberty and Head, *Working Cowboy*, 51. The screw-worm is the flesh-eating, larval form of the parasitic fly *Cochliomyia hominivorax*. Ward, *Cowboy at Work*, 61; see also Erickson, *Modern Cowboy*, 105–6; Jacobs, *Cattle and Us*, 34–36.
73. Liberty and Head, *Working Cowboy*, 51–52; see also Jacobs, *Cattle and Us*, 34–35.
74. Liberty and Head, *Working Cowboy*, 51–52.
75. Ward, *Cowboy at Work*, 62.
76. Westermeier, *Man, Beast, Dust*, 54.
77. Dary, *Cowboy Culture*, 148–57.
78. "Roping Texas Steers," *Cheyenne Daily Leader*, June 26, 1890.
79. Baxter, "Sport on the Rio Grande," 250; Baxter, "Ropers and Rangers," 318, 327. In the Southwest, the steer was given a seventy-five or one-hundred-yard head start, further north only fifty, which produced quicker roping times in areas with a smaller pool of expert ropers.
80. H. D. Gough, "Steer Busting," *Wyoming State Tribune* (Cheyenne), July 27, 1907.
81. Doss, "Shoot-Out," in *Redrawing Boundaries*, 50–51; Goetzmann, *West of the Imagination*, 267–73.
82. Tyler, *Prints of the West*, 130; see also Dippie, "Chop! Chop!: Progress in the Presentation of Western Visual History," 492, 496. In books and folios published in the 1880s and 1890s featuring the latest photography, photographers and their publishers often combined plain, documentary images of landscape or people with

"inventive engravings" that, Martha Sandweiss shows, evoked "western violence, a theme so deeply ingrained in popular literature and myth about the West (and so utterly absent from eyewitness photographs) that audiences would not only *expect* such imagery but would be predisposed to accept its veracity" because it told a familiar story about the West. Sandweiss, *Print the Legend*, 288–89, 323–24.
83. Tyler, *Prints of the West*, 130. See also Dippie, "Visual West," in Milner et al, eds. *Oxford History of the American West*, 692; Hassrick, ed. "Where's the Art in Western Art?" in *Redrawing Boundaries*, 9–10; Angela Miller, "Chasing the Phantom: Cultural Memory in the Image of the West," in *Redrawing Boundaries*, 71; Murdoch, *American West*, 34–42.
84. Goetzmann and Goetzmann, *West of the Imagination*, 238–39. See also Derry, "Corset and Broncs," 4; Kasson, *Buffalo Bill's Wild West*, 110–11, 225–36; Rosa and May, *Buffalo Bill*, 33–45, 110, 133.
85. "Cowboy's Fall," *Temple Daily Times* (TX), October 19, 1887.
86. Some historians have replicated this sort of doublethink tactic in their writing as well; see, for instance, Thornton, "San Diego's First Cabrillo Celebration," 177.
87. Rowe, *Sport, Culture and the Media*, 122–23.
88. Sandweiss, *Print the Legend*, 323.
89. "Roping Texas Steers," *Cheyenne Daily Leader*, June 26, 1890.
90. Nance, "Game Stallions," 364.
91. "The Acme of Success," *Weekly Democratic Statesman* (Austin, TX), November 2, 1882; see also Hough, *Cowboy*, 104–6.
92. Starrs, *Let the Cowboy Ride*, 27–29.
93. "Cowboy Reunion," *Daily Inter-Ocean* [Chicago], August 31, 1896.
94. "Numerous Papers throughout the State," *Salida Mail* (CO), September 21, 1897.
95. "Objects to Wild West Exhibits," *Daily Capital Journal* (Salem, OR), November 23, 1912. See also "Busting Steers for Amusement," *Oregonian* (Portland), July 18, 1909.
96. "Cowboy's Bad Work," *Salt Lake Herald*, November 23, 1895.
97. Baxter, "Sport on the Rio Grande," 258.
98. Westermeier, "Cowboy Sports and the Humane Society," 244.
99. Beers, *For the Prevention of Cruelty*, 85–90.
100. Westermeier, "Cowboy Sports and the Humane Society," 241.
101. Pearson, *Rights of the Defenseless*, 80–81
102. Goetzmann and Goetzmann, *West of the Imagination*, 265–66.
103. "Austin Fair," *San Marcos Free Press* (TX), October 4, 1883.
104. Baxter, *Cowboy Park*, 116, 118, 126, 136; Jordan, *North American Cattle-Ranching Frontiers*, 267–72; LeCompte, "Hispanic Roots of American Rodeo," 62.
105. "A Needed Exhibition," *Austin Weekly Statesman* (TX), October 18, 1883; "Numerous Papers throughout the State," *Salida Mail* (CO), September 21, 1897; Baxter, "Ropers and Rangers," 339.
106. "The Portland Telegram," *The Athena Press* (OR), October 23, 1903.
107. Cothran, *Remembering the Modoc War*, 116–39.

108. "Busting Steers for Amusement," *Oregonian* (Portland, OR), July 18, 1909. The *Oregonian* article was reprinted in part in various places, for instance, "A Cruel Sport," *Rathdrum Tribune* (ID), July 22, 1910.
109. Westermeier, *Man, Beast, Dust*, 228–29.
110. Baxter, "Ropers and Rangers," 339–40; Pearson, *Rights of the Defenseless*, 80–81.
111. Chuck Walters, "My Favorite Rodeo Story," *Rodeo Sports News*, June 15, 1955.
112. *Penal Code and Code of Criminal Procedure of the State of Texas*, 1906 supplement, 28–29.
113. "Law Affecting Roping Contests," *The Cattleman* (June 1948), 8. See also Hoy, "Origins and Originality of Rodeo," 31.
114. "Objects to Wild West Exhibits," *Daily Capital Journal* (Salem, OR), November 23, 1912.
115. "Busting Steers for Amusement," *Oregonian* (Portland), July 18, 1909.
116. C. G. Coutant, quoted in Larson, *History of Wyoming*, 313, 319.
117. Larson, *History of Wyoming*, 374, see also 375–78.
118. Larson, *History of Wyoming*, 313–14, 349–51, 369–70.
119. "Busting Steers for Amusement," *Oregonian* (Portland), July 18, 1909; see also Harding [Barrow], "Passing of 'Busting,'" 139; Wyoming State Board, *Biannual Report, 1912*, 43. A few years later, one humane advocate explained the thinking in the anti-cruelty community about how the new cowboy sports damaged society: "Each year that [cowboy tournaments] go uncensored the performances become worse, exhibiting more brutality and newer and more cruel abuses. Cowboys grow bolder and the public more hardened. . . . Cruelty, someone has said, grows upon those who witness it. If we are so placed that we see cruel and brutal sights constantly we soon become calloused to them. It is much easier to cultivate a taste for cruelty than it is to create a sentiment against it." "Objects to Wild West Exhibits," *Daily Capital Journal* (Salem, OR), November 23, 1912.
120. "No More Roping Contests," *Daily East Oregonian* (Pendleton, OR), September 16, 1907.
121. "Busting Steers for Amusement," *Oregonian* (Portland, OR), July 18, 1909; reprinted in part in various places, including "A Cruel Sport," *Rathdrum Tribune* (ID), July 22, 1910.
122. H. D. Gough, "Steer Busting," *Wyoming Tribune* (Cheyenne), July 27, 1907.
123. "No More Roping Contests," *Daily East Oregonian* (Pendleton, OR), September 16, 1907.
124. Wyoming State Board, *Biannual Report*, 42–43.
125. Westermeier, *Man, Beast, Dust*, 242.
126. "Bar 'Busting,'" *Wyoming Tribune* (Cheyenne), July 26, 1907.
127. H. D. Gough, "No Roping," *Wyoming Tribune*, September 4, 1907.
128. There are countless examples, but see for instance: "Rides Maddened Steer," *Morning Oregonian*, October 8, 1903; "The Portland Telegram," *The Athena Press* (OR), October 23, 1903; "Busting Steers for Amusement," *Oregonian* (Portland, OR), July 18, 1909; "A Cruel Sport," *Rathdrum Tribune* (ID), July 22, 1910; "Objects

to Wild West Exhibits," *Daily Capital Journal* (Salem, OR), November 23, 1912; *Florence Tribune* (AZ) quoted in Baxter, "Ropers and Rangers," 340.
129. Baxter, *Cowboy Park*, 66–67; Baxter, "Ropers and Rangers," 342–43; Westermeier, *Man, Beast, Dust*, 45; Chuck Walters, "My Favorite Rodeo Story," *Rodeo Sports News*, June 15, 1955; Westermeier, "Cowboy Sports and the Humane Society," 247.
130. In those years, the society's provisions still allowed WHS officers to intervene to interrupt or prevent acts that mutilated, tortured, or tormented livestock, which would potentially have regulated branding, ear cutting, castration, and any cowboy tournament event employing a resistant horse or steer. *Wyoming Laws 1911*, 10–13. Yet, by 1920, the WHS had additionally stated publicly that the concepts of cruelty and mutilation in Wyoming animal protection did not apply to the known-painful dehorning of cattle. *Wyoming Laws 1920*, 11. Regarding the Wyoming Humane Society members' concerns about neglect and abuse of cattle and horses on remote ranches (although they were hardly in a position to police the problem), see for instance, Wyoming State Board, *Biannual Report 1912*, 30–31.
131. Westermeier, "Cowboy Sports and the Humane Society," 247.

## Chapter 2

1. Moulton and Moulton, *Steamboat*, 118–19.
2. Clayton Danks, quoted in Helen Clark, "Clayton Danks," *Western Horseman* (June 1961): 50–52, 96–99.
3. "Thrills and Throbs for State Fair Visitors," *Salt Lake Telegram*, September 30, 1914.
4. "Thrills and Throbs for State Fair Visitors," *Salt Lake Telegram*, September 30, 1914; "State Fair Program," *Salt Lake Telegram*, October 6, 1914; "Sensational Midway in Full Swing at State Fair," *Salt Lake Telegram*, October 6, 1914.
5. "State Fair to Close in Blaze of Glory," *Salt Lake Tribune*, October 10, 1914; "Rain Will Not Stop Fair Races Today," *Salt Lake Tribune*, October 10, 1914.
6. Gillespie and Burns, *Steamboat*, 10. Rodeo horses "receive bite wounds from other horses; kick wounds from over-crowded corrals; and tears and abrasions as a result of their contact with trailers and chutes. Unfortunately for the animal, the skin and hair covers bruises and broken ribs. . . . Transport injuries and fighting are major causes of injuries in horses. Rodeo horses are constantly in transit." Larson, "Rodeo Is Cruel Entertainment," 117.
7. Paul Hansen quoted in "Steamboat Sleeps at Old City Dump," *Wyoming State Tribune*, June 2, 1955.
8. Gillespie and Burns, *Steamboat*, 10. In an even more gruesome but possibly untrue retelling, Clayton Danks explained that Steamboat had been stabled in Cheyenne favoring his painful and swollen limb. At one point, he had gotten spooked and jumped up on his good rear leg, shattering it. Helen Clark, "Clayton Danks," *The Western Horseman* (June 1961): 50–52, 96–99.

9. "Old Steamboat Put to Death," *Billboard*, October 24, 1914; "Old Steamboat, World's Worst Bucking Broncho, Mercifully Shot Today," *Wyoming Tribune* (Cheyenne), October 14, 1914; "Old Steamboat Killed to End His Suffering," *Cheyenne State Leader*, October 15, 1914.
10. Gillespie and Burns, *Steamboat*, 11.
11. "Old Steamboat, World's Worst Bucking Broncho, Mercifully Shot Today," *Wyoming Tribune* (Cheyenne), October 14, 1914.
12. Moulton and Moulton, *Steamboat*, 32–33. On Tom Horn, see, for instance, Larson, *History of Wyoming*, 372–74.
13. Gillespie and Burns, *Steamboat*, 11.
14. One writer described the sunfisher thusly, "a hoss that twisted his body into a crescent, or, in other words, when he seemed to try to touch the ground with first one shoulder and then the other, lettin' the sunlight hit his belly. Such pitchin' was called 'sunfishin'." (Adams, *Old Time Cowhand*, 298).
15. Allen, *Rodeo Cowboys*, 112–15, 123–24.
16. LeCompte, *Cowgirls*, 9; Reba Perry Blakely, "The Three Studnick Brothers," *Rodeo News* (September 1978): 24, Rodeo Material Scrapbooks—"Rodeo Old-Timers" I (Cowgirls), 1937–1981, box 46, folder 7, PAL; Fred Nelson, "Heller in Skirts," *Outdoor Nebraskaland* (April 1965), 16–18, Rodeo Material Scrapbooks, "Rodeo Old-Timers" I (Cowgirls), 1937–1981, box 46, folder 7, PAL; Reddin, *Wild West Shows*, 192–93; Tavegia, "Sam Brownell," 9–11; Trolinger, "Samuel Thomas 'Booger Red' Privett," 142–51; Young, "Recalling a Texas Legend," 6.
17. LeCompte, *Cowgirls*, 2, 8.
18. "Wild West Shows Barred," *Billboard*, November 14, 1914.
19. W. G. Brown, "Rodeos, Past and Present Entertainments and What They Signify," reprinted in *The Billboard*, July 5, 1924, 71.
20. Reddin, *Wild West Shows*, 147, 151.
21. Bridger, *Buffalo Bill and Sitting Bull*, 13. The Miller Brothers 101 Ranch show was a demonstration specifically of ranch life, not the frontier, with multiple units on different routes and offering Indigenous and Mexican performers, cowboy sports, parades, and Cody-style dramas like staged hunting or Indian attack scenarios. Reddin, *Wild West Shows*, 162–65.
22. Trolinger, "Samuel Thomas 'Booger Red' Privett," 144–46; see also, Young, "Recalling a Texas Legend," 8; Reddin, *Wild West Shows*, 163.
23. Reba Perry Blakely, "The Three Studnick Brothers," *Rodeo News* (September 1978): 24, Rodeo Material Scrapbooks, "Rodeo Old-Timers" I (Cowgirls), 1937–1981, box 46, folder 7, PAL.
24. LeCompte, *Cowgirls*, 13–14, 36–69.
25. Tavegia, "Sam Brownell," 9; see also LeCompte, *Cowgirls*, 87; Smith, "Hoosier Hollywood Cowboys," 10; Young, "Recalling a Texas Legend," 10.
26. Andrea Galliher, "Rodeo Was Their Business," *Fence Post*, May 18, 1987, Rodeo Material Scrapbooks, "Rodeo Old-Timers" I (Cowgirls), 1937–1981, box 46, folder 7, PAL.

27. Nash, *American West in the Twentieth Century*, 26–27.
28. "Grandmother Recalls How She Rode Broncs," [newspaper title missing], December 4, 1977, Rodeo Material Scrapbooks, "Rodeo Old-Timers" I (Cowgirls), 1937–1981, box 46, folder 7, PAL. See also LeCompte, *Cowgirls*, 2.
29. Gillespie and Burns, *Steamboat*, 7.
30. "C. B. Irwin's adopted son, Roy Kivett, got killed in steer roping when his horse turned a somersault over him and crushed him to death. It was a very sad time for the Irwin family and sad for all who attended the show." Reba Perry Blakely, "The Three Studnick Brothers," *Rodeo News* (September 1978): 24, 34, Rodeo Material Scrapbooks, "Rodeo Old-Timers" I (Cowgirls), 1937–1981, box 46, folder 7, PAL.
31. Interviewed in the 1970s, Frank said his brother Bob had "died by his own hand in 1963" due to old rodeo injuries. "He had arthritic hips and broke the left one which would not heal and then injured the other hip. He went through indescribable pain and did not live long enough to benefit from modern plastic replacements that could have saved his life." Reba Perry Blakely, "The Three Studnick Brothers," *Rodeo News* (September 1978): 34, Rodeo Material Scrapbooks, "Rodeo Old-Timers" I (Cowgirls), 1937–1981, box 46, folder 7, PAL.
32. LeCompte, *Cowgirls*, 29–31, 78.
33. Gillespie and Burns, *Steamboat*, 2.
34. Young and Sparks, *Cattle in the Cold Desert*, 217.
35. Dobie, *Mustang*, 128; Young and Sparks, *Cattle in the Cold Desert*, 217.
36. Hämäläinen, "Rise and Fall of Plains Indians Horse Cultures," 851. See also Carr Childers, *Size of the Risk*, 156.
37. Siringo, *Texas Cow Boy*, 328–36.
38. Dobie, *Mustang*, 132–34; Carr Childers, *Size of the Risk*, 157.
39. Carr Childers, *Size of the Risk*, 159; de Steiguer, *Wild Horses*, 43–45; Wyman, *Wild Horse of the West*, 264–67; Young and Sparks, *Cattle in the Cold Desert*, 218–20.
40. Hämäläinen, "The Rise and Fall of Plains Indians Horse Cultures," 838–41.
41. Flores, *American Serengeti*, 64.
42. Flores, *American Serengeti*, 70.
43. Jordan, *North American Cattle-Ranching Frontiers*, 155.
44. Flores, *American Serengeti*, 74; see also 67–69.
45. Larson, *History of Wyoming*, 168, 178.
46. Veterinarian Peggy Larson said of such horses used in smaller, more remote rodeos in the 1980s that they were "usually not given grain regularly if at all, receive[d] little or no veterinary care, and many receive[d] inferior hay or fend[ed] for themselves in winter by pawing for feed in the snow." Larson, quoted in Clifton, "Anti-Rodeo Vet Was Performer."
47. Dean and Wilson, "Horse Power in the Modern City," 105; Greene, *Horses at Work*, 69–70, 194–96; Tarr and McShane, *Horse in the City*, 35, 58, 137.
48. The story continues, "Sam Moore, foreman of the Swan Company, bought the young horse and trimmed away the protruding bone. The horse was left with a peculiar whistle. Cowboy Jimmy Danks told the Swan foreman that the horse

'sounds like a steamboat.' With that, the bucking horse had a name." "The Bucking Horse on the License Plate," Wyoming State Archives, https://www.wyohistory.org/encyclopedia/wyomings-long-lived-bucking-horse, See also Gillespie and Burns, *Steamboat*, 13.
49. Beutler, "Broncs, Bulls and Contracts," 48–52; Reba Perry Blakely, "Pauline Irwin Sawyer—Trainer, Winner," *World of Rodeo and Western Heritage* (February 1980): 27–28.
50. "Grandmother Recalls How She Rode Broncs," [newspaper title missing], December 4, 1977, Rodeo Material Scrapbooks, "Rodeo Old-Timers" I (Cowgirls), 1937–1981, box 46, folder 7, PAL.
51. Woerner, Belly *Full of Bedsprings*, 35.
52. "Cowboys Contest," *Rocky Mountain News* (Denver), October 15, 1887.
53. "Cowboys Contest," *Rocky Mountain News* (Denver), October 15, 1887.
54. "Exposition Premiums Awarded," *Rocky Mountain News* (Denver), October 15, 1887.
55. "Cowboy Tournament," *Northwestern Live Stock Journal* (Cheyenne), October 21, 1887.
56. Lawrence, *Hoofbeats and Society*, 83.
57. Examples are too numerous to note here, but see for example, "Cowboys' Work and Ways," *Frank Leslie's Illustrated Newspaper*, April 9, 1887, 118; George Pattullo, "Corazón," [Illustrations by C. M. Russell] *McClure's Magazine* 35 (June 1910): 300–307; Slatta, *Cowboys of the Americas*, 75.
58. Slatta, *Cowboys of the Americas*, 77.
59. Westermeier, *Man, Beast, Dust*, 174.
60. Pattullo, "Corazón," 306.
61. Westermeier, *Man, Beast, Dust*, 173.
62. This literature is sizeable and growing. See, for instance, Fowler, Kennedy, and Marlin, "A Comparison of the Monty Roberts Technique," 302.
63. Platt, "'Ride 'em Cowboy!,'" 59. On the longer history of horse taming through gentling and positive reinforcement see, for instance, Davis, *Gospel of Kindness*, 15, 38; Nance, *Entertaining Elephants*, 78.
64. Westermeier, *Man, Beast, Dust*, 172–74; see also Slatta, *Cowboys of the Americas*, 136.
65. Platt, "'Ride 'em Cowboy!,'" 59; Trolinger, "Samuel Thomas 'Booger Red' Privett," 144.
66. Westermeier, *Man, Beast, Dust*, 173; see also, Slatta, *Cowboys of the Americas*, 75–77.
67. Slatta, *Cowboys of the Americas*, 74.
68. Gilbreath, "I Was a Cowboy Once," 16.
69. Ewers, *Horse in Blackfoot Indian Culture*, 60–64.
70. Everett Brisendine, quoted in Griffith, "Cowboy Poetry of Everett Brisendine," 38.
71. Ed Strickland, quoted in Barker, ed., "History of the Strickland and Taylor Families," 17; Santee, *Men and Horses*, 169.
72. Platt, "'Ride 'em Cowboy!,'" 58–59; see also Slatta, *Cowboys*, 77–78.

73. Sheppard, "Bronco Busters," 251.
74. Griffith, "Cowboy Poetry of Everett Brisendine," 39.
75. Brownell, *Rodeos*, 37.
76. Brandon, "Bernalillo County," 70. See also, for instance, "The Bucking Horse," *Frank Leslie's Illustrated Newspaper*, May 18, 1889, 259.
77. Platt, "'Ride 'em Cowboy!,'" 53.
78. Jimmy Danks, quoted in *Laramie Republican Boomerang*, 1901; Moulten and Moulten, *Steamboat*, 20.
79. Moulten and Moulten, *Steamboat*, 50.
80. Pattullo, "Corazón," 302.
81. "Thirty-Sixth Annual State Fair Complete," *Salt Lake Tribune*, October 3, 1914.
82. Hydrocyanic gas was produced by dropping potassium cyanide into sulfuric acid and water. See "Bisulphate of Carbon and Tree-Root Lice," *The Chanute Times* (Kansas), July 21, 1899; "To Destroy Ground Hogs," *Meade County News* (Kansas), September 14, 1911.
83. Howard, *Montana*, 237–38. See also Clancy, *My Fifty Years in Rodeo*, 66–67.
84. In California, just a few years after steer busting had supposedly been abolished, rodeo people suffered another public scandal, in California. Rodeo Salinas, founded 1911, had in early August 1912 produced an especially gruesome event in which many animals were killed, visibly injured, and gratuitously terrorized. Nonetheless the State Fair Association asked Salinas producer Frank Griffin to ship the whole show to the state capitol for the third week of September that year. "Big Cowboy Show State Fair Plan," *Sacramento Union*, August 4, 1912. When they visited the Sacramento State Fair thereafter, Hennessey and some colleagues insisted the cowboys required "unrelenting surveillance . . . to prevent abuse of their animals." "Objects to Wild West Exhibits," *Daily Capital Journal* (Salem, OR), November 23, 1912.
85. "Objects to Wild West Exhibits," *Daily Capital Journal* (Salem, OR), November 23, 1912.
86. "Objects to Wild West Exhibits," *Daily Capital Journal* (Salem, OR), November 23, 1912. These reports came from a San Francisco SPCA investigation and letters to their offices, which appeared in their publication *Our Animals* and were reprinted in at least one friendly newspaper in Oregon. The state fair in Sacramento had drawn the attention of humane advocates for some time. "Society Condemns Fair Exhibition," *San Francisco Call*, August 26, 1911.
87. Westermeier, *Man, Beast, Dust*, 200.
88. "Objects to Wild West Exhibits," *Daily Capital Journal* (Salem, OR), November 23, 1912.
89. A generation after the publication of *Black Beauty* and almost half a century after Henry Bergh and other advocates had first begun checking on the health of Boston's work horses, issuing citations and advice to negligent drivers, out West many middle-class citizens in Canada and the U.S. believed that a civilized society was kind to animals. They argued that public displays of intentional

animal teasing, suffering, and injury were unnecessary and detrimental to all of society. "Each year that [cowboy tournaments] go uncensored the performances become worse, exhibiting more brutality and newer and more cruel abuses. Cowboys grow bolder and the public more hardened and more accustomed to the spectacles they present . . . It is much easier to cultivate a taste for cruelty than it is to create a sentiment against it," said one animal advocate. In that view, rodeo people were actively creating animal suffering, and with considerable public support. "Objects to Wild West Exhibits," *Daily Capital Journal* (Salem, OR), November 23, 1912.
90. Swanton quoted in Westermeier, "Cowboy Sports and the Humane Society," 247.
91. "Banishing Cruelties from the Rodeo," *National Humane Review* 8, no. 11 (November 1920): 218; see also Westermeier, "Cowboy Sports and the Humane Society," 246.
92. Fred Nelson, "Heller in Skirts," *Outdoor Nebraskaland* (April 1965), 16–18, Rodeo Material Scrapbooks, "Rodeo Old-Timers" I (Cowgirls), 1937–1981, box 46, folder 7, PAL.
93. There appear to be no veterinary or animal welfare studies of the flank strap's effect on horses, just the practical experience of people who have worked with them and see that the strap or rope behind the ribs causes horses to kick up and back more dependably, although it does not have that effect on all horses. Countless rodeo advocates insist the bucking strap causes no physical pain to animals. See, for instance, Corey, "Welfare Issues in the Rodeo Horse," 257; Schonholtz, "Animals in Rodeo," 1248. Others counter that on horses, the strap causes anxiety or fear that drives horses to kick into their rear blind spot. See, for instance, Franzky et al, "Animal Welfare Legal Aspects of Rodeo Events," 94.
94. Jack Burrows, "The Greatest Bronc Buster Who Ever Lived: Manny Airola of Angels Camp," *American West* 20, no. 3 (1983): 55.
95. "Cowboy Reunion," *Daily Inter-Ocean* [Chicago], August 31, 1896.
96. "Cowboy Reunion," *Daily Inter-Ocean* [Chicago], August 31, 1896; Brownell, *Rodeos*, 78–79.
97. Brownell, *Rodeos*, 78–79.
98. Trolinger, "Samuel Thomas 'Booger Red' Privett," 142.
99. Tavegia, "Sam Brownell," 10.
100. Westermeier, "Cowboy Sports and the Humane Society," 246.
101. "The Useless Spur," *National Humane Review* 7, no. 11 (November 1919): 214.
102. Sydney H. Coleman, "The Wild West Round-Up Must Go," *National Humane Review* 7, no. 11 (November 1919): 204 [203–4, 218–19].
103. Moulton and Moulton, *Steamboat*, 58.
104. "World's Best Riders in Final Contests," *Wyoming Tribune*, August 21, 1909. *Union Pacific Magazine* joked that bucking horses at the 1927 Pendleton Round-Up were "anarchists" determined to unseat cowboy kings and queens (i.e., riders). Vincent H. Hunter, "The Pendleton Round-Up September 14–17," *Union*

*Pacific Magazine* (September 1927): 15, Rodeo Material Scrapbooks, "Rodeo Old-Timers" I (Cowgirls), 1937–1981, box 46, folder 7, PAL. See also, Siringo, *Lone Star Cowboy*, 120.
105. Bertha French Ratliff, "Cheyenne's Champion Cowgirl," *Denver Post*, July 24, 1966 in Rodeo Material Scrapbooks, "Rodeo Old-Timers" I (Cowgirls), 1937–1981, box 46, folder 7, PAL.
106. "Made in America," *Eastern Utah Advocate*, October 15, 1914; "Old Steamboat, World's Worst Bucking Broncho, Mercifully Shot Today," *Wyoming Tribune* (Cheyenne), October 14, 1914.
107. Gillespie and Burns, *Steamboat*, 2.
108. Gillespie and Burns, *Steamboat*, 2.
109. Westermeier, "Cowboy Sports and the Humane Society," 245–47.
110. Hough, *Story of the Cowboy*, 176–77.
111. Gail Downing, quoted in Rowdy Waddy, "The Corral," *The Billboard*, May 13, 1916.
112. LeCompte, *Cowgirls*, 10–11.
113. LeCompte, 10–12; Livingstone, *Cowboy Spirit*, 65, 71; Westermeier, *Man, Beast, Dust*, 50.
114. *Wyoming Tribune*, Oct. 14–15, Dec. 15, 1914.
115. *Wyoming Tribune*, Oct. 14–15, Dec. 15, 1914.
116. "Steamboat Sleeps at Old City Dump," *Wyoming State Tribune*, June 2, 1955.
117. Gillespie and Burns, *Steamboat*, i.
118. Gillespie and Burns, *Steamboat*, 11.
119. "Rodeo Material Scrapbook 'Steamboat' ca. 1904–1992," PAL.
120. Gillespie and Burns, *Steamboat*, 4.
121. Gillespie and Burns, *Steamboat*, 10.

### Chapter 3

1. Guy Weadick to James A. Shoemaker, 25 July 1912, Calgary Exhibition & Stampede correspondence, 1912–1953, WEA.
2. Kelm, *Wilder West*, 25; Livingstone, *Cowboy Spirit*, 14, 33.
3. "Calgary Turns Back Clock to Rough and Ready Frontier Days," and "Indians and Old Timers Colorful in Big Parade," *Calgary Herald*, 11 July 1927, 9; "A Welcome to Our Visitors," *Calgary Herald*, 11 July 1927, 10; Lounsberry, "Wild West Shows and the Canadian West," 147–48, 151–52.
4. Colpitts, *Game in the Garden*, 103–8; Wetherell, "Making Tradition," 29; Campbell, "The Stampede," 105–6. See also Konrad, "Barren Bulls and Charging Cows," 153; Seiler, "Riding Broncs and Taming Contradictions," 179–82. At the turn of the century, some complained that Alberta was "the mild West," instead of a Wild West, due to its (supposed) lack of range wars and other interpersonal violence, which were guaranteed by the Royal Canadian Mounted Police. The myth that the Canadian West experienced no real violence as settlers colonized the place is

a persistent one, which I discuss further in the epilogue. Katerberg, "A Northern Vision"; Francis, *National Dreams*, 29–51; Oosterom, "Mild West."
5. Derry, *Horses in Society*, 46–48.
6. Leisl Carr Childers explains, "Horses became objects of consumption rather than partners in work." Carr Childers, *Size of the Risk*, 171; see also Little, "Ox and Horse Power," 86–87.
7. Kelm, *Wilder West*, 22.
8. Campbell, "The Stampede: Cowtown's Sacred Cow," 103–4; Konrad, "Barren Bulls and Charging Cows," 145–64.
9. Derry, *Ontario's Cattle Kingdom*, 116–48; Hoganson, "Meat in the Middle," 1031–35.
10. Brado, *Cattle Kingdom*, 155–57, 176–93; Elofson, *So Far and Yet So Close*, 7–24, 143–64; Elofson, *Cowboys, Gentlemen, and Cattle Thieves*, 7–15; Foran, "Land Speculation and Urban Development," 203–20; Wise, *Producing Predators*, 39, 69–71, 82.
11. Morris, "Fort Macleod of the Borderlands." Rodeo managers across the North American West communicated by mail, sent schedule and purse announcements to be posted one another's bulletin boards, and visited one another's shows. Thus did they slowly build a supportive network that drove a uniformity of rodeo performance conventions, but would keep all the community rodeos afloat since rodeo competitors, contract acts, and stock suppliers might make a part-time living by traveling the network. Westermeier, *Man, Beast, Dust*, 50.
12. Various participant lists, 1912, 1925–1930, STA.
13. Pomeroy, *In Search of the Golden West*, 175–81.
14. Kelm, *Wilder West*, 27–28.
15. Kelm, *Wilder West*, 33.
16. Woerner, *Belly Full of Bedsprings*, 35.
17. Kelm, *A Wilder West*, 71.
18. LeCompte, *Cowgirls*, 70, 82.
19. "Canadian Twisters Turn from Decorating to Dogging and Thoroughly Trounce U.S. Top Steer Wrestlers," *Rodeo Sports News*, May 15, 1957.
20. Fredriksson, *American Rodeo*, 151; Wetherell, "Making Tradition," 26–28.
21. Only a small number of Canadian venues in Alberta and Saskatchewan adopted chuckwagon racing, which went unsanctioned by any of the broad rodeo administrative bodies, and has come to be governed by the World Professional Chuckwagon Association and the Canadian Professional Chuckwagon Association. Nonetheless, although the sport is very expensive for competitors, purses are unusually high among rodeo events for the handful of teams involved. Competitive chuckwagon races are not to be confused with the activities of the American Chuck Wagon Association, which sponsors gatherings and cook-offs featuring restored chuck wagon outfits from the era of open-grass ranching.
22. LeCompte, *Cowgirls*, 14.
23. Burstyn, *Rites of Men*, 107–9.
24. Woerner, *Belly Full of Bedsprings*, 30–32.

25. LeCompte, *Cowgirls*, 70–76, 86–88.
26. Wetherell, "Making Tradition," 21–45.
27. "Big Opening Day," *Calgary Herald*, August 27, 1919, 12.
28. "Ridin' Pretty" and "Used Cars—Stampede Visitors Look!!" *Calgary Herald*, July 9, 1927, 29.
29. "Stampede Twister and Expert Navigator," *Calgary Herald*, July 12, 1927, 1.
30. "The Stampede," *New York Times*, August 2, 1916; "'Stampede' Seeks $35,000," *New York Times*, August 14, 1916; "Stampeders Get Some Pay," *New York Times*, August 17, 1916. Rodeos outside the West often took place inside arenas and venues designed for other sports, like baseball, and thus did not include a carnival or Indian village feature. LeCompte, *Cowgirls*, 9–10.
31. Kelm, *Wilder West*, 13.
32. Little, "Ox and Horse Power," 74.
33. Kelm, *Wilder West*, 70–71; Livingstone, *Cowboy Spirit*, 76–87.
34. Little, "Ox and Horse Power," 74; Thistle, *Resettling the Range*, 54–61.
35. Tavegia, "Sam Brownell," 11. See also Reba Perry Blakely, "The Three Studnick Brothers," *Rodeo News* (September 1978): 16, Rodeo Material Scrapbooks, "Rodeo Old-Timers" I (Cowgirls), 1937–1981, box 46, folder 7, PAL. The business correspondence of the Calgary Stampede contains dozens of letters from rodeo competitors who wrote asking if the rodeo needed any "bad ones" and offering up horses for lease or sale.
36. Jordan, *Rodeo History and Legends*, 12.
37. Dick [Howard Steen] to Guy Weadick, June 20, 1930, "Events Records—1930," M2160/94, STA.
38. Guy Weadick to F. R. Martin, August 12, 1929, "Correspondence with Guy Weadick, 1928–1930," M2160/71, STA.
39. See for instance, "Bucking Horse List," "Events Records—1930," M2160/97, STA.
40. "List of Bucking Horses—1926 Stampede," "List of Stock Delivered to Clem Gardiner July 18, 1927," "List of Horses Purchases by Calgary Exhibition Co.," "Bucking Horse List 1927 Stampede," and "Bucking Horses 1927," series 7—"Events Records 1927," M-2160-89, STA. On Gardiner see Faulknor, *Turn Him Loose*, 95.
41. Webb, *Great Plains*, 252–53.
42. Nance, "Who Was Greasy Sal?" 384. On bucking horse names as a way to satirize gender relations, see Kelm, *Wilder West*, 44.
43. The Calgary horse lists show that only a few of the names expressed the publicly rampant xenophobia or racism of the period, presumably to keep rodeo at arm's length from contemporary politics, although a "Pappoose" or "Sambo" appeared occasionally.
44. Kelm, *Wilder West*, 110–13.
45. "1927 Bucking Horses List Office Copy," series 7—"Events Records 1927," M-2160-89, STA; "1929 Bucking Horses List," series 7—"Events Records 1927," M-2160-91(a), STA. Greasy Sal and the other rough stock horses were valued

from $100.00 to $200.00 each. Clem Gardiner to Guy Weadick, 8 July 1927, series 7—"Events Records 1927," M-2160-89, STA.
46. Guy Weadick to F. R. Martin, August 12, 1929, "Correspondence with Guy Weadick, 1928–1930," M2160/71, STA.
47. [unsigned] to E. L. Richardson, July 18th, 1933, "Bucking Horse Records—1933," M2160/111, STA.
48. A "distorted image of him in his most reckless moments, in his hours of gross merry-making, when he toned down his constitution with frontier whisky and rode his horse into saloons and caracoled crazily through the town, shooting and whooping." "The Cowboys," *Billboard*, October 2, 1915.
49. William E. Hawks, "The West That Was," *Billboard*, October 2, 1915. The degree to which rodeo sports misrepresented actual range work was also a worry in the 1920s and 1930s. Barrows, *Ubet*, 152.
50. LeCompte, *Cowgirls*, 75–76.
51. Livingstone, *Cowboy Spirit*, 50, 74.
52. Woerner, *Belly Full of Bedsprings*, 30.
53. Kelm, *Wilder West*, 110–12.
54. Larson, "Rodeo Is Cruel Entertainment," 117.
55. "Calls Rodeos Cruel," *New York Times*, June 29, 1934.
56. White, "Tony the Wonder Horse," 294, 348n.25.
57. "Oppose Chicago Rodeo," *New York Times*, July 12, 1925.
58. For instance, see the pamphlet *The Wild West Round-Up Must Go*, a reprint of a story from the November 1919 issue of the *National Humane Review*, publication of the American Humane Association.
59. Fredriksson speculates that anti-rodeo committees and activists were mostly opportunists "exploiting the cruelty angle" to shut down rodeos simply because they disliked the transient cowboys who invaded town at rodeo time. I do not find this view reflected in the considerable record of critics and reformers working with rodeos to refine them, rather than simply abolishing them, which Fredriksson herself notes. Fredriksson, *American Rodeo*, 152.
60. Fredriksson, *American Rodeo*, 154; Kelm, *Wilder West*, 113; Westermeier, "Cowboy Sports and the Humane Society"; Woerner, *Belly Full of Bedsprings*, 28.
61. "List of Contracted Bucking Horses," and handwritten note re: Sid Bannermann, series 7—"Events Records 1929," M-2160-92, STA.
62. "Bucking Horse List," "List of Bucking Horses Owned by Calgary Exhibition Association, June 27th, 1930," "Bucking Horse Contracts and Entries," all in "Events Records 1930," M2160/97, STA.
63. Brandon, "Bernalillo County," 70.
64. Fred Nelson, "Heller in Skirts," *Outdoor Nebraskaland* (April 1965), 16–18, Rodeo Material Scrapbooks, "Rodeo Old-Timers" I (Cowgirls), 1937–1981, box 46, folder 7, PAL.
65. Gary Moran, "A Rodeo with Fifty Candles," *The Dakota Farmer*, June 21, 1969, in folder 2/2 "Belle Fourche, South Dakota, 1969–1986," POR; see also Tipperary

monument, National Cowboy and Western Heritage Museum, Oklahoma City, Oklahoma.
66. Brownell, *Rodeos*, 125; "Early Belle Area Cowboy Heritage Basis for Modern Hills Roundup," n.d., unidentified newspaper article, "Belle Fourche, South Dakota, 1969–1986," POR.
67. Hell's Angel monument, National Cowboy and Western Heritage Museum, Oklahoma City, Oklahoma; see also ProRodeo Hall of Fame, "Hell's Angel," http://www.prorodeohalloffame.com/inductees/by-category/livestock/hells-angel.
68. Furlong, *Let 'Er Buck*, xii; see also Barrows, *Ubet;* Allen, *Rodeo Cowboys*, 109–30.
69. Clark, "Horseface Minstrelsy"; see also White, "Tony the Wonder Horse."
70. Marsden, "Rise of the Western Movie," 21–22; White, "Tony the Wonder Horse."
71. Lippman, *Public Opinion*, 64–69, 224.
72. "List of Stock Delivered to Clem Gardiner July 18, 1927," series 7—"Events Records 1927," M-2160-89, STA.
73. Dick Cosgrove to Guy Weadick, 24 May, 1930, series 7, "General Correspondence A—H 1930," M-2160-98, STA.
74. Guy Weadick to Dick Cosgrove, 30 May, 1930, series 7, "General Correspondence A—H 1930," M-2160-98, STA.
75. "List of Bucking Horses Owned by Calgary Exhibition Assoc. June 27, 1930," series 7, "Events records 1930," M-2160-97, STA.
76. In 1930, Greasy Sal was still owned by Exhibition Company, delivered to manager Dick Cosgrove "Horses Delivered to Dick Cosgrove," Stampede Fonds, series 7, "Events records 1930," M-2160-97, STA; but she did not appear on events records for 1930 or 1931: "Bucking Horses Calgary Stampede 1930," "Mr. Dillon's Bucking Horse List 1930," "Office Copy Bucking Horse List Stampede 1931," series 7, "Events records 1931," M-2160-97 and M-2160-101, STA.
77. Thomas, *Man and the Natural World*, 243, 303.
78. Greg Evans, quoted in "Cast-Off Calgary Stampede Horses Sent to Slaughterhouse," *CTV News*, May 31, 2012, https://www.ctvnews.ca/cast-off-calgary-stampede-horses-sent-to-slaughterhouse-1.833809.
79. Cindy Bray [comment] for "Cast-Off Calgary Stampede Horses Sent to Slaughterhouse," *CTV News*, May 31, 2012, https://www.ctvnews.ca/cast-off-calgary-stampede-horses-sent-to-slaughterhouse-1.833809.

### Chapter 4

1. Atherton, "Cattleman and Cowboy," 3.
2. Lex Connelly, quoted in Lamb, *Rodeo: Back of the Chutes*, 6.
3. Bernstein, *Wild Ride*, 115.
4. Burbick, *Rodeo Queens*, 54.
5. Wells, *Car Country*, 253–87.
6. Montana ranchman, quoted in Lawrence, *Hoofbeats and Society*, 87.

7. Carr Childers, *Size of the Risk*, 160; Little, "Ox and Horse," 85; Stillman, *Mustang*, 244–45; Westermeier, *Man, Beast, Dust*, 167; Wyman, *Wild Horse of the West*, 96–97, 132–36, 174–75; Young and Sparks, *Cattle in the Cold Desert*, 231. Similar patterns emerged in Canada, as well. See, for instance, Thistle, *Resettling the Range*, 54–61.
8. Quaker Oats Company, *Rockford: The Pet Food Story*, 3–6.
9. Edwards, "Horse Story"; Quaker Oats Company, *Rockford: The Pet Food Story*, 3–6.
10. Stillman, *Mustang*, 242–43; see also Carr Childers, *Size of the Risk*, 160; Wyman, *Wild Horse of the West*, 157, 204–8.
11. Wyman, *Wild Horse of the West*, 220–42; Young and Sparks, *Cattle in the Cold Desert*, 221.
12. Don Bell, "During Those Depression Days," manuscript, "Don Bell Rodeo Memoirs and Brief Histories," BEL.
13. Animal welfare science researchers would refer to this phenomenon as "confinement-induced aggression." Many species suffer from it in small spaces where natural hierarchies or social relations cannot take place. Even captive "tame" horses will at times exhibit aggression toward other horses if that horse is unfamiliar or if horses are confined to too small a space. Fureix, et al, "Exploring Aggression Regulation," 221.
14. See also, for instance, Geri Pursley, "The Man Behind Some of the PRCA's Greatest Broncs," *ProRodeo Sports News*, October 30, 1991, 38–39.
15. Barker, ed. "History of the Strickland and Taylor Families," 14.
16. Barker, ed. "History of the Strickland and Taylor Families," 18.
17. Young and Sparks, *Cattle in the Cold Desert*, 222–23. See also Carr Childers, *Size of the Risk*, 156.
18. Dobie, *Mustang*, 199.
19. MacDonald, "'Kid' Foss and the Birth of Rodeo," 59.
20. Carr Childers, *Size of the Risk*, 171.
21. Little, "Ox and Horse," 85.
22. Westermeier, *Man, Beast, Dust*, 167; Wooden and Ehringer, *Rodeo in America*, 117.
23. Lamb, *Rodeo Cowboy*, 165.
24. Lawrence, *Hoofbeats and Society*, 81; Westermeier, *Man, Beast, Dust*, 174.
25. Don Bell, "North of Yellowstone," and "Nostalgia," manuscripts, "Don Bell Rodeo Memoirs and Brief Histories," BEL.
26. Richardson, *Casey Tibbs*, 112.
27. Hank Christensen, quoted in "They Made It Possible," *Rodeo Sports News*, February 1, 1958, 2.
28. Deb Copenhaver, quoted in Richardson, *Casey Tibbs*, 112–13.
29. Gillespie and Burns, *Steamboat*, 5.
30. Westermeier said of killers actually having "no place in the sport" because they were dangerous to people and other horses: "The horses seen in the arena are, in

most cases, halter-broken and are gentle until an attempt is made to ride them." Westermeier, *Man, Beast, Dust*, 189–90.
31. Gillespie and Burns, *Steamboat*, 5.
32. "Steamboat and Midnight Rated Greatest of Rodeo Broncs," [newspaper not named], July 25, 1939, "Cheyenne Frontier Days 1903–1982, 2/11, POR.
33. See, for instance, "Harry Tompkins, Dublin, Texas, All-Around World Champion Cowboy; 1952 Triple Champion," *Rodeo Sports News*, January 1, 1953, 1.
34. Cy Taillon, quoted in McFadden, *Rain or Shine*, 119.
35. Fredriksson, *American Rodeo*, 89; see also, Kelm, *Wilder West*, 138–41.
36. Richards, *Casey Tibbs*, 158–60.
37. "Champ Rider," *Life* 31, no. 17 (October 22, 1951), 123–29.
38. Savitt, *Rodeo*, 46.
39. Robertson, *Rodeo*, 32.
40. Carr Childers, "National Finals Rodeo," 273–75; LeCompte, *Cowgirls*, 15.
41. Comparison of 1910s-era editions of the early trade journal, *The Wild Bunch*, with *Rodeo Sports News*, forty years later, reveals how artificial was the exclusively male nature of rodeo leadership at mid-century.
42. Burstyn discusses this trend with respect especially to the 1970s and 1980s, but the trends were visible two decades earlier in which "sport formed a countermovement of men . . . powered by impulses to exclude women, weave a masculine generating myth, and create patriarchal identifications and values. Such impulses have substantial political implications." Burstyn, *Rites of Men*, 121.
43. LeCompte, "Home on the Range," 339, 343; LeCompte, *Cowgirls*, 104.
44. Woerner, "History of Barrel Racing."
45. "A Glimpse Behind the Scenes at Round-Up," *East Oregonian* [Pendleton, OR], September 24, 1913.
46. LeCompte, *Cowgirls*, 104.
47. "Trick & Fancy Riding" plaque, Lynn Hickey American Rodeo Gallery, National Cowboy and Western Heritage Museum, Oklahoma City, Oklahoma; Westermeier, *Man, Beast, Dust*, 71.
48. Lawrence, *Hoofbeats and Society*, 80.
49. Bernstein, *Wild Ride*, 109; Haney, *Ride 'em Cowgirl*, 114; Gray, "Florence Hughes Randolph, Part I," 50. Mary Lou LeCompte says of Vera McGinnis, relay race and trick rider, "With her horse in an open trailer, she bumped along dirt roads, and like others in the business, sometimes slept in tent cities along the way to the next rodeo." (LeCompte, *Cowgirls*, 97).
50. LeCompte, *Cowgirls*, 103–4.
51. Greene, *Horses at Work*, 144.
52. Don Bell, "Animal Rights," manuscript, "Don Bell Rodeo Memoirs and Brief Histories," BEL.
53. "It's a Fact," *Rodeo Sports News*, February 1, 1956, 3; Westermeier, *Man, Beast, Dust*, 222.

54. Casey Tibbs, "The Quality and Quantity of Today's Bucking Horses Good as Those of Old Days," *Rodeo Sports News*, June 1, 1957, 7.
55. Casey Tibbs, "The Quality and Quantity of Today's Bucking Horses Good as Those of Old Days," *Rodeo Sports News*, June 1, 1957, 7; see also Woerner, *Belly Full of Bedsprings*, 110–11.
56. Corey, "Welfare Issues in the Rodeo Horse," 286–88.
57. "A few simple rules make rodeo travel easier on horses," *ProRodeo Sports News*, March 7, 1990, 25; Campion, *Rodeo*, 37, 45–48.
58. Temple Grandin, paraphrased by Larson, "Rodeo Is Cruel Entertainment," 117.
59. "Over 200 Rodeos Approved for 1958 at Denver Convention," *Rodeo Sports News*, February 1, 1958, 3.
60. Casey Tibbs, quoted in Woerner, *Belly Full of Bedsprings*, 110.
61. The ProRodeo Hall of Fame note on her induction was, until very recently, illustrated with a photograph of the horse climbing up the wall of a bucking chute. ProRodeo Hall of Fame, "Miss Klamath," http://www.prorodeohalloffame.com/inductees/by-category/livestock/miss-klamath/.
62. Tooke, "Bill Ward and Miss Klamath," in *Moments in Rodeo*, chapter 19.
63. "Miss Klamath Is Dead!" *Rodeo Sports News*, August 15, 1955, 1.
64. Deb Copenhaver, quoted in "King of the Cowboys," *Fortnight: Magazine of the Pacific Coast* 19, no. 4 (April 1956): 50. See also Burstyn, *Rites of Men*, 111.
65. Anonymous rodeo cowboy quoted in Lawrence, *Hoofbeats and Society*, 88.
66. Westermeier, *Man, Beast, Dust*, 192–93.
67. Westermeier, *Man, Beast, Dust*, 191–94, 242–45.
68. Robertson, *Rodeo*, 30; Savitt, *Rodeo*, 48–49.
69. Savitt, *Rodeo*, 45–47.
70. Savitt, *Rodeo*, 48.
71. Savitt, *Rodeo*, 40.
72. Savitt, *Rodeo*, 43.
73. Richards, *Casey Tibbs*, 163.
74. Tibbs, *Born to Buck*.
75. Robertson, *Rodeo*, 30. In 1985, Kristine Fredriksson dismissed then-contemporary concerns over spurring of bucking broncs by disparaging rodeo's critics as disingenuous. "Humane groups like to have the public believe that spurs cause the horse to perform the action of bucking, which is instead natural and instinctive for American range-bred horses." Fredriksson, *American Rodeo*, 155.
76. Henry Fonda narration in Tibbs, *Born to Buck*; Richards, *Casey Tibbs*, 162.
77. Henry Fonda narration in Tibbs, *Born to Buck*.
78. Mellis, *Riding Buffaloes*, 23, 29.
79. Iverson, *When Indians Became Cowboys*, 31–37.
80. Faulknor, *Turn Him Loose*, 67.
81. Kay Doering, "War Paint: The Grand Marshall," *Western Horseman* (June 1971), 56; Faulknor, *Turn Him Loose*, 39; Geronimo Productions, *War Paint*; ProRodeo Hall of Fame, "War Paint"; Tootoosis, "This Was One of the Predictions," 331.

82. Iverson, *When Indians Became Cowboys*, 76–79; Mellis, *Riding Buffaloes*, 148–55.
83. Richards, *Casey Tibbs*, 164.
84. Richards, *Casey Tibbs*, 162.
85. "From the Rodeo Information Commission," *Rodeo Sports News*, May 1, 1956, 4.
86. Carr Childers, "Leisl Carr Childers on the Gus Bundy Photographs," 605, 609–13.
87. Carr Childers, *Size of the Risk*, 180; see also 173–82.
88. Carr Childers, "Leisl Carr Childers on the Gus Bundy Photographs," 605; Gibson, "Beasts of Burden," 39–41. The Wild Free-Roaming Horses and Burros Act would not come about until 1971, but it expanded and elaborated earlier laws protecting wild equids.
89. Marino, "'Wind Blew Down,'" 40–42.
90. Lawrence, *Hoofbeats and Society*, 93.
91. Savitt, *Rodeo*, 46; Weiland, *100 Years of Rodeo Stock Contracting*; Wooden and Ehringer, *Rodeo in America*, 119.
92. Lawrence, *Hoofbeats and Society*, 94.
93. See, for instance, "Stock Contractors Invite Rule Changes," *Rodeo Sports News*, February 1, 1958, 10.
94. Gene Autry, "Introduction," in Weiland, *100 Years of Rodeo Stock Contracting*, vii.
95. Wooden and Ehringer, *Rodeo in America*, 117–18.
96. Lamb, Rodeo: *Back of the Chutes*, 5.
97. Robertson, *Rodeo*, 30; Woerner, *Belly Full of Bedsprings*, 111.
98. Gray, *Ranch Economics*, 202–3.
99. See Sayre, *Ranching*, 121; see also Horowitz, *Putting Meat on the American Table*, 15–18, 41; Starrs, *Let the Cowboy Ride*, 74–76; White, "It's Your Misfortune," 496–507, 520–52.
100. See for instance, "Auction Sale—Walter Plugge," *Rodeo Sports News*, April 1, 1957; "Two Day Auction Hoover's Ox-Yoke Rodeo," *Rodeo Sports News*, September 1, 1957.
101. Tooke, "Tooke Bucking Horses," 878; Wooden and Ehringer, *Rodeo in America*, 118.
102. Tooke, *Moments in Rodeo*, chapter 15.
103. Lawrence, *Hoofbeats and Society*, 90–97.
104. "From the Rodeo Information Commission," *Rodeo Sports News*, May 1, 1956, 4.
105. Savitt, *Rodeo*, 49. See also Geri Pursley, "The Man Behind the PRCA's Greatest Broncs," *ProRodeo Sports News*, October 30, 1991, 38–39.
106. Today, most born-to-buck broncs at the higher levels of rodeo are about 50% thoroughbred with Shire or Percheron lineage to produce a sturdy, tall, athletic horse. Campion, *Rodeo*, 48.

107. Dobie, *Mustangs*, 139; Lawrence, *Hoofbeats and Society*, 85–86.
108. Carr Childers, *Size of the Risk*, 154–55; Young and Sparks, *Cattle in the Cold Desert*, 217, 225–27.
109. Richards, *Casey Tibbs*, 162.
110. The company fell upon hard times around 1980 due to declining revenue and perhaps some mismanagement. It was bought and sold several times by teams of investors, until being closed down in 1989 after a very long tenure in the trade. "Christensen Brothers," ProRodeo Hall of Fame, http://www.prorodeohalloffame.com/inductees/by-category/stock-contractors/christensen-brothers/; see also, "Christensen Brothers Rodeo Company," Ellensburg Rodeo Hall of Fame, http://erhof.com/inductees/christensen-brothers-rodeo-company; Weiland, *100 Years of Rodeo Stock Contracting*, 160–61.
111. Richards, *Casey Tibbs*, 117–18.
112. Bernstein, *Wild Ride*, 109–10.
113. Tooke, *Moments in Rodeo*, chap. 11; see also Robertson, *Rodeo*, 30.
114. Robertson, *Rodeo*, 30–32.
115. Henry and Bobby Christensen quoted in Robertson, *Rodeo*, 32.
116. "Bucking Horse of the Year Trophy Awarded to 'War Paint' at Denver," *Rodeo Sports News*, February 1, 1958, 1.
117. "Bucking Horse of the Year Trophy Awarded to 'War Paint' at Denver," *Rodeo Sports News*, February 1, 1958, 1.
118. "Bucking Horse of the Year Trophy Awarded to 'War Paint' at Denver," *Rodeo Sports News*, February 1, 1958, 1.
119. "Tibbs to Try 'War Paint' at Red Bluff," *Rodeo Sports News*, April 15, 1958, 1.
120. "Stock Contractors Invite Rule Changes," *Rodeo Sports News*, February 1, 1958; "They Made It Possible," *Rodeo Sports News*, February 1, 1958, 10.
121. "They Made It Possible," *Rodeo Sports News*, February 1, 1958, 2.
122. Woerner, *Belly Full of Bed Springs*, 103; Geronimo Productions, *War Paint*, Youtube.com, https://www.youtube.com/watch?v=2sKzhcKV8GU; Ellensburg Rodeo Hall of Fame, "War Paint," http://erhof.com/inductees/warpaint/.
123. Devere Helfrich, photographer. National Cowboy and Western Heritage Museum, Oklahoma City, OK.
124. ProRodeo Hall of Fame, "War Paint," http://www.prorodeohalloffame.com/inductees/by-category/livestock/war-paint/; Geronimo Productions, *War Paint*.
125. Doering, "War Paint: The Grand Marshall," 116.
126. Woerner, *Belly Full of Bed Springs*, 103.
127. Tooke, *Moments in Rodeo*, chapter 40.

## Chapter 5

1. Peter Richmond, "Death of a Cowboy," *National Sports Daily*, July 22, 1990; Kendra Santos, "Friends Recall Love for Lane Frost," "It's Hard to Say Goodbye," and "Lane Frost Scored 85 Points," all in *ProRodeo Sports News*, August 16, 1989; see

also interviews with friends and family of Frost in *The Ride with Cord McCoy: Lane Frost*.
2. "John Growney Talks About Red Rock, Lane Frost, and Clovis Rodeo's 100th Anniversary."
3. "Growney Interview"; "John Growney Talks About Red Rock, Lane Frost, and Clovis Rodeo's 100th Anniversary."
4. Levi Green, quoted in *The Ride with Cord McCoy: Lane Frost*.
5. Kendra Santos, "Friends Recall Love for Lane Frost," *ProRodeo Sports News*, August 16, 1989.
6. Westermeier, *Trailing the Cowboy*, 346.
7. Jordan, *Rodeo History and Legends*, 13; Woerner, *Cowboy Up*, 2.
8. Woerner, *Cowboy Up*, 5–6.
9. "Oh, Shucks! You Can't Kill a California Cowpuncher!" *San Francisco Call*, August 2, 1912.
10. Unlabeled newspaper article, folder 2/4 "Fort Worth, Texas, 1935–1981," POR; Gary Moran, "A Rodeo with Fifty Candles," *The Dakota Farmer*, June 21, 1969, folder 2/2 "Belle Fourche, South Dakota, 1969–1986," POR.
11. American Brahman Breeders Association, "Why Use Brahman," https://www.brahman.org/about/benefits-of-brahman/.
12. Lawrence, *Rodeo*, 182; Woerner, *Cowboy Up*, 7.
13. Stratton, *Chasing the Rodeo*, 14; Woerner, *Cowboy Up*, 72–73.
14. "*PBR 101: Spurs*," Professional Bull Riders, Youtube.com, June 18, 2013, https://www.youtube.com/watch?v=pbS-gscDlqI.
15. "NFR—1967," *RCA Rodeo Sports News Annual* 16, no. 3 (January 1968): 12.
16. Stratton, *Chasing the Rodeo*, 14. See also Woerner, *Cowboy Up*, 135.
17. Stern and Stern, "Raging Bulls," 101.
18. Reg Kesler, quoted in Gail Woerner, "A True Rodeo Champion," *Way Out West Blog* (blog), July 25, 2016, http://www.gailwoerner.com/way-out-west-blog/a-true-rodeo-champion-v61.
19. "Quintana Tops V61 at Gladewater!" *ProRodeo Sports News*, July 1, 1971.
20. Reg Kesler, quoted in Gail Woerner, "A True Rodeo Champion," *Way Out West Blog* (blog), July 25, 2016, http://www.gailwoerner.com/way-out-west-blog/a-true-rodeo-champion-v61.
21. "The Bull of the Year," *Life*, October 23, 1970, 75.
22. Back in the 1940s Clifford Westermeier noted that while some particularly intimidating "Brahma celebrities," as one rodeo paper described them, did receive names, the practice of numbering bulls predominated for decades. Even Bodacious would be known simply as J-31 for a time in the early 1990s. Westermeier, *Man, Beast, Dust*, 250n.1.
23. Ellis and Irvine, "Reproducing Dominion," 29.
24. Slatta, *Cowboys of the Americas*, 192–93.
25. Brickey, "Buying the Bull"; Jeffords, *Remasculinization of America*, 127–30; Reports circulated that in a number of large Texas bars live bulls were employed

in place of the mechanical bulls that people had seen in *Urban Cowboy*. Two correspondents for the *New Yorker* called them "pitiful creatures" who found themselves "transported from a grassy field to a smoke-filled room rocked by people doing the Texas Two-Step" and "shocked, prodded, and provoked mercilessly, then ridden until all their fight is gone, whereupon they are replaced. There are no veterinarians in attendance or on call. . . . Unlike the prized bucking bulls of the pro-rodeo circuit, such animals are expendable—worth their weight as dog food once they are used up for sport." Stern and Stern, "Raging Bulls," 100.

26. Rupert Wilkinson, quoted in Jeffords, *Hard Bodies*, 3; see also, Burstyn, *Rites of Men*, 103–4; 49–50, 175.
27. Burstyn, *Rites of Men*, 175.
28. Woerner, *Cowboy Up*, chap. 8, p. 137.
29. LeCompte, *Cowgirls*, 189–93; Glory Ann Kurtz, "Scamper Inducted into Pro Rodeo Hall of Fame," *Barrel Horse News* (October 1996); Willard H. Porter, "Charmayne Rides into Rodeo History," *The Oklahoman*, December 9, 1990, https://newsok.com/article/2340681/charmayne-rides-into-rodeo-history.
30. On Title IX and women's college rodeo, see Mahoney, *College Rodeo*, 106.
31. "Mr. T Retires in California," *ProRodeo Sports News*, February 6, 1991.
32. John Growney, quoted in Wooden and Ehringer, *Rodeo in America*, 119–20.
33. John Growney, quoted in Wooden and Ehringer, *Rodeo in America*, 119–20.
34. Ty Murray, quoted in *Professional Bull Riders: 8 Seconds—Bred for Greatness*. Professional Bullriders / Image Entertainment. 2006.
35. Groves, *Ropes, Reins, and Rawhide*, 57; Jones, "Eight Seconds to Midnight: Not all Bulls Buck Out of Instinct," *National Post*, 19 November 1999; Lawrence, *Rodeo*, 181–82; Professional Rodeo Cowboys Association, *Humane Facts: The Care and Treatment of Professional Rodeo Livestock* (Colorado Springs, CO: Professional Rodeo Cowboys Association, n.d.), 4; Wooden and Ehringer, *Rodeo in America*, 119–21.
36. Wooden and Ehringer, *Rodeo in America*, 120.
37. Reddin, *Wild West Shows*, 95, 161–63, 186.
38. Gene Pruett, "Rodeo '67," *RCA Rodeo Sports News Annual* 16, no. 3 (January 1968): 10.
39. In the 1960s, rodeo had been entirely banned in Ohio (that law was eventually ruled unconstitutional), with other bills up for votes in nine other states, mostly in the Northeast and Midwest, and also California. Rodeo advocates had called state representatives and otherwise lobbied successfully against these proposed bans throughout the decade. Woerner, *Rope to Win*, 126.
40. Bob Norris, "Committee Rep. Writes Open Letter," *Rodeo Sports News*, July 1, 1971, 20.
41. "Confronting the Animal Rights Beast," *ProRodeo Sports News*, July 31, 1991, 10. In Canada, similarly, officials of the CPRA had been talking since the 1950s

about how to address the activities of the 'new' animal advocacy organizations that appeared at mid-century. Kelm, *Wilder West*, 143–44.
42. "Confronting the Animal Rights Beast," *ProRodeo Sports News*, July 31, 1991, 10.
43. "An interview with Chairman Bob Thain," *Prorodeo Sports News*, April 3, 1991, 14–15.
44. "Animal Welfare Issues," *ProRodeo Sports News*, October 7, 1992, 24.
45. "Animal Welfare Issues," *ProRodeo Sports News*, June 3, 1992, 16; "Animal Welfare Issues," *ProRodeo Sports News*, June 17, 1992, 18.
46. "Animal Welfare Issues," *ProRodeo Sports News*, September 23, 1992, 25.
47. "Animal Welfare Issues," *ProRodeo Sports News*, December 2, 1993, 32.
48. Rollin, "Rodeo and Recollection," 3.
49. Rollin, "Rodeo and Recollection," 2.
50. In 2006 the Animal Enterprise Act of 1992 was amended and rewritten as the Animal Enterprise Terrorism Act, which increased penalties and the range of animal facilities under protection, as well as expanding the range of possible activities that industry and government considered "terrorism." It would be followed by state "ag-gag" anti-whistleblower laws that criminalized the recording of animal use in laboratories or animal facilities, which animal advocates, among others, worried was a way to criminalize free speech. Sorenson, *Constructing Ecoterrorism*, 52–60.
51. "Animal Welfare Issues," *ProRodeo Sports News*, February 24, 1993, 23.
52. Jeffords, *Remasculinization of America*, 127–30; Jordan, "Politics of Cowboy Culture," 41–42. In Canada, this dynamic was especially so in Alberta. Due to heavy American in-migration in the late nineteenth and early twentieth century, the province had a uniquely conservative political culture. Citizens there elected a series of governments and parties united by "frontier liberalism"–style themes: "individualism, stressing the importance of personal responsibility, free enterprise, private-sector development, entrepreneurship, a strong work ethic, the evils of socialism, and the protection of individual rights and liberties." Wesley, *Code Politics*, 56; see also 55–103. Examples of "subsidies" for rural living might include national highway systems, tax breaks for the agricultural sector, federal management and repair of public lands such as overgrazed public ranges, irrigation, and land reclamation projects that states and provinces would never afford alone, as well as grazing leases that propped up countless ranching operations, big and small, by preventing a collapse of rangelands similar to the 1880s–1900s. Although many western states and provinces have had a net inflow of federal dollars into their economies over the years, resentment against "government meddling and interference" have been perennial political issues in many places due to many rural westerners' belief in themselves as self-sufficient economic actors rather than, for instance, "welfare ranchers." Peterson, "What Cattle Grazing Does to Public Land," *New York Times*, August 12, 1991; Sharman Apt Russell, "Myth of the Welfare Rancher," *New York Times*, July 19, 1991; Russell, *Kill the Cowboy*, 15-25.

53. Starrs, *Let the Cowboy Ride*, 76–79.
54. Childers, *Colorado Powder Keg*, 149–50; Sorenson, *Constructing Ecoterrorism*, 65.
55. Wooden and Ehringer, *Rodeo in America*, 130.
56. Wooden and Ehringer, *Rodeo in America*, 130–32.
57. McInnis, "War on the West," *Beef*, January 1, 1999.
58. McInnis, "War on the West," *Beef*, January 1, 1999; see also Hasselstrom, *Between Grass and Sky*, 81, 157–59.
59. Fredriksson, *American Rodeo*, 147, 152; Woerner, *Cowboy Up*, 120.
60. Burbick, *Rodeo Queens*, 7. See also Wooden and Ehringer, *Rodeo in America*, 132–34.
61. Stern and Stern, "Raging Bulls," 99.
62. Fredriksson, *American Rodeo*, 148; Kendra Santos, "Bull Riding Goes Big Time," *American Cowboy* (May/June 1996): 72–73; "An Interview with Bob Thain," *Pro-Rodeo Sports News*, April 3, 1991, 14–15.
63. Kendra Santos, "Lewis Field Hits Rodeo's Magical Mark," *ProRodeo Sports News*, March 21, 1990, 3–4; see also "Dee Pickett Joins PRCA's Most Exclusive Club," *ProRodeo Sports News*, October 31, 1990.
64. Johnston and Cartwright, *Professional Bull Riders*, 76.
65. Peter, *Fried Twinkies*, 139–43.
66. Wooden and Ehringer, *Rodeo in America*, 235, 237.
67. For current winnings ranking, see: Professional Bull Riders, "All Time Money Earners," *PBR.com*, https://www.pbr.com/en/riders/all-time-money-earners.aspx. Although there would be power struggles and griping that stock contractors and PBR executives had too much power to favor some bulls and some riders, it was an improvement in profit sharing. Peter, *Fried Twinkies*, 96.
68. Peter, *Fried Twinkies*, 93.
69. "Kirby Rodeo School," *ProRodeo Sports News*, March 11, 1992, 33.
70. Haney and Pearson, "Rodeo Injuries," 449–50.
71. Thor, "Realities of Rodeo," 52; see also, Haney and Pearson, "Rodeo Injuries," 447.
72. Haney and Pearson, "Rodeo Injuries," 445.
73. Haney and Pearson, "Rodeo Injuries," 445–49; Schmoldt, "Lasting Legacy: Lane Frost and the Rodeo Community," *Casper Star Tribune*, July 11, 2009; Woerner, *Cowboy Up*, 207.
74. Faulkner, "Their Own Brand of Misery," 252.
75. Larry Mahan quoted in Merrill, dir., *Great American Cowboy*.
76. Fredriksson, *American Rodeo*, 87, 210.
77. Allen, *Rodeo Cowboy*, 32–33.
78. Jane Stern and Michael Stern, "Raging Bulls," *New Yorker*, September 14, 1992, 99.
79. Stern and Stern, "Raging Bulls," 99–100.
80. Derrick, "J-31 Bodacious, Rodeo's Master of Disaster," accessed 5 May, 2006, http://www.andrewsrodeoco.com/Bodacious.html; Brett Hoffman, "Bodacious:

1,800 Pound Bad Boy of Rodeo Stock is Dead," *FreeRepublic.com*, accessed May 7, 2006, http://www.freerepublic.com/forum/a392d65f33b51.htm.
81. Woerner, *Cowboy Up*, 8, 56; Westermeier, *Man, Beast, Dust*, 189.
82. Peter, *Fried Twinkies*, 105.
83. Derrick, "J-31 Bodacious." See also the Bodacious DVD, *Bodacious: Master of Disaster*; and Lynn Montgomery, "Stock Contractor Details Latest Crop of Buckers," *Country World* (Texas), March 26, 2004; Peter, *Fried Twinkies*, 109.
84. Groves, *Ropes, Reins, and Rawhide*, 57; Robertson, *Rodeo*, 81.
85. Peter, *Fried Twinkies*, 109.
86. Derrick, "J-31 Bodacious"; *Bodacious: Master of Disaster*.
87. *Bodacious: Master of Disaster*.
88. Lawrence, *Rodeo*, 169–80; Wayne and Ehringer, *Rodeo in America*, 109.
89. Jim McLain, Professional Bullfighters Tour representative, quoted in Groves, *Ropes, Reins, and Rawhide*, 65–66.
90. Freeman Gregory, "Some Kinda Bull!" *H Magazine*, August 1999, accessed July 5, 2006, http://www.hlsr.com/hmagazine/99aug/f-bull.html. See also Weiland, *100 Years of Rodeo Stock Contracting*, vii.
91. "They're Sort of Like Mike," *New York Times*, 17 January 1999.
92. Derrick, "J-31 Bodacious."
93. *Bodacious: Master of Disaster*.
94. *Bodacious: Master of Disaster*; Woerner, *Cowboy Up*, 220–21.
95. *Bodacious: Master of Disaster*.
96. For footage of this ride, see *Bodacious*. See also Santos, *Ring of Fire*, 94–97.
97. Tuff Hedeman quoted in *Bodacious*.
98. Doug Abraham, "Top Bull Rider Meets Match in Bodacious," *Calgary Herald*, 9 December, 1995, D8.
99. Cody Snyder, quoted in Dwayne Erikson, "Outlaw 56, Cowboys 0: This Bull's One Tough Hombre," *Calgary Herald*, July 8, 2003.
100. "Champion Bucking Bull Retires," *Calgary Herald*, December 27, 1995.
101. Gregory, "Some Kinda Bull!" In recognition of his retirement, and as a sort of consolation prize for the Andrews and Bodacious' management team, Bodacious was voted 1995 Bull of the Year by the PRCA. "Cowboys Choose Top Bucking Stock," *ProRodeo Sports News*, November 1, 1995.
102. Derrick, "J-31 Bodacious."
103. John Growney interviewed in "John Growney Talks About Red Rock, Lane Frost, and Clovis Rodeo's 100th Anniversary."
104. Johnstone and Cartwright, *Professional Bull Riders*, 4. See also Claire Atkinson, "An 8-Second Ride Lures Sponsors Beyond the Rodeo," *New York Times*, December 11, 2007.
105. Claire Atkinson, "An 8-Second Ride Lures Sponsors Beyond the Rodeo," *New York Times*, December 11, 2007.

106. PBR officials state that these totals included including seventeen million viewers in China who watched the PBR World Finals broadcast from Las Vegas. Johnston and Cartwright, *Professional Bull Riders*, 4.
107. David L. Andrews and Steven J. Jackson, "Introduction: Sport Celebrities, Public Culture, and Private Experience," in Andrews and Jackson, ed., *Sport Stars*, 4–5, 7.
108. Murray entitled his autobiography—another obligatory accoutrement for celebrity self-promotion—*King of the Cowboys: The Autobiography of the World's Most Famous Rodeo Star*, indicating how diligently he and his publicists were working to encourage consumers to follow his activities. *Sports Illustrated* and *Reader's Digest* called him "The Best Danged Rodeo Cowboy of 'Em All," and "The Greatest Cowboy Ever." E. M. Swift, "Whoopee Ty Yay!" *Sports Illustrated*, December 24, 1990, 49–53; Skip Hollandsworth, "The Greatest Cowboy Ever," *Reader's Digest* 156, no. 935 (2000): 70–75.
109. *ProRodeo Sports News*, May 16, 1990.
110. Johnston and Cartwright, *Professional Bull Riders*, 76.
111. Nance, "A Star is Born to Buck."
112. "Talented Bulls and Broncs Star at NFR," *ProRodeo Sports News*, March 24, 1993, 32.
113. Johnston and Cartwright, *Professional Bull Riders*, 76.
114. Johnston and Cartwright, *Professional Bull Riders*, 77.
115. Mary Bridges, "Bull Market," *Upstart Business Journal*, August 13, 2007.
116. Johnston and Cartwright, *Professional Bull Riders*, 77.
117. *The Ride with Cord McCoy: Lane Frost*.
118. Woerner, *Cowboy Up*, 162.
119. "PBR Press Release: Getting Off on the Payne: Major Payne Continues to Confound Riders," PBRNOW.com, December 9, 2010, http://www.pbrnow.com/release/?id=7003.
120. In 2010, Major's Payne's partial itinerary from a PBR press release included in January: Baltimore, MD; New York, NY; Tampa, FL; February: Winston-Salem, NC; Arlington, TX; St. Louis, MO; March: Glendale, AZ; Fresno, CA; Albuquerque, NM; April: New Orleans, LA; Nampa, ID; Las Vegas, NV; Billings, MT; Rapid City, SD; May: Wichita, KS; Pueblo, CO. "PBR Press Release: Getting Off on the Payne: Major Payne Continues to Confound Riders," PBRNOW.com, December 9, 2010, http://www.pbrnow.com/release/?id=7003.
121. "Bull Biz Briefs: Super Duty Injures Leg During BRT Championship Round," *Buckin' Stock Magazine*, April–May 2011, 6.
122. Ducharme, "Stifle Injuries in Cattle," 59–84.
123. "PBR Press Release: Super Duty Possibly Injured, World Champion Contender Under Expert Care," PBRNOW.com, March 1, 2011, http://www.pbr.com/release/?id=7226.
124. E. M. Swift, "Bucking for Big Bucks," *Sports Illustrated*, December 20, 1993, 46. See also, Haney and Pearson, "Rodeo Injuries," 444–45; White, "The Meaning of Injury in Rough Stock Rodeo Cowboys," 128–29.
125. See for instance, "Attention Bull Riders," *Rodeo Sports News*, February 1, 1960.

126. Peter, *Fried Twinkies*, 100–101, 112–13.
127. Derry, *Bred for Perfection*, 15; Oppenheimer, *Cowboy Economics*, vi, 12; Orland, "Turbo-Cows," 167–69.
128. American Bucking Bull, "Our History," https://www.americanbuckingbull.com/about/history/; NBBA—National Bucking Bull Association, January 7, 2015, Facebook.com, https://www.facebook.com/NBBA-NATIONAL-BUCKING-BULL-ASSOCIATION-390870891419/.
129. John Shull quoted in *The Ride with Cord McCoy: The Making of a World Champion Bucking Bull*.
130. Johnston and Cartwright, *Professional Bull Riders*, 76.
131. Rudy E. Vela quoted in Stern and Stern, "Raging Bulls," 99.
132. *Bodacious: Master of Disaster*.
133. See, for instance, *Bodacious: Master of Disaster*; James Drew, "The Stockyard Bull Sheet: Smokeless Wardance," *Pro Bull Rider* (May 2006): 67; Weiland, *100 Years of Rodeo Stock Contracting*, 31–32.
134. Gary Leffew quoted in Joris Debeij, *The Bull Rider: New York Times Op-Docs*, April 8, 2015, https://www.nytimes.com/2015/04/08/opinion/the-bull-rider.html. H. D. Page, PBR bull producer, former bull rider, and a proprietor of D & H Cattle Company in Dixon, Oklahoma talked of this phenomenon, which was successful with some bulls and not others. Some remained dangerous and one would venture into an enclosed space with them only on horseback. Others he had gentled down, including one of his winning bulls, Hot Stuff. Distracted with a tub of feed, Hot Stuff appeared for an interview in a pen with Page, his young daughter, and bull rider, Cord McCoy. Page assured McCoy how tame the bull was away from the bucking chute. H. D. Page quoted in *The Ride with Cord McCoy: The Making of a World Champion Bucking Bull*.
135. *PBR 101: Flank Strap*.
136. Dale Butterwick, quoted in Marty Klinkenberg, "Eight Seconds: The Life and Death of a Cowboy," *Globe and Mail*, November 11, 2017, https://beta.theglobeandmail.com/sports/ty-pozzobon-concussion-bull-riding/article36842612/.
137. "There are those people who've won championships and had their names here and there. . . . Most of those people have worked from the bottom-up and they know what it takes to work your way up. And most of those people are great people who want to see other people succeed and do well. So, they lend a hand and encourage. Ty Pozzobon was that person. He was always there for the little kids and he became this huge hero." Barrel Racer Katie Garthwaite quoted in "Rodeo 'Family' Back in Town for 71st Annual Cloverdale Rodeo and County Fair," *Vancouver Sun*, May 14, 2017.
138. Butterwick quoted in Klinkenberg, "Eight Seconds."

## Chapter 6

1. Roberts, *Man Who Listens to Horses*, 85.
2. Roberts's full statement on bronc riding explains that "the distress that some people feel for broncs is misplaced. The bronc is not just any wild animal; he is

a highly prized specialist. Not many horses are suited for the work. Far from being a cruel sport, this is a competition event in which the horse truly enjoys himself. The champion bronc is a valuable animal who gets the best care and nutrition. He is not bored by repetitive exercises, like many horses working in other rodeo events or in the Western show-horse categories. He is respected as a bronc. He is a wild thing, and nobody spends hours trying to bend his will. He quickly learns that he has nothing to fear." Roberts, *Man Who Listens to Horses*, 85.

3. In a 2013 study, Shannon Nicholson, a University of Guelph graduate student in animal welfare science, visited rodeos in Ontario and Quebec to conduct a survey about tie-down roping and the nature of calf welfare, or "well-being," as the questionnaire phrased it. Herself a barrel racer, she interviewed fellow competitors in barrel racing as well as family members, fans, and rodeo competitors in other events. Interestingly, Nicholson discovered that most of her informants did not actually know much about the welfare needs of calves on ranches or behind the chutes since they were mostly horse people. Nor was there a consensus about how or whether calf roping should be changed. A few interviewees said the event should be abolished but were not doing anything about it. If you visit many rodeos you will find that despite the many marriages between female barrel racers and male rodeo competitors (an aspect of rodeo's long role in rural matchmaking), there exist parallel and overlapping subcultures divided by event, ethnicity, and class. Nicholson, "Rodeo Participants' Perception of Roping Calf Welfare." More broadly, the diversity of opinion among rodeo people about which events are especially taxing for or dangerous to livestock and which should be phased out, like calf roping or steer roping, is a topic that requires more research, especially for the period after World War II, when more suburban and urban people became involved in the sport. In the meantime, see, for instance, Larson, "Thinks Calf Roping, Steer Tripping Inhumane"; Roberts, *Man Who Listens to Horses*, 85–86; Stratton, *Chasing the Rodeo*, 35; Wooden and Ehringer, *Rodeo in America*, 130.

4. Westermeier, *Man, Beast, Dust*, 45. At least one rodeo experimented with competitive branding, sometime between about 1905 and 1914. The wife of one the cowboys associated with Steamboat remembered, "One year the Frontier Committee [in Cheyenne] asked Guy to get a crew of cowboys together to compete against other crews to brand a certain number of calves. But the smell of burning hair proved offensive so wasn't popular." Mrs. Guy Holt quoted in Gillespie, *Steamboat*, 15.

5. LeCompte, "Home on the Range," 331.

6. Woerner, *Rope to Win*, 134.

7. Starrs, *Let the Cowboy Ride*, 10.

8. Calf roping created the appearance that "animals were rarely hurt" "because the roper was required to dismount and throw the calf by hand to make the tie." Baxter, "Ropers and Rangers," 345.

9. Westermeier, *Man, Beast, Dust*, 213. "These times [from 1910s] will not sound very fast to today's steer ropers, who often rope and tie steers in fifteen seconds and under, but when one considers the generally smaller, slower horses of sixty years ago, the bigger, faster steers (800 to 1000 pound three- and four-year-old longhorns), and the grass ropes that soften in the heat and hardened in the cold as they hung on saddle horns all day long, these are creditable times indeed." Hoy, "From Folk Game to Professional Sport," 147.
10. Ellis and Irvine, "Reproducing Dominion," 28–31.
11. Brownell, *Rodeos*, 114.
12. LeCompte, *Cowgirls*, 8.
13. Wooden and Ehringer, *Rodeo in America*, 132.
14. R. C. Patterson, quoted in Kendra Santos, "August is the Season," *ProRodeo Sports News*, September 4, 1991. The sport needed city kids, too, a PRCA business director would counsel, "The bulk of our population today is urban raised. They don't appreciate the skill in rodeo or the opportunities in rodeo for themselves. I think it's possible to get the message across, but it's going to take a lot of work and a lot of money." Eldon Evans, quoted in "Eldon Evans Specializes in the Business End of Rodeo," *ProRodeo Sports News*, August 21, 1991.
15. So did the film *8 Seconds* famously remind viewers that Lane Frost began his bull riding career in Little Britches calf riding competitions sponsored by the sport's junior event network. Allen, *Rodeo Cowboy*, 32–33.
16. Fredrickson, *American Rodeo*, 135.
17. Stratton, *Chasing the Rodeo*, 34.
18. See, for example, Andy Wright, "6 Seconds and a Sheep: Welcome to the World of Mutton Busting," *Modern Farmer* (December 2013), https://modernfarmer.com/2013/12/mutton-busting/; Kate Linthicum, "Where Rodeo Is King, Parents Sign Young Children Up for Mutton Busting," *Vancouver Sun*, August 24, 2009.
19. Faulkner, "Their Own Brand of Misery," 254.
20. Wright, "6 Seconds and a Sheep."
21. See for instance, "Mutton Busting: Crossover to Child Abuse," SHARK: Showing Animals Respect and Kindness, www.sharkonline.org/index.php/rodeo-events/711-mutton-busting; Jenny Kutner, "Rodeo Side-Show Mutton Busting: Bad for Kids, Bad for Sheep?," *The Dodo*, March 30, 2014, https://www.thedodo.com/rodeo-side-show-mutton-busting-490292697.html.
22. Kati Muirheld, commenter, "Kids and Animals Get Rights Trampled at Rodeos," *Modern Dog* Carreen Blog, March 1, 2014, https://moderndogmagazine.com/blogs/carreen/kids-and-animals-get-rights-trampled-rodeos.
23. Westermeier, *Man, Beast, Dust*, 243–45; Westermeier, "Cowboy Sports and the Humane Society."
24. Jack Scott, "Our Town," *Vancouver Sun*, May 27, 1949.
25. Jack Scott, "Our Town," *Vancouver Sun*, May 27, 1949.
26. Personal—[Br—?] 1925—Vancouver 1926—Prince George—Prince Rupert, AM 1614-: 2011-002.4, Sound Recording and Moving Image Collection, City of

Vancouver Archives, Vancouver, BC, https://searcharchives.vancouver.ca/personal-br-1925-vanc-ouver-1926-prince-george-prince-rupert.
27. Barman, *West Beyond the West*, 287, 302–6; Morley, *Vancouver*, 202–15.
28. See, for instance, "Man riding a bucking horse at the Callister Park rodeo," AM1184-53-: CVA 1184-696, Jack Lindsay Ltd. Photographers fonds, City of Vancouver Archives, Vancouver, BC, https://searcharchives.vancouver.ca/man-riding-bucking-horse-at-callister-park-rodeo-4.
29. "The Rodeo," 1944, AM1487-MI191, Sound Recording and Moving Image Collection, City of Vancouver Archives, Vancouver, BC.
30. Ken McConnell, "They Are Careful of the Stock," *Vancouver Province*, May 17, 1949.
31. "Linder Says Rodeo Fair to Animals," *Vancouver Province*, May 18, 2018.
32. "Three Rodeo Riders Find Steeds Rough," *Vancouver Province*, May 23, 1949.
33. "Five Charged with Cruelty to Animals in Local Rodeo," *Vancouver Sun*, May 30, 1949.
34. Linder finally prevailed through an appeal (funded by the Calgary Stampede, the Canadian Stampede Managers Association, the International Rodeo Association, the Rodeo Cowboys Association, and other industry organizations) to overturn a British Columbia Supreme Court ruling that briefly banned flank straps in the province and "posed a threat to a multi-million-dollar industry," some worried a bit hyperbolically. Faulknor, *Turn Him Loose*, 98, 102–5.
35. Faulknor, *Turn Him Loose*, 100.
36. It is difficult to say with accuracy, but it appears that probably a large minority of the citizens of Vancouver were sympathetic to various kinds of animal advocacy and, presumably, opposed rodeos. My point here is speculative and twentieth-century public opinion regarding rodeos and other modes of animal use is a subject that cries out for further research. Still, Vancouver seems to have earned a reputation after World War II as home to an unusually large proportion of opponents to forms of animal use that expanded in the twentieth century. For instance, a 1956 survey taken in the city showed that 17 percent of respondents were opposed to animal experimentation at the local university. McMillan, "Conflict over Animal Experimentation in Vancouver," 9–10. See also Kelm, *Wilder West*, 142.
37. Jack Scott, "Our Town," *Vancouver Sun*, May 27, 1949.
38. "Stampede Continues in Court," *Vancouver Province*, May 30, 1949; "One Charge of Cruelty Against Rodeo Promoters Dismissed," *Vancouver Sun*, June 2, 1949; Westermeier, *Man, Beast, Dust*, 217.
39. "One Charge of Cruelty against Rodeo Promoters Dismissed," *Vancouver Sun*, June 2, 1949.
40. "One Charge of Cruelty against Rodeo Promoters Dismissed," *Vancouver Sun*, June 2, 1949; "Promoter of Rodeo Acquitted," *Vancouver Province*, June 2, 1949.
41. Faulknor, *Turn Him Loose*, 105–6.
42. Kelm, *Wilder West*, 142–43.

43. "Cowboys at Work," *Frank Leslie's Illustrated Newspaper*, April 30, 1887, 166.
44. Dummitt, "Finding a Place for Father"; Hoganson, "Meat in the Middle," 1030; Horowitz, *Putting Meat on the American Table*, 17.
45. Burbick, *Rodeo Queens*, 51–52.
46. Gray, *Ranch Economics*, 197.
47. Hasselstrom, *Between Grass and Sky*, 163.
48. Oppenheimer, *Cowboy Economics*, 23–24.
49. Gray, *Ranch Economics*, 69.
50. Ellis, "Boundary Labor," 99–102; Ellis and Irvine, "Reproducing Dominion," 27–31; Wilkie, *Livestock/Deadstock*, 129.
51. Starrs, *Let the Cowboy Ride*, 75.
52. Gray, *Ranch Economics*, 13.
53. Gray, *Ranch Economics*, 161.
54. Gray, *Ranch Economics*, 162.
55. Hasselstrom, *Between Grass and Sky*, 163. See also Rollin, "Rodeo and Recollection," 6.
56. Wilkie, *Livestock/Deadstock*, 10. See also Jeffrey Rushen, et al., *The Welfare of Cattle*, 202.
57. Joby Warrick, "They Die Piece by Piece," *Washington Post*, April 10, 2001.
58. Burbick, *Rodeo Queens*, 52; Stoeltje, "Power and the Ritual Genres, 144–45.
59. For instance, in the 1980s and 1990s, the Anchor D Ranch of Coldwater, Kansas, held a yearly "Roping Calf Sale" of longhorn and longhorn cross heifers and steers. "All consignments welcome" they advertised of the free traffic in juvenile cattle. See, for instance, "9th Annual Anchor D. Ranch Roping Calf Sale," *ProRodeo Sports News*, January 13, 1993.
60. Groves, *Ropes, Reins, and Rawhide*, 121. See also Westermeier, *Man, Beast, Dust*, 216.
61. Mansfield, *Calf Roping*, 8.
62. Mansfield, *Calf Roping*, 7–8; see also Larson, "Rodeo Is Cruel Entertainment," 118.
63. Cooper, *Calf Roping*, 8. Competitors can seriously damage shoulders from swinging the rope, hips from straddling calves, back and arms from flanking (hoisting calves in the air to drop them on their sides), knees and ankles while jumping from a running horse, and hands and digits from catching them in a taut rope. Groves, *Ropes, Reins, and Rawhide*, 119.
64. Cooper, *Calf Roping*, 126–28; Ehringer, *Rodeo Legends*, 53–61. See also "Roy Cooper Calf Roping School Inc.," *ProRodeo Sports News*, May 15, 1991.
65. Cooper, *Calf Roping*, 90.
66. Text of the 1969 PRCA regulations; Mansfield, *Calf Roping*, 55.
67. Cooper, *Calf Roping*, 92–95.
68. Gavin Ehringer, "The Mud, the Blood & the Poop: A Rodeo Insider Takes You behind the Chutes of America's Cowboy Sport," *Colorado Springs Independent* online edition 12, no. 34 (August 19, 2004), accessed June 25, 2006, https://www.csindy.com/coloradosprings/the-mud-the-blood-and-the-poop/Content?oid

=1124891. Veterinarian and calf roper T. K. Hardy similarly explains that, in the words of fellow vet Peggy W. Larson, "calf roping is an expensive sport. . . . two or three calves are injured in each practice session and have to be replaced." Larson, "Rodeo Is Cruel Entertainment," 118.
69. Calgary Stampede stock voucher, Aleck Hartell, "Bucking Horse Records—1948," M2160 / 160, STA.
70. "Attention—All Calf Ropers," *ProRodeo Sports News*, February 10, 1993. Similar products are still available at some tack and roping suppliers. See, for example "Calf Saver Collars," 2C Custom Tack, http://2ccustomtack.com/item_47/Calf-Saver-Collars.htm; "Cactus Ropes Stran Smith Double S Calf Collar," NRS Ranch, https://www.nrsworld.com/cactus-ropes/cactus-ropes-stran-smith-double-s-calf-collar-7464.
71. A study conducted in 1977 determined that calves run up to twenty-seven miles per hour and at that speed the stop shock "caused severe damage," especially as practice-pen stock were routinely roped repeatedly in a single day or on consecutive days. Lawrence, *Rodeo*, 176. See also James Naviaux and Robert Miller, "Is Rodeo Cruel?, *Horse Lover's National Magazine* 21: 7–10.
72. Bob Welch, "Buying Roping Steers," *The Team Roping Journal*, March 31, 2005, https://teamropingjournal.com/rodeo-road/buying-roping-steers.
73. Lawrence, *Rodeo*, 176.
74. Westermeier, *Man, Beast, Dust*, 215n.1.
75. Westermeier, *Man, Beast, Dust*, 215, n. 1. See also Faulknor, *Turn Him Loose*, 38–40, 85; Groves, *Ropes, Reins, and Rawhide*, 116.
76. Woerner, *Rope to Win*, 141.
77. Westermeier, *Man, Beast, Dust*, 214–15.
78. Westermeier, *Man, Beast, Dust*, 215.
79. Groves, *Ropes, Reins, and Rawhide*, 119.
80. Kelm, *Wilder West*, 143–46.
81. A debate ensued over whether it was a case of simple correction or whipping in frustration since the horse had been slow out of the box, and thus whether the Stampede's ruling was warranted or productive for the sport. "Cooper Disqualified from the Calgary Stampede for Mistreatment of Horse," *CBC News Calgary*, July 9, 2015, https://www.cbc.ca/news/canada/calgary/tuf-cooper-disqualified-from-the-calgary-stampede-for-mistreatment-of-horse-1.3145638; "Tie-Down Roper Disqualified from Calgary Stampede Over Alleged Mistreatment of Horse," *CTV News Calgary*, July 9, 2015, https://calgary.ctvnews.ca/tie-down-roper-disqualified-from-calgary-stampede-over-alleged-mistreatment-of-horse-1.2462320.
82. Ed Pajor quoted in Calgary Stampede, *An Interview with Dr. Ed Pajor about the Animal Care Advisory Panel*. See also "New Animal Care Approaches for Calgary Stampede," *Meristem Land & Science*, May 23, 2013, http://www.meristem.com/feature_articles-fac/2013/fa_2013_23.php.
83. Groves, *Ropes, Reins, and Rawhide*, 116.
84. Pooley-Ebert, "Species Agency," 160–62.

85. Lawrence, *Rodeo*, 152–55.
86. PRCA, *Animal Welfare*, 3.
87. Woerner, *Rope to Win*, 10. In Rhode Island, various bills circulated, some outlawing calf roping entirely, some allowing "traditional" (tie-down) calf roping but requiring experienced veterinarians to be on site at all rodeos, and one that allowed breakaway roping but also require veterinarians to be present. "Calf Roping Outlawed in Rhode Island," *ProRodeo Sports News*, August 2, 1989. The PRCA lobbied successfully against a 1973 bill that would have banned all roping events in the state of Colorado. "Meet Bob Ragsdale," Friends of Rodeo, https://www.friendsofrodeoinc.com/bob-ragsdale.
88. "Confronting the Animal Rights Beast," *ProRodeo Sports News*, July 31, 1991, 10.
89. Larson, "Dr. Larson Responds," 595; *Action for Animals Testimony to Hearing before the Subcommittee on Department Operations, Research, and Foreign Agriculture of the Committee on Agriculture*, House of Representatives, July 8, 1992, 613, https://hdl.handle.net/2027/umn.31951d00303920d; Regan, *Empty Cages*, 153.
90. "Confronting the Animal Rights Beast," *ProRodeo Sports News*, July 31, 1991, 10.
91. Westermeier, *Man, Beast, Dust*, 215n.1.
92. "Calf Roping Outlawed in Rhode Island," *ProRodeo Sports News*, August 2, 1989. Often this data has been put forward by industry advocates, for instance, Schonholz, "Animals in Rodeo"; Furman, "Rodeo Cattle's Many Performances." A more recent veterinarian's defense of rodeo employs many of the familiar arguments pioneered in the 1980s without addressing specific cases of animals injured, killed, or traumatized in the arena or at the breeding ranch. Doug Corey, "Welfare Issues in the Rodeo Horse," in McIlwraith and Rollin, *Equine Welfare*, 275–301.
93. "Calf Roping Outlawed in Rhode Island," *ProRodeo Sports News*, August 2, 1989; Schonholz, "Animals in Rodeo," 1247–48.
94. "Confronting the Animal Rights Beast," *ProRodeo Sports News*, July 31, 1991, 10; see also Furman, "Rodeo Cattle's Many Performances," 1395; Furman, "Dr. Furman Responds," 167; Ryan, "Rodeos Put Animal Care Front and Center"; Schonholz, "Animals in Rodeo," 1247–48.
95. Ryan, "Rodeos Put Animal Care Front and Center."
96. There are many examples of this phenomenon. See, for instance, Campion, *Rodeo*, 44; Canadian Professional Rodeo Association, *Animal Welfare*; *PRCA Media Guide*. The PRCA, for one, did acknowledge the possibility of compromised welfare at the two-thirds of rodeos in the U.S. not sanctioned by the PRCA, explaining, "Unfortunately, unsanctioned events do take place. The PRCA has no control over those events and urges anyone who witnesses improper treatment of animals to report the offending action to local animal welfare agencies." PRCA, *Animal Welfare*, 16.
97. Furman, "Rodeo Cattle's Many Performances," 1395.
98. Larson, "Thinks Calf Roping, Steer Tripping Inhumane," 166.

99. Taylor, "More Thoughts on Calf Roping, Steer Tripping," 594. A Canadian Veterinary Medical Association statement on rodeos, proposed but never formally adopted, maintained that "it is not possible for the profession to positively embrace the practices which are integral to rodeos. The success of rodeos inevitably rests on the exploitation of animals' reactions to pain, noise and fear, and the animals' desire to escape." Veterinarians have always balanced the needs of animal patients against their owners' financial needs or cultural beliefs. Sometimes compromises had to be made. Continued the CVMA, "veterinarians are rarely able to find perfect worlds in which to operate, and . . . the animals' lot is not likely to be improved by having veterinarians 'opt out.'" Instead, more veterinarians should be involved in the planning and running of rodeos, although how that would take place at the hundreds of small-town amateur rodeos, the CVMA did not appear to have any practical plan. "Canadian Veterinary Medical Association Statement on Rodeos," xvii.
100. Grandin, *Animals in Translation*, 189–92.
101. Jones, *Valuing Animals*, 63–114.
102. Larson, "Rodeo Is Cruel Entertainment," 117–18.
103. Larson, "Rodeo Is Cruel Entertainment," 117–18.
104. Morrow-Tesch, "Evaluating Management Practices for Their Impact on Welfare," 1374.
105. Grandin, "Welfare of Cattle," 1377.
106. Sinclair et al, "Behavioral and Physiological Responses of Calves," 9. Scientific studies by ethologists and veterinarians of calf welfare in rodeo have been very slow to appear. More research might refute or support the very narrow pro-rodeo definitions of calf "injury," put forward by rodeo committees and governing bodies, restricting calf harm to visibly crippling physical trauma, such as bone breaks or being rendered unconscious in the immediate seconds after roping in the arena. One recent study found elevated levels of both acute and long-lasting stress hormones in experienced calves upon being roped and, among "naïve" calves, even just from being herded through an arena by a pickup rider. This study took place in a quiet arena with no music or audience noise to disturb the calves and with experienced professional ropers. Still it found elevated stress levels and behaviors indicating discomfort and disorientation, like a failure to stand up after being roped, coughing and head shaking, rolling the eyes to show the whites. Researchers estimated that the effects among practice pen stock or calves roped by novice ropers would have been considerably elevated since the roping would take longer.
107. Daryl Slade, "Calf Roping Gains a New Sensitivity," *Calgary Herald*, July 9, 2003.
108. See for instance, Mike Rogozinski, "Not My Idea of a Good Time," *Coquitlam Now*, May 15, 2006. Regarding local newspapers in and around Vancouver and the city's unusually prominent history of public animal advocacy, see Colby, "Cetaceans in the City," 294–305; McMillan, "Conflict Over Animal Experimentation in Vancouver," 35–38.

109. Debra Probert, "The Rodeo Debate: Against," *Vancouver Sun*, May 16, 2006.
110. "What Is the Vancouver Humane Society Asking Surrey Council to do about the Cloverdale Rodeo?," Vancouver Humane Society to City of Surrey Council, May 8, 2006, VHS.
111. Debra Probert, "Putting Spurs to Cloverdale's Brutal Rodeo," *Animal Writes*, 35 (Summer 2006): 6-7.
112. "Having Fun?," Vancouver Humane Society Press Release, May 14, 1992; "Airplane to Fly Over Surrey Rodeo Protesting Cruelty to Animals," Vancouver Humane Society Press Release, May 19, 2005, VHS.
113. "No One Likes an 8 Second Ride," Vancouver Humane Society Press Release, May 19, 2006, VHS.
114. "Pamela Anderson Tells Sponsors to Buck the Cloverdale Rodeo," Vancouver Humane Society Press Release, May 18, 2007, VHS.
115. Eva Salinas, "Rodeo Spurs Animal-Rights Furor," *Globe and Mail*, May 20, 2006.
116. Laura Balance, "The Rodeo Debate: For," *Vancouver Sun*, May 16, 2006.
117. "Cloverdale Rodeo Announces Major Changes to Event Programming," Cloverdale Rodeo and Exhibition press release, May 22, 2007; Nicholas Read, "Ban on Roping Events Is a Rodeo First," *Vancouver Sun*, May 23, 2007: Jane Armstrong, "B. C. Rodeo Nixes Roping, Wrestling and Milking Events," *Globe and Mail*, May 24, 2007.
118. "Cloverdale Rodeo Announces Major Changes to Event Programming," Cloverdale Rodeo and Exhibition press release, May 22, 2007; "Calf-Roping Banned at Cloverdale Rodeo after Calf Dies," Vancouver Humane Society press release, May 22, 2007; "Cloverdale Rodeo cancels calf-roping events after death of animal," News 1130 radio broadcast transcript, May 22, 2007, http://www.animaladvocates.com/watchdog.pl?page=1;md=read;id=9171.
119. See for instance, Morisset kids Mutton Bustin at the Cloverdale Rodeo, Youtube.com, June 2, 2017, https://youtu.be/8CC04sFm49Q.
120. Wooden and Ehringer, *Rodeo in America*, 130.
121. Bernie Rollin, quoted in Alexis Kienlen, "Don't Write Off Animal Welfare Advocates as Vegans and 'Crazies,' Says Expert," *Alberta Farm Express*, April 11, 2011.
122. Bernie Rollin, quoted in Alexis Kienlen, "Don't Write Off Animal Welfare Advocates as Vegans and 'Crazies,' Says Expert," *Alberta Farm Express*, April 11, 2011.

## Epilogue

1. Lutz, *Makúk*, 119.
2. There followed almost a century of overgrazing of British Columbia's grasslands that saw their carrying capacity for cattle spiral downward. Thistle, *Resettling the Range*, 116-17, 132-35.
3. Lutz, *Makúk*, 131-41. The Chilcotin War was representative of countless similar moments of armed conflict fueled by the provocative and sometimes downright outrageous behavior of miners, homesteaders, road building crews, and other settlers who trespassed on Indigenous land in British Columbia. Canadian Prime

Minister Justin Trudeau recently apologized formally and exonerated in Parliament the six chiefs, explaining, "They were acting as one independent nation engaged in war with another when they attacked and killed members of a road crew that trespassed on their territory." Trudeau agreed to make his way to the formal ceremony marking the official apology riding a black horse. The horse was symbolic of a black horse ridden by one of the chiefs to meet for peace talks. When the chief was arrested, his horse fled and returned to a Tsilhqot'in chiefs' camp. Amy Smart, "Trudeau Apologizes to B.C. Indigenous Community for 1864 Hanging of Chiefs," *Globe and Mail*, November 2, 2018; Tsilhqot'in National Government, *Bringing the Spirit Home*, November 17, 2018, YouTube.com, https://www.youtube.com/watch?time_continue=55&v=zkwDq9Im-Bg.
4. Furniss, *Burden of History*, 169.
5. Kelm, *Wilder West*, 16–17, 52–53; Furniss, *Burden of History*, 4–11, 164–65.
6. Iverson, *Riders of the West*, 14–15, 28.
7. Furniss, *Burden of History*, 183; Kelm, *Wilder West*, 12; Mellis, *Riding Buffaloes*, 35–42; Penrose, "When all the Cowboys are Indians."
8. "Redstone Rodeo Rider Killed in Mountain Race Identified by Coroner," *CBC News British Columbia*, August 20, 2014, https://www.cbc.ca/news/canada/british-columbia/redstone-rodeo-rider-killed-in-mountain-race-identified-by-coroner-1.2741753.
9. Gabo Gasztonyi Studio, April 12, 2018, Facebook.com, https://www.facebook.com/events/1815541728747338/?active_tab=discussion.
10. Lutz, *Makúk*, 146; see also Iverson, *Riders of the West*, 28.
11. British Columbia Rodeo Association, *2018 BCRA Rodeo Guide*, 16.

# Works Cited

### Archives and Libraries

City of Vancouver Archives, Vancouver, BC
Dickinson Research Library, National Cowboy and Western Heritage Museum, Oklahoma City, OK
Glenbow Museum Archives, Calgary, AB
Special Collections and University Archives, Stanford University Libraries, Stanford, CA
University of Wyoming American Heritage Center, Laramie, WY
Vancouver Humane Society, Vancouver, BC
Wyoming State Archives, Cheyenne, WY

### Manuscript Collections

BEL  Don Bell Collection, Dickinson Research Center, National Cowboy and Western Heritage Museum, Oklahoma City, Oklahoma, https://nationalcowboymuseum.org/finding-aids/don-bell/.

HAN  Robert D. Hanesworth Papers, University of Wyoming American Heritage Center, Laramie, WY, http://uwcatalog.uwyo.edu/record=b2135240~S3.

PAL  Joseph S. Palen Papers, University of Wyoming American Heritage Center, Laramie, WY, http://uwcatalog.uwyo.edu/record=b2139860~S3.

POR  Willard H. Porter Rodeo Collection, Dickinson Research Center, National Cowboy and Western Heritage Museum, Oklahoma City, Oklahoma, https://nationalcowboymuseum.org/finding-aids/porter/.

STA  Stampede Fonds, Glenbow Museum Archives, Calgary, Alberta, http://www.glenbow.org/collections/search/findingAids/archhtm/stampede.cfm.

WEA  Guy Weadick Fonds, Glenbow Museum Archives, Calgary, Alberta, http://www.glenbow.org/collections/search/findingAids/archhtm/weadick.cfm.

## Periodicals

*Alberta Farm Express*
*Animal Writes*
*Arizona Republican* (Phoenix)
*Aspen Tribune*
*The Athena Press* (OR)
*Barrel Horse News*
*Bastrop Advertiser* (TX)
*Beef*
*The Billboard*
*Buckin' Stock Magazine*
*Calgary Herald*
*The Cattleman*
*Cheyenne Daily Leader*
*Cheyenne Daily Sun*
*Chico Enterprise* (CA)
*Colorado Springs Independent*
*Colorado Transcript* (Golden)
*Coquitlam Now*
*Country World*
*Daily Alta California* (San Francisco)
*Daily Capital Journal* (Salem, OR)
*Daily East Oregonian* (Pendleton)
*Daily Inter-Ocean* (Chicago)
*Dalles Daily Chronicle* (OR)
*Denver Post*
*Deseret Evening News* (Salt Lake City)
*The Dodo*
*Eastern Utah Advocate* (Price, UT)
*Fort Morgan Times* (CO)
*Frank Leslie's Illustrated Newspaper*
*Free Press* (KS)
*Galveston Daily News*
*Globe and Mail*
*Harper's Weekly*
*Heppner Gazette* (OR)
*Herald Democrat* (Leadville, CO)
*H Magazine*
*Hoofs 'N Horns*
*Horse Lover's National Magazine*
*Life*
*McClure's Magazine*

*Meristem Land and Science*
*Modern Dog*
*Modern Farmer*
*National Humane Review*
*National Post*
*National Sports Daily*
*New York Sun*
*New York Times*
*New York Tribune*
*New Yorker*
*Northwestern Livestock Journal* (Cheyenne, WY)
*The Oklahoman*
*Oregonian* (Portland)
*Pro Bull Rider*
*ProRodeo Sports News*
*Rathdrum Tribune* (ID)
*Reader's Digest*
*Rocky Mountain News* (Denver)
*Rodeo Sports News* [continues as *ProRodeo Sports News*]
*Sacramento Daily Union*
*Salida Mail* (CO)
*Salt Lake Herald* (UT)
*Salt Lake Telegram* (UT)
*Salt Lake Tribune* (UT)
*San Francisco Call*
*San Marcos Free Press* (TX)
*Sports Illustrated*
*Team Roping Journal*
*Temple Daily Times* (TX)
*Upstart Business Journal*
*Vancouver Province*
*Vancouver Sun*
*Washington Post*
*Weekly Democrat Statesman* (Austin, TX)
*Western Horseman*
*The Wild Bunch*
*World of Rodeo and Western Heritage*
*Wyoming State Tribune* (Cheyenne)

## Published Primary Sources

Adams, Andy. *The Log of a Cowboy: A Narrative of the Old Trail Days*. Boston: Houghton, Mifflin and Company, 1903.

Adams, Ramon F. *The Old-Time Cowhand*. New York: Macmillan Company, 1961.
American Humane Association. *The Wild West Round-Up Must Go*. Albany, NY: American Humane Association, 1919. Hathi Trust Digital Library, https:/catalog.hathitrust.org/Record/012477600.
Barker, Marcia, ed. "History of the Strickland and Taylor Families: An Oral History with Edward Burton Strickland." *Northeastern Nevada Historical Society Quarterly* 96, no.1 (1996): 1–23.
Barrows, John R. *Ubet*. Caldwell, ID: Caxton, 1934.
Blunt, Judy. *Breaking Clean*. New York: Vintage, 2002.
Branch, Edward Douglas. *The Cowboy and His Interpreters*. New York: D. Appleton, 1926.
Brandon, William. "Bernalillo County." *American West* 11, no. 2 (1967): 28–29, 70–71.
British Columbia Rodeo Association. *2018 BCRA Rodeo Guide*. Cache Creek: British Columbia Rodeo Association, 2018.
Brisendine, Everett. *Old Cowboys Never Die*. n.p.: Everett Brisendine, 1984.
Brownell, Sam. *Rodeos and "Tipperary."* Denver: Big Mountain Press, 1961.
Canadian Professional Rodeo Association. *Animal Welfare*. Airdrie, AB: Canadian Professional Rodeo Association, 2010, http://www.rodeocanada.com/pdfs/2010animalwelfare.pdf
Clancy, Foghorn. *My Fifty Years in Rodeo: Living with Cowboys, Horses, and Danger*. San Antonio: Naylor Company, 1952.
Cooper, Roy. *Calf Roping*. Colorado Springs: Western Horseman, 1984.
CPRA. *See* Canadian Professional Rodeo Association
Darden, Jim. *Scrappy: A Rodeo Bull*. Pine Bluffs, WY: Rodeo Studio, 1985.
Edwards, Jim, and Helen Edwards. "A Horse Story and a Lesson to Remember." *Montana Standard* (Butte). March 1, 2005, https://mtstandard.com/special-section/local/a-horse-story-and-lesson-to-remember/article_5be65162-a656-55fa-995e-2b7dc60b54be.html.
Faulkner, Steven. "Their Own Brand of Misery," *Southwest Review* 100, no. 2 (Spring 2015), 244–62.
Faulknor, Cliff. *Turn Him Loose! Herman Linder, Canada's Mr. Rodeo*. Saskatoon, SK: Western Producer Prairie Books, 1977.
Furlong, Charles Wellington. *Let 'Er Buck*. 1921; New York: Overlook, 2007.
Gilbreath, C. T. "I Was a Cowboy Once (A True Story)," *American West* 13, no. 2 (1976): 14–17, 62.
Gillespie, A. S. "Bud," and R. H. "Bob" Burns. *Steamboat: Symbol of Wyoming Spirit*. Laramie: University of Wyoming Steamboat Monument Project, 1952.
Harding, Frank [Frank Barrow]. "The Passing of 'Busting' as a Sport." *Pacific Monthly* (August 24, 1910), 139–43.
Hasselstrom, Linda M. *Between Grass and Sky: Where I Live and Work*. Reno: University of Nevada Press, 2002.
Hennessey, Paul. *Tipperary: The Diary of a Bucking Horse, 1905–1932*. Belle Fourche, SD: Sand Creek Printing, 1989.

Hough, Emerson. *The Cowboy.* New York: Brampton Society, 1897.
Jacobs, Frank. *Cattle and Us, Frankly Speaking.* Calgary, AB: Detselig Enterprises, 1993.
Johnstone, Jeffrey, and Keith Ryan Cartwright. *Professional Bull Riders: The Official Guide to the Toughest Sport on Dirt.* Chicago: Triumph Books, 2009.
"King of the Cowboys," Fortnight: Magazine of the Pacific Coast 19, no. 4 (April 1956): 50.
Knight, Darrell. *Pete Knight: The Cowboy King.* Walnut Springs, TX: Wild Horse Press, 2004.
Lamb, Gene. *Rodeo: Back of the Chutes.* Denver: The Bell Press, 1956.
———. *Rodeo Cowboy.* San Antonio: Naylor, 1959.
Mansfield, Toots. *Calf Roping.* Colorado Springs: Western Horseman, 1961.
McCoy, Joseph G. *Historic Sketches of the Cattle Trade of the West and Southwest.* Kansas City: Ramsey, Millett & Hudson, 1874.
McFadden, Cyra. *Rain or Shine: A Family Memoir.* Lincoln: University of Nebraska Press, 1986.
Moulton, Candy Vyvey, and Flossie Moulton. *Steamboat: Legendary Bucking Horse.* Glendo, WY: High Plains Press, 1992.
Norbury, Rosamond. *Behind the Chutes: The Mystique of the Rodeo Cowboy.* Vancouver: Whitecap Books, 1992
*Penal Code and Code of Criminal Procedure of the State of Texas,* 4th ed., 2 vol., with 1906 supplement. St. Louis: Gilbert Book Company, 1896, 1906.
Peter, Josh. *Fried Twinkies, Buckle Bunnies and Bull Riders: A Year Inside the Professional Bull Riders Tour.* New York: Rodale, 2005.
Platt, Kenneth B. "'Ride 'em Cowboy!'—or WALK: Was Situation on Salmon River in 1910." *Pacific Northwesterner* 17, no. 3 (1973): 51–60.
PRCA. *See* Professional Rodeo Cowboys Association
Professional Rodeo Cowboys Association. *Animal Welfare: The Care and Treatment of Professional Rodeo Livestock.* Colorado Springs: Professional Rodeo Cowboys Association, n.d.
———. *Humane Facts: The Care and Treatment of Professional Rodeo Livestock.* Colorado Springs: Professional Rodeo Cowboys Association, 1994.
———. *2006 PRCA Media Guide.* Colorado Springs: Professional Rodeo Cowboys Association, 2006.
Quaker Oats Company—Rockford Pet Foods Division, Inc. *Rockford: The Pet Food Story, 1923–87.* Rockford, IL: Rockford Pet Foods Division, Quaker Oats Co., 1987.
*Review of U.S. Department of Agriculture's Enforcement of the Animal Welfare Act, Specifically of Animals Used in Exhibitions: Hearings before the Subcommittee on Department Operations, Research, and Foreign Agriculture of the Committee on Agriculture, House of Representatives.* 102nd Cong., 2nd sess. July 8, 1992. Action for Animals testimony.
Richards, Rusty. *Casey Tibbs: Born to Ride.* Wickenburg, AZ: Moonlight Mesa, 2010.
Robertson, M. S. *Rodeo: Standard Guide to the Cowboy Sport.* Berkeley, CA: Howell-North, 1961.

Rollins, Philip Ashton. *The Cowboy: His Characteristics, His Equipment, and His Part in the Development of the West.* New York: Charles Scribner's sons, 1922.
Santee, Ross. *Men and Horses.* 1921; Lincoln: University of Nebraska Press, 1977.
Santos, Kendra. *Ring of Fire: The Guts and Glory of the Professional Bull Riders Tour.* Chicago: Triumph Books, 2000.
Savitt, Sam. *Rodeo: Cowboys, Bulls, and Broncos.* New York: Doubleday, 1963.
Siringo, Charles A. *A Lone Star Cowboy.* Santa Fe: Chas. A. Siringo, 1919.
———. *A Texas Cow Boy; or, Fifteen Years on the Hurricane Deck of a Spanish Pony.* Chicago: Siringo and Dobson, 1886.
Stanley, Clark. *The Life and Adventures of the American Cow-boy.* Providence: n.p., 1897. Hathi Trust Library, https://hdl.handle.net/2027/njp.32101074864578.
Tooke, Ernest. *Moments in Rodeo* (Ekalaka, MT: n.p., 1992), reproduced at https://www.facebook.com/media/set/?set=a.270207933148326.107374 1876.192768134225640&type=3.
———. "Tooke Bucking Horses." *Shifting Scenes* 2 (1978): 878–80.
Ward, Fay E. *The Cowboy at Work.* 1958; repr. Mineola, NY: Dover Publications, 2003.
Weiland, Victoria Carlyle. *100 Years of Rodeo Stock Contracting.* Reno, NV: Professional Rodeo Stock Contractors Association, 1997.
*Wyoming Laws for the Protection of Children and Animals.* Laramie: Wyoming Humane Society and State Board of Child and Animal Protection, 1911, 1920.
Wyoming State Board of Child and Animal Protection. *Biannual Report of the Wyoming Humane Society and State Board of Child and Animal Protection.* Cheyenne, WY: The Board, 1912.

## Books, Chapters, Articles

Alagona, Peter S. *After the Grizzly: Endangered Species and the Politics of Place in California.* Berkeley: University of California Press, 2013.
Allen, Michael. "Real Cowboys? The Origins and Evolution of North American Rodeo and Rodeo Cowboys. *Journal of the West* 37, no. 1 (January 1998): 69–79.
———. *Rodeo Cowboys in the North American Imagination.* Reno: University of Nevada Press, 1998.
———. "Yakima Canutt: From Colfax to Hollywood and Beyond." *Columbia* 12, no. 2 (Summer 1998): 38–43.
Anderson, Virginia De John. *Creatures of Empire: How Domestic Animals Transformed Early America.* New York: Oxford University Press, 2004.
Andrews, David L., and Steven J. Jackson, eds. *Sport Stars: The Cultural Politics of Sporting Celebrity.* New York: Routledge, 2001.
Arluke, Arnold, and Robert Bogdan. "Taming the Wild: Rodeo as Human-Animal Metaphor." In James Gillett and Michelle Gilbert, eds. *Sport, Animals, and Society.* New York: Routledge, 2014, 15–34.
Aron, Stephen. "Lessons in Conquest: Towards a Greater Western History." *Pacific Historical Review* 63, no. 2 (May 1994): 125–48.
Atherton, Lewis. "Cattleman and Cowboy: Fact and Fancy." *Montana* 11, no. 4 (1964): 2–17.

Barman, Jean. *The West Beyond the West: A History of British Columbia*, 3rd ed. Toronto: University of Toronto Press, 2007.

Barrow, Mark V., Jr. *Nature's Ghosts: Confronting Extinction from the Age of Jefferson to the Age of Ecology*. Chicago: University of Chicago Press, 2009.

Baxter, John O. *Cowboy Park: Steer-Roping Contests on the Border*. Lubbock: Texas Tech University Press, 2008.

———. "Ropers and Rangers: Cowboy Tournaments and Steer Roping Contests in Territorial Arizona." *Journal of Arizona History* 46, no. 4 (Winter 2005): 315–48.

———. "Sport on the Rio Grande: Cowboy Tournaments at New Mexico's Territorial Fair, 1885–1905." *New Mexico Historical Review* 78, no. 3 (Summer 2003): 244–63.

Beers, Diane L. *For the Prevention of Cruelty: The History and Legacy of Animal Rights Activism in the United States*. Athens: Swallow Press/The Ohio University Press, 2006.

Bennett, Lyn, and Scott Abbott. "Barbed and Dangerous: Constructing the Meaning of Barbed Wire in Late Nineteenth-Century America." *Agricultural History* 88, no. 4 (Fall 2014): 566–90.

Bernstein, Joel H. *Wild Ride: The History and Lore of Rodeo*. Salt Lake City: Gibbs Smith, 2007.

Beutler, Randy L. "Broncs, Bulls and Contracts: The Rodeo World of the Beutler Brothers." *Chronicles of Oklahoma* 63, no. 1 (1985): 48–57.

Boatright, Mody C. "The American Rodeo." *American Quarterly* 16, no. 2, part 1 (1964): 195–202.

Bold, Christine. *The Frontier Club: Popular Westerns and Cultural Power, 1880–1924*. New York: Oxford University Press, 2013.

———. *Selling the Wild West: Popular Western Fiction, 1860–1960*. Bloomington: Indiana University Press, 1987.

Brado, Edward. *Cattle Kingdom: Early Ranching in Alberta*. Vancouver: Douglas & McIntyre, 1984.

Brickey, Michael Charles. "Buying the Bull: Gender, Class, and the Implied Politics of Urban Cowboy (1980)." Paper presented at the Western Literature Association Conference, St. Louis, MO, October 2018.

Bridger, Bobby. *Buffalo Bill and Sitting Bull: Inventing the Wild West*. Austin: University of Texas Press, 2002.

Brown, Frederick L. *The City Is More than Human: An Animal History of Seattle*. Seattle: University of Washington Press, 2016.

Brown, Mark H., and W. R. Felton. *Before Barbed Wire: L. A. Huffman, Photographer on Horseback*. New York: Henry Holt and Company, 1956.

Budiansky, Stephen. "The Ancient Contract." *U.S. News & World Report* 106, no. 11 (March 20, 1989): 74.

Burbick, Joan. *Rodeo Queens and the American Dream*. New York: Public Affairs, 2002.

Burrows, Jack. "The Greatest Bronc Buster Who Ever Lived: Manny Airola of Angels Camp." *American West* 20, no. 3 (1983): 54–58.

Burstyn, Varda. *The Rites of Men: Manhood, Politics, and the Culture of Sport*. Toronto: University of Toronto Press, 1999.

Butler, Anne M. "Selling the Popular Myth." In Milner, Clyde A., II, Carol A. O'Connor, and Martha A. Sandweiss, eds., *The Oxford History of the American West*. New York: Oxford University Press, 1994, 771–79.

Campbell, Colin S. "The Stampede: Cowtown's Sacred Cow." In Chuck Reasons, ed., *Stampede City: Power and Politics in the West*. Calgary: Between the Lines, 1984, 106–13

"Canadian Veterinary Medical Association Statement on Rodeos," *Canadian Veterinary Journal* 26, no. 5 (May 1985): xvii.

Carlson, Paul H. "Myth and the Modern Cowboy." In Paul H. Carlson, ed. *The Cowboy Way: An Exploration of History and Culture*. Lubbock: Texas Tech University Press, 2000.

Carr Childers, Leisl. "Leisl Carr Childers on the Gus Bundy Photographs and the Wild Horse Controversy." *Environmental History* 18, no. 3 (July 2013): 604–20.

———. "The National Finals Rodeo." *Nevada Historical Society Quarterly* 51, no. 4 (Winter 2008): 267–91.

———. *The Size of the Risk: Histories of Multiple Use in the Great Basin*. Norman: University of Oklahoma Press, 2015.

Childers, Michael W. *Colorado Powder Keg: Ski Resorts and the Environmental Movement*. Lawrence: University Press of Kansas, 2012.

Christiansen, Larry D. "The Extinction of Wild Cattle in Southern Arizona." *Journal of Arizona History* 29, no. 1 (Spring 1988): 89–100.

Clark, J. J. "The Slave Whisperer Rides the Frontier: Horseface Minstrelsy in the Western." In Sarah E. McFarland and Ryan Hediger, ed. *Animals and Agency: An Interdisciplinary Exploration*. Leiden, The Netherlands: Brill, 2009, 159–81.

Clifton, Merritt. "Anti-Rodeo Vet Was Performer." *Animal People* 3, no. 6 (July-August 1994), https://newspaper.animalpeopleforum.org/1994/07/01/anti-rodeo-vet-was-performer/

Colby, Jason. "Cetaceans in the City: Orca Captivity, Animal Rights, and Environmental Values in Vancouver." In Joanna Dean, Darcy Ingram, and Christabelle Sethna, eds. *Animal Metropolis: Histories of Human-Animal Relations in Urban Canada*. Calgary: University of Calgary Press, 2017, 285–308.

Coleman, James T. *Vicious: Wolves and Men in America*. New Haven: Yale University Press, 2006.

Colpitts, George. *Game in the Garden: A Human History of Wildlife in Western Canada to 1940*. Vancouver: University of British Columbia Press, 2002.

Corey, D. "Welfare Issues in the Rodeo Horse." In C. W. McIlwraith and B. E. Rollin. *Equine Welfare*. Oxford: Wiley-Blackwell, 2011, 275–301.

Cothran, Boyd. *Remembering the Modoc War: Redemptive Violence and the Making of American Innocence*. Chapel Hill: University of North Carolina Press, 2014.

Cronin, J. Keri. *Manufacturing National Park Nature: Photography, Ecology, and the Wilderness Industry of Jasper*. Vancouver: University of British Columbia Press, 2011.

Cronon, William. *Nature's Metropolis: Chicago and the Great West*. New York: W. W. Norton, 1991.

Cronon, William, George Miles, and Jay Gitlin, eds. *Under an Open Sky: Rethinking America's Western Past*. New York: W. W. Norton, 1992.
Dant, Sara. *Losing Eden: An Environmental History of the American West*. Hoboken: Wiley & Sons, 2017.
Dary, David. *Cowboy Culture: A Saga of Five Centuries*. Lawrence: University Press of Kansas, 1981.
Davis, Janet M. *The Gospel of Kindness: Animal Welfare and the Making of Modern America*. New York: Oxford University Press, 2016.
Davis, Susan G. *Parades and Power: Street Theatre in Nineteenth-Century Philadelphia*. Berkeley: University of California Press, 1986.
Dawson, Michael. *Selling British Columbia: Tourism and Consumer Culture, 1890–1970*. Vancouver: University of British Columbia Press, 2004.
Dean, Joanna, and Lucas Wilson. "Horse Power in the Modern City." In Ruth W. Sandwell, ed. *Powering Up Canada: A History of Power, Fuel, and Energy from 1600*. McGill-Queen's University Press, 2016, 99–128.
Derry, Kathryn. "Corset and Broncs: The Wild West Show Cowgirl, 1890–1920," *Colorado Heritage* (Summer 1992): 2–16.
Derry, Margaret. *Bred for Perfection: Shorthorn Cattle, Collies, and Arabian Horses since 1800*. Baltimore: Johns Hopkins University Press, 2003.
———. *Horses in Society: A Story of Animal Breeding and Marketing Culture, 1800–1920*. Toronto: University of Toronto Press, 2006.
———. *Ontario's Cattle Kingdom: Purebred Breeders and Their World, 1870–1920*. Toronto: University of Toronto Press, 2001.
De Steiguer, J. Edward. *Wild Horses of the West: History and Politics of America's Mustangs*. Tucson: University of Arizona Press, 2011.
Dippie, Brian W. "'Chop! Chop!': Progress in the Presentation of Western Visual History." *The Historian* 66, no. 3 (Fall 2004): 491–500.
———. "The Visual West." In Milner, Clyde A., II, Carol A. O'Connor, and Martha A. Sandweiss, eds., *The Oxford History of the American West*. New York: Oxford University Press, 1994, 677–705.
Dobie, Frank J. "The First Cattle in Texas and the Southwest: Progenitors of the Longhorns." *Southwestern Historical Quarterly* 42, no. 3 (January 1939): 171–97.
———. *The Longhorns*. 1941; repr. New York: Bramhall, 1982.
———. *The Mustangs*. Boston: Little, Brown, 1952.
———. *The Voice of the Coyote*. 1949; repr. Lincoln: University of Nebraska Press, 2006.
Doss, Erika. "Shoot-Out: Poking Fun and Challenging Myths in Western American Art." In *Redrawing Boundaries: Perspectives on Western American Art*. Denver: Institute of Western American Art, Denver Art Museum/University of Washington Press, 2007, 44–55.
DuBose, Robert W., Jr. "Updating the Cowboy." *Southern Folklore Quarterly* 26, no. 3 (1962): 187–98.
Dummitt, Chris. "Finding a Place for Father: Selling the Barbecue in Postwar Canada." *Journal of the Canadian Historical Association* 9, no. 1 (1998): 209–223.

Ehringer, Gavin. *Rodeo Legends: 20 Extraordinary Athletes of America's Sport.* Colorado Springs: Western Horseman, 2001.

Ellis, Colter. "Boundary Labor and the Production of Emotionless Commodities: The Case of Beef Production." *Sociological Quarterly* 55, no. 1 (2014): 92–118.

Ellis, Colter, and Leslie Irvine. "Reproducing Dominion: Emotional Apprenticeship in the 4-H Youth Livestock Program." *Society and Animals* 18, no. 1 (2010): 21–39.

Elofson, Warren E. *Cowboys, Gentlemen and Cattle Thieves: Ranching on the Western Frontier.* Montreal: McGill-Queens University Press, 2000.

———. *Frontier Cattle Ranching in the Land and Times of Charlie Russell.* Seattle: University of Washington, 2004.

———. *So Far and Yet So Close: Frontier Cattle Ranching in Western Prairie Canada and the Northern Territory of Australia.* Calgary: University of Calgary Press, 2015.

Erickson, John R. *The Modern Cowboy,* 2nd ed. Denton, TX: University of North Texas Press, 2004.

Etulain, Richard W. *Telling Western Stories: From Buffalo Bill to Larry McMurtry.* Albuquerque: University of New Mexico Press, 1999.

Ewers, John Canfield. *The Horse in Blackfoot Indian Culture.* Washington, DC: Smithsonian Institution, 1955.

Ewing, Solon E., Donald C. Lay, Jr., and Eberhard Von Borell, *Farm Animal Well-Being: Stress Physiology, Animal Behavior, and Environmental Design.* Upper Saddle River, New Jersey: Prentice Hall, 1999.

Fischer, John Ryan. *Cattle Colonialism: An Environmental History of the Conquest of California and Hawai'i.* Chapel Hill: University of North Carolina Press, 2015.

Fleharty, Eugene D. *Wild Animals and Settlers on the Great Plains.* Norman: University of Oklahoma Press, 1995.

Flores, Dan. *American Serengeti: The Last Big Animals of the Great Plains.* Lawrence: University Press of Kansas, 2016.

Foer, Jonathan Safran. *Eating Animals.* New York: Little, Brown and Company, 2009.

Food and Agriculture Organization of the United Nations, *Livestock's Long Shadow* 2006. http://www.fao.org/3/a0701e/a0701e00.htm.

Foran, Max. "Land Speculation and Urban Development: Calgary 1884–1912." In *Frontier Calgary: Town, City, and Region, 1875–1914,* ed. Anthony W. Rasporich and Henry C. Klassen. Calgary: McClelland and Stewart, 1975, 203–20.

Fowler, Veronica, Mark Kennedy, and David Marlin. "A Comparison of the Monty Roberts Technique with a Conventional UK Technique for Initial Training of Riding Horses." *Anthrozoös* 25, no. 3 (2012): 301–21.

Francis, Daniel. *National Dreams: Myth, Memory, and Canadian History.* Vancouver: Arsenal Pulp Press, 1997.

Franzky, F., W. Bohnet, F. Kuhne, and J. Luy. "Animal Welfare Legal Aspects of Rodeo Events." *Deutsche Tierarztliche Wochenschrift* 112, no. 3 (March 2005): 92–94.

Fraser, David. *Understanding Animal Welfare: The Science in its Cultural Context.* London: Wiley-Blackwell, 2008.

Fredriksson, Kristine. *American Rodeo: From Buffalo Bill to Big Business*. College Station: Texas A&M University Press, 1986.
Fudge, Erica. *Animal*. London: Reaktion Books, 2002.
Fureix, Carole, Marie Bourjade, Séverine Henry, Carol Sankey, and Martine Hausberger. "Exploring Aggression Regulation in Managed Groups of Horses *Equus caballus*. *Applied Animal Behaviour Science* 138 (2012): 216–28.
Furman, J. W. "Dr. Furman Responds." *Journal of the American Veterinary Medical Association* 220, no. 2 (January 15, 2002): 167.
——. "Rodeo Cattle's Many Performances," *Journal of the American Veterinary Medical Association* 219, no. 10 (November 15, 2001): 1394–97.
Furniss, Elizabeth. *The Burden of History: Colonialism and the Frontier Myth in a Rural Canadian Community*. Vancouver: University of British Columbia Press, 1999.
Gibson, Abraham H. "Beasts of Burden: Feral Burros and the American West." In Susan Nance, ed. *The Historical Animal*. Syracuse: Syracuse University Press, 2015, 38–53.
Gillett, James, and Michelle Gilbert, ed. *Sport, Animals, and Society*. New York: Routledge, 2014, 15–34
Glassberg, David. *Sense of History: The Place of the Past in American Life*. Amherst: University of Massachusetts Press, 2001.
Goetzmann, William H., and William N. Goetzmann. *The West of the Imagination*. Norman: University of Oklahoma Press, 2009.
Grandin, Temple, and Catherine Johnson. *Animals in Translation: Using the Mysteries of Autism to Decode Animal Behavior*. New York: Harcourt, 2005.
Grandin, Temple. "Welfare of Cattle During Slaughter and the Prevention of Nonambulatory (Downer) Cattle." *Journal of the American Veterinary Medical Association* 219, no. 10 (November 15, 2001): 1377–82.
Gray, James R. *Ranch Economics*. Ames: Iowa State University Press, 1968.
Greene, Anne Norton. *Horses at Work: Harnessing Power in Industrializing America*. Cambridge: Harvard University Press, 2008.
——. "War Horses: Equine Technology in the American Civil War." In Susan R. Schrepfer and Philip Scranton, ed. *Industrializing Organisms: Introducing Evolutionary History*. London: Routledge, 2004, 143–65.
Griffith, James S. "The Cowboy Poetry of Everett Brisendine: A Response to Cultural Change," *Western Folklore* 42, no. 1 (1983): 38–45.
Groves, Melody. *Ropes, Reins, and Rawhide: All About Rodeo*. Albuquerque: University of New Mexico Press, 2006.
Gruen, J. Philip. *Manifest Destinations: Cities and Tourists in the Nineteenth-Century American West*. Norman: University of Oklahoma Press, 2014.
Hämäläinen, Pekka. "The Rise and Fall of Plains Indians Horse Cultures." *Journal of American History* 90, no. 3 (December 2003): 833–62.
Haney, C. Allen, and Demetrius W. Pearson. "Rodeo Injuries: An Examination of Risk Factors." *Journal of Sport Behavior* 22, no. 4 (December 1999): 443–66.

Harrod, Howard L. *The Animals Came Dancing: Native American Sacred Ecology and Animal Kinship.* Tucson: University of Arizona Press, 2000.

Hassrick, Peter H. "Where's the Art in Western Art?" In *Redrawing Boundaries: Perspectives on Western American Art.* Denver and Seattle: Institute of Western American Art, Denver Art Museum and University of Washington Press, 2007, 9–11.

Hixson, Walter L. *American Settler Colonialism.* New York: Palgrave Macmillan, 2013.

Hoganson, Kristin. "Meat in the Middle: Converging Borderlands in the U.S. Midwest, 1865–1900." *Journal of American History* 98, no. 4 (March 2012): 1025–51.

Horowitz, Roger. *Putting Meat on the American Table: Taste, Technology, Transformation.* Baltimore: Johns Hopkins University Press, 2006.

Howard, Joseph Kinsey. *Montana: High, Wide, and Handsome.* New Haven: Yale University Press, 1943.

Hoy, James F. "From Folk Game to Professional Sport: Early Rodeo in Kansas." *International Folklore Review* 3 (Summer 1983): 143–51.

———. "The Origins and Originality of Rodeo." *Journal of the West* 17, no. 3 (1978): 16–33.

Hurt, R. Douglas. *The Big Empty: The Great Plains in the Twentieth Century.* Tucson: University of Arizona Press, 2011.

Igler, David. *Industrial Cowboys: Miller & Lux and the Transformation of the Far West, 1850–1920.* Berkeley: University of California Press, 2001.

Institute of Western American Art, Denver Art Museum. *Redrawing Boundaries: Perspectives on Western American Art.* Denver and Seattle: Institute of Western American Art, Denver Art Museum/University of Washington Press, 2007.

Isenberg, Andrew C. *The Destruction of the Bison: An Environmental History, 1750–1920.* Cambridge: Cambridge University Press, 2000.

Iverson, Peter. *Riders of the West: Portraits from Indian Rodeo.* Seattle: University of Washington Press, 1999.

———. *When Indians Became Cowboys: Native Peoples and Cattle Ranching in the American West.* Norman: University of Oklahoma Press, 1994.

Jacoby, Karl. *Crimes against Nature: Squatters, Poachers, Thieves, and the Hidden History of American Conservation.* Berkeley: University of California Press, 2001.

Jeffords, Susan. *Hard Bodies: Hollywood Masculinity in the Reagan Era.* New Brunswick: Rutgers University Press, 1993.

———. *The Remasculinization of America: Gender and the Vietnam War.* Bloomington and Indianapolis: Indiana University Press, 1989.

Jensen, Per, ed. *The Ethology of Domestic Animals: An Introductory Text,* 3rd ed. Wallingford, Oxfordshire, UK: CABI International, 2017.

Johnson, Dirk. *Biting the Dust: The Wild Ride and Dark Romance of the Rodeo Cowboy and the American West.* Lincoln: University of Nebraska Press, 1994.

Johnson, Lindgren. "To 'Admit All Cattle without Distinction': Reconstructing Slaughter in the Slaughterhouse Cases and the New Orleans Crescent City Slaughterhouse." In Paula Young Lee, ed. *Meat, Modernity, and the Rise of the Slaughterhouse.* Durham: University of New Hampshire Press, 2008, 198–215.

Jones, Karen R. *Wolf Mountains: A History of Wolves along the Great Divide.* Calgary: University of Calgary Press, 2002.
Jones, Susan D. *Valuing Animals: Veterinarians and Their Patients in Modern America.* Baltimore: Johns Hopkins University Press, 2003.
Jordan, Bob. *Rodeo History and Legends.* Montrose, CO: Rodeo Stuff, 1993.
Jordan, Philip. "Pistol Packin' Cowboy: From Bullet to Burial." *Red River Valley Historical View* 2, no. 1 (1975), 64–91.
Jordan, Terry G. *North American Cattle-Ranching Frontiers: Origins, Diffusion, and Differentiation.* Albuquerque: University of New Mexico Press, 1993.
Kahn, Margot. *Horses That Buck: The Story of Champion Bronc Rider Bill Smith.* Norman: University of Oklahoma Press, 2008.
Kasson, Joy S. *Buffalo Bill's Wild West: Celebrity, Memory, and Popular History.* New York: Hill and Wang, 2000.
Katerberg, William H. "A Northern Vision: Frontiers and the West in the Canadian and American Imagination." *American Review of Canadian Studies* 33, no. 4 (2003): 543–63.
Kelm, Mary-Ellen. "Riding into Place: Contact Zones, Rodeo, and Hybridity in the Canadian West, 1900–1970." *Journal of the Canadian Historical Association* 18, no. 1 (2007): 107–32.
———. *A Wilder West: Rodeo in Western Canada.* Vancouver: University of British Columbia Press, 2011.
Kleber, Louis C. "The Era of the American Cowboy." *History Today* 22, no. 5 (May 1972): 338–45.
Konrad, Herman W. "Barren Bulls and Charging Cows: Cowboy Celebrations in Copal and Calgary." In Frank E. Manning, ed. *The Celebration of Society: Perspectives on Contemporary Cultural Performance.* Bowling Green, OH: Bowling Green University Popular Press, 1983, 145–64.
Laegreid, Renée M. *Riding Pretty: Rodeo Royalty in the American West.* Lincoln: University of Nebraska Press, 2006.
Laird, Pamela Walker. *Advertising Progress: American Business and the Rise of Consumer Marketing.* Baltimore: Johns Hopkins University Press, 2001.
Larson, Peggy W. "Dr. Larson Responds." *Journal of the American Veterinary Medical Association* 220, no. 5 (March 1, 2002): 594–95.
———. "Rodeo Is Cruel Entertainment." *Pace Environmental Law Review* 16, no. 1 (Winter 1998): 115–23.
———. "Thinks Calf Roping, Steer Tripping Inhumane." *Journal of the American Veterinary Medical Association* 220, no. 2 (January 15, 2002): 166–67.
Larson, T. A. *History of Wyoming,* 2nd ed. Lincoln: University of Nebraska Press, 1978.
Lause, Mark A. *The Great Cowboy Strike: Bullets, Ballots, & Class Conflicts in the American West.* New York: Verso, 2017.
Lawrence, Elizabeth Atwood. *Hoofbeats and Society: Studies of Human-Horse Interactions.* Bloomington: Indiana University Press, 1985.

———. *Rodeo: An Anthropologist Looks at the Wild and the Tame.* Chicago: University of Chicago Press, 1982.

LeCompte, Mary Lou. "Cowgirls at the Crossroads: Women in Professional Rodeo, 1885–1922." *Canadian Journal of History of Sport* 20, no. 2 (1989): 27–48.

———. *Cowgirls of the Rodeo: Pioneer Professional Athletes.* Urbana-Champaign: University of Illinois Press, 2000.

———. "The First American Rodeo Never Happened." *Journal of Sport History* 9, no. 2 (Summer 1982): 89–96.

———. "The Hispanic Influence on the History of Rodeo, 1823–1922." *Journal of Sport History* 12, no. 1 (Spring 1985): 21–38.

———. "Hispanic Roots of American Rodeo." *Studies in Latin American Popular Culture* 13 (1994): 57–75.

———. "Home on the Range: Women in Professional Rodeo: 1929–1947." *Journal of Sport History* 17, no. 3 (Winter 1990): 318–46.

———. "Wild West Frontier Days, Roundups and Stampedes: Rodeo Before There Was Rodeo." *Canadian Journal of the History of Sport* 16, no. 2 (1985): 54–67.

Lee, Paula Young, ed. *Meat, Modernity, and the Rise of the Slaughterhouse.* Durham: University of New Hampshire Press, 2008.

Liberty, Margot, and Barry Head. *Working Cowboy: Recollections of Ray Holmes.* Norman: University of Oklahoma Press, 1995.

Limerick, Patricia Nelson. *The Legacy of Conquest: The Unbroken Past of the American West.* New York: W. W. Norton, 1987.

Limerick, Patricia Nelson, Clyde Milner II, and Charles E. Rankin, eds. *Trails: Toward a New Western History.* Lawrence: University Press of Kansas, 1991.

Lippman, Walter. *Public Opinion.* 1922; New York: Free Press/Simon & Schuster, 1997.

Little, J. I. "Ox and Horse Power in Rural Canada." In Ruth W. Sandwell, ed. *Powering Up Canada: A History of Power, Fuel, and Energy from 1600.* Montreal: McGill-Queen's University Press, 2016, 59–98.

Livingstone, Donna. *The Cowboy Spirit: Guy Weadick and the Calgary Stampede.* Vancouver: Greystone Books, 1996.

Lockwood, Randall. "Anthropomorphism Is Not a Four-letter Word." In R. J. Hoage, ed. *Perceptions of Animals in American Culture.* Washington, DC: Smithsonian Institution Press, 1989, 41–56.

Lounsberry, Lorraine. "Wild West Shows and the Canadian West." In Simon Evans, Sarah Carter, and Bill Yeo, eds. *Cowboys, Ranchers and the Cattle Business: Cross-Border Perspectives on Ranching History.* Calgary: University of Calgary Press, 2000, 139–52.

Lutz, John S. *Makúk: A New History of Aboriginal-White Relations.* Vancouver: University of British Columbia Press, 2008.

MacDonald, Marie. "'Kid' Foss and the Birth of Rodeo." *Montana* 21, no. 3 (1971): 56–63.

MacLachlan, Ian. "Humanitarian Reform, Slaughter Technology, and Butcher Resistance in Nineteenth-Century Britain." In Paula Young Lee, ed. *Meat, Modernity, and the Rise of the Slaughterhouse.* Durham: University of New Hampshire Press, 2008, 107–26.

Maher, Daniel R. *Mythic Frontiers: Remembering, Forgetting, and Profiting with Cultural Heritage Tourism.* Gainesville: University Press of Florida, 2016.

Mahoney, Sylvia Gann. *College Rodeo: From Show to Sport.* College Station: Texas A&M University Press, 2004.

Marino, Stephen. "'Wind Blew Down'/'Wind Came Up': *The Misfits* and the Imagery of Arthur Miller." *Nevada Historical Society Quarterly* 52, no. 1 (Spring 2009): 33–47.

Marsden, Debbie. *How Horses Learn.* London: J. A. Allen, 2005.

Marsden, Michael T. "The Rise of the Western Movie: From Sagebrush to Screen." *Journal of the West* 22, no. 4 (1983): 17–23.

Marx, Leo. *The Machine in the Garden: Technology and the Pastoral Ideal in America.* New York: Oxford University Press, 1967.

McFerrin, Randy, and Douglas Wills. "Searching for the Big Die-Off: An Event Study of 19th Century Cattle Markets." *Essays in Economic and Business History* 31 (2013): 33–52.

McIlwraith, C. Wayne, and Bernard E. Rollin, eds. *Equine Welfare.* Chichester, UK: Wiley-Blackwell, 2011.

McMillan, Robert Edward. "The Conflict over Animal Experimentation in Vancouver, 1950–1990." M.A. thesis, University of British Columbia, 2004.

McShane, Clay, and Joel A. Tarr. *The Horse in the City: Living Machines in the Nineteenth Century.* Baltimore: Johns Hopkins University Press, 2007.

Mellis, Allison Fuss. *Riding Buffaloes and Broncos: Rodeo and Native Traditions in the Northern Great Plains.* Norman: Oklahoma University Press, 2003.

Milner, Clyde A., II, Carol A. O'Connor, and Martha A. Sandweiss, eds., *The Oxford History of the American West.* New York: Oxford University Press, 1994.

Mitchell, Lee Clark. *Westerns: Making the Man in Fiction and Film.* Chicago: University of Chicago Press, 1998.

Mohs, Clinton. "'The Man Was Forever Looking for That Which He Never Found': The Western and Automotive Tourism in the Early Twentieth Century." *Western American Literature* 50, no. 3 (Fall 2015): 225–49.

Morley, Alan. *Vancouver: From Milltown to Metropolis,* 2nd ed. Vancouver: Mitchell Press, 1969.

Morris, Peter S. "Fort Macleod of the Borderlands: Using the Forty-Ninth Parallel on the Southern Ranching Frontier." In *One West, Two Myths: A Comparative Reader.* ed. Carol Higham and Robert Thacker. Calgary: University of Calgary Press, 2004, 149–73.

Morrow-Tesch, Julie L. "Evaluating Management Practices for Their Impact on Welfare." *Journal of the American Veterinary Medical Association* 219, no. 10 (November 15, 2001): 1374–76.

Murdoch, David Hamilton. *The American West: The Invention of a Myth.* Cardiff: Welsh Academic Press, 2001.

Murray, Robin L., and Joseph K. Heumann. *Gunfight at the Eco-Corral: Western Cinema and the Environment*. Norman: University of Oklahoma Press, 2012.

Myres, Sandra L. *The Ranch in Spanish Texas, 1691–1800*. El Paso: Texas Western Press, 1969.

Nance, Susan. *Animal Modernity: Jumbo the Elephant and the Human Dilemma*. Houndmills, Basingstoke: Palgrave Macmillan, 2015.

———. *Entertaining Elephants: Animal Agency and the Business of the American Circus*. Baltimore: Johns Hopkins University Press, 2013.

———. "Game Stallions and Other 'Horseface Minstrelsies' of the American Turf." *Theatre Journal* 65, no. 3 (October 2013): 355–72.

———. "A Star Is Born to Buck: Animal Celebrity and the Marketing of Professional Rodeo," in *Sport, Animals and Society*, edited by Michelle Gilbert and James Gillett. New York: Routledge, 2013, 173–91.

———. "Who Was Greasy Sal? Outlaw Horses and the Spirit of Calgary in the Automobile Age." *Histoire sociale/Social History* 49, no. 99 (June 2016): 371–89.

Nash, Gerald D. *The American West in the Twentieth-Century: A Short History of an Urban Oasis*. Albuquerque: University of New Mexico Press, 1977.

Nicholson, Shannon. "Rodeo Participants' Perception of Roping Calf Welfare Before, During and After 'The Show.'" Master's thesis, University of Guelph, 2013.

Oosterom, Nelle. "The Mild West." *Canada's History*. 96, no. 2 (April-May 2016): 31.

Oppenheimer, Harold L. *Cowboy Economics: Rural Land as an Investment*. Danville, IL: Interstate Printers & Publishers, 1966.

Orland, Barbara. "Turbo-Cows: Producing a Competitive Animal in the Nineteenth and Early Twentieth Centuries." In Susan R. Schrepfer and Philip Scranton, ed. *Industrializing Organisms: Introducing Evolutionary History*. New York: Routledge, 2004, 167–89.

Pacyga, Dominic A. "Chicago: Slaughterhouse to the World." In Paula Young Lee, ed. *Meat, Modernity, and the Rise of the Slaughterhouse*. Durham: University of New Hampshire Press, 2008, 153–66.

Park, Roberta J. "San Franciscans at Work and at Play, 1846–1869." *Journal of the West* 22, no. 1 (January 1983): 44–51.

Pate. J'Nell L. *America's Historic Stockyards: Livestock Hotels*. Fort Worth: Texas Christian University Press, 2005.

Pearson, Susan J. *The Rights of the Defenseless: Protecting Animals and Children in Gilded Age America*. Chicago: University of Chicago Press, 2011.

Penrose, Jan. "When All the Cowboys Are Indians: The Nature of Race in All-Indian Rodeo." *Annals of the Association of American Geographers* 93, no. 3 (2003): 687–705.

Pomeroy, Earl. *In Search of the Golden West: The Tourist in Western America*. New York: Alfred A. Knopf, 1957.

Premo, Bianca. "Recreating Identity: Recreation on the Arizona-Sonora Border, 1880–1930." *Studies in Latin American Popular Culture* 16 (1997): 31–52.

Price, Jennifer. *Flight Maps: Adventures with Nature in Modern America*. New York: Basic Books, 2000.

Pooley-Ebert, Andria. "Species Agency: A Comparative Study of Horse-Human Relationships in Chicago and Rural Illinois." In Susan Nance, ed. *The Historical Animal*. Syracuse: Syracuse University Press, 2015, 148–65.

Rainey, Buck. "The 'Reel' Cowboy: Myth versus Realism." *Red River Valley Historical Review* 2, no. 1 (1975): 24–63.

Reddin, Paul. *Wild West Shows*. Urbana: University of Illinois Press, 1999.

Regan, Tom. *Empty Cages: Facing the Challenge of Animal Rights*. Rowman & Littlefield, 2004.

Richardson, Rusty. *Casey Tibbs: Born to Ride*. Moonlight Mesa, 2010.

Ringley, Tom. *Rodeo Time in Sheridan Wyo: A History of the Sheridan-Wyo-Rodeo*. Greybull, WY: Pronghorn Press, 2004.

Ritvo, Harriet. *The Animal Estate: The English and Other Creatures in Victorian England*. Cambridge: Harvard University Press, 1989.

Robbins, William G. *Colony and Empire: The Capitalist Transformation of the American West*. Lawrence: University Press of Kansas, 1994.

———. "In Pursuit of Historical Explanation: Capitalism as a Conceptual Tool for Knowing the American West." *Western Historical Quarterly* 30 (Autumn 1999): 277–93.

Roberts, Monty. *The Man Who Listens to Horses: The Story of a Real-Life Horse Whisperer*. 1996; repr. New York: Ballantine Books, 2008.

Robertson, M. S. *Rodeo: Standard Guide to the Cowboy Sport*. Berkeley, CA: Howell-North, 1961.

Robinson, Forrest G., ed. *The New Western History: The Territory Ahead*. Tucson: University of Arizona Press, 1998.

Rodeo Cowboys Association, *RCA Rodeo Sports News Annual* 16, no. 3 (January 1968).

Rollin, Bernard E. "Rodeo and Recollection—Applied Ethics and Western Philosophy." *Journal of the Philosophy of Sport* 23 (1996): 1–9.

Rosa, Joseph G., and Robin May. *Buffalo Bill and His Wild West: A Pictorial Biography*. Lawrence: University Press of Kansas, 1989.

Rowe, David. *Sport, Culture and the Media: The Unruly Trinity*, 2nd ed. Buckingham and Philadelphia: Open University Press, 2004.

Rushen, Jeffrey, Anne Marie de Passillé, Marina A. G. von Keyserlingk, and Daniel M. Weary. *The Welfare of Cattle*. Dordrecht, The Netherlands: Springer, 2008.

Russell, Sharman Apt. *Kill the Cowboy: A Battle of Mythology in the New West*. Lincoln: University of Nebraska Press, 1993.

Ryan, Jennifer. "Rodeos Put Animal Welfare Front and Center." *Beef*, March 5, 2013, https://www.beefmagazine.com/cattle-handling/rodeos-put-animal-care-front-center.

Ryan, Mary P. *Civic Wars: Democracy and Public Life in the American City during the Nineteenth Century*. Berkeley: University of California Press, 1997.

Ryder, Richard D. "Measuring Animal Welfare." *Journal of Applied Animal Welfare Science* 1, no. 1 (1998): 75–80.

Sacks, Benjamin. "Charles Fletcher Lummis at Hotel Del Coronado: The Spanish Fiesta Spring 1894." *Southern California Quarterly* 78, no. 2 (1996): 139–74.

Sands, Kathleen Mullen. *Charrería Mexicana: An Equestrian Folk Tradition*. Tucson: University of Arizona Press, 1993.

Sandweiss, Martha A. "Interpretation." In Milner, Clyde A., II, Carol A. O'Connor, and Martha A. Sandweiss, eds., *The Oxford History of the American West*. New York: Oxford University Press, 1994.

———. *Print the Legend: Photography and the American West*. New Haven: Yale University Press, 2002.

Sayre, Nathan Freeman. *Ranching, Endangered Species, and Urbanization in the Southwest: Species of Capital*. Tucson: University of Arizona Press, 2002.

Schonholz, Cynthia M. "Animals in Rodeo—A Closer Look." *Journal of the American Veterinary Medical Association* 216, no. 8 (April 15, 2000): 1246–49.

Schrepfer, Susan R., and Philip Scranton, ed. *Industrializing Organisms: Introducing Evolutionary History*. London: Routledge, 2004.

Scully, Matthew. *Dominion: The Power of Man, the Suffering of Animals, and the Call to Mercy*. New York: St. Martin's, 2002.

Seiler, Tamara Palmer. "Riding Broncs and Taming Contradictions: Reflections on the Uses of the Cowboy in the Calgary Stampede." In Max Foran, ed. *Icon, Brand, Myth: The Calgary Stampede*. Edmonton, AB: Athabasca University Press, 2008, 179–82.

Serpell, James. *In the Company of Animals: A Study of Human-Animal Relationships*. 1986; repr. New York: Cambridge University Press, 1996.

Sinclair, Michelle, Tamara Keeley, Anne-Cecile Lefebvre, and Clive J. C. Phillips. "Behavioral and Physiological Responses of Calves to Marshalling and Roping in a Simulated Rodeo Event." *Animals* 6 (2016): 30–41.

Slatta, Richard W. *Cowboys of the Americas*. New Haven and London: Yale University Press, 1990.

———. "Long Hours and Low Pay: Cowboy Life on the Northern Plains." *South Dakota History* 32, no. 3 (Fall 2002): 194–216.

Slotkin, Richard. *Gunfighter Nation: The Myth of the Frontier in Twentieth-Century America*. Norman: University of Oklahoma Press, 1992.

———. *Regeneration through Violence: The Mythology of the American Frontier, 1600–1860*. Norman: University of Oklahoma Press, 1973.

Smalley, Andrea L. *Wild by Nature: North American Animals Confront Colonization*. Baltimore: Johns Hopkins University Press,

Smith, David L. "Hoosier Hollywood Cowboys: The Careers of Buck Jones and Ken Maynard." *Traces of Indiana and Midwestern History* 18, no. 1 (2006): 4–21.

Smith, Henry Nash. *Virgin Land: The American West as Symbol and Myth*. New York: Vintage, 1957.

Sorenson, John. *Constructing Ecoterrorism: Capitalism, Speciesism, and Animal Rights*. Halifax: Fernwood Publishing, 2016.

Specht, Joshua. "The Rise, Fall, and Rebirth of the Texas Longhorn: An Evolutionary History." *Environmental History* 21 (2016): 343–63.
Starrs, Paul F. *Let the Cowboy Ride: Cattle Ranching in the American West.* Baltimore: Johns Hopkins University Press, 1998.
Stillman, Deanne. *Mustang: The Saga of the Wild Horse in the American West.* Boston: Mariner Books, 2008.
Stoeltje, Beverly J. "Power and the Ritual Genres: American Rodeo." *Western Folklore* 52, no. 2/4 (April—October 1993): 135–56.
———. "Rodeo: From Custom to Ritual." *Western Folklore* 48, no. 3 (July 1989): 244–55.
Strand, Rod, and Patti Strand. *The Highjacking of the Humane Movement.* Wilsonville, OR: Doral Publishing, 1993.
Stratton, W. K. *Chasing the Rodeo: On Wild Rides and Big Dreams, Broken Hearts and Broken Bones, and One Man's Search for the West.* New York: Harcourt, 2006.
Tarr, Joel A., and Clay McShane. *Horse in the City: Living Machines in the Nineteenth Century.* Baltimore: Johns Hopkins University Press 2007.
Tavegia, Merle. "Sam Brownell Was a Bronco Buster." *Bits and Pieces* 7, no. 2 (1971): 8–13
Taylor, Mark B. "More Thoughts on Calf Roping, Steer Tripping." *Journal of the American Veterinary Medical Association* 220, no. 5 (March 1, 2002): 594.
Tenório Vasconcelos, Orivaldo, Antônio Carlos Alessi, Cesar Roberto Esper, and Paulo Henrique Franceschin. "Avaliação técnico-científica da utilização do sedém em bovinos de rodeio" ["Evaluation of Flank Strap Effects on Professional Rodeo Cattle."] *Revista de Educacao Continuada.* 3, no. 2 (2000): 72–77.
Thistle, John. *Resettling the Range: Animals, Ecologies, and Human Communities in Early British Columbia.* Vancouver: University of British Columbia Press, 2015.
Thomas, Keith. *Man and the Natural World: Changing Attitudes in England, 1500–1800.* New York: Penguin Books, 1984.
Thor, James. "Realities of Rodeo." *The Lancet* 362 (December 2002): S52-S53.
Thornton, Sally Bullard. "San Diego's First Cabrillo Celebration, 1892." *Journal of San Diego History* 30, no. 3 (1984): 167–80.
Tootoosis, Wilf. "This Was One of the Predictions, That Our Traditions Will Come Back Some Day." In Peter Kulchyski, Don McCaskill, and David Newhouse, ed. *In the Words of Elders: Aboriginal Cultures in Transition.* Toronto: University of Toronto Press, 1999, 311–61.
Trolinger, Boyd. "Samuel Thomas 'Booger Red' Privett: Cowboy, Showman, and Early Rodeo Pioneer." *West Texas Historical Association Year Book* 72 (1996): 142–51.
Tyler, Ron. *Prints of the West.* Golden, CO: Fulcrum Publishing, 1994.
Van Nuys, Frank. *Varmints and Victims: Predator Control in the American West.* Lawrence: University Press of Kansas, 2015.
United Nations Environment Program International Panel for Sustainable Resource Management, *Assessing the Environmental Impacts of Production and Consumption,*

www.unep.org/resourcepanel/Portals/24102/PDFs/PriorityProducts AndMaterials_Report.pdf

Warren, Louis S. *Buffalo Bill's America: William Cody and the Wild West.* New York: Vintage, 2006.

Wetherell, Donald G. "Making Tradition: The Calgary Stampede, 1912–1939." In Max Foran, ed. *Icon, Brand, Myth: The Calgary Stampede.* Edmonton, AB: Athabasca University Press, 2008, 21–46.

Webb, Walter Prescott. *The Great Plains.* New York: Grosset and Dunlap, 1931.

Weiland, Victoria Carlyle. *100 Years of Rodeo Stock Contracting.* Reno, NV: Professional Rodeo Stock Contractors Association, 1997.

Wells, Christopher W. *Car Country: An Environmental History.* Seattle: University of Washington Press, 2012.

Wesley, Jared J. *Code Politics: Campaigns and Cultures on the Canadian Prairies.* Vancouver: University of British Columbia Press, 2011.

West, Elliot. "Selling the Myth: Western Images in Advertising." In Richard Aquila, ed. *Wanted Dead or Alive: The American West in Popular Culture.* Urbana: University of Illinois Press, 1998, 269–91.

Westermeier, Clifford P. "The Cowboy—His Pristine Image." *South Dakota History* 8, no. 1 (1977): 2–23

———. "Cowboy Sports and the Humane Society." *Colorado Magazine* 26, no. 4 (October 1949): 241–52.

———. *Man, Beast, Dust: The Story of Rodeo.* 1947; repr. Lincoln: University of Nebraska Press, 1987.

———. *Trailing the Cowboy: His Life and Lore as Told by Frontier Journalists.* Caldwell, ID: Caxton Printers, 1955.

White, Courtney. "Tony the Wonder Horse: A Star Study." In Susan Nance, ed. *The Historical Animal.* Syracuse: Syracuse University Press, 2015, 209–37.

White, Marshia. "The Meaning of Injury in Rough Stock Rodeo Cowboys: The Lived Experience." *Journal of Emergency Nursing* 32, no. 2 (April 2006): 128–29.

White, Richard. "Animals and Enterprise." In Clyde A. Milner II, Carol A. O'Connor, and Martha A. Sandweiss, eds., *The Oxford History of the American West.* New York: Oxford University Press, 1994, 237–73.

———. *"It's Your Misfortune and None of My Own": A New History of the American West.* Norman: Oklahoma University Press, 1991.

Wilkie, Rhoda M. *Livestock/Deadstock: Working with Farm Animals from Birth to Slaughter.* Philadelphia: Temple University Press, 2010.

Williams, Jeff. "Prolegomenon for a Field of Rodeo Studies." *Journal of the West* 45, no. 3 (Summer 2006): 3–7.

Wilson, Laurel E. "'I Was a Pretty Proud Kid': An Interpretation of Differences in Posed and Unposed Photographs of Montana Cowboys." *Clothing and Textiles Research Journal.* 9, no. 3 (Spring 1991): 49–58.

Winson, Anthony. *The Industrial Diet: The Degradation of Food and the Struggle for Healthy Eating.* Vancouver: University of British Columbia Press, 2013.6

Wise, Michael D. *Producing Predators: Wolves, Work, and Conquest in the Northern Rockies*. Lincoln: University of Nebraska Press, 2016.
Woerner, Gail Hughbanks. *Belly Full of Bedsprings: The History of Bronc Riding*. Austin, TX: Eakin Press, 1998.
———. *Cowboy Up: The History of Bull Riding*. Austin, TX: Eakin Press, 2001.
———. "The History of Barrel Racing." *Way Out West Blog*, October 28, 2014, http://www.gailwoerner.com/way-out-west-blog/the-history-of-barrel-racing.
———. *Rope to Win: The History of Steer, Calf, and Team Roping*. Austin, TX: Eakin Press, 2001.
———. "A True Rodeo Champion," *Way Out West Blog*, July 25, 2016, http://www.gailwoerner.com/wayout-west-blog/a-true-rodeochampion-v61.
Wooden, Wayne S., and Gavin Ehringer. *Rodeo in America: Wranglers, Roughstock and Paydirt*. Lawrence: University Press of Kansas, 1996.
Worcester, Don. *The Texas Longhorn: Relic of the Past, Asset for the Future*. College Station: Texas A&M University Press, 1987.
Worster, Donald. *Under Western Skies: Nature and History in the American West*. New York: Oxford University Press, 1992.
Wrobel, David M. *Global West, American Frontier: Travel, Empire, and Exceptionalism from Manifest Destiny to the Great Depression*. Albuquerque: University of New Mexico Press, 2013.
Wyman, Walker D. *The Wild Horse of the West*. Lincoln: University of Nebraska Press, 1945.
Young, James A., and B. Abbott Sparks. *Cattle in the Cold Desert*, expanded edition. Reno: University of Nevada Press, 2002.
Young, Jerry. "Recalling a Texas Legend: Samuel Thomas 'Booger Red' Privett." In Kenneth L. Untiedt, ed. *Cowboys, Cops, Killers, and Ghosts: Legends and Lore in Texas*. Denton: University of North Texas Press, 2013, 3–13.

### Film and Video

*Bodacious: Master of Disaster*. DVD. Directed by Stephan Corey. Broncs Boys Inc., 2004.
Calgary Stampede, *An Interview with Dr. Ed Pajor about the Animal Care Advisory Panel*. Youtube.com, June 30, 2015, https://www.youtube.com/watch?v=UL7Y_Jl6qHY.
Carle, Mollie. *Born to Buck*. Directed by Casey. Casey Tibbs Inc., 1966.
Debeij, Joris. *The Bull Rider: New York Times Op-Docs*, April 8, 2015, https://www.nytimes.com/2015/04/08/opinion/the-bull-rider.html.
Geronimo Productions. *War Paint*. Youtube.com, July 1, 2011, https://www.youtube.com/watch?v=2sKzhcKV8GU.
*John Growney Talks about Red Rock, Lane Frost, and Clovis Rodeo's 100th Anniversary*. Will R, Youtube.com, February 9, 2014, https://www.youtube.com/watch?v=mA6bZuDsRKs
*The Last Stronghold: The Miles City Bucking Horse Sale*. Stronghold Productions, 2004.

Merrill, Keith. *The Great American Cowboy*. Directed by Keith Merrill. American National Enterprises, Merrill-Rodeo Film Productions, 1973.

Miller, Arthur. *The Misfits*. Directed by John Huston. Seven Arts Production, 1961.

*PBR 101: Flank Strap*. Professional Bull Riders, Youtube.com, June 13, 2013, http://www.youtube.com/watch?v=tXpwwUBsVyU.

*PBR 101: Spurs*. Professional Bull Riders, Youtube.com, June 18, 2013, https://www.youtube.com/watch?v=pbS-gscDlqI.

*Professional Bull Riders: 8 Seconds—Bred for Greatness*. DVD. Professional Bull Riders and Image Entertainment. 2006.

Reeve, Josef, *Hard Rider*. Directed by Josef Reeve. National Film Board of Canada, 1972, https://www.nfb.ca/film/hard_rider/.

*The Ride with Cord McCoy: Lane Frost*. Cow Horse Productions, 2013, Youtube.com, https://www.youtube.com/watch?v=kAHqcZKrWO0.

*The Ride with Cord McCoy: The Making of a World Champion Bucking Bull*. Cow Horse Productions, 2014, Youtube.com, https://www.youtube.com/watch?v=1dAwPPqD6V0.

Studiowestmarketing. *Growney Interview*. Youtube.com, April 24, 2014, https://www.youtube.com/watch?v=J5V59Oy2Bjk.

Tsilhqot'in National Government, *Bringing the Spirit Home*, Youtube.com, November 17, 2018, https://www.youtube.com/watch?time_continue=55&v=zkwDq9Im-Bg.

## Websites

ProRodeo Hall of Fame, "War Paint," http://www.prorodeohalloffame.com/inductees/by-category/livestock/war-paint/.

Universities Federation for Animal Welfare, https://www.ufaw.org.uk/.

# Index

agricultural fairs, 21, 52, 77, 80, 183, 188
Alexis Creek First Nation, 213, 214
Allen, Rex, 122
Alves, Silvano, 170
American Bucking Bull Inc. (ABBI), 172
Anderson, Pamela, 208
Andrews, Sammy, 163, 165, 173
Andrews Rodeo Company, 161, 164
animal advocates, 13–14, 23, 43, 46, 67–68, 93, 99; British Columbia, 185, 187–89, 207–11; California, 37, 66, 68; post-1960, 153–55, 208; Wyoming, 41, 44, 46, 70
Animal Advocates (BC), 207, 209. *See also* animal advocates
Animal Agriculture Alliance, 155
animal behavior, misinterpreted, 9, 10–11, 20, 29–30, 33, 51, 68–70, 145, 148, 169, 173, 190, 206
animal consent: and "ancient contract," 9, 177; and animal "athlete," 137, 148, 151–52, 165, 167–70, 172; and born-to-buck programs, 101, 144, 173–74; myth of, 9, 12, 49–51, 54, 65, 70, 95, 98, 122, 144, 177, 216; myth of critiqued, 59, 61, 93; and partnership ideal, 10, 36, 95, 113, 173–74, 202; and rodeo livestock awards, 133
Animal Enterprise Act, 154
Animal Liberation Front (ALF), 14. *See also* animal advocates

animals: and Richard White's "great divide," 5; and violence in the West, 4, 6; westerners' views of, 12
*Animals in Rodeo: A Closer Look* (video), 160
animal welfare, 124–25, 169, 171, 172–73, 205–6; variously defined, 15–16, 204
Animal Welfare Act (U.S.), 154
anti-cruelty groups. *See* animal advocates
Anti-Rodeo League (Chicago), 92. *See also* animal advocates
Aron, Stephen, 6
Austin, Tex., 20–21, 53, 82
Autry, Gene, 112, 127

Baby Doll (horse), 96
Bad Company Rodeo stock contracting company, 142
Bailey, Nat, 187
Baldy (horse), 115
Ballance, Laura, 210
Bannerman, Sid, 93
Barnum, Phineas T., 67
barrel racing, 112
Beebe, Fred, 82
Beef Bonanza bubble, 19, 20, 26, 58
beef industry, 8, 15, 19, 27, 32, 128, 157, 171, 189, 192–93; American "midwestern system," 26, 28, 79, 190; Canadian, 79; controversy over, 15–56. *See also* ranchers

Bell, Don, 105, 107, 115
Benny Clegg (horse), 116
Bernard, Randy, 157
Beutler Brothers (stock contractors), 127
Big Country Toys, 141, 142
Big Die-Up, 22, 26, 39
Bill Pickett Invitational Rodeo, 150
Black Diamond (horse), 94
Blunt, Judy, 3
Bodacious (bull), 143, 161–66, 172, 173–74, 175, 247n22
Booger Red's Wild West Show, 53
*Born to Buck* (film), 122–25
born-to-buck programs: bulls, 143, 151, 161, 171–74; horses, 100–101, 103, 108, 123, 129–30, 137. *See also* animal consent
breakaway roping, 178, 203, 207–8, 212, 259n87
Breding, Scott, 165
Brisendine, Everett, 25, 63
British Columbia Rodeo Association, 214
bronco busting. *See* bronc riding
bronc riding (bareback), 80, 85
bronc riding (saddle), 51, 85, 130, 178; criticized, 65–69, 91–92, 99; horses injured and killed in, 66, 67, 70, 71, 91, 93–94, 119, 187; matched rides, 107–8, 133; technical description of, 59–60, 68, 70, 71, 81, 87, 90–91, 120–21
broncs, 87–88, 106, 201; disposition after rodeo, 96–98, 99; as diving bronc, 100, 103, 133; "double-tempered," 103, 108–9, 119, 132; imagined as "outlaw," 48, 49, 59, 65, 68, 70, 94–95, 108; naming conventions, 86–87; sourcing of for rodeo, 59, 64, 85–86, 88–89, 94, 105, 108, 119, 120–25, 126, 127–28; as symbolic of the West, 76. *See also* horses; sunfisher
Brown, Freckles, 146

Brownell, Sam, 69
bucking (bull and horse behavior), 76, 78, 82–84, 91, 95, 98, 120, 133; means of producing in bulls, 160, 161–62; means of producing in horses, 66–67, 68–70, 71, 89–90, 129; as presumed indicator of animal consent, 9, 11, 64, 87, 103, 108, 167–69. *See also* born-to-buck programs
Bucking Horse of the Year Award, 101, 131, 133
Budiansky, Stephen, 9
bulldogging. *See* steer wrestling
bullfighters (bull riding), 145
bullfighting (Spanish and Mexican), 23, 39
Bull of the Year Award, 144, 148, 169
bull rider, 157–58; as stoic, adrenalin seeker, 149–50, 157–59, 171; women, 144, 157. *See also* cowboy; cowgirl
Bull Riders Only Tour, 157. *See also* Professional Bull Riders (PBR)
bull riding, 144–46, 149, 153, 156–57; bulls injured in, 154, 160–61, 167, 170–71; risks and injuries to riders in, 146, 158, 171, 175; technical description of, 143–46, 161–63
bull rope (surcingle), 145, 162–63, 171
bulls: behavior of, 143–44, 145–46, 161, 162–65, 167, 172–75; "double-tempered," 173–74; as "droppy" bull, 148, 168; imagined as animal "athletes," 143–44, 151, 159–60, 167, 169–71; naming conventions, 149; as rank bulls, 145; as rodeo celebrities, 143, 144, 149, 151, 169, 173
bull tailing, 23
Bundy, Gus, 125, 126
Burbick, Joan, 102, 156, 190
Bureau of Indian Affairs, 123
Bureau of Land Management (U.S.), 3, 11
Buttermilk (horse), 95

INDEX 287

calf riding, 182
calf roping, 46, 80, 154, 180, 197, 211–12; ambivalence among rodeo people regarding, 178, 189, 206, 211; calves injured and killed in, 179, 187, 188, 195–97, 198, 199, 205–6, 208; criticized, 184, 203, 208; devices for protecting roping calves in, 199; injuries to ropers in, 197; "no jerk down" rules in, 195, 199–200; technical description of, 177–78, 195, 197–98, 200; veterinarians' controversy over, 203–4
Calgary, Alb., 76–77, 82, 91
Calgary Exhibition Company, 87. *See also* Calgary Stampede
Calgary Industrial Exhibition Company, 85
Calgary Red (cowboy), 144
Calgary Stampede, 4, 8, 14, 76, 78–79, 93, 99, 103, 175, 198, 206; Animal Care Advisory Panel, 201; early programs, 79–80, 81
California State Humane Association, 66, 68. *See also* animal advocates
Callister Park Rodeo (Vancouver), 185, 186
calves, 177, 181, 189, 191–92, 200, 209; as "babies," 208, 211; behavior of, 189, 195, 197–98; calf-crop percentage, 192; images of clotheslined, 190, 203, 209–10; imagined inability to feel pain or fear, 182–83, 202, 208; pain and fear defined as injuries to, 205–6; as practice pen stock, 194–98. *See also* ranching
Cameron, Goldie, 68
Canadian Crown, 3, 123, 214
Canadian Professional Rodeo Association (CPRA), 80, 101, 127, 150, 157, 158, 168, 207, 209
Capital State Fair (Austin, Tex.), 21–22, 39

Cariboo Chilcotin (B.C.), 213–14
Catlin, George, 33
cattle, 45; behavior of, 28–29, 30; Brahma, 140, 145, 146, 148, 151, 161, 173, 189, 195, 228n64; feedlot welfare, 193; slaughterhouse welfare, 193–94, 205
cattlemen. *See* ranchers
cattle prod. *See* "hot shot"
cattle trade. *See* beef industry
Cavanaugh, Mary, 92
CBC Corporation, 104. *See also* Chappel Brothers Company
Center for Consumer Freedom, 155
Challenge of Champions bull-riding tour, 140–41, 143
Champion (horse), 95
Chappel Brothers Company, 104, 105
*charreada*, 5, 7, 23
Cheyenne, Wyo., 43, 48–49, 73–74
Cheyenne Frontier Days, 1, 4, 14, 37, 41, 43–44, 45, 70, 72, 141, 160, 206, 211
Cheyenne Nation Rodeo, 124
chicken pull (vaquero game), 23, 93
Chilcotin War, 214
children: and rodeo, 44, 179, 181–84, 185; as critics of rodeo, 185
Christensen, Babe, 130
Christensen, Bobby, 127, 130
Christensen, Henry, 127, 130
Christensen Brothers Rodeo Company, 119, 130–31, 133, 135–36
chuckwagon racing, 81
civic festivals, 21, 22, 82
Cloverdale Rodeo (Surrey, B.C.), 179, 207–11
cockfights, 21, 39
Code Blue (bull), 170–71
Cody, William, 21, 25, 33
comedy act horses, 113–14. *See also* horses
comedy teams (human and animal), 112–13

Connelly, Lex, 128
Coon (horse), 94
Cooper, Roy "Super Looper," 197–98
Cooper, Tuf, 201
Cooper, Tuffy Dale, 197, 201
Copenhaver, Deb, 107, 108
Cosgrove, Dick (aka Dick Cosgrave), 94, 96, 97, 199, 213
Coutlee, Jason, 215
cowboy, 52: in advertising, 133; attitudes toward livestock, 22, 177, 182–83, 199; costuming of, 20, 66; as martyr, 141–42, 143, 150, 175; as mythical figure, 9, 24, 141–42; as professional athlete, 101, 103, 110, 120–21, 159; as wild man, 23, 24–25, 89; as working cowboy, 20, 22–23, 25, 109
cowboy tournaments, 5, 20, 34, 37; as grotesquerie of range labor, 23, 34–36, 60, 68; origins of, 19. *See also* rodeo
Cowboy Turtles Association, 111. *See also* Rodeo Cowboys Association (RCA)
cowgirl, 52, 64, 68, 73, 79, 111, 113, 144, 157: as mythical figure, 9; marginalized in rodeo, 111–12, 150–51; as professional athlete, 150–51
cow pony. *See* horses
cowpuncher, 23. *See also* cowboy
Craver, William "Pecos," 71
Creed, Gene, 115
Creed, Loyce, 53
Creed, Mary, 53
Creed, Shorty, 115
Cremer, Leo, 108
cruelty, varying definitions of, 39, 42, 93, 155, 188
Cyclone (bull), 148, 149
Cyclone (horse), 77, 94

*Dancing with the Stars* (television program), 167
Danks, Jimmy, 58, 65, 71, 74

deer, 21–22, 39, 122
Denver Stock Show, 120, 183
Department of Agriculture, U.S. (USDA), 160, 193–94
Dillinger (bull), 143, 171
Dobie, James Frank, 27, 105
dog fighting, 46
dominionism, 10, 11; and emotional distancing from livestock, 149, 182–83

Earth First!, 156
Earth Liberation Front, 14, 156
eco-terrorism, 156
Ehringer, Gavin, 198, 211
*8 Seconds* (film), 141
Elliot, Vern, 116–17, 119, 145
environmental change: and extensive ranching, 3, 8, 22, 26, 179; and human predation, 6. *See also* wild horses
Erwin, Chuck, 188, 199
Etienne, Myron "Doc," 153, 203
Evans, Greg, 99

Faulknor, Cliff, 187, 188–89
Field, Lewis, 157
Five Minutes to Midnight (horse), 120
flank rope. *See* flank strap
flank strap: bulls, 144, 146, 162; horses, 68–69, 90, 91, 129, 162, 185
Flores, Dan, 57
Flying A Rodeo Company, 112
Fonda, Henry, 122, 123, 130
Forest Service (U.S.), 3, 11, 43, 123
Foss, Frank, 55
Fredriksson, Kristine, 156
Frost, Elsie, 141
Frost, Lane, 140–41, 143, 144, 146, 150, 151, 157, 159, 166, 175
Furman, James, 204

Gang Ranch, 213
Gardiner, Clem, 86, 94, 96, 99
Gasztonyi, Gabor, 216

Gay, Donnie, 158
Gillespie, Bud, 49, 70–71, 75
Girl's Rodeo Association, 112. *See also* Women's Professional Rodeo Association
goat tying, 182
gophers, 65, 122
Gore, Al, 155
Grandin, Temple, 118, 205, 206
Gravedigger (horse), 77
Greasy Sal (horse), 77–78, 84, 86, 89, 90, 93, 96–97, 99, 103
Greenwood, Russ, 94
Greer, Terri, 154–55
Growney, John, 141, 142, 151–52
Growney Brothers Rodeo Company, 142, 160

Hall-Studnick Wild West Show, 53
Hansen, Paul, 48, 74
Harry Knight Rodeo Company, 148
Hart, J. W., 174
Hartell, Aleck, 198
Hasselstrom, Linda, 193
Hastings Park Rodeo (Vancouver), 185
Hedeman, Tuff, 165, 166
Hell's Angel (horse), 94
Hennessey, M. F., 66
"high-life" (bisulphate of carbon), 65–66, 144
Hispanic peoples, treatment of livestock. *See* vaqueros
Hixson, Walter, 10
Horn, Tom, 49, 58
horse breaking, 60–62, 64; and persona of bronc buster, 62
horse racing, 21, 22
horses, 36, 77, 85, 102, 106, 139, 213; behavior of, 59, 60–62, 64, 68–69, 70, 96, 106–7, 130; injured and killed in transport, 115–16, 118, 124; markets for, 57, 59, 104–6; theft of in rodeo, 124; transport for rodeo, 54, 114–16, 117–18

"hot shot," 160, 167, 215
Hough, Emerson, 26, 72
Houston Livestock Show and Rodeo, 164
Howard, Joseph, 65
HR 3252 (Kostmeyer bill), 154
humane associations, 38. *See also* animal advocates
Humane Slaughter Act, 193–94
Humane Society of the United States (HSUS), 14, 38, 153, 155. *See also* animal advocates
Hurricane (bull), 148, 149
Hussy, Shirley, 108

Indigenous Peoples: attitudes toward animals, 5, 12, 63, 216–17; horses stolen from, 124; reservation lands, 123–33; rodeos, 124, 214–15, 217. *See also* rodeo
International Gay Rodeo Association, 150
Irwin, Charlie, 48, 49, 54, 58, 59
Irwin, Floyd, 48
Irwin, Frank, 49
*I Witness Video* (television program), 154

James, Charmayne, 8
James, Will, 52
Jardine, O., 86
Johnson, Velma "Annie," 125
Johnson, Col. W. T., 94
Joker (horse), 133
Jones, Buck, 53
J-31 (bull). *See* Bodacious (bull)
Junior Rodeo. *See* children

Katich, Karlene, 170
Katich, Steve, 169
Kimball, Vern, 8
Kirby's Rodeo School, 158
Kish, Don, 151

Kivett, Roy, 54
Klamath Indian Reservation, 124
Kostmeyer bill (HR 3252), 154

LaDue, Florence "Flores," 85
Lady Luck (horse), 93
Laine, Frankie, 189
Lakota Sioux Nation, 124
Lamb, Gene, 106
Lambert, Cody, 159
lang, k.d., 155
Larson, Peggy, 205–6
LaRue, Walt, 52
Lawrence, Bruce
Lawrence, Elizabeth Atwood, 4, 8, 113, 120, 199, 202
LeCompte, Mary Lou, 112
Lee, Bob, 48
Leffew, Gary, 174
*Let 'Er Buck* (1921), 95
Liberation BC, 207, 208. See also animal advocates
Linder, Herman, 186–88, 189, 199
Linderman, Bill, 107–8, 186
Lippmann, Walter, 95
Little Yellow Jacket (bull), 143, 169
Long, Bert, 86
longhorn cattle, 27–28. See also cattle

Madison Square Garden Rodeo, 82, 109, 194
Mahan, Larry, 157, 159, 182
Major Payne (bull), 169–70
Mansfield, Toots, 194–97, 198
mares, 56, 100. See also horses
Marpole Rotary Club Stampede (Vancouver), 185–89, 198, 207
McBride, Justin, 158
McConnell, Ken, 186
McCarroll, Bonnie, 111
McGonigal, Clay, 42
McInnis, William, 188
McNab, Jim, 86

Mexican American rodeo. See Mexican rodeo
Mexican rodeo, 24, 39–40. See also *charreada*
Midnight (horse), 77, 94, 116, 132
Miles City, Mont., 106
Miles City Bucking Horse Sale and Rodeo, 104
Miller, Arthur, 126
*The Misfits* (film), 126
Miss Klamath (horse), 119, 135
Mix, Tom, 95, 144
Modoc War, 41
Montana State Fair, 76
mountain race, 4, 215–16
Mr. Ed (horse), 113
Mr. T (bull), 143
Mudslinger (bull), 143, 172
Mulhall, Lucille, 8, 53, 111
Murray, Ty, 8, 151–52, 167, 174
mustanging. See wild horses
mustangs. See wild horses
mutton busting, 182, 183–84, 211; criticized, 184
"myth of the garden," 3–4, 22

National Bucking Bull Association (NBBA), 172
National Cowboy and Western Heritage Museum, 113, 148
National Finals Rodeo, 111, 119, 136, 146, 165
Neff, John, 20
Nelson, Alvin, 133, 135
New Western History, 6, 10
New York Women's League for Animals, 92. See also animal advocates
Northern Cheyenne Nation, 124
North of Yellowstone (horse), 107

Omak Stampede (Wash.), 4
101 Ranch Wild West show, 53

Oregon Humane Society, 68. *See also* animal advocates
Oscar (bull), 143, 151, 159, 175

Pacific National Exhibition (Vancouver), 188
Palen, Joseph, 74
Parry, Arthur, 24, 26
Pendleton Round-Up, 68, 111, 133
Pendleton Round-Up and Happy Canyon Hall of Fame, 100, 138
People for the Ethical Treatment of Animals (PETA), 2, 14, 153, 155; 198. *See also* animal advocates
pickup horses, 107. *See also* horses
pickup men (riders), 1, 12, 32, 106, 167
Pine Ridge Rodeo, 124
Pinnacle Bull Group, 170
Plaga, Otto, 71
Pozzobon, Ty, 175–76, 215
Prince (horse), 129
Privett, "Booger Red," 53, 69
Privett, Mollie, 53
Probert, Debra, 207–11
Proctor, Alexander Phimister, 52
Professional Bull Riders (PBR), 143, 151, 157, 159–60, 162, 166–72, 175, 202
Professional Rodeo Cowboys Association (PRCA), 42, 80, 101, 112, 127, 145, 150, 153, 157, 158, 168; response to animal advocacy criticism, 153–55, 160, 174, 198, 202–3, 205
ProRodeo Hall of Fame, 131, 133, 142
Protect the Harvest, 155
Pruett, Gene, 153

"quarrel with the land," 3, 11, 15
Quintana, John, 148

Rambo, 149
ranchers: as critics of rodeo, 42–43, 44–45; as perceived exploiters of working cowboys, 25–26, 152; and rural politics, 15, 19, 44, 154–56; women as, 112. *See also* ranching; stock contractors
ranching, 54, 79, 102, 128–29, 179; British Columbia, 213; cow-calf operations, 179, 190–94; livestock management in, 171–73, 178–79, 190–91
Rankin, Lawyer, 108
*Rawhide* (television program), 189–90
Reagan, Ronald, 143, 149
Red Head (horse), 96
Red Rock (bull), 140–43, 151, 161, 166, 167, 169
Redstone Rodeo, Gymkhana, and Mountain Race, 213–16
Remington, Frederick, 52
Republican National Convention (1980), 149
Rick, Johnny, 48
Rifkin, Jeremy, 155
Roberts, Monty, 177–78
Roddy, Jack, 156
rodeo: academic interpretations, 4, 75; as adrenalin sport, 51, 52, 54, 146, 159d, 166; All-Indian, 124, 214; as "big business," 102, 113; children in, 150, 179; as civic branding festival, 21, 22, 41, 77, 98; community-sponsored, 51, 76, 79–80, 81–82, 90; and consumer society, 8; contract acts, 112–13; contradictions within, 6–7, 217; criticism of, 12, 45, 47, 67–68, 69–70, 92, 144, 155, 184; diversity within, 7, 15, 214; historical sources for, 14–15, 78, 87–88, 93, 152, 179–80, 189; Indigenous Peoples marginalized in, 124, 214; masculinism within, 112, 143, 149–51, 175–76; professionalization of, 100, 101–2, 109–10, 111, 119–20; urban-rural divide and appeal, 40–41, 156, 157–58, 179, 184–85, 215; and western identity, 3, 13, 15, 19, 44; women marginalized in, 110–12, 150–51

Rodeo Association of America (RAA), 42, 80, 81, 111
rodeo clowns. *See* bullfighters
Rodeo Cowboys Association (RCA), 101, 102, 111, 136
Rodeo Information Committee, 101, 129
rodeo people: as community, 6, 7, 9, 13, 54, 171; defined, 3, 7, 8, 219n2; mobility of, 102, 114–16, 126, 138–39; responses to animal advocates and critics, 13, 40, 93, 115, 154–56, 159–60, 166, 175, 186–87, 188–89, 199–200, 202–3, 211
Rodeo Salinas, 4, 66
rodeo schools, 157, 158, 160, 167, 195–98
Rodman, Charmayne James, 150
Rollin, Bernie, 211
roping horses, 36, 114, 180, 200–202. *See also* horses
Rosebud Rodeo, 124
Rosser, Cotton, 126
rounder, 110, 182. *See also* cowboy
"running W" scandal, 92
Russell, Charles M., 39, 52, 62

Sacramento State Fair Rodeo, 66
Saddle Bronc of the Year Award, 135. *See also* Bucking Horse of the Year Award
Santee, Ross, 52, 63
Savitt, Sam, 121, 129
Sawyer, Pauline Irwin, 59
Scamper (horse), 150
Scott, Jack, 185, 188
sheep, 44, 54, 183–84
Sheepshead Bay Speedway Rodeo, 85
Shoemaker, James, 76
shorthorn cattle, 28, 30
Shoulders, Jim, 146–47
Showing Animals Respect and Kindness (Shark), 14. *See also* animal advocates
Shivers, Chris, 169
Shull, John, 172
Silver (horse), 95
Siringo, Charles, 56
Smith, Henry Nash, 3–4
Snowflake (horse), 129
Snyder, Cody, 165
Society for the Prevention of Cruelty to Animals (SPCA), 14, 38; British Columbia, 187–89, 208–9. *See also* animal advocates
spurs, 61, 68, 69, 90, 121, 146, 162, 171
stallions, 56. *See also* horses
Stampede Ranch, 85, 99
Stanley, Dick, 74
Starrs, Paul, 3, 139
Steamboat (horse), 48, 54–58, 65, 70–73, 77, 94, 109, 118, 141; death of, 48–49, 73; fame of, 49, 74–75; imagined consent to use in rodeo, 49–51, 65, 75
steer busting: controversy over, 41–45, 47, 67, 93; criticized, 18, 37–38, 45; legislation against, 43, 45; origins of, 20; as satire, 23, 24; steers injured and killed in, 36–37, 44–45, 93, 205; technical description of, 17–18, 24–25, 32–33, 36
steer decorating, 81
steer riding, 144. *See also* bull riding
steer roping, 46, 80, 81, 179. *See also* steer busting
steers, 30, 31–33, 35, 45, 199; as capital, 26, 31–32, 42; imagined as dangerous and inherently western, 20, 26–27, 33, 41, 45; imagined as representatives of the Southwest, 30. *See also* cattle; longhorn cattle; shorthorn cattle
steer wrestling, 39, 80, 210
Stern, Jane, 156, 160
Stern, Michael, 156, 160
stock contractors, 3, 58, 86, 93–94, 99, 100–101, 103, 108–9, 114, 116–17, 118–20, 124, 125–32, 145, 171–72, 178, 180, 200, 202, 205, 209, 214; as

INDEX    293

critics of cowboys, 127, 171; as icons of patrilineal family ranch, 127–28, 143, 153; as promoters of stock and rodeo, 107, 127, 131, 133, 135–36, 143, 146, 148, 151–52, 161, 163
stockmen. *See* ranchers
Streak (horse), 115
Strickland, Ed, 63, 105
Strickland, Hugo, 105
Strickland, Mabel, 8, 105
Studnick, Frank, 54
suicide race, 4, 215–16
Sumner, Phil, 161
Sumpter, Ore., 41
sunfisher, 52, 68, 95; meaning of, 51, 77, 82–83; Steamboat as, 51, 74. *See also* broncs
Super Duty (bull). *See* Major Payne (bull)
Surrey, B.C., 179, 207; city council, 208–9
Swan Land and Cattle Company, 57–58
Swanton, F. W., 68

Taillon, Cy, 110
Tanglefoot (horse), 69
Takin' Care of Business (bull), 141, 142, 161
Taylor Grazing Act (1934), 104
team roping, 41–42, 46, 210
Thain, Bob, 154
Thomas, Keith, 98
Threepersons, Tom, 8
Tibbs, Casey, 8, 103, 107–8, 116–17, 119, 120, 122–26, 129–31, 132, 135–36; celebrity of, 110–11
tie-down roping, 206, 207. *See also* calf roping
Tipperary (horse), 69, 94, 108, 132
Tip Top (horse), 94
Tomkins, Harry, 109–10
Tony the Wonder Horse, 95
Tooke, Earnest, 126, 129, 133

Tornado (bull), 143, 146, 148, 149, 151
Travolta, John, 149
trick and fancy roping, 113
trick riding, 112–14
trick riding horses, 113. *See also* horses
Trigger (horse), 95, 113
Tŝideldel. *See* Alexis Creek First Nation
Tsilhqot'in Nation, 213–17
Twister (bull), 148, 149
Tyler, Ron, 33

*Ubet* (1934), 95
University of British Columbia, 207
University of Wyoming, 52, 74, 75
*Urban Cowboy* (film), 149
Utah State Fair, 48

Vancouver, B.C., 179, 185, 207
Vancouver Humane Society (VHS), 207–11. *See also* animal advocates
vaqueros, 23, 33, 62–63, 69. *See also* cowboy
Vason, Lu, 150
Vela, Rudy, 148–49, 173
veterinarians, 117, 118, 133, 188, 194, 203–6
VH (horse), 115
violence: animals as surrogates for and subjects of, 6, 11, 19, 33–36, 49, 60, 71; and myth of animal consent, 10, 44, 47, 74; in rodeo, 81, 93, 113–14; in rodeo and concern about children, 44, 93, 184, 185; and western history, 6, 7, 10, 214. *See also* western rural identity
Vold, Harry, 126
V61 (bull), 143, 147–48, 149, 169

Walters, Chuck, 42
War Paint (horse), 100–101, 103, 117, 120, 124, 125, 130, 132–39, 148; fame of, 132–38

Ward, Ray, 28
wastage, 61, 78, 96, 143, 152, 161, 167
Watts, Dianne, 210
Weadick, Guy, 53, 76, 77, 78, 79, 80, 81, 82, 85, 86, 87, 89, 96, 98
Weld, Mrs. Edward, 92
West: defined, 7; in popular culture, 7–8, 10
West, Terry Don, 162, 164–65
West Coast Rodeo Company, 185
Westermeier, Clifford, 45, 61, 66, 72, 120, 199, 200, 203
Western genre, 11, 33, 95, 152; in advertising, 150; cinema, 92, 95, 222n41; as civic branding theme, 22, 77; television, 122, 189–90
western rural identity: in Canada, 207, 216–17; defined by danger and violence, 4, 33, 65, 72, 148; defined by emotional distance from livestock, 181, 182–83, 192; defined by ranching, 109, 127, 143, 154; defined by struggle and fortitude, 3, 11–12, 60, 102, 114, 181, 184; indicated by resistant animals, 19, 27, 33, 75, 95, 114, 122–23, 125–26; vulnerability symbolically purged from by rodeo sports, 179, 180–82, 184, 194, 200, 212
Western Wishes (bull), 169
White, Richard, 5, 6

Whitfield, Fred, 8
wild cow milking, 81, 184, 209, 210
Wild Horse Annie (aka Velma "Annie" Johnson), 125
Wild Horse Annie Act, 125
wild horse race, 1–2, 39, 67, 93, 107
wild horses, 1–2, 51, 53–57, 103–4, 122–23; behavior of, 55–56, 106–7; capture of, 56–57, 104–6, 125; defined, 106; employed as broncs, 107–9, 119; perceived as nuisance, 104, 106; symbolic of the West, 125. *See also* horses
Wild West shows, 21, 51, 52–53, 58, 66, 80, 112
Wilkie, Rhoda, 193
Williams, Sloan, 148
Williams Lake (B.C.), 213, 216
Winters, Charlie, 148
Wister, Owen, 53
Woerner, Gail, 144, 203
women, rodeo competitors. *See* cowgirl
Women's Professional Rodeo Association, 150
Wooden, Wayne, 211
Worster, Donald, 4
Wyoming Humane Society, 41, 44, 46, 70. *See also* animal advocates

Yore, Jack, 24, 26

www.ingramcontent.com/pod-product-compliance
Lightning Source LLC
Chambersburg PA
CBHW031429160426
43195CB00010BB/667